The Cambridge Companion to Me W

The Cambridge Companion to Medieval Women's Writing seeks to recover the lives and particular experiences of medieval women by concentrating on various kinds of texts: the texts they wrote themselves as well as texts that attempted to shape, limit, or expand their lives. The first part investigates the roles traditionally assigned to medieval women (as virgins, widows, and wives); it also considers female childhoods and relations between women. The second part explores social spaces, including textuality itself: for every surviving medieval manuscript bespeaks collaborative effort. It considers women as authors, as anchoresses 'dead to the world', and as preachers and teachers in the world (staking claims to authority without entering a pulpit). The final section considers the lives and writings of remarkable women, including Marie de France, Heloise, Joan of Arc, Julian of Norwich, Margery Kempe, and female lyricists and romancers whose names are lost, but whose texts survive.

Carolyn Dinshaw is Professor of English and Director of the Center for the Study of Gender and Sexuality at New York University. She is the author of *Chaucer's Sexual Poetics* (1989) and *Getting Medieval: Sexualities and Communities, Pre- and Postmodern* (1999).

David Wallace is Judith Rodin Professor and Chair of English at the University of Pennsylvania. He is the editor of *The Cambridge History of Medieval English Literature* (1999, 2002), and the author of *Chaucerian Polity* (1997).

THE CAMBRIDGE COMPANION TO

MEDIEVAL WOMEN'S WRITING

EDITED BY

CAROLYN DINSHAW AND DAVID WALLACE

CAMBRIDGE
UNIVERSITY PRESS

CAMBRIDGE UNIVERSITY PRESS
Cambridge, New York, Melbourne, Madrid, Cape Town, Singapore, São Paulo, Delhi

Cambridge University Press
The Edinburgh Building, Cambridge CB2 8RU, UK

Published in the United States of America by Cambridge University Press, New York

www.cambridge.org
Information on this title: www.cambridge.org/9780521796385

First published 2003
Reprinted 2006

A catalogue record for this publication is available from the British Library

ISBN 978-0-521-79188-5 hardback
ISBN 978-0-521-79638-5 paperback

Transferred to digital printing 2009

The editors gratefully acknowledge the assistance of Leif Sorensen in compiling this volume.

CONTENTS

CONTRIBUTORS

CHRIS AFRICA, University of Iowa

ALEXANDRA BARRATT, University of Waikato, New Zealand

CHRISTOPHER BASWELL, University of California, Los Angeles

ALCUIN BLAMIRES, Goldsmiths College, University of London

CHRISTOPHER CANNON, Pembroke College, Cambridge

CAROLYN DINSHAW, New York University

DYAN ELLIOTT, Indiana University

RUTH EVANS, University of Stirling

BARBARA A. HANAWALT, Ohio State University

DAVID F. HULT, University of California, Berkeley

DANIEL T. KLINE, University of Alaska, Anchorage

ROBERTA L. KRUEGER, Hamilton College, New York

KARMA LOCHRIE, Indiana University

SARAH McNAMER, Georgetown University

NADIA MARGOLIS, Independent scholar

SARAH SALIH, University of East Anglia

JENNIFER SUMMIT, Stanford University

DAVID WALLACE, University of Pennsylvania

NICHOLAS WATSON, Harvard University

Date	
c. 425	Anglo-Saxon incursions into England begin.
476	Romulus Augustulus, considered the last of the Roman emperors of Western Europe, is deposed by the German general, Odoacer.
c. 481	Clovis the Frank establishes his hegemony as ruler of northern Gaul (parts of France and Germany). Under the influence of his Christian wife, Clotilda, Clovis converts to Christianity some time between 496 and 508.
512	Caesarius, Bishop of Arles (France), writes a rule, *Regula virginum*, for his sister Caesaria's convent.
523	In prison, Italian philosopher and theologian Boethius writes *De consolatione philosophiae*, treating classical literary and philosophical ideas from a Christian perspective. It becomes a widely known text.
c. 525–87	Frankish Queen Radegund (518–87) establishes a convent in Poitiers with herself as its first abbess. Radegund's circle includes the poet, later Bishop of Poitiers, Venantius Fortunatus. Fortunatus and Baudonivia, a sister of the convent, both write lives of Radegund.
529	Benedict of Nursia founds a monastery at Monte Cassino (Italy). Benedict's programme for the community, including regular periods of prayer, work, and study, becomes the model for European monastic communities.
547	Gildas, *Liber querulus de excidio Britanniae*.
565	Irish monk Columba founds a monastery on the island of Iona (off Scotland) after founding others at Derry (546), Durrow (c. 556), and probably Kells.
590–604	Pope Gregory I establishes the basic institutions of the Roman papacy.

591	Gregory of Tours, *Decem libri historiarum*.
597	Pope Gregory dispatches Augustine to England. With the support of King Aethelbert of Kent's Christian wife, Bertha (Clotilda's great-granddaughter), Augustine converts Aethelbert to Christianity.
622	Mohammed's *hegira* from Mecca to Medina, starting date of the Islamic calendar.
c. 630–50	The Irish author known as Pseudo-Cyprian epitomizes the *femina sine pudicitia*, 'the woman without modesty', in *De duodecim abusivis saeculi*, a text that becomes well known in medieval Europe.
636	Publication of Isidore of Seville's influential encyclopaedia, the *Etymologiae*.
664	At Whitby, in a double monastery headed by Abbess Hilda, the Northumbrian King Oswy convenes a synod to determine whether English Christians will follow the Roman Catholic or Celtic Christian calendar for observing Easter.
665–75	Barking Abbey founded, with Aethelburg as first abbess. First Anglo-Latin author, Aldhelm, writes *De virginitate* for the nuns and their second abbess, Hildelith.
710	Muslims from North Africa invade the Spanish peninsula.
716–57	English monk Boniface (born Wynfrith) corresponds with nuns Bucge and Eangyth, Ecgburg, Eadburg, and Leoba during his mission to Germany.
731	Bede, *Historia ecclesiastica gentis Anglorum*.
732	Charles Martel checks the Muslim advance north of the Pyrenees at Tours.
744	Foundation of the Benedictine abbey of Fulda by Boniface.
761–74	Paul the Deacon writes his *Historia Romana* for Adelpurga, Duchess of Benevento.
768–814	Charlemagne's reign; c. 781–2, Charlemagne assembles a group of scholars, including Alcuin of York, at his court at Aachen. Charlemagne's sister Gisele, Abbess of Chelles, is one of Alcuin's most enthusiastic correspondents.
800	Charlemagne crowned Holy Roman Emperor by Pope Leo III in Rome.
c. 830	Einhard writes his biography of Charlemagne, *Vita Karoli Magni*.
c. 840–3	Carolingian noblewoman, Dhuoda, writes the *Liber manualis* for her son, William.

871–99	Reign of Alfred the Great of England. Alfred may have initiated the *Anglo-Saxon Chronicle* which began during his reign.
889	Marriage of Alfred's daughter Aethelflaed to Aethelraed of Mercia, marking the reconciliation of Wessex and Mercia.
c. 900	*Beowulf*.
911	Aethelflaed, 'the Lady of the Mercians', assumes rule of Mercia from her husband's death until her own in 918. Her brother Edward ousts her daughter Aelfwynn and merges Mercia with Wessex after Aethelflaed's death.
960s	Hrotswith of Gandersheim, author of dramas, poems, biographies, and histories.
960–90	'The Wife's Lament', 'Wulf and Eadwacer'.
983–91	Empress Theophanu regent for Otto III.
c. 1000	Sei Shonagon, *Makura no Soshi* [The Pillow Book].
c. 1010	Murasaki Shikibu, *Genji Monogatari*.
1022	Trial of Jacoba Felicie in Paris for practising medicine.
c. 1050–c. 1300	Period of growth in population, agricultural production, trade, and urbanization in Europe.
1065–7	*Vita Aedwardi* dedicated to Edith, wife of Edward the Confessor (reigned 1042–66).
1066	William the Conqueror's Normans invade England.
Late 1060s–mid 1090s	The Bayeux Tapestry depicting the events of the Norman Conquest is designed and executed.
1072–85	Pontificate of reform-minded Gregory VII; objectives include stricter enforcement of clerical celibacy.
c. 1082	Goscelin of St Bertin writes his *Liber confortatorius* for Eve of Angers.
1086–7	*Domesday Book*, compiled by the order of William the Conqueror, provides a detailed picture of England at the time of the survey.
1095	At the Council of Clermont, Urban II calls for an offensive to recapture Christian holy sites from the Muslims.
1096	Robert d'Arbrissel establishes a monastery for women and men at Fontevrault.
1097–8	Robert d'Arbrissel establishes a monastery at Cîteaux.
1100	(11 November) Edith of Scotland marries Henry I of England. As Queen Matilda she acts as regent for Henry when he is in Normandy.
1106	Hildegard of Bingen, aged eight, joins recluse Jutta of Sponheim at the monastery of St Disibod.

1109–26	Urraca Queen Regnant of Castile.
1116–17	Correspondence between Peter Abelard and his student, then lover, Heloise. In 1118–19, Heloise takes vows and becomes prioress at Argenteuil.
1122	Abelard, *Sic et non* [Yes and No].
1125	William of Malmesbury, *Gesta regum Anglorum*.
1126	Bernard of Clairvaux, *De diligendo deo*.
1129	King Baldwin II of Jerusalem's daughter, Melisende, marries Fulk V, Count of Anjou. After Fulk's death in 1143, Melisende rules as regent and then jointly with her son, Baldwin III, until 1161.
1129–34	Evicted from Argenteuil, Heloise, in collaboration with Abelard, establishes a new community at the Paraclete.
1131	Gilbert of Sempringham founds a Cistercian community that includes a women's house, although Bernard of Clairvaux refuses to admit them to the Cistercian order.
1135	Geoffrey of Monmouth, *Historia regum Britanniae*.
1137	Marriage of Eleanor of Aquitaine and Louis VII of France (annulled 1152).
1138–48	Civil war in England, 'the Anarchy', as Henry I's daughter, Matilda, and her cousin, Stephen of Blois, contest succession after Henry I's death in 1135. Stephen wins militarily, but Matilda's son, Henry, succeeds Stephen as king in 1154.
c. 1140	Gratian, a Bolognese monk, produces the *Concordance of Discordant Canons*, or *Decretum*, which becomes the basic textbook of canon (Church) law. The survival of Roman and customary law provides grounds for ongoing competition for authority, especially between the Church, which claimes supremacy, and secular rulers.
c. 1140–1240	Period of *trobairitz* writing in the Occitan language of the south of France. There is historical evidence for the Countess of Die, Castelloza, Azalais de Porcairagues, and Clara d'Anduza.
1141	Orderic Vitalis, *Historia ecclesiastica*.
1144	Capture of Edessa by the Muslims leads Eugene III to call a new crusade.
c. 1145	Construction of a priory at Markyate headed by Christina of Markyate (c. 1096–1165).

c. 1148	Anna Komnena's *Alexiad*, a history of her father Alexius I Komnenus's reign.
1151	Hildegard of Bingen completes her *Scivias* and moves to a new monastery at Rupertsburg.
1152	Marriage of Eleanor of Aquitaine to Henry of Anjou (future Henry II of England).
	Elisabeth of Schönau (1129–65) begins to have her visions recorded by her brother and secretary Ekbert in three *Libri visionum* [Books of Visions]: *Liber viarum Dei* (1157), *Revelatio* (Ursula and the 1100 virgins), and *Visio de resurrectione Beate Virginis Maria* (1159).
1155	Wace, *Roman de Brut*.
1158	Hildegard of Bingen, *Liber vite meritorum*.
1160	Aelred of Rievaulx writes *De institutione inclusarum* for his sister.
1160–1215	Marie de France, *Lais*, *Fables*, and *Espurgatoire seint Patriz*.
1167–95	Abbess Herrad of Landsberg directs production of the *Hortus deliciarum*.
c. 1170	Nun of Barking, *Vie d'Edouard le Confesseur*.
c. 1170–8	Chrétien de Troyes's romances, including *Erec et Enide*, *Cliges*, *Yvain*, *Lancelot*, written at Marie of Champagne's court.
1173	Waldo, merchant in Lyons (France), having given up his worldly wealth to minister to the poor, has the Gospels translated into Provençal. Waldo and his followers, the Waldensians, receive papal approval for their vows of poverty. The Waldensians also preach, an activity forbidden to the laity, and in 1184 their beliefs are declared heretical.
	Hildegard of Bingen, *Liber divinorum operum*.
c. 1175	Clemence of Barking, *Life of St Katherine*.
c. 1180	Andreas Capellanus, *De arte honeste amandi*, on courtly love.
1187	Third Crusade.
1198–1204	Fourth Crusade. Crusaders divert to Constantinople, which the French and Italians capture and loot.
1199–1216	Reign of King John. In March 1215, the English barons force him to confirm their feudal rights in Magna Carta.
c. 1200	*Nibelungenlied*, German epic.

1201	Roger of Howden, *Chronica majora*.
1207	Giovanni Bernardone of Assisi vows himself to poverty and, as Francis of Assisi, asks for papal sanction, in 1211, of a rule of absolute poverty for himself and his followers.
	Geoffroi de Villehardouin, *Conquête de Constantinople*.
1208	Pope Innocent III proclaims a crusade against the Cathar movement centred in southern France near Albi – the Albigensian Crusade.
c. 1210	Gottfried von Strassburg, *Tristan und Isolt*.
	Wolfram von Eschenbach, *Parzival*.
1214	Women followers of Francis of Assisi receive a rule for a cloistered order from Francis, with Clare of Assisi as first Abbess of the Poor Clares.
1215	Recognition of the association, *universitas*, of Parisian teachers that evolves into the University of Paris. The future University of Oxford is in a similar state of development. The University of Cambridge originates with scholars who left Oxford. In Bologna, groups of students form associations to make agreements with teachers, primarily of law. The emergence of universities, which are not open to women, as the new educational centres of medieval Europe bar women from participation in the intellectual life and emerging professions in Europe.
	The Fourth Lateran Council makes annual confession and communion obligatory. It also requires declarations of mutual consent to make a marriage valid. The requirement for confession leads to the production of guides for priests to hearing confessions and assigning penances.
	Jacques de Vitry, *Vita Mariae Oigniancensis* (biography of beguine Mary of Oignies). He obtains Pope Honorius III's permission for beguines to live in common.
1216	Pope Honorius III recognizes the Order of Preachers (Dominican friars).
c. 1220	*Ancrene Wisse* (*Ancrene Riwle*), manual for anchoresses.
c. 1220–40	Active period of Flemish beguine poet and mystic Hadewijch.
1223–6	Blanche of Castile regent for Louis IX of France.
c. 1225	The 'Wooing Group', *Wohung of ure Lauerd*, *On Lofsong of ure Louerde*, *On Ureison of ure Louerde*, and

	the 'Katherine Group', *Hali Meiðhad*, *Sawles Ward*, *vitae* of St Juliana, St Margaret, and St Katherine.
1227–9	Fifth Crusade led by Frederick II, Emperor of Germany and King of Sicily.
c. 1230	Guillaume de Lorris begins the *Roman de la Rose* as a courtly romance.
	Roger of Wendover, *Flores historiarum*.
c. 1241	Circle of devout lay women forms around Douceline de Digne (1215/16–74) in Hyères. Around 1250, Douceline establishes a second community in Marseilles.
1244	Albigensian Crusade ends with the massacre at Montsegur.
1254	Louis IX expels Jews from his domain; expulsion repeated by Philip IV in 1306.
1259	Matthew Paris, *Chronica majora*.
c. 1265	Jacobus de Voragine, *Legenda aurea* [The Golden Legend] (collection of saints' lives).
c. 1270	Jean de Meun completes the *Roman de la Rose*, abandoning the courtly romance and taking a misogynistic turn that draws criticism from Christine de Pizan in the early fifteenth century.
1274	Death of Thomas Aquinas, leaving his *Summa theologica* incomplete.
c. 1280	Mechthild of Magdeburg, *Das fliessende Lichte der Gottheit*.
1289	The Benedictine nun, Gertrud the Great of Helfta, *Legatus memorialis abundantiae divinae pietatis* (only Book 2 written by Gertrud; Books 3–5 probably partially dictated, and with introductory Book 1 added posthumously).
1290	Edward I expels Jews from England.
1291–8	*Liber spiritualis* (or *Specialis gratiae*), revelations of Mechthild of Hackeborn written down by Gertrud the Great.
1290s	Period of cold, wet weather in Europe leading to poor harvests and the Great Famine.
1303	Robert Mannyng of Brunne, *Handlynge Synne*.
c. 1304	Dante Alighieri, *De vulgari eloquentia*.
1305	College of Navarre, University of Paris, created by a bequest from Jeanne of Navarre.

1309	Jean de Joinville, *Mémoires; ou histoire de chronique du très chrétien roi St Louis*.
1310	Marguerite Porete burned as a heretic in Paris.
1311	Council of Vienne orders the suppression of beguines and beghards.
c. 1315	*Li vida de la benaurada sancta Doucelina*, biography of Douceline de Digne, in Provençal, possibly by Philippine Porcellet.
1321	Death of Dante Alighieri.
1328	Marriage to Edward III of Philippa of Hainault, patron of the chronicler Froissart and future founder of Queen's College, Oxford.
1330	Edward III assumes personal rule of England after his mother, Isabella, and her lover, Roger de Mortimer, have ruled for him since his accession in 1327.
1336–8	Elizabeth de Clare (Lady de Burgh) founds Clare College, Cambridge.
1337	Beginning of the Hundred Years' War between France and England.
1346	Battle of Crécy.
1347–9	Bubonic plague, the Black Death, spreads westward from Constantinople, reaching England by 1349. Mortality rates range from a quarter to a half, with the highest rates in urban populations. Plague returns in 1358, 1361, 1368–9, and 1374–5. In the wake of the plague, measures such as the Statute of Labourers, enacted in England in 1351, attempt to regulate wages and prices.
1348–51	Giovanni Boccaccio, *Decameron*.
1352	Ranulf Higden, *Polychronicon* (a history of the world).
1356	Bridget of Sweden (1302/3–73) founds the Brigittine Order in Vadstena, Sweden. Bridget canonized in 1391.
c. 1361–2	Giovanni Boccaccio, *De mulieribus claris*, for Andrea Acciaiuoli, Countess of Altavilla.
Late 1360s	William Langland's first version of *The Vision of William Concerning Piers the Plowman*.
1369	Geoffrey Chaucer, *The Book of the Duchess*.
c. 1370	Bridget of Sweden, *Liber celestis*.
1373	Julian of Norwich experiences visionary episodes; she is an anchoress by 1393 and writes into the fifteenth century.

1374	The *Devotio moderna* [Modern Devotion] begins with Geert Grote in Deventer (Netherlands). Houses of Brothers and Sisters of the Common Life observe a religious life but members do not take formal religious vows. Books of Sisters from the late fifteenth century record short biographies of inhabitants to serve as examples and inspiration.
1376–8	John Wyclif, *De civili dominio* and *De potestate papae*. Wyclif contests the need for clerical mediation in worship and in biblical interpretation. Wyclif attracts followers, known as Lollards, including many women who take an active role.
1378	Catherine of Siena, *Dialogo della Divina Provvidenza*. Beginning of the Great Schism in the papacy. From Rome and Avignon (France), rival claimants dispute each other's legitimacy until 1417, when Martin V is elected at the Council of Constance.
1379	John Wyclif, *De Eucharistia*.
1382	(20 January) Marriage of Anne of Bohemia and Richard II. She and her entourage bring contemporary French and Italian cultural influences with them to England.
c. 1382	Geoffrey Chaucer, *The Parliament of Fowls*.
c. 1383	John Gower, *Vox clamantis*.
c. 1385	Chaucer, *Troilus and Criseyde*; Thomas Usk, *The Testament of Love*.
1387–1400	Chaucer, *The Canterbury Tales*.
c. 1390	John Gower, *Confessio amantis*. Archbishop Arundel reportedly allows Queen Anne (d. 1394) to use an English Bible.
1390s	British Library, MS Cotton Nero A.x, containing *Sir Gawain and the Green Knight*, *Pearl*, *Patience*, *Cleanness*.
c. 1396	Walter Hilton, *The Scale of Perfection*, ostensibly composed for a woman recluse.
1399	(30 September) Henry Bolingbroke deposes Richard II and becomes the first Lancastrian king of England.
1400	John Lydgate, *The Damage and Dystruccyon of Realmes*.
1400–1	Christine de Pizan, *Epistre Othea*.
1404	Christine de Pizan, *Le Livre des faicts et bonnes meurs du sage roi Charles* (Charles V of France).
1405	Christine de Pizan, *Le Livre de la cité des dames*, *Le Livre de trois vertus*, and *L'Avision-Christine*.

1412	Christine de Pizan, *Le Livre de paix*.
1413	John Hus, *De ecclesia*. Bohemian scholars take Wyclif's ideas back from Oxford. Hus disseminates them among the Czechs in Bohemia until the Council of Constance has him burned as a heretic.
1415	Battle of Agincourt. Henry V founds Syon, the only English house of Bridget of Sweden's Order of the Holy Saviour (Bridgettines).
c. 1415–30	John Lydgate, author of *The Siege of Thebes*, *Troy Book*, and *The Fall of Princes*, addresses several of his other works, including *The Life of St Margaret*, *An Invocation to St Anne*, *The Fifteen Joys of Our Lady*, *Guy of Warwick*, and *The Virtues of the Mass*, to the women who commissioned them.
1418	Christine de Pizan addresses her *Epistre de la prison de vie humaine* to Marie, Duchess of Bourbon, whose father was killed at Agincourt.
1422	(30 August) Accession of Henry VI. After Henry becomes insane in 1453, his wife Margaret of Anjou fights to protect his position and their son Edward's succession.
c. 1425	Thomas à Kempis, *De imitatione Christi*.
1429	Christine de Pizan, 'Ditié en l'honneur de Jeanne d'Arc'.
1431	(30 May) Execution of Joan of Arc.
c. 1436	Margery Kempe, *The Book of Margery Kempe*.
1445	Osbern Bokenham, *Legendys of Hooly Wummen*.
1446	Margaret of Anjou (wife of Henry VI) and Elizabeth Woodville (wife of Edward IV) found Queens' College, Cambridge.
1451	Isotta Nogarola, *De pari aut impari Evae atque Adae peccato* (dialogue on the relative fault of Adam and Eve).
1453	Sultan Mohamedd II's forces seize Constantinople. The Hundred Years' War ends.
1455	Beginning of the Wars of the Roses between the houses of Lancaster and York in England following the mental collapse of Henry VI.
1456	Johann Gutenberg completes printing his 42-line Bible.
c. 1459–84	Most of the Paston letters exchanged between Margaret Paston, her husband John, and sons John II and John III.
1470	Thomas Malory, *Le Morte d'Arthur*.
1474	William Caxton prints *Recuyell of the Historyes of Troye* in Bruges.

1476	Caxton begins printing in England, at Westminster, with *The Dictes or Sayengis of the Philosophres* (1477) followed by Chaucer's *Canterbury Tales* and *Parliament of Fowls* and Boethius' *De consolatione philosophiae* (1478). Lady Margaret Beaufort is a patron of Caxton and Wynken de Worde.
1485	(August) Henry Tudor becomes King Henry VII of England after defeating Richard III at Bosworth Field, ending the Wars of the Roses.
1492	With the patronage of Queen Isabella of Spain, Christopher Columbus sets off for Asia and finds the Americas in his path.
1505	Lady Margaret Beaufort, mother of Henry VII, endows Christ's College, Cambridge. In 1511, she founds St John's College, Cambridge. She also endows theology lectureships at both Cambridge and Oxford.

ABBREVIATIONS

BL	British Library
EETS	Early English Text Society
ES	Extra Series
MED	Middle English Dictionary
OED	Oxford English Dictionary
OS	Original Series
SS	Special Series

CAROLYN DINSHAW AND DAVID WALLACE

Introduction

This volume explores medieval women's involvement with textual culture. The women of our study are chiefly those living in England, viewed as part of a greater medieval Europe. To do full justice to such involvement, our title would need to be very long indeed; the whole volume might in fact be seen as an attempt to qualify or tease out the meanings of 'medieval women's writing'. The image featured as frontispiece and paperback cover of this book speaks eloquently to many of these issues, hence provides ways of beginning.

The painting, now in the Philadelphia Museum of Art (Johnson Collection 402), dates from c. 1500–20. Although not painted in England, its subject would have been recognized by English observers: for it depicts scenes from the life of Mary Magdalene deriving from *The Golden Legend* of Dominican friar Jacobus de Voragine (compiled 1259–66).[1] Chaucer drew on this *Legenda aurea* for his tale of St Cecilia (and perhaps for his lost Magdalene legend); the early English printer William Caxton produced his own edition from Latin, French, and English sources (subsequently reprinted by Wynkyn de Worde, Pynson, and Notary). Our image and this spread of dates thus suggest a culture that, while alive to local and temporal particulars – as detailed in the fashionable costumes – nonetheless preserves some remarkable continuities in experience over time and space. Continuities may also be read across the essays of this volume, suggesting that 'medieval women's writing' provides (with due account taken of experiences differentiated by age, class, and marital status) viable terms of analysis.

The immediately problematic term here is 'writing': for few medieval women could write, and nothing survives in Middle English that is indisputably the work of a female religious. As Nicholas Watson observes here, the *Revelation of Love* of Julian of Norwich is 'the earliest work in English we are sure is by a woman', and it dates from the late fourteenth century. And yet all women, from agrarian worker to queen, maintained relationships with textual culture: everything from records of birth and death to pardons, romances, and Sunday sermons. Women rarely had pens in their hands; the power to fashion a text of one's own was not readily obtained. And yet, of course, many medieval English women – most famously Margery Kempe – did manage to get texts made. The actual business of pushing a pen across a page – which we tend to think of as the supreme declaration of authorial independence – was not so highly rated in the Middle Ages: as professional copyist Thomas Hoccleve complained, working with dead animal skins was not a glamorous pursuit.[2] More relevant for medievals was the aggregation of *auctoritas*: the recognition by others of a witnessing to time-honoured truths in a particular individual. In our painting it is a woman who attests truths, or *the* medieval truth, to male and female bystanders: Mary Magdalene, the first person on earth to whom the risen Christ chose to reveal himself. Church Fathers could hardly dispute Christ's decision: for St Ambrose, Mary Magdalene was to be acknowledged as *apostolorum apostola*, 'apostle to the apostles'. And later exegetes, such as Friar James, could hardly imagine such a personage resting on her laurels; she is thus depicted, in this painting as in his text, on the road, preaching the gospel.

Medieval clerics, however, were reluctant to concede that a woman, any woman, could be appointed to preach, as Alcuin Blamires in this volume demonstrates; and their coyness is shared by our painter. In *The Golden Legend*, Mary is said to preach in cities, at Marseilles and at Aix; here, however, she is set in the countryside. And is she actually *preaching*? She seems, rather, to breathe forth the perfumed word of God (as if become the canister of perfumed ointment that is her identifying iconographic sign). She, alone of all the foreground figures, seems withdrawn from the very scene that, visually, she dominates: as if, perhaps, already transported to the next scene of her life, the thirty-year solitariness in a desert landscape where, borne up by angels, she levitates between heaven and earth seven times a day. The man on her right clasps what might be a pilgrim's staff; the man on her left raises his hand in a classic sermonizing gesture, responding to the questioning implicit in the woman by his side. Lines of sight leading from women sitting in the foreground bring us to these men (excepting the woman bottom left, who gazes abstractedly out of the frame, scratching her baby's head while handing him an apple). Although the authority of witness emanates from the female saint, then, powers of exegesis and containment seem to be accorded to the men who frame her.

But although the painting busily works to augment masculine authority, there is no doubt that this woman, Mary from Magdalum, is preaching: for she stands in a pulpit. The concession is not, of course, made with great fanfare: Mary is not accorded an ecclesiastical setting, and her elevated position (she rises above the men who flank her) does not immediately suggest a pulpit. But the wooden crossbar between two trees – upon which the preaching saint's left hand lightly rests – explicitly concedes the point: this is a pulpit. Illuminator Jean Poyet, in imagining the rural preachings of his John the Baptist (fo. 173), finds just the same visual solution.[3] Clerical commentators did indeed concede that Mary was licensed to preach (*praedicare*) in Marseilles; and they also worried about what precedents images of a preaching woman might set. Some emphasized (as with another Mary) her historical uniqueness. Others conceded that this Mary had indeed preached after Pentecost, but that St Paul had brought such female preaching to an end. Nonetheless, a space opens for speculation: a medieval female viewer of our painting, drawn to identify with the protagonist's wearing of contemporary dress, might further imagine the active life to be led in such clothes. Sarah McNamer suggests similar processes of identification among female readers of romances. If then, why not now, or now again?

It is traditionally the task of historians to eschew subjunctives as they police the limits of such speculation: after all, the painting might well have spent four hundred years in a monastery, hidden from female sight. Two of the five essays in the first part of this *Companion*, entitled 'Estates of Women', are written by historians: Dyan Elliott writes on marriage, and Barbara Hanawalt on widowhood; the others are by literary scholars. Both historians marshal an impressive range of materials to give a concrete sense of conditions constraining medieval wives and widows. Local and national factors here assume considerable importance: women marrying in medieval London could look forward to happier lives as widows than their counterparts in medieval Florence, say (or, Hanawalt ultimately argues, in Renaissance London). But even here, the categories by which medieval women were enjoined to live prove highly problematic: the perfect paradigm of marriage, as Elliott notes, was one (as in the holy family) never consummated. The third traditional 'estate' of women, that of virginity, proves even more problematic: its history might be written, although empirical data will prove hard to find. Even medievals (Ruth Evans notes) acknowledged that a doubting Salomé, following in the tracks of doubting Thomas, took things too far in wishing to ascertain that the Virgin Mary was indeed *intacta*. And yet, of course, the hymning of virginity (almost always female) forms one of the most distinctive features of Middle English literature; its discursive obsolescence – as proclaimed in *A Midsummer Night's Dream* – will form a powerful marker of historical change. For Shakespeare's Theseus, perpetual,

prayerful inclaustration is wasted promise – a fate to threaten upon a wayward daughter, such as Hermia:

> You can endure the livery of a nun,   [habit]
> For aye to be in shady cloister mewed,   [ever; caged up in]
> To live a barren sister all your life,
> Chanting faint hymns to the cold fruitless moon.[4]

The triad of virginity, widowhood, and wifehood (to list them by declin-
ing rate of spiritual return) was sufficiently concrete a social structure for
Chaucer to imagine a female parliament assembled to judge the knight rapist
of *The Wife of Bath's Tale*:

> Ful many a noble wyf, and many a mayde,
> And many a wydwe, for that they been wise,
> The queene hirself sittynge as a justise,
> Assembled been, his answere for to here.
>
> (3.1026–9)[5]

To these three medieval 'estates' of women we have added two more, exploring other conditions of female life which fascinated medieval audiences:
childhood and relations between women. We include Daniel Kline's account of female childhood both because it is important not to confuse the
strong category of 'virginity' with notions of 'childish innocence', and because medieval imaginative, educational, and medical literatures clearly treat
childhood as a distinct phase of life. And we consider strong and intimate
relationships between women because this, too, is a recurrent topic of medieval literature. In the *Roman de la Rose* and in Chaucer, for example,
female friendship hints at traditions of handed-down knowledge, linking
female generations, escaping and indeed threatening equivalent masculine,
text-based traditions. And in *Sir Gawain and the Green Knight*, the close
pairing of young and old women, fair and foul (lines 943–69), hints that the
lone hero is outmatched – a recognition voiced in his final, extraordinary
misogynist outburst:

> Bot, hit is no ferly thagh a fole madde
> And thurgh wiles of wimmen be wonen to sorwe,
> For so was Adam in erde with one bigiled
> And Salamon with fele sere and Samson eftsones –
> Dalida dalt him his wyrde – and Davith therafter
> Was blended with Barsabe, that much bale tholed.[6]

> But it is no wonder if a fool be flummoxed,
> And be brought to grief through women's tricks:
> For earthly Adam was beguiled by one such [woman],

And Solomon by many such, and Samson too –
Delilah dealt him his fate – and after this David
Was duped by Bathsheba, and [he] suffered much misery.

All this (and there is more; Gawain goes on for nine more lines) speaks of, or precisely from, masculine fears; the art of Karma Lochrie's chapter is to consider what happens between female subjects, as she puts it, 'she and she'.

The four chapters of our second part explore social spaces, including textuality itself: for every surviving medieval manuscript bespeaks a history of collaborations, from first commission or inspiration through composition, compilation, scribing, copying, reading, and centuries of conservation. Texts authored in the Middle Ages present particular challenges to modern understanding, beginning with the notion of authorship itself. It is thus necessary for Jennifer Summit to refine Foucault by asking: 'What *is* a medieval author?' Again, our modern assumption that the more of herself a writer puts into a text, the more authoritative it will be, must be challenged: for if the first author of a visionary text is God, the chief imperative of the second, human author is to diminish rather than assert personal identity. In our painting we see the female evangelist somewhat removed from the representational moment, still dwelling perhaps before the divine presence which called her name from beyond the grave. The men who flank her, denied such an encounter, nonetheless play a role in the ways that her experience will be mediated to the world. Analogous roles played out in the army of masculine exegetes (interpreters and commentators), scribes, and compilers attending female visionaries (and now embedded in medieval texts). It is naive, however, to try to separate authentic female voices from masculine textual operations. (And women, we should remember, themselves took active roles in various aspects of textual production.) But it is important to note, with Summit and McNamer, the tendency of such masculine mediators to accentuate the importance of their own roles, or to occlude aspects of female involvement. Some of this echoes through modern disputes over the 'authenticity' of particular medieval women's texts (this lyric or letter is astonishing: could a woman have written it?); such arguments rarely appear in gender-reverse.

Perhaps the most challenging locus for the life of self-annihilation sought by certain medieval women is the anchorhold. The anchoress is dead to the world, entombed for the duration of her natural life before the burial of her body. And yet such a woman occupies central and prominent social space: for her cell is typically built into the fabric of a church in a market town or city. Her paradoxical aim is thus, Christopher Cannon argues, to perform an ascetic flight from the world while living in its midst and drawing upon it for sustenance. The texts abetting such an undertaking, such as

Ancrene Wisse, attend to the complex business of constructing inner and outer boundaries (corresponding in part to those of stone walls and fleshly body): a process of self-fashioning at once far removed from and instructively contiguous to more recent accounts of identity formation. Regulation of orifices, particularly eyes and windows, consumes much imaginative energy both in anchoritic texts and in accounts of feminine occupation of domestic space. In Chaucer's *Troilus and Criseyde* and in Lydgate's heated recollections of it, Sarah Salih notes, appearances at windows crackle with erotic disturbance; in Boccaccio's *Decameron*, the gendered battle for control of domestic openings – windows and doors – sustains the Seventh Day's comedy from beginning to end. Keys, too, are crucial signifiers: medieval poets and painters are scrupulous in observing their possession and passage. For Margery Kempe, Salih observes, recovery of full mental sanity can only be achieved through the recovery of household keys.

Some medieval households were metaphorical, almost metaphysical, concepts that might shift from one physical building to another: for where the lord goes, so too goes his household, configuring itself around his physical person. Queens and magnate women were accompanied by households or attendant circles of their own; their experiences within domestic interiors differed and were to some extent shielded from that of their spouses. At lower social levels, work and domestic spaces might overlap, leading to more fluid and continuous movement in, out of, and around the house (to feed chickens; to cook; to check on children). In medieval literary texts, however, the entering and exiting of domestic space bears considerable imaginative charge: as in Chaucer's *Clerk's Tale*, for example, when Griselde sets down her water pot 'as she wolde over hir thresshfold gon' (4.288). The Latin for 'threshold' is *limen*; medieval audiences were alert to the suggestive power of liminal spaces long before anthropologists coined the term.

Medieval women, like Margery Kempe, might wander the world with a freedom scarcely conceivable in post-medieval centuries (such being the enabling power of pilgrimage). Whether crossing the world or their native village, the most likely or plausible destination for women exiting their homes was a church. And here they would sit or stand before a man preaching from a pulpit. The pulpit was (indeed perhaps still is) the most potent signifier of masculine authority over women: for it is the point of delivery, in a society of restricted literacy, of forms of common knowledge scripted by men. And yet not every pardoner or friar ascending one of Chaucer's pulpits is to be trusted; nor is masculine monopoly of church preaching, Alcuin Blamires argues, a sure thing. Abbesses might preach; St Paul's oft-cited strictures against women teaching were subjected to scrutiny. And astute women, such as Margery Kempe and Anne Askew, might argue that they were indeed teachers, but not preachers. The more extravagant the misogynistic material emanating from pulpit-like places, the more likely – so Chaucer suggests – its comic overturn or subjection to counterclaim, as in the Wife of Bath's view of a painting of a lion killed by a man:

> Who peyntede the leon, tel me who?
> By Godde, if wommen hadde writen stories,
> As clerkes han withinne hire oratories,
> They wolde han writen of men moore wikkednesse
> Than al the mark of Adam may redresse.
>
> (3.692–6)

These celebrated, oft-cited lines bespeak supreme masculine complacency: for even in acknowledging gendered monopolization of artistic viewpoint, the masculine artist – the poet Chaucer – continues to practise his craft while purporting to speak for, indeed as, a woman. Poems and paintings, however, continue to hold interpretive possibilities for female readers once men depart the scene. Even the author of *Ancrene Wisse*, the most programmatically controlling text considered in this volume, knows that the women for whom he writes will navigate personal pathways through his text once it passes through their window.

Particular medieval women's lives and texts – the brilliance of which defies any characterization of this era as 'the so-called Dark Ages' for 'the female imagination' – unfold in part III.[7] These are lives that touched and transformed English textual traditions in some way: from Marie de France's dedication of her *Lais* to (most likely) the Plantagenet Henry II, and her claim to have translated her *Fables* from a translation by King Alfred; to Heloise, who made it into Jankyn's 'book of wikked wyves', containing the textual tradition that underlies the creation of the Wife of Bath herself (*Wife of Bath's Prologue*, 3.677, 685); to Christine de Pizan, literary adversary of the monumentally influential *Romance of the Rose*, a work she viewed as obscene, misogynist, and dangerously ambiguous, and that Chaucer had translated; to Joan of Arc – about whom Christine wrote her last poem – who wrote pugnaciously to the King of England and the Duke of Bedford as the virgin defender of France, and who inspired the loathing of Caxton (among other Englishmen); to Julian of Norwich and Margery Kempe, who spent 'many days' conversing and communing in the love of Christ, a meeting recorded in *The Book of Margery Kempe*; to, finally, the women who may have written Middle English lyrics and romances, cannily responding to literary conventions without, however, leaving their names.

We have presented both lives and texts here; indeed, these two are concepts difficult to disentangle. There are at least two reasons for the difficulty:

first, we know everything we do of these lives through texts, of course, be they documentary or recreational; and second, the lived lives themselves are constituted by bits and pieces of texts. Margery Kempe seems to have modelled herself on various saints, including her near contemporary Bridget of Sweden (whose *Revelations* she knew), and her scribe, further, may have fashioned her narrative to fit into the tradition of written lives of other holy devouts. Julian of Norwich, as an anchoress, used the rule of anchoritic life in order to constitute her self. Lives are made up of texts in other ways as well: they are conducted through the exchange of texts (the letters of Joan of Arc, and of Heloise and Abelard; the polemics of Christine de Pizan). Lives can be saved by texts: from the searingly depressive effects of reading misogynistic Matheolus, Christine turns to building a metaphorical city of ladies in words to save her very spirit. And lives – or parts of lives – can be lost by texts, of course: Abelard's books were burned, and he was castrated for keeping company with Heloise as her instructor, the two of them reading books as a cover for amorous pursuits; Joan of Arc was condemned for (among other things) wearing the wrong kind of *textus* (fabric, clothing); the threat of heresy loomed dangerously around Margery Kempe and, presumably, the scribes who wrote down her story.

Each woman realized the power of writing in different ways. Roberta Krueger finds the strength of Marie de France's texts – created in the flourishing literary culture of England in the twelfth century – in their bold claims to teach, using a female voice that interrupts masculine traditions, and in their provocation of the reader to interpretation and self-knowledge. Heloise, as Christopher Baswell observes, chooses to assume a remarkable range of identities – sister, daughter, lover, wife, whore, abbess – through epistolary form. Julian of Norwich's powerful shaping of her book is explicated by Nicholas Watson in his discussion of her relentless interpretation and theologizing about her visions (experienced in her anchorhold in the last decades of the fourteenth century). *The Book of Margery Kempe* was created in the charged atmosphere of the early fifteenth century in which vernacular prose was a suspect medium; Margery triumphs over political and practical obstacles to produce a document, as Carolyn Dinshaw argues, at once of its time and profoundly out of its time. Even less educated than Margery, Joan of Arc used writing to rally support and intimidate her enemies in the Hundred Years' War against England, in sometimes 'bloodthirsty' prose, as Nadia Margolis vividly puts it. In contrast to Joan's short life, Christine's long career as a professional writer, David Hult finds, in France in the late fourteenth and early fifteenth centuries, encompasses her shifting positions on literary style as well as on the oppressive power of misogyny she denounced early in her writings. Certainly not professional writers, the women who may have written lyrics and romances nonetheless would probably have had a good grasp of literary conventions, as Sarah McNamer suggests, particularly when it came to gender.

The range of literary engagements shown here is wide, as is the range of personal religious belief. Life in medieval England, as in the rest of Western Europe, was founded on and structured by Christianity, of course, but within that structure operated a range of practices and beliefs, devotion and doctrine, as can be seen throughout this volume: Julian of Norwich developed her concept of Jesus as Mother, for example (echoing St Bernard of Clairvaux), in a theology differing markedly from that of Thomas Aquinas; Margery Kempe annoyed almost everyone around her with her devotional extremes, but was never formally accused of heresy; Joan was convicted of heresy, blasphemy, and other charges, and burned. During the time of the Great Schism (1378–1417), two and then even three popes competed for legitimacy; even though the Council of Constance in 1417 resolved the schism at last with the election of Pope Martin V, two others continued in their claims: Joan of Arc was herself asked which one was to be followed (she did not give an answer, too preoccupied with battling the English was she). The Church of the late medieval period was fractious and multiplex, riven by tensions that would later erupt in full-scale nationalist and religious conflicts. At the same time, it was heterogeneous and capacious, allowing for greater local variations of practice than would be possible under later panoptical papacies.

Internal threats divided Christians, but external threats in some sense held them together. The alienness of those other great religious systems of the time, Judaism and Islam, was itself doubted but nonetheless imposed: Jews were expelled from England in 1290, in an action that might be seen as an attempt to make the people whose religion preceded and enabled Christianity clearly external to it; Muslims were geographically more clearly other, but there was considerable learned debate about whether Islam was a Christian heresy (a position Langland in *Piers Plowman* accepted [B 15, C 17])[8] or a paganism (adopted by romances, including Chaucer's *Man of Law's Tale*). It is important in any case to acknowledge the shaping forces of both Judaism and Islam on Christianity, witnessed in their pervasive but sometimes shadowy presence in later medieval English texts. In the most celebrated examples, Chaucer's *Prioress's Tale* and *Man of Law's Tale*, their presence is marked by gender and sexuality – not a coincidence, since Jewish and Muslim bodies were believed to be fundamentally different from Christian bodies, but rather a clear indication that this arena will richly repay further inquiry, and deserves more attention than we are able to give it in this volume. For now, we can note that in *The Book of Margery Kempe*, Margery's pilgrimage to the Holy Land brings her into pleasant contact with 'Saracens': they make much of her and treat her better than do her own companions – and she notes in passing that one is good-looking, to boot. Just as Langland finds Mohammed to be an example for the Pope (c 17.239–49), so Margery's experience here must be a comment on the craven Christianity of her fellows.

Margery's pilgrimage brought her to the very place where Mary Magdalene saw Christ after his resurrection, and this brings us, finally, back to our frontispiece. The Magdalene whom Margery saw in her various visions was not the Magdalene as preacher, however, serenely detached in her communication of God's words, but the Magdalene of the gospels, the one whom Christ warned, 'Touch me not.' In that role she provided another kind of model for women – of decorous, even happy acceptance of earthly limitations – which Margery, for all her devotional dependence on biblical narrative, in fact refused to accept. This volume will help us understand the conditions in which women encountered and produced possibilities for their lives in texts, and will lead us to think further about the conditions in which texts must be left behind.

NOTES

1. See Jacobus de Voragine, *The Golden Legend*, selections ed. Richard Hamer (London: Penguin, 1998).

2. See *The Regement of Princes*, lines 932–1044 (esp. lines 1013–15), conveniently available in *Chaucer to Spenser: An Anthology*, ed. Derek Pearsall (Oxford: Blackwell, 1999), pp. 327–31.

3. See Roger S. Wieck, William M. Voelkle, and K. Michelle Hearne, *The Hours of Henry VIII: A Renaissance Masterpiece by Jean Poyet* (New York: George Braziller, in association with The Pierpont Morgan Library, 2000), pp. 138–9.

4. *A Midsummer Night's Dream*, in *The Norton Shakespeare. Based on the Oxford Edition*, ed. Stephen Greenblatt et al. (New York: Norton, 1997), 1.1.70–3.

5. All references to Chaucer in this volume follow *The Riverside Chaucer*, ed. Larry D. Benson (Boston: Houghton Mifflin, 1987).

6. *Sir Gawain and the Green Knight*, ed. Richard H. Osberg (New York: Peter Lang, 1990), lines 2414–19; our translation.

7. *The Norton Anthology of Literature by Women: The Traditions in English*, ed. Sandra M. Gilbert and Susan Gubar, 2nd edn (New York: Norton, 1996), p. 14.

8. *Piers Plowman: The B Version*, ed. George Kane and E. Talbot Donaldson, rev. edn (London: Athlone and Berkeley: University of California Press, 1988); *Piers Plowman by William Langland: An Edition of the C-Text*, ed. Derek Pearsall (Berkeley: University of California Press, 1982).

I

ESTATES OF WOMEN

I

DANIEL T. KLINE

Female childhoods

Medieval persons showed nuanced awareness of human lifespan development. The familiar 'ages of man' texts generally followed one of three conceptual systems: the biologists' theory of three ages (youth, maturity, and old age); the physiologists' theory of four ages (childhood, youth, maturity, and old age), corresponding to the four humours, seasons, and elements; and the astrologers' theory of seven ages (infancy, childhood, adolescence, youth, maturity, old age, decrepitude) following the Ptolemaic structure of the universe.[1] By the later Middle Ages a stable set of terms divided childhood into seven-year segments: *infantia* (infancy), *pueritia* (childhood), and *adolescentia* (adolescence). These demarcations were based primarily upon age but also considered the social, emotional, and mental development of the individual. Prior to the age of seven or *infantia*, an infant girl was not considered to be a fully rational and responsible agent. The transition to *pueritia* was marked by growing personal awareness and social accountability, and the move into *adolescentia* was marked by the onset of menarche and secondary sexual characteristics. At *adolescentia*, regarded as twelve for girls and fourteen for boys, young people could marry according to canon law or could break a marriage contract arranged in their childhood by paying a fine equivalent to the value of the marriage.[2] Although remaining unmarried was a possibility, the life options available to most girls were limited to marriage, religious vocation, or some form of domestic employment or household management. The social ideal, of course, was for young medieval girls to marry and have children, for the normative course of secular life led a girl directly from her father's house as a child and daughter to her husband's house as a wife and mother.

Infantia: conception and parturition

In concert with the relatively limited life options available to maturing young women, a female infant in the Middle Ages faced gendered assumptions even prior to birth. Medieval medical tradition, derived from Aristotle, viewed the creation of a female child as the unsuccessful attempt to generate a male. One important medieval treatise calls a girl

> *puella*, as it were clene and pure as þe blake of þe yȝe, as seiþ Isidre. For among all þat is iloued [beloved] in a wench chastite and clennes is iloued most. Men schal take hede of wenches for þey bene hote and moist of complexioun; and tender, small, pliaunt, and faire of disposicioun of body; shame fast, fereful, and mury, touching þe affeccioun; delicat in clothinge. For as Senec seiþ, semelich [modest] cloþinge bysemeþ hem wel þat beþ chast wenchis.[3]

The references to learned authorities here legitimate the discursive construction of the nascent girl; the description of her physiognomic and humoral characteristics quickly lapses into an evaluation of the girl's fragility, as opposed to the boy, who is 'clepid *puer* when he is iwanied [weaned] from melk and departed from þe brest and þe tete, and knoweþ good and euel. þerefore he is able to fonge [undertake] chastisinge and lore [learning], and þanne hi is iput and sette to lore vnder tutours'.[4] While young boys are defined according to their separation from feminine nurture and are prepared for schooling and the lifelong discipline of hard work, girls are defined by their sexuality, held to be emotionally labile, and marked by suitable clothing. Children, especially girls, were often seen as fully fledged subjects from the perspective of what they would become as adults, rather than as subjects in their own right.[5]

Infantia: birth and baptism

Birth was the province of women: as in the Nativity play of the N-Town cycle (to be performed in aNy-Town),[6] medieval women gave birth in the presence of female friends and relations under the care of a midwife, who was empowered to baptize critically ill newborns in extreme emergencies.[7] Baptism itself served a number of important long- and short-term social functions for the newly born girl. The infant daughter was given her Christian name and ushered into the religious community while surrounded by her family, godparents and extended kin, and family friends. Parents provided for the young girl's physical needs, while the godparents taught the basic tenets of the Church ('Here [their] pater noster and here crede'),[8] and both were enjoined to protect the youngster from accidents like drowning, burning, trampling, and smothering.[9] Since godparents often later served as guardians, parents might choose godparents of a higher social status who could serve as the girl's advocate or employer in adolescence.[10] Nonetheless, young girls did not earn income as did boys prior to their majority; therefore, raising a daughter and marrying her off meant that her family lost money, often in the form of a dowry, while a son's labour and eventual marriage brought wealth into the household.

The medieval double vision regarding female children – their coincident social disapprobation and ideological elevation – and the social and theological necessity of infant baptism is depicted most potently in the elegiac dream vision *Pearl*. An apology for the innocence of young children that subverts conventional medieval hierarchies, the poem features a dead infant girl who summons a 'theology of childhood' in educating the adult narrator, even though she knows 'nawþer Pater ne Crede' (line 485).[11] The *Pearl*-child's 'theology of childhood' is refracted through the 'materiality of childhood' in a veiled account of her birth, brief life, death, and burial. Swathed in the scent of rose-water at birth and wearing the pearl-encrusted crysom of infant baptism, the *Pearl*-child is a 'faunt', a young child who was nearer to the Dreamer than aunt or niece (line 233), whose relationships extended to godparents and even the wider parish community, and who died before she could learn the rudiments of Christian faith. The *Pearl*-child's argument is that she should be valued for who she is, an infant girl, and not just for what she might become – a paramour, an object of sexual desire, a bride. Bolstered by biblical texts from Matthew to Revelation, the *Pearl*-child admonishes the Dreamer to internalize permanently the cultural inversion indicated by Jesus' saying, 'The last shall be first and the first last.' By extension, a culture that devalues the young girls stands equally rebuked: as Jesus tells the disciples, 'Hys ryche no wyȝ myȝt wynne / Bot he com þyder ryȝt as a chylde' (lines 722–3).[12]

Pueritia: education and training

Infant girls were ushered into the social world through rituals surrounding birth and baptism. In contrast to the *Pearl*-child, who does not attain the rudiments of Christian teaching, the young Virgin Mary is often depicted as the obedient daughter and perfect student, as in the N-Town *Mary Play*, a previously self-contained play now incorporated into the N-Town cycle.[13] Mary's obedience to her parents and to God is an object lesson for the young, while her parents' devotion to her and to the Church is a paradigm for adult emulation. Mary's exemplary life itself becomes the basis for two prayers, the 'ave' and 'Our Lady's Psalter' (which includes the pater noster, or 'Lord's Prayer'). These prayers not only formed the basis of medieval piety, they also provided the educational foundation of medieval youth. One late fourteenth-century school primer begins with a symbol of the cross (✠), which signalled the student to cross herself with the saying, 'Christ's cross me speed'. This is then followed by an ABC, a denunciation of the devil, the paternoster, the ave Maria, the Apostle's Creed, the Ten Commandments, the seven deadly sins, the seven principal virtues, the seven works of bodily mercy, the seven works of spiritual mercy, the five bodily wits, the four cardinal virtues, the seven gifts of the Holy Spirit, 1 Corinthians 13, the Beatitudes, and the Sayings of St Augustine.[14]

Medieval education focused primarily upon training boys in basic literacy for ecclesiastical and professional duties; girls had access to more informal instruction. Young boys might attend a grammar school (to train in Latin) or a song school, as do the 'litel clergeon' and his older 'felawe' in Chaucer's *Prioress's Tale* (7.495–536),[15] before moving on to higher studies. Girls might receive instruction at a local nunnery; from a nurse, chaplain, clerk, or priest; or from local charitable institutions. By the late fourteenth century, guilds or other fraternities began to sponsor local schools.[16] Nunneries appear to have regularly instructed their novices, and about two thirds of English nunneries intermittently took young children of both sexes as boarders, despite ecclesiastical prohibitions.[17] In *The Reeve's Tale*, Symkin's wife

> . . . thoughte that a lady sholde hire spare   [be aloof]
> What for hire kynrede and hir nortelrie   [nurture; education]
> That she hadde learned in the nonnerie.
> (1.3966–8)

Young gentlewomen probably learned enough Latin to read their psalters or books of hours, but more likely received sufficient instruction in the vernacular (French and, into the fourteenth century, English) to run a household, read popular or religious literature, manage business affairs, and conduct themselves well in polite company.[18] Widely copied over several centuries, Bibbesworth's *Treatise*, a thirteenth-century lexicon of English phrases written for the Duchess of Pembroke to educate her children, provided the vocabulary necessary for young Anglo-Norman nobles to converse in polite society (terms describing the weather, health, and courtly pursuits, for example) and for young women to run a large household (expressions for lighting a fire, setting a table, and preparing food, among others).[19]

Pueritia: courtesy, conduct, and manners

In fact, Chaucer's Prioress appears to have gained just such a practical education, combining proper manners and religious piety in a bilingual context (1.118–62). She learned French 'After the scole of Stratford atte Bowe' (Anglo-Norman French rather than the Parisian dialect (1.125)), and while her Latin was minimal she could sing the divine service (1.122) and participate in the religious observances of her house. Above all, however, the Prioress is cheerful, considerate, courteous, and has exquisite table manners, reflecting the most important aspect of a young medieval girl's education, her instruction in morals and manners.[20] Providing a model for socializing children, courtesy literature articulated the 'rudimentary traits [which] were felt to lay the groundwork for a child's future success in schooling, apprenticeship, service, career, and marriage'.[21] These texts could range from sayings collections like 'The ABC of Aristotle' to courtesy books like 'The Young Children's Book' or extensive compilations like *The Book of the Knight of the Tower*.[22] Hagiographical collections like *The Golden Legend* or *The South English Legendary* also served as courtesy texts by including youthful episodes in the saint's life as examples of pious conduct in the face of temptation.[23]

Most conduct literature was aimed at young men or at both sexes, although some texts were directed exclusively at girls. 'How the Good Wijf Tauȝte Hir Douȝtir', a popular poem recopied into the fifteenth century,[24] demonstrates how a young girl's physical desirability, religious practice, conventional piety, and gentle manners together create a marriageable young woman. The poem charts the young girl's life from childhood to the marriage offer, into marriage and relations with her husband, to her management of the household and of her reputation in town, and finally to the birth and disciplining of her own children. Ultimately, a good daughter's purpose is to become a good mother, and a good mother prepares her daughter for 'spowsynge' by gathering a dower and dispensing womanly advice from the moment of her birth.

Adolescentia: *raptus* and marriage

Perhaps better than any other literary text, Chaucer's *Physician's Tale* problematizes the multiple tensions of growing up female in late medieval England, for it presents a marriageable young woman caught between mutually exclusive masculine desires: the lust of judge Apius and the paternal control exerted by Virginius over his daughter and heiress. Described as a living courtesy book (6.107–9), the exemplary fourteen-year-old Virginia is portrayed exactly at the moment of social transition from childhood to marriageability: in fact, she is actually shown walking with her mother from their home to the temple as Apius plots his seizure or 'raptus'. Chaucer's explicit linkage of Virginia with courtesy (or 'good conduct') literature – which goes beyond anything in his sources – marks her as an important socio-economic asset: family status might rise through Virginia's good marriage.

While *The Physician's Tale* shares the basic plot of each of the analogues, Chaucer adds to the source drawn from Livy (*Ab urbe condita*) via

Boccaccio's *De mulieribus claris* (ch. 56) two major sections of material, the advice to parents and governesses (6.73–104) and the dialogue between Virginius and Virginia prior to her murder (6.212–50). In addition, Chaucer notably changes and particularizes the charges brought against Virginius in court, thus grounding *The Physician's Tale* in issues concerning marriage, wardship, and child custody in late medieval England. These adaptations explore the tensions surrounding female childhood in aristocratic circles and critique the forms of violence necessary to perpetuate that patriarchal system.

Depending upon their family's wealth, class, and social aspirations, young girls might also enter service in the household of another family to work or to be educated; in other cases girls learned a skilled trade or craft, especially in the textile arts, as cloth-maker, embroiderer, or seamstress. Service in a well-to-do household groomed a girl socially and increased her marriageability, while the craft work she learned carried over easily into the household. An unmarried female Londoner could practise her trade, or, if married, could conduct business, contract debts, and settle legal cases, under London's *feme sole* provision.[25] Service, like apprenticeship, provided lateral mobility between equally placed families, while both arrangements also created the opportunity for a daughter to marry up the social scale. Unfortunately, young girls in service could be mistreated, the most commonly heard complaint in the legal record being the girl's sexual exploitation.[26]

While girls were most often taught at home, in some cases well-born girls and boys might be educated together in a noble household not their own,[27] and these early relationships later bore fruit through marriage and other associations. The early, mixed affinities of noble young boys and girls, and the attendant household intrigues, love relationships, political careers, and labyrinthine exertions to establish or reassert their own 'gentle' identities are a staple of much medieval courtly literature, particularly the romance. The widely diffused poetic romance *Floris and Blancheflur* depicts two noble children, a Saracen boy and Christian girl, raised inseparably and educated together;[28] in accord with the well-worn story of lovers separated and reunited, the youthful pair overcomes a series of misadventures to be reunited as king and queen. One of the delights of this genre lies in the ingenious plot twists that take the young people away from their native lands and the even more outlandish scenarios that return them home. One of its negative traits is the tendency to represent young girls as objects of exchange between men, facilitating patriarchal power as potential mothers and wives. In the apt phrase of Constance in *The Man of Law's Tale*, 'Wommen are born to thraldom and penance, / And to been under mannes governance' (2.286–7). The plot elaborations of the romance genre demonstrate the degree to which marriage seems to be an inevitable, unavoidable, even universal outcome for young medieval women. Even virginal saints eventually become brides of Christ.

Conclusion

Medieval authors, mostly men, struggled with conflicting imperatives in their considerations of female childhood. On one hand, the successful rearing of healthy young women was both essential for the social and reproductive needs of the culture in general and necessary to the maintenance of family lineage and inheritance in particular. On the other hand, the social disenfranchisement of young girls placed them on the lowest rung of the social ladder and the conditions of medieval life often left them physically at risk. And yet these contending imperatives of female childhood create possibilities for resistance, agency, and surprise. In the *Pearl*-child's spirited 'Sir, ȝe haf your tale mysetente' (line 257) or Virginia's trenchant 'Pardee' (7.240) in response to her father, we hear the echo of young medieval girls opposing, even if for only a short time, the powerful forces that compelled them to conform to conventional social roles or to accept coercive personal situations.

NOTES

1. See J. A. Burrow, *The Ages of Man: A Study in Medieval Writing and Thought* (Oxford: Clarendon Press, 1986), pp. 1–54.
2. Sue Sheridan Walker, 'Free Consent and Marriage of Feudal Wards in Medieval England', *Journal of Medieval History* 8 (1982): 123–34.
3. 'De puella'. In *On the Properties of Things: John of Trevisa's Translation of Bartholomaeus Anglicus De Proprietatibus Rerum*. Gen. ed. M. C. Seymour. 3 vols. (Oxford University Press, 1975–88), p. 301.
4. 'De puero'. In *On the Properties of Things*, p. 300.
5. Jacques Le Goff, ed., *The Medieval World*, trans. Lydia G. Cochrane (London: Collins and Brown, 1990), pp. 16–17.
6. See Play 15 in Stephen Spector, ed., *The N-Town Play: Cotton MS Vespasian D.8*. EETS ss 11–12 (Oxford University Press, 1991), pp. 152–63.
7. John Myrc, *Instructions for Parish Priests*, ed. Edward Peacock, EETS os 31 (London: Kegan Paul, 1902. New York: Greenwood, 1969), lines 87–140.
8. Ibid., line 153.
9. *English Fragments from Latin Medieval Service Books*, ed. Henry Littlehales, EETS es 90 (London: Kegan Paul, Trench, Trubner, 1903), p. 5.
10. Barbara Hanawalt, *Growing Up in Medieval London: The Experience of Childhood in History* (London: Oxford University Press, 1993), pp. 48–9.
11. All references to *Pearl* are from Malcolm Andrew and Ronald Waldron, eds., *The Poems of the Pearl Manuscript*. York Medieval Texts, 2nd ser. (Berkeley: University of California Press, 1978). Henceforth line numbers will be cited parenthetically in the text.

12. See Matthew 18: 1–3.

13. Peter Meredith, *The Mary Play from the N-Town Manuscript* (New York: Longman, 1987).

14. Jo Ann Hoeppner Moran, *The Growth of English Schooling, 1340–1548: Learning, Literacy, and Laicization in Pre-Reformation York* (Princeton University Press, 1985), p. 43.

15. Henceforth, Chaucer fragment and line numbers are indicated parenthetically in the text.

16. John Lawson and Harold Silver, *A Social History of Education in England* (London: Methuen, 1973), p. 44.

17. Eileen Power, *Medieval English Nunneries* (Cambridge University Press, 1922), pp. 264–5.

18. See Moran, *Growth of English Schooling*, pp. 69–70; and Nicholas Orme, *English Schools in the Middle Ages* (London: Methuen, 1973), pp. 52–5.

19. William Rothwell, ed., *Walter de Bibbesworth: Le Tretiz* (London: Anglo-Norman Text Society), 1990.

20. See Norbert Elias, *The Civilizing Process: Sociogenetic and Psychogenetic Investigations*, rev. edn (London: Blackwell, 2000), pp. 45–182; and Suzanne W. Hull, *Chaste, Silent, and Obedient: English Books for Women, 1475–1640* (San Marino, CA: Huntington Library, 1982).

21. Hanawalt, *Growing Up in Medieval London*, p. 70.

22. Frederick J. Furnivall, ed., *Early English Meals and Manners*, EETS OS 32 (London, 1868; rpt New York: Kraus, 1969), pp. 11–12, 16–25; M. Y. Offord, ed., *The Book of the Knight of the Tower*, EETS SS 2 (London: Oxford University Press, 1971).

23. Jacobus de Voragine, *The Golden Legend: Readings on the Saints*, ed. and trans. William Granger Ryan. 2 vols. (Princeton University Press, 1993); Charlotte D'Evelyn and Anna J. Mill, eds., *The South English Legendary*. 3 vols. (Oxford University Press, 1956–9).

24. Furnivall, *Early English Meals*, pp. 36–47; and Tauno F. Mustanoja, ed., *The Good Wife Taught Her Daughter, The Good Wyfe Wold a Pylgremage, and The Thewis of Gud Women* (Helsinki: Suomalaisen Kirjallisuuden Seuran, 1948), pp. 158–72.

25. See Judith Bennett, 'Medieval Women, Modern Women: Across the Great Divide', in *Culture and History, 1350–1600: Essays on English Communities, Identities, and Writing*, ed. David Aers (Detroit: Wayne State University Press, 1992), pp. 154–5.

26. P. J. P. Goldberg, ed., *Women in England, c. 1275–1525* (Manchester University Press, 1995), pp. 252 ff.

27. Nicholas Orme, *From Childhood to Chivalry: The Education of the English Kings and Aristocracy, 1066–1530* (London: Methuen, 1984), pp. 28–36.

28. J. Rawson Lumby, ed., *King Horn, Floriz and Blanchflur, The Assumption of Our Lady*, re-edited by George H. McKnight, EETS OS 14, 1866 (London: Oxford University Press, 1901), pp. 71–110.

2

RUTH EVANS

Virginities

How do you know that someone is a virgin? This question is implicitly posed in the *Nativity* pageant of the N-town collection of biblical drama, just after Mary has given birth. Salomé, one of the two midwives attendant on Mary, refuses to believe that the Virgin is still a virgin.[1] She insists on 'touching' Mary's body. Terrifyingly, her hand turns 'ded and drye [withered] as claye [earth]' (line 256). An angel appears, and orders her to touch Jesus' swaddling-clothes. Frightened, Salomé obeys the angel and the hand is miraculously restored to health. But a number of questions are left unanswered. Since female roles were all played by men, the scene calls for some ingenuities of staging and suspension of audience disbelief. Readers today may wonder why Mary's virginity, and medieval virginities in general, are invested with such powers of magic and danger. And what exactly does Salomé touch? Does she really touch inside Mary's body? Surely (we think now) this is sacrilege – or bad taste? In the Chester version, the figure of Expositor steers the audience towards a general moral, 'that unbeleeffe [lack of faith] is a fowle [evil] sinne' (line 721), keeping the audience from pondering too closely the troubling complexities of Mary's physiology.

But the N-town pageant goes out of its way to emphasize physical 'touch'. Zelomye, the other midwife, asks to 'towch and fele' Mary's body to see if she needs medicine, and Mary invites her to '[t]ast [feel] with ȝoure hand' to find out if she is a 'clene mayde and pure virgyn' (lines 224–5). The Latin stage directions say that Zelomye '*palpat . . . Beatam Virginem . . .*' [feels the Blessed Virgin]. Though the exact form of verification is unclear, Zelomye is satisfied: 'Here opynly I fele and se: / A fayr chylde of a maydon is born' (lines 238–9). But sceptical Salomé demands to 'preve' [test] Mary's virginity by 'hand towchynge' (line 247). Mary assents: 'Towch with ȝoure hand and wele asay [find out]' (line 251). She goes even further, inviting Salomé to '[w]ysely [with discretion] ransake [examine] and trye [find out] þe trewthe owth' (line 252). 'Ransake' also suggests violence (*MED*: 'to plunder, ransack, steal; to treat roughly, mistreat'), evoking the popular medieval image of Mary (and the consecrated virgin) as a 'tower' to be defended. And 'ransake' can also mean 'to examine a wound' (*MED*), a sense that presages the risen Christ's invitation to Doubting Thomas to probe his wounds in the N-town *Appearance to Thomas*, an invitation that also plays on the binary of wholeness and incompleteness that marks Salomé's testing: 'Put þin [your] hool [whole] hand into my ryght syde' (line 339). Yet the N-town stage direction only says that Salomé '*tangit* [touches]' Mary, leaving the form of the touching inexplicit. Instead, the touch takes its place within a system of correspondences and resemblances: the *touching* of Jesus' clothes (a detail not present in the Chester *Nativity*); Christ's later injunction to Mary Magdalene *not* to touch, in *The Appearance to Mary Magdalene*: 'Towche me not as ʒett [yet], Mary' (line 42). *Noli me tangere*: the words that so dismay Margery Kempe when she has a vision of Mary Magdalene and Christ in the garden, for she cannot imagine herself being happy if Christ had spoken to her as he had to Mary, if he had refused *her* touch.[2]

Virginity is a category that the Middle Ages found indispensable to think with: unsettling and yet enormously productive. Salomé's faithless touch makes Mary's virginity the locus of a number of broad and compelling concerns: the meaning of faith; how to show devotion; the limits of knowledge and of recognition. It is implied that Zelomye must have found some physical proof: the hymen perhaps? But how can Mary's body offer irrefutable empirical proof of her virginity? Only Salomé's shrivelled hand can do that, ironically signifying the Virgin's wholeness. Despite Salomé's explorations, virginity can never be a sure thing. Faith and miracle plug the gap between suspicion and certain knowledge, but they only displace the questions on to other sites, other bodies, other texts. In *Getting Medieval*, Carolyn Dinshaw explores 'contiguity and displacement' as signs of what she calls the 'the queer': a disruptive excess that shakes the foundations of representation but which also makes connections, 'knock[ing] signifiers loose, ungrounding bodies, making them strange, working in this way to provoke perceptual shifts and subsequent corporeal response in those touched'.[3] Whether or not we want to call Mary's virginity queer, the N-town pageant articulates what is both disturbing and powerful about virginity: a state that refuses representation, whose 'truth' cannot be spoken by the body, yet which acts as a relay-point for faith, devotion, and knowledge.

Although some famous men were virgins – Christ, St John the Evangelist, St Alexis – virginity and chastity are overwhelmingly viewed in the Middle Ages as female concerns. Why? Partly because of increased devotion to Mary and the rise of women in monasticism; partly because virginity was a precious object to be guarded by the senses and the feminine was synonymous with the sensual; partly for economic reasons: within medieval systems of inheritance and land tenure, the woman's body is male property and the virgin wife guarantees the purity of the family line. Virginity's yearning for purity owes a great deal to clerical anxieties about ritual pollution, anxieties that are linked to the misogynistic view of women – and women's sexuality in particular – as dirt. Yet virginity in the Middle Ages cannot be reduced to fetish or abject 'Thing'. Women of all estates and ages, lay and in orders, virgins or otherwise, appropriated its representations in bold and sometimes radical ways.

The memory of virgins was everywhere in late medieval English culture: in biblical drama, in popular story-collections, in lyrics and poems, in sermons, in rules and treatises for enclosed women, in manuscript illuminations, in manuals of pastoral instruction to the laity, in court poetry, interspersed with romances in household miscellanies. Chaucer's Wife of Bath could presume that her late fourteenth-century audience were sufficiently familiar with the high value put on virginity for her to challenge that valuation. The virgin-martyr saints (Katherine, Margaret, Barbara, Cecilia, Lucy, Agnes, Agatha, Christine, Petronilla/Parnel, etc.) were widespread and multivalent cultural symbols, their stories recycled in various modes and genres over centuries; their names regularly given to children (generations of Paston women were called Agnes, Margaret, and Elizabeth; Henry VI's mother was called Katherine); their feast-days used as date-markers in the 'kalendars' of the Church year in medieval Primers; their images painted on the stained glass and rood screens of parish churches in East Anglia and Devon with money provided by the pious and prosperous laity. Katherine of Alexandria was the most popular, with Margaret of Antioch a close second. Their statues even flanked the image of Our Lady on the shrine at Walsingham.

Medieval women used these virgin saints in highly personal ways. In a letter to her husband, John Paston I, in 1441, the young wife Margaret Paston, from a prominent bourgeois family in Norfolk, urges him to 'wear the ring with the image of Saint Margaret that I sent you for a remembrance till ye come home'.[4] As an object commemorating both a famous historical virgin martyr and Margaret's role as wife, the ring carries sexualized and collective memories that bind together husband and wife within their community. Margaret was the patron saint of childbirth because of her miraculous escape from the dragon's belly, suggesting that medieval women read the virgin-martyr lives symbolically as well as literally. When Margery Kempe feels troubled because of her lack of virginity, Christ reassures her that she is numbered with the virgin martyrs: 'Dowtyr, I be-hote [promise] þe [you] þe same grace þat I be-hyte [promised] Seynt Kateryne, Seynt Margarete, Seynt Barbara . . . in so mech þat [in that] what creatur in erth [if any creature on earth] vn-to þe Day of Dom [Judgment Day] aske þe [you] any bone [favour] & belevyth þat God lovyth þe [you] he xal [shall] haue hys bone or ellys

[else] a better thyng.'[5] The miracle-working of the virgin saints was an ideal to aspire to – and even, sometimes, to surpass.

Just as virginity belies a singular definition, so its literature resists easy categorization: the plural 'virginities' in my title signals the material's heterogeneity. It has been traditional to trace a chronology within this long period from a 'militant' to a 'bridal' virginity, to use Sarah Salih's terms: from the virgin as a virago – a woman acting like a man (ninth to eleventh centuries), to the feminized virgin (twelfth to fourteenth centuries): a romance heroine married to Christ.[6] But, as Salih points out, these narratives do not displace each other chronologically, but are the effects of spaces and places – and, I would add, of genres and audiences.

The sheer variety of texts witnesses to the all-pervasiveness of virginity as a model for medieval women. It is central to the so-called Katherine Group of virgin-martyr lives and their associated texts, the *Ancrene Wisse* [*Guide for Anchoresses*] and the treatise *Hali Meiðhad* [*Letter on Virginity*] (both early thirteenth century), addressed in the first instance to three aristocratic enclosed women.[7] But there are numerous later treatises on virginity addressed to lay people. Women of the seigneurial classes, lay and religious, consumed female virgin-martyr hagiography, such as Lydgate's *Legend of Seynt Margarete* (1415–26), or the Augustinian friar John Capgrave's extraordinarily ambitious *Life of Saint Katherine* (c. 1445), or lives in devotional miscellanies, such as Auchinleck (Edinburgh, National Library of Scotland MS Advocates 19.2.1; c. 1330–40), and orthodox sermon collections, such as John Mirk's *Festial*.[8] The heretical Lollards (their name was first an abusive term), a socially diverse group who broadly followed the radical tenets of John Wyclif (c. 1330–84), were opposed to lurid narratives, so the virgin-martyr lives are not included in the sermons on saints' days in the standard Wyclifite sermon cycle. In *The Second Nun's Tale* and *The Physician's Tale* Chaucer writes the passionate suffering of female virgins, although the latter is curiously unclassifiable: offered as an 'historial [historical] thyng notable [famous]' (6.155–6), it is neither *passio* nor hagiography. Virginity also enters medieval romances: *Sir Eglamour of Artois* has a chaste heroine, and Eglamour kills a dragon at Rome, which links his narrative to that of St Margaret (copies of both are in the Auchinleck manuscript).[9] Medieval medical texts offer receipts for the reconstruction of the hymen that bear witness to a cultural preoccupation with the intact female body.[10] And *The Book of Margery Kempe* (c. 1436) records in part the desires and struggles of its bourgeois East Anglian author to be a born-again virgin. Yet this obsession with virginity must be put into perspective. In the legendaries male saints outnumber female ones, and Mary Magdalene – who was *not* a virgin – is only second in popularity to Katherine of Alexandria.

Despite the fact that a large number of the legends were written for or at the behest of women, women did not write them. But there are important exceptions, although they concern texts that were not written in English: Clemence of Barking's twelfth-century Anglo-Norman *Life of St Katherine*, and Christine de Pizan's *Cité de dames* [Book of the City of Ladies] (1405), a third of which is devoted to virgins.[11] De Pizan's work was popular with English women book collectors: Chaucer's granddaughter, Alice, owned a copy and so probably did Cecily Neville, Duchess of York (mother of Edward IV).

Why virginity?

In the traditional division of medieval women's 'estates', virginity offers the greatest heavenly returns. To be a chaste wife is good, to be a chaste widow is better, but to be a virgin is best. As the author of *Hali Meiðhad* puts it: 'For wedlac haueð hire frut þrittifald in heouene; widewehad, sixtifald; meiðhad wið hundretfald ouergeað baþe. [For marriage has its reward thirtyfold in heaven; widowhood, sixtyfold; virginity, with a hundredfold, surpasses both.]'[12] These precise (and conventional) arithmetical ratios, as well as the female career-hierarchy that they support, owe their values to St Jerome. Virginity represents the closest thing on earth to prelapsarian purity. And not just for career virgins. Rather, virginity is a spectrum of ideals, one that includes the related category of chastity: a vanquishing of sexual temptation by the sexually active – a practice not synonymous with virginity but sometimes overlapping with it. *Of þe Mirrour of Chastite* (c. 1380), part of a longer work known as *Pore Caitif*, addresses laymen and women, arguing that chastity brings them nearer to the angels: 'gostly [spiritual] virtues ben aungels þinges, and principally chastite is aungels þinge. Be [Through] chastite men and wymmen ben lickened to aungels, whanne kynde [human nature] is ouercomen þoruʒ [through] virtues.'[13] Virginity is by no means a flight from the tempestuous stirrings of the body: virginity's value lies precisely in the fact that it inhabits the frail flesh but that its 'wilful' [willing, determined] subjects are engaged in a war against the flesh that they overcome through virtue. *Of Maydenhede* (c. 1450) argues that the state of virginity is 'so hiʒe as þat þat nexte is God' [so high that it is next to God], and because 'harde þinge it is to make man or woman to life angelis life', so Christ made for himself 'a newe folke þat nexte hym schuld be as his moste loued seruauntes, þat as he was worschipid in heuene of [by] angelis, so þat he haue angelis, þat is clene [pure] maydens, to worschipe hym in erþe'.[14] Virginity surpasses matrimony and widowhood because it overcomes both nature and the battle of temptation: as St Jerome says, to live in the flesh without the action that the nature of flesh asks is not earthly life but angel's life and heavenly (fo. 140v).

Virginity is often represented as an immensely valuable possession. As the treatise *Hali Meiðhad* puts it, 'Meiðhad [Virginity] is þet [that] tresor þet [which], beo hit eanes forloren [once it is lost], ne bið hit neauer ifunden [it will never be found again]' (8/34–5). Hang on to your virginity, because you will never get it back. Virginity is famously described in *Ancrene Wisse* as 'a precious liquor, a valuable liquid like balm, in a fragile vessel'. The vessel represents 'women's flesh' and the balm 'is maidenhood held within it (or chaste purity once maidenhood is lost)'. And 'this brittle vessel is nonetheless as brittle as any glass; for if it is once broken, it is never mended to the wholeness it had, any more than glass. But it breaks more easily than brittle glass does.'[15] Yet this comparison struggles to maintain the distinction between inner and outer upon which its hierarchy of values depends: if virginity is an inner, spiritual quality and the outer vessel which contains it is women's despised flesh, then virginity cannot exist without its corporeal container, its liquidity suggesting a problematic overflowing rather than the potential for containment. How can the container be broken without virginity also being broken? And where does that put '*chaste* purity'? Here the play of exteriority and interiority, far from confirming boundaries, confounds them. Small wonder, then, that Margery Kempe cannot understand why her desire to be a virgin is so misunderstood: non-virginity is supposedly irreversible, but you *can* – just about – become a virgin again, by willing yourself to live chastely.

Wilful virgins

Kempe certainly knew enough about the value of virginity to want to recast herself as a 'wilful virgin'. I adapt this phrase from *Pore Caitif's Of the Mirrour of Chastite*, which asserts that

> a souereyne vertu and quene of al vertues to be perfite is wilful [purposeful, done willingly] chastite, þe whiche is in þre wiles [desires]: þe vnweddid to kepe hem from alle lecherie in wille, worde and dede; þe weddid to kepe hem [themselves] chaste to her [their] / wifes wiþouten any auouterie [adultery] bodily eiþer gostly [in mind] in þe holy termes þat God him self haþ lette [prevented]. But as þe briȝt schynynge sonne passiþ [surpasses] in clerenesse [brightness] þe liȝt of þe mone [moon] and þe sterres, so doþ clene virginite þese oþer two degrees[16]

'Clene virginite' is here considered the best, but '*wilful* chastite' is highly esteemed, for the chaste spouse or the chaste person awaiting marriage. Kempe, of course, understands her desired brand of virginity not as a return to a state of bodily intactness but as the recuperation of a spiritual state that stands outside the temporality of virginity as we normally understand it. In its context in *Pore Caitif*, 'wilful' has a positive sense, 'purposeful, done willingly', but it can also mean, as it does today, 'governed by will without regard to reason; determined to take one's way; obstinately self-willed or perverse' (*OED*). Although Kempe sees herself as a 'purposeful' virgin, her detractors see her as nothing if not perverse in her determination to achieve virginity, so much so that the Archbishop of York reads her wearing of white clothes as a sign of heresy.[17]

Just as the fundamental indeterminacy of virginity is not capable of being fully written in/on the body, so it is also marked by a strangely disjunctive temporality: one that Kempe exploits. Questions of temporality are, of course, linked to the body and its cycles of change and decay. But the temporality of virginity is something apart from this. On the one hand, virginity represents the fantasy of an escape from the human condition: from bodily change and pollution. But narratives of virginity (like Kempe's) often fail to maintain this fantasy as bounded or fixed. The strange temporality of virginity shakes the foundations of linear chronology, calling into question the proprieties of 'before' and 'after'. Medieval commentators insist that virginity is chiefly a *spiritual* state and a matter of *will*. But it has degrees: *Of Maydenhede* defines three 'degrees' of virgins – those who are pure in body but who like to talk about sex or indulge in 'vnleful [unlawful] touchynge'; those who are pure in body and speech, but who do not intend to remain virgins for ever (the chaste pre-marrieds); and those 'gostly [in spirit] maydens' who are not corrupt in either word or will but who intend to live chaste for ever.[18] Of these three categories, the last are the best. Even if they are raped and no longer technically virgins, they will nevertheless get all the *rewards* of virginity if they resist their rapists: 'þouȝ þei þurȝ strengþe be rauesched and defouled of wicked men aȝeynes her wille . . . for ouȝt þat wicked men wiþ hem done, noþinge þei losen of maydens mede ȝif þei wiþstande wiþ her myȝt and sufferen aȝeynes her wille [even if they are forcibly raped and defiled by wicked men against their will, . . . despite anything that wicked men do to them, they lose nothing of the reward of virginity if they resist with their power and endure it against their will]' (fos. 137r–v). Bodily intactness is less important than the will to remain chaste. The virginal female subject *wills* her virginity, overturning the proprieties of linear chronology. Virginity disorganizes temporal sequence.

Margery Kempe, mother of fourteen children, exploits the possibilities of the non-sequential temporality of virginity to remake herself as a virgin. Uncannily echoing the language of *Of Maydenhede*, Christ's unorthodox words of reassurance to Kempe – unorthodox in that they implicitly deny that technical virgins are better – explicitly mention 'will': '"trow þow rygth wel [rest assured] þat I lofe wyfes also, and specyal [specially] þo wyfys [those wives] whech woldyn levyn chast [who would live chaste], ȝyf [if] þei mygtyn haue her wyl, & don her besyness [do all they can] to plesyn me as þow dost [you do]"'.[19] And Kempe has Christ say to her, immediately before he expresses his desire that she wear white clothes: "'I xal [shall] kepe þe [you] fro alle wykked mennys power. And, dowtyr, I sey to þe I wyl [that I want] þat þu were clothys of whyte [white clothes] non oþer colowr, for þu xal ben arayd aftyr my wyl [for you shall dress according to my will]"' (32 [67]). Kempe's version of the 'wilful virgin' may not be exactly what the purveyors of pastoral teaching had in mind but it is – just about – compatible with it. Her *Book* reveals how one medieval woman attempts to live out the contradictory temporality of virginity, in which the apparently irreversible effects of sexual experience can be overridden by an effort of will. Despite the railings against her by the Mayor of Leicester, by the English priest on her way to Rome, by the townspeople of Lynn, it is not Kempe who is incoherent in her desire to remake virginity, but the cultural meanings of virginity itself.

Although it is ostensibly Mary's virginity which supports the notion of prelapsarian purity, through the traditional exegesis of the virgin birth as a joyful reversal of the sin that Eve brought into the world, the purity signified by virginity may not be so much opposed to the dirt of women as to the dirt of sodomy. In the thirteenth-century *Golden Legend* (the source for the Salomé episode) we learn that on Christmas Eve '"even the sodomites gave witness by being exterminated wherever they were in the world on that night", as Jerome says: "A light rose over them so bright that all who practiced this vice were wiped out; and Christ did this in order that no such uncleanness might be found in the nature he had assumed."'[20] So the cleanness of (Christ's) virginity wards off sodomy and heresy, those notorious bedfellows, suggesting that we might need to rethink the special value of virginity for (heterosexual) men and women, turning our attention instead to virginity's role in the disruptive discourses of same-sex desire.

Clean and pure

The N-town Christ, unlike all other newborns, 'nedyth [needs] no waschinge' (line 230), for Mary's body is so utterly clean. The obsession with virgin cleanness is graphically presented through its opposite in a much earlier piece of reportage: the mid-twelfth-century story of the Nun of Watton, reviled by her fellow nuns when she becomes pregnant.[21] Safely delivered (in both senses) of her illegitimate child (she gives birth but the child is miraculously taken away in a vision by the very bishop who had originally committed her to life in the monastery), she is subjected to a humiliating body-search by her prison guards who believe she has murdered the baby:

> They felt her belly: such slenderness had replaced the swelling that you would have thought her back was stuck to her front. They squeezed her breasts but elicited no liquid from them. Not sparing her, they pressed harder, but expressed nothing. They ran their fingers over every joint, exploring everything, but found no sign of childbirth, no indication even of pregnancy. They called the others, and they all found the same thing: everything restored, everything proper, everything beautiful. (p. 457)

In this ruthless exacting of the signs of purity we see the obverse of Salomé's testing of Mary – the kind of fate that Mary, as the mother of a child born out of an adulterous (so to speak) relationship, might have been subjected to, had she not been the mother of Christ. Ironically, it is Mary who so often in English vernacular narratives presides over the miraculous spiriting away of the illegitimate children of consecrated virgins and the restoration of their virginal bodies, as in the widespread story of the pregnant abbess that circulated in Latin and Middle English from the twelfth century: a version of this 'miracle of the Virgin' appears in the popular fifteenth-century *Alphabet of Tales*.[22] Furthermore, some of the tortures inflicted on the hapless Nun of Watton by her fellow nuns uncannily resemble those by which – as we shall see – the virgin martyr is tested by pagans (stripped, whipped, thrown into prison, fettered with heavy chains, starved, verbally abused, beaten) (p. 454). But where the virgin martyr triumphs, the Nun of Watton is abjected. The frenzy with which her fellow-nuns set about disciplining her body into virginal channels suggest something of the force that virginity as an ideal exerted on this particular medieval community of nuns – or perhaps more accurately on its clerical author, Aelred, and on Gilbert, the father of the convent – and also something of the misery brought about when individual medieval women failed to take or live up to virginity as *their* ideal. The Nun of Watton's newly purified, non-pregnant body *occupies no space*: it was as if 'her back was stuck to her front'. But such is the force of the ideology of virginity that this curiously diminished and organless body is described as 'proper' and 'beautiful'.

Mary's virginity

Mary's virginal body is often figured as a sacred, enclosed, and inviolate space: the *porta clausa* (locked door) in Ezekiel's vision of the new temple (Ezekiel 44: 1–2), a 'fountain sealed', a 'spring shut up'.[23] Lydgate's poem 'To Mary, the Queen of Heaven' speaks of her as 'Hool & vnbroken by virgynal clennesse', and praises 'The cristal cloistre of thy virginyte'.[24] Devotion to Mary reached unprecedented heights of intensity by the fifteenth century. Books of Hours, especially popular among the devout laity in this century, prescribed a semi-liturgical devotional routine based on the Little Office of the Blessed Virgin, a routine that included the recitation of multiple ave Marias and prayers to the Virgin, based on that laid out in the *Ancrene Wisse*.

Hoccleve's *Legend of the Virgin*, a poem once attributed to Chaucer, alludes to the spatial symbolism of wholeness signified by Mary's body.[25] Mary, wearing a sleeveless dress, appears to a monk in France, asking him to rectify her dishabille by trebling the number of ave Marias he repeats, and by adding a paternoster to every tenth ave. This he faithfully does; in the next vision Mary's garment has sleeves. Eventually the monk is made abbot. In this miracle of sartorial completeness, social degree as well as piety is at stake: since Mary is Queen of Heaven, she must be dressed royally. Servants would often sew a garment's detachable sleeves into the bodice in the process of dressing a lady: because Mary is metaphorically 'clothed' in the prayers of the faithful, her 'servants' must appropriately complete her dressing. Because faith restores Mary's wholeness, the tale parallels Salomé's physical testing. Mary's body hovers between the fullness of virginity and the incompleteness signalled by her clothing, its contradictions marking yet another paradox of virginity: a wholeness that wards off lack but which simultaneously conceals an anxiety about lack.

The numerous lyrics that extravagantly praise the Virgin, with their elaborate litanies of aves, sorrows and joys, seem designed to freeze Mary and to multiply her, Warhol-like, in a series of repeated but ever-so-slightly varied images. They present a Virgin who defends against temporality and change – sometimes bathetically, as when Lydgate claims she will 'vs diffende [defend us] with hir mylk virgynal'.[26] But the fifteenth-century Sloane lyric 'I singe of a maiden' is exceptional in acknowledging the play of the eternal *and* the temporal in Mary and her history, enacted through its use of alternating tenses in each stanza. Pared down to its essentials, the incarnation becomes nothing more than the secret visiting of the beloved by her divine lover in human guise:

> He cam also stille   to his moderes bour   [as silently]
> As dew in April   that falleth on the flour.[27]

But this is nonetheless *queer*: after all, this is mother and son; and the surprise reversal of the lyric's second line – in which the maiden 'chese' (*chose*) the 'King of alle kinges' to be her son – further confounds temporality. And the metaphors of the Old Testament prophecies of the virgin birth (Judges 6:

36–40, Psalm 71: 6, Deuteronomy 32: 2, Isaiah 45: 8) are treated not as events to come but as events that have already happened and are still happening. The virgin birth represents a disjunctive coexistence of temporalities and sexualities that belies the singularity ('a maiden that is makeless'; 'was never non but she') and rigid hierarchies of inner and outer with which Mary's virginity is usually invested.

Virgin-power?

Increased devotion to the cult of Mary is paralleled by a burgeoning interest in the *vitae* of the virgin-martyr saints, especially those of Katherine and Margaret. In these narratives, a beautiful, virtuous Christian virgin has her faith tested by pagan adversaries: tortured, imprisoned, her flesh stripped, her body dismembered, her breasts torn off, boiling oil poured over her, the virgin remains miraculously alive, her narrative of survival the very revelation of her true (Christian) self: unchangeable, indestructible, incorruptible. Her pagan opponents are converted or destroyed.

How can we understand these often sensationalist stories? Their heroines have either been seen as victims, bearers of medieval culture's misogynistic fear of the female body, or as triumphant and autonomous protofeminist subjects – like the various incarnations of Katherine, proving her 'clergie' [scholarship] before fifty learned men, or Chaucer's St Cecilia, answering the tyrannical prefect Almachius with absolute poise, and still teaching the faith after her throat has been sliced through: models of intelligence, learning, and fortitude. But it is too reductive to read this material as either affirming or denying the 'power' conferred by virginity, whatever that might be. The Katherine Group's St Juliana is tortured first by her father, then by Eleusius, and then by the devil Belial, in a manner that seems designed to exact from her body some sort of 'truth' about women.[28] But she survives even being broken upon the wheel, emerging 'ase fischhal as þah ha nefde nohwer hurtes ife let' (53/570–1) [as whole as a fish, as though she had never felt injury anywhere (p. 317)], the fish image suggesting perhaps the teasingly non-human nature of her resistance. These repeated tortures suggest that the texts *stage* gender as fluid and performative: not as an essence but as a continual acting out of female sexual and social identity.

The versions vary enormously in length, genre, and detail. Capgrave's little-studied *Katherine* is almost novelistic in impulse, rivalling Chaucer's *Troilus* in design, length, and psychological motivation.[29] And paratextual material (prologues, dedications, moralizations, ballades) positions the versions in widely divergent ways. The *vitae* offer virginity as fantasy of a wholeness that binds together late medieval Christian communities, one that bears comparison with that other broad signifier of the wholeness and inviolacy of the Christian faith: the Eucharist. Indeed, the lives of Katherine, Margaret, Juliana, Christine, Dorothy, and others are strikingly similar to those of the popular anti-Semitic host-desecration narratives, circulating at the same time and often in the same collections.[30] In the best-known of these narratives, the so-called Paris version, a Jew obtains the host and tests its much-vaunted properties by subjecting it to abuse and torture: striking it, piercing it until it bleeds, burning and boiling it. The host's miraculous intactness brings about the conversion of onlooking Jews. The frequent etymologizing of Margaret's name invokes the symbolism of the Eucharistic wafer: in Osbern Bokenham's Prologue to his legend of *Margaret* (1443–7), her Latin name (*margarita*, 'pearl') signifies that she is 'whyht, lytyl, and eek verteuous'.[31]

What pleasures did women derive from these narratives? One fifteenth-century anthology for devout laywomen, Cambridge University Library MS Fo.2.38, intersperses legends of Katherine and Margaret with various Middle English romances, suggesting that women readers liked romancing their virgin martyrs, liked the foreign, the supernatural, the marvellous. But as Diane Elam argues, romance is self-divided, a category that can unsettle by muddling classificatory and aesthetic boundaries.[32] Perhaps their appeal lies in their *social* narratives: their espousing of a woman's right to choose her marriage partner, and their explicit challenge to family values. Christina of Markyate, when challenged on behalf of her parents by the prior Fredebertus to defend her refusal to marry her suitor Burthred ('"Nor should you think that only virgins are saved: for whilst many virgins perish, many mothers of families are saved, as we well know"'), convincingly and disarmingly refutes him: '"if many mothers of families are saved, which you likewise say, and it is true, certainly virgins are saved more easily"'.[33]

Because the *vitae* focus in varying degrees on the dismemberment and mutilation of female bodies, they seem pornographic. But before we dismiss pornographic readings as reductive, anachronistic, or antifeminist, it is crucial to recognize that medieval women readers could accept these narratives simultaneously as 'pornographic' *and* as warnings to readers about the dangers of sexuality. Furthermore, the 'pornographic' scenes in these narratives are more nuanced than is generally recognized, to the extent that they position their audiences (inside and outside the text) as powerless and yet complicit, and that they speak of a *female* enjoyment that cannot be fully represented. Various versions of Margaret's legend, for example, *stage* the spectator's impotence within the text: in the Katherine Group version, Margaret's beatings are witnessed by a helpless heathen audience who 'remden of reowðe [wept for compassion] ant meanden þes meiden [pitied this maiden], ant summe of ham [them] seiden: "Margarete, Margarete, meide swa muche wurð ʒef þu wel waldest [maiden who might be worth so much if you wanted to be], wa is us [we are sorry] þet we seoð þi softe leofliche lich [lovely body] toluken se ladliche [so cruelly torn to pieces]!'"[34] As Slavoj Žižek suggests, the (male) observer is represented as passive and impotent because 'his desire is split, divided between fascination with enjoyment and repulsion at it; or – to put it another way – because his yearning to rescue the woman from her torturer is hindered by the implicit knowledge that the victim is *enjoying* her suffering'.[35] Margaret's ecstasies indeed suggest this disturbing *feminine* enjoyment, provoking ambivalent reactions for its onlookers within a complex dialectic of gaze and power.

Not being seen

Seeing is indeed at the heart of it. '[L]ove your windows as little as you possibly can', the author of *Ancrene Wisse* warns his early thirteenth-century audience of anchoresses.[36] To see was to risk being seen. And to be lusted after was a fate worse than death, as Chaucer's *Physician's Tale* suggests. Virginia gets her head chopped off by her father for nothing more than getting in the sightline of the 'false juge' Apius (6.154). Because the woman is held responsible for arousing the male gazer, she must be punished for *his* improper arousal. Because male desire is troublesome, men make her guilty for their guilt. But what if the virgin returns the gaze? These texts may evoke the substance of Freud's 1917 essay on virginity, namely that 'with the taboo of virginity primitive man is defending himself against a correctly sensed, although psychical, danger', that of an 'archaic reaction of hostility' that will be unleashed by the woman towards the man for deflowering her.[37] The castrating power of virgins may be implied in the name of St Petronilla's unsuccessful suitor: in Lydgate's retelling, 'Erle Flaccus' [flabby, not stiff].[38] Medieval virginity treatises often reinforce the warning not to look by reference to the Old Testament *exemplum* of Dyna, the daughter of Lya, who goes out to visit the women of her land and is seen by the prince's son Sychym, who rapes her. The *Ancrene Wisse* provides one of the best-known instances. In a late fourteenth-century recension (c. 1380–c. 1400) of the *Ancrene Wisse* in the Vernon Manuscript, the author underlines the meaning of the *exemplum*: 'And al þe euel of Dyna þat I speek er [before] of [about], al com not forþi þat [because] þe wommon lokede folyliche [foolishly] vppon men, ac þorw þat heo schewede hire [showed herself] in monnes eiʒe-sihte [before the sight of men], and duden [behaved] wherþorw [in such a way that] heo [she] mouhten [could] fallen in synne.'[39] Dyna's 'sin', then, is not that *she* cast desiring glances upon men, but that she made herself an object of desire. But medieval authors did not always distinguish between the sin of looking and the sin of being looked at. *Pore Caitif*'s *Of þe Mirrour of Chastite* bids its unnamed addressee to 'kepe wel þi siȝt [guard well your sight] for it is þe messanger of þi soule, be it clene eiþer ellis [whether it be pure or otherwise]. Dyna, for [because] she vnwarly [incautiously] lokid, leste [lost] þe floure [precious thing] of her maydenhode.'[40] Dyna loses her virginity through heedless looking. But 'vnwarly' can also mean 'innocently'. The virgin is caught in a double bind: whichever way the gaze travels, there is no such thing as an innocent look.

But this idea is not central to most of the vernacular virgin-martyr lives of the period: Almachius' gaze on Cecilia, Olibrius' on Margaret, Maxentius' on Katherine, in the various Middle English retellings of their *vitae*, are indeed sexualized gazes, but their narrative purpose is to get the virgin noticed so that she can defend her Christianity. The virgin martyr may (eventually) get her head chopped off, but these narratives simply do not obey the logic of desire suggested by the Dyna *exemplum*, whereby the looked-at virgin is as guilty as the looker. Chaucer's *Physician's Tale*, then, is something of an anomaly. At first glance, it certainly reads like a textbook case of the logic of desire. In this tale of patriarchal wrangling over a virgin's body, Apius plans to enlist the help of the low-born 'cherl' Claudius to outwit Virginia's father and gain possession of her. Effectively despoiled by Apius' glance, the hapless Virginia is given two choices by her father: 'outher [either] deeth or shame, / That thou most suffre' (6.214–15), and since 'shame' is the worst, he tells her he must 'smyten of [smite off] thyn [your] heed' (6.226). But this only shows to what extent Virginia's virginity is valued by her *father* (as representative of patriarchal culture), that is, as long as nobody else sees it and it remains his exclusive property. Moreover, Virginia does not authorize the meanings of her narrative as the female virgin martyrs do. Katherine, Margaret, Cecilia meet the male tyrant's lustful gaze with defiance: they answer back.

Nor is it always the category of the body that is at stake in the look upon the virgin. In Mirk's retelling of St Margaret, for example, Olibrius wants to know if she is 'gentyll' [noble] – for then he will marry her – or 'þrale' [slave], for then he will take her as his 'leman' [mistress].[41] Social class here, like virginity, is not 'visible' and cannot be read on the body. Similarly, in Bokenham's *St Margaret*, there is concern for social status: the tyrants always ask some version of Olibrius' question: 'Sey me, damysel, of what kyn thou art / And whethyr thou be bonde [a serf] or ellys fre [noble]' – and this question mobilizes the opposition between pagan (and secular) and Christian values, since the heroine always responds that she is no slave but a Christian, bringing two different codes (one religious, one to do with social degree) into collision.[42] The tyrant expects an answer to do with social degree, because he is thinking of her status as a worldly object of desire; but the virgin seizes this opportunity to exploit analogical thinking: non-Christians, however noble, are slaves, and only Christians are truly 'fre' [noble]. In *The Physician's Tale*, Apius tells his fall-guy, the 'cherl' Claudius, that if he reveals Apius' plot he will 'lese his heed' (6.145). Churls lose their heads if they betray their lords; virgins lose their (maiden)heads if they are seen. Anxiety about virginity in *The Physician's Tale* is also a displacement of anxiety about social mobility.

English virginities?

Earlier I claimed that the memory of virgins and virginities was everywhere in medieval English culture. The Middle Ages was fundamentally a 'memorial culture', in which memory was a sacred, affective and living presence. But there is an important sense in which the *vitae* of the female virgin martyrs served as versions of what Pierre Nora calls 'memory-places' [*lieux de mémoire*], subject to the injunction to remember.[43] For Nora, the memorial impulse is tied up with the desire to remember the nation. Virginities were symbolic memory-places upon which the emerging nation of 'England' was fastened. Lydgate writes a Valentine poem to the Virgin Mary in which he invokes Mary for nationalist and royalist purposes, beseeching her to show grace to Henry VI and his mother, Katherine, and 'þeyre noble bloode'.[44] And in 1501, at a civic triumph in London to celebrate the marriage of Henry VII's eldest son, Prince Arthur, to Katharine of Aragon, symbols of Englishness (Lancastrian roses; lions rampant holding metal plates with the arms of England painted on them) are juxtaposed with a representation of the royal wife's virgin-martyr namesake: 'a faire yong lady with a wheel in hir hand in liknes of Seint Kateryne', with many virgins about her.[45] Jocelyn Wogan-Browne observes that in the fifteenth-century vernacular *Life of Edith of Wilton*, a virgin saint, Edith's post-mortem wholeness is contrasted with images of menstruating Jews, arguing that 'the long-expelled Jewish nation of England becomes an upturned and feminized anti-body to Edith's monastic and national purity'.[46] In Lydgate's fifteenth-century lyric 'Ave Regina Celorum', Mary's chaste self is asked to intercede for England: 'That no perylous plage of pestilence, / . . . / Entyr in Englond . . .!'[47] This sounds like a staking out of the nationalistic ground that Elizabeth I will later occupy. But the issues are complex: as Helen Hackett argues, 'Celebration of [Elizabeth's] virginity was less an attempt to replicate the cult of the Virgin than an effort to turn to nationalistic use enduring superstitions which associated the virgin female body with purity and the sexually active female body with pollution and mortality'.[48]

The memory of virgin martyrs persisted into the Reformation. Elizabeth Barton, the 'Holy Maid of Kent' (1506–34), a former servant who modelled herself explicitly on Bridget of Sweden and Catherine of Siena and became a Benedictine nun at the convent of St Sepulchre's in Canterbury, contributed to resistance to the Reformation.[49] And although Foxe's *Book of Martyrs* (1563) has no Margaret or Juliana,[50] it does have Katherine. Foxe regards her legend as a farrago of 'incredible' and 'impudent' fictions, accusing hagiographers generally of having 'mingle mangled their stories and liues' (1, 95), but he nevertheless imagines an audience that desires to hear her story. And he imposes Katherine's narrative upon his Protestant female martyrs. A certain Elizabeth Young, arrested for smuggling books from the continent and examined on thirteen different occasions (nine of which Foxe transcribes), disputed with learned doctors, so impressing her interrogators that one exclaimed, 'Twenty pounds, it is a man in woman's clothes! twenty pounds it is a man!'[51] If virginity has ceased to be what is at stake in this account, we can nevertheless recognize here a continuity with the cross-gendering of the medieval virgins: their power to unsettle and confound social and sexual expectations.

NOTES

1. *The N-town Play*, 2 vols., ed. Stephen Spector, EETS ss 11 (text) and 12 (apparatus) (Oxford University Press, 1991). The episode also appears in the Chester Nativity pageant: *The Chester Mystery Cycle*, ed. R. M. Lumiansky and David Mills, EETS ss 3 and 4 (Oxford University Press, 1974). References are to line numbers of the particular plays.
2. *The Book of Margery Kempe*, ed. Sanford Brown Meech and Hope Emily Allen, EETS os 212 (Oxford University Press, 1940), p. 197; *The Book of Margery Kempe*, trans. Barry A. Windeatt (Harmondsworth: Penguin, 1985), p. 238.
3. Carolyn Dinshaw, *Getting Medieval: Sexualities and Communities, Pre- and Postmodern* (Durham, NC: Duke University Press, 1999), p. 151.
4. Norman Davis, ed., *The Paston Letters: A Selection in Modern Spelling* (Oxford University Press, 1999), p. 5.
5. Meech and Allen, *Book of Margery Kempe*, p. 52; Windeatt, *Book of Margery Kempe*, p. 87.
6. Sarah Salih, 'Performing Virginity: Sex and Violence in the Katherine Group', in *Constructions of Widowhood and Virginity in the Middle Ages*, ed. Cindy L. Carlson and Angela Jane Weisl, The New Middle Ages Series (Basingstoke: Macmillan, 1999), pp. 95–112 (p. 99).
7. For text and translation of *Hali Meiðhad* and of Parts 7 and 8 of *Ancrene Wisse* see *Medieval English Prose for Women*, ed. Bella Millett and Jocelyn Wogan-Browne, rev. edn (Oxford: Clarendon Press, 1992), pp. 2–43, 110–49. *Ancrene Wisse* is translated in *Anchoritic Spirituality: Ancrene Wisse and*

Associated Works, trans. Anne Savage and Nicholas Watson (New York: Paulist Press, 1991), pp. 41–207.

8. *Seynt Margaret*, in *The Minor Poems of John Lydgate*, Part 1, ed. Henry Noble MacCracken, EETS ES 107 (London: Kegan Paul, Trench, Trübner and Oxford University Press, 1911), pp. 173–92; John Capgrave, *The Life of Saint Katherine*, ed. Karen A. Winstead, TEAMS Middle English Texts (Kalamazoo: Western Michigan University, Medieval Institute Publications, 1999); John Mirk, *Mirk's Festial: A Collection of Homilies*, ed. Theodor Erbe, EETS ES 96 (London: Kegan Paul, Trench, Trübner, 1905).

9. *Sir Eglamour of Artois*, ed. F. E. Richardson, EETS OS 256 (Oxford University Press, 1965).

10. Alexandra Barratt, ed., *Women's Writing in Middle English* (London: Longman, 1992), pp. 37–8; Jocelyn Wogan-Browne, 'The Virgin's Tale', in *Feminist Readings in Middle English Literature: The Wife of Bath and All Her Sect*, ed. Ruth Evans and Lesley Johnson (London: Routledge, 1994), pp. 165–94, p. 168.

11. *The Life of Saint Catherine by Clemence of Barking*, ed. William MacBain, ANTS 18 (Oxford: Blackwell, 1964); *The Book of the City of Ladies*, trans. Earl Jeffrey Richards (London: Pan, 1983).

12. Millett and Wogan-Browne, *Medieval English Prose for Women*, p. 20/19–21.

13. Sister Mary Brady, 'The Pore Caitif: Edited from MS Harley 2336 with Introduction and Notes', PhD diss., Fordham University, 1954. I have edited this work's treatise *Of þe Mirrour of Chastite* from Glasgow University Library MS Hunter 496, fos. 146v–164r (fo. 158r).

14. British Library MS Arundel 286, fos. 134v–148r (fo. 138r). For an edition of this treatise, see Lorna R. L. Stevenson, 'Fifteenth-Century Chastity and Virginity: Texts, Contexts, Audiences', unpublished PhD thesis, University of Liverpool, 1992, pp. 367–97. I have edited the text myself from the manuscript.

15. Savage and Watson, *Anchoritic Spirituality*, p. 109.

16. See n. 13 (fos. 151v–152r).

17. Meech and Allen, *Book of Margery Kempe*, p. 124; Windeatt, *Book of Margery Kempe*, p. 162.

18. See n. 14 (fo. 135r).

19. Meech and Allen, *Book of Margery Kempe*, p. 49; Windeatt, *Book of Margery Kempe*, p. 84.

20. Jacobus de Voragine, *The Golden Legend: Readings on the Saints*, ed. and trans. William Granger Ryan, 2 vols. (Princeton University Press, 1993), 1.41.

21. Aelred of Rievaulx, 'The Nun of Watton', *Patrologia Latina* 195: 780–96, trans. John Boswell, in *The Kindness of Strangers: The Abandonment of Children in Western Europe from Late Antiquity to the Renaissance* (Harmondsworth: Penguin, 1989), pp. 452–8. Henceforth page nos. will be cited parenthetically in the text.

22. *An Alphabet of Tales*, ed. Mary Macleod Banks, EETS OS 126–7 (London: Kegan Paul, Trench, Trübner, 1904).

23. Marina Warner, *Alone of All Her Sex: The Myth and Cult of the Virgin Mary* (London: Picador, 1990), p. 73.

24. MacCracken, *Minor Poems of John Lydgate*, pp. 284–7, lines 12 and 20.

25. Thomas Hoccleve, *Legend of the Virgin and her Sleeveless Garment*, ed. Arthur Beatty, The Chaucer Society (London: Kegan Paul, Trench, Trübner, 1902).

26. 'To Mary, the Queen of Heaven', in MacCracken, *Minor Poems of John Lydgate*, pp. 284–7, line 71.

27. John Burrow, ed., *English Verse 1300–1500* (London: Longman, 1977), p. 301 (BL, MS Sloane 2593).

28. *Þe Liflade et te Passiun of Seinte Iuliene*, ed. S. T. R. O. d'Ardenne, EETS OS 248 (London: Oxford University Press, 1961); trans. Savage and Watson, *Anchoritic Spirituality*, pp. 306–21.

29. See n. 8.

30. Miri Rubin, *Gentile Tales: The Narrative Assault on Late Medieval Jews* (New Haven: Yale University Press, 1999), pp. 40–69.

31. Osbern Bokenham, *Vita S. Margaretae*, in *Legendys of Hooly Wummen*, ed. Mary S. Serjeantson, EETS OS 206 (London: Oxford University Press, 1938), pp. 7–38, line 251.

32. Diane Elam, *Romancing the Postmodern* (London: Routledge, 1992), p. 17.

33. *The Life of Christina of Markyate, a Twelfth-Century Recluse*, ed. and trans. C. H. Talbot (Oxford: Clarendon Press, 1959, repr. 1987), pp. 61, 63.

34. *Seinte Margarete*, in Millett and Wogan-Browne, *Medieval English Prose for Women*, pp. 44–85 (p. 52/26–9).

35. Slavoj Žižek, *The Metastases of Enjoyment: Six Essays on Women and Causality* (London: Verso, 1994), p. 75.

36. Savage and Watson, *Anchoritic Spirituality*, p. 66.

37. Sigmund Freud, 'The Taboo of Virginity' (1918 [1917]), in *On Sexuality: Three Essays on the Theory of Sexuality and Other Works*, vol. 8, The Pelican Freud Library, trans. James Strachey, ed. Angela Richards (Harmondsworth: Penguin, 1977), pp. 261–83 (pp. 274, 282).

38. *The Legende of St Petronilla*, in MacCracken, *Minor Poems of John Lydgate*, pp. 154–9, line 75.

39. *The English Text of the Ancrene Riwle: The 'Vernon' Text*, ed. Arne Zittersten and Bernhard Diensberg, EETS OS 310 (Oxford University Press, 2000), p. 22.

40. See n. 13 (fos. 147r–v).

41. Erbe, *Mirk's Festial*, p. 200.

42. Serjeantson, *Legendys of Hooly Wummen*, pp. 14–15, lines 512–13.

43. 'Between Memory and History', in Pierre Nora, ed., *Realms of Memory: The Construction of the French Past*, vol. 1: *Conflicts and Divisions*, European Perspectives: A Series in Social Thought and Cultural Criticism (New York: Columbia University Press, 1996), pp. 1–20.

44. John Lydgate, 'A Valentine to Her that Excelleth All', in MacCracken, *Minor Poems of John Lydgate*, pp. 304–10 (line 137).

45. *The Receyt of the Ladie Kateryne*, ed. Gordon Kipling, EETS OS 296 (Oxford University Press, 1990).

46. 'Outdoing the Daughters of Syon?: Edith of Wilton and the Representation of Female Community in Fifteenth-Century England', in *New Trends in Feminine Spirituality: The Holy Women of Liège and Their Impact*, ed. Juliette Dor, Lesley Johnson, and Jocelyn Wogan-Browne, Medieval Women: Texts and Contexts 2 (Turnhout: Brepols, 1999), pp. 393–409, pp. 402–3.

47. MacCracken, *Minor Poems of John Lydgate*, pp. 291–2, lines 13–15.

48. Helen Hackett, *Virgin Mother, Maiden Queen: Elizabeth I and the Cult of the Virgin Mary* (Basingstoke: Macmillan, 1995), p. 240.

49. Diane Watt, 'Of the Seed of Abraham: Elizabeth Barton, the "Holy Maid of Kent"', *Secretaries of God: Women Prophets in Late Medieval and Early Modern England* (Cambridge: D. S. Brewer, 1997), pp. 51–80.

50. John Foxe, *Actes and Monuments of matters most speciall and memorable, happening in the Church, with a Vniuersall history of the same* [Foxe's *Book of Martyrs*] [1563], 3 vols., 4th edn. (London: John Daye, 1583).

51. Watt, *Secretaries of God*, p. 116.

3

DYAN ELLIOTT

Marriage

Marriage contained and shaped the lives of the vast majority of the medieval populace of both sexes. By 1200, moreover, the jurisdiction over this quintessentially lay institution was firmly in the hands of the clergy, who were, by definition, male. This clerical/masculine primacy corresponds to the official ideology of marriage. As guardians of the institution, the clergy in no way challenged its traditional patriarchal structure. Although the Church would from time to time attempt to curb the more brutal manifestations of the husband's prerogatives over the wife, the reintroduction of Roman law into the canon law of the Church in the high Middle Ages tended to ratify the husband's position of authority.

The married woman's position was additionally compromised by the clergy's traditional bias in favour of celibacy, which assigned to marriage a less estimable position in the hierarchy of salvation than either virginity or chaste widowhood. The Middle Ages inherited the patristic reckoning which accorded virgins a hundred-fold reward in the kingdom of heaven, consecrated widows sixty-fold, and matrons a mere thirty-fold.[1] Awareness of this distinction was ever present to the spiritually ambitious women of the period. Thus Christina of Markyate (died between 1155 and 1166), a daughter of well-to-do burghers who struggled to extricate herself from a forced marriage in order to preserve her virginity for Christ, gives an unassailable response to her clerical interlocutor's contention that both matrons and virgins would be saved: "'Nor do I think that virgins only will be saved . . . [But] if many mothers of families are saved, which you likewise say, and it is true, certainly virgins are saved more easily.'"[2] Christina's appreciation of the hierarchical relation of virgin to matron is repeatedly acknowledged by Chaucer's Wife of Bath, albeit with humorous complacency.

This chapter examines some of the theoretical and practical implications of the ecclesiastical imprint on marriage. The first section discusses the formation of the bond through consent and some of the complications raised by the consensual definition of marriage. The second addresses the way the bond establishes the husband's total authority over the wife, and the gender roles which thus ensue. An exemplary court case is then adduced as a kind of worst-case scenario, suggesting the way that the consensual theory of marriage, in conjunction with patriarchal authority, can have so numbing an effect on a woman's freedom of consent that the union's validity is ultimately placed in jeopardy. We then consider the exercise of married sexuality – the one sphere of theoretical freedom between the couple. In thus introducing the medieval institution of marriage, my purpose is to acquaint the reader with a wide array of primary sources while pointing to how these sources correspond to various analogues in literature.

The formation of a marriage: consent versus coercion

The high Middle Ages saw the triumph of a consensual definition of marriage which was indebted both to the Roman perspective regarding the essence of a contract and to a Christian interpretation of a spiritual bond between spouses.[3] In fact, the theological vision of the unconsummated marriage of Mary and Joseph was upheld as the unlikely model for the ideal Christian marriage.[4] This spiritualization of the bond corresponded, in turn, to the gradual sacramentalization of marriage, which opened the way for its eventual inclusion among the emerging list of seven sacraments. Thus the exchange of consent between spouses was sufficient for a legally binding marriage from an ecclesiastical perspective. Parental consent, marriage banns, the presence of witnesses, an officiating priest (all of which were certainly highly desirable), or even sexual consummation were not essential to the integrity of the union. Consent to marriage was understood as a performative utterance, which theoretically created an indissoluble bond. Such privately contracted marriages, referred to as clandestine unions, were valid but illicit, and the couple was generally required to undergo a subsequent, public ceremony, which in England was performed at the church door for enhanced publicity.[5]

Some scholars have argued that the triumph of this consensual theory of marriage corresponded with the new-found emphasis on the individual associated with the twelfth century.[6] From this perspective, children are supposedly supported in opposing, and perhaps even encouraged to resist, familial pressures concerning the choice of a spouse.[7] The consensual definition has been construed as especially advantageous to young women, who, due to their presumably enhanced dependency from an economic and social standpoint, were considered to be more susceptible to coercion than were their male counterparts.

Yet the principle of consensuality could also work to the opposite purpose. Already in the twelfth century its potentially disadvantageous consequences are apparent in the plight of Christina of Markyate. In a moment of weakness, Christina yielded to her parents' aggressive inducements and exchanged vows with Burthred.[8] When her bridegroom attempted to consummate the marriage, however, Christina tried to convert him to a spiritual marriage. This implies an agreement between spouses to remit all sexual relations in accordance with the model of St Cecilia and her husband Valerian, a model best known to students of literature through Chaucer's later *Second Nun's Tale*. Though Christina recounted the saint's life with vigour, she encountered strenuous resistance and was forced to flee the wedding chamber to avoid a forced consummation.[9] Yet despite Christina's protestations that the marriage was forced – a fact which the unrelenting parents nevertheless corroborated – the marriage was perceived by most of the ecclesiastical authorities she encountered as binding. It was at least four years before Burthred finally agreed to release Christina from her vows, at which point the marriage was finally annulled and Burthred declared free to remarry.[10] Canon law would ultimately ratify the unilateral dissolution of an unconsummated marriage, providing the resistant spouse entered a monastery. The permitted timespan was drastically narrowed to two months, however. After this interval, ecclesiastical authorities would uphold the husband's right to consummate the marriage.[11]

Clearly the matrimonial ambiance of Christina's time was still in transition. The various clerics she consulted seemed sensitive to the view that the exchange of vows created an indissoluble bond, yet were insufficiently appreciative of the invalidity of a coerced vow. Even the Bishop of Lincoln, who was initially sympathetic to Christina's case – before accepting a bribe from her parents, that is – thought that the marriage should be set aside on the basis of Christina's pre-existing vow of chastity, not because of undue coercion.[12] But the most progressive canon lawyers of the period had already begun to determine that consent to marriage must be given freely. Even so, what constituted *free* consent would remain a problem throughout the Middle Ages. It was to be expected that parents would have strong views on whom their child would marry, while canonical authorities were agreed that filial piety should generally support parental views.[13] Most of medieval society would be deeply sympathetic to the protestations of Christina's parents when they said: "'If she resists our authority and rejects it, we shall be a laughing-stock of our neighbours, a mockery and derision to those who are round about.'"[14] Nor would it be seen as particularly unusual for recalcitrant daughters to be chastised. The fifteenth-century example of Elizabeth Paston is sobering in this context. In a situation emulating the classic case of the January/May relation of Chaucer's *Merchant's Tale*, Elizabeth was a lively twenty-year-old naturally averse to marrying the fifty-year-old misshapen widower that her family had selected for her. She was accordingly imprisoned in her room and subjected to daily beatings.[15]

Fortunately for Elizabeth, the attempted match was eventually abandoned by the family. But supposing she had been forced to acquiesce to her parents' wishes: could she then have petitioned for an annulment on the basis of coercion? Perhaps, but the success of such a plea was by no means certain. The guideline adopted by canonists for what degree of threat and force constituted an impediment to marriage centred on the rather fanciful criterion of what would have weakened the resolve of the hypothetical 'constant man' or 'constant woman'. But the evidence of the ecclesiastical courts indicates that this legal abstraction set something of a heroic standard which many women might not attain, especially since the legal age of marriage was twelve for women, versus fourteen for men. In fact, petitions for the dissolution of marriage – technically a *divortium a vinculo matrimonii* (literally, 'divorce from the chain of marriage'), which signified that no marriage had existed in the first place – were comparatively rare.[16]

Thus far I have been emphasizing how consensuality contributed to the ecclesiastical vision of stable and indissoluble unions. But there is also a very real sense in which the emphasis on consent alone, and the ensuing toleration of clandestine matches, had a destabilizing effect on the institution of marriage. Michael Sheehan has shown that the vast majority of cases of marriage litigation before the ecclesiastical courts concerned efforts to enforce a marriage that one party denied, while a large proportion of these cases involved actual bigamy.[17] A clandestine union was thus frequently being alleged against a subsequent and public union. If the contention could be proved, the second couple had to separate – even if it was a longstanding match with a public wedding which had produced a number of children. But if there were no witnesses to the prior union, and the recalcitrant spouse refused to confess, the subsequent union was permitted to remain intact – despite the fact that the couple was not really married before God's eyes and that one of the members was most certainly living in mortal sin. The party who had brought the charge of precontract, moreover, must henceforth remain chaste.

Despite the complications generated by this definition of marriage, there were undeniable instances in which consensuality's potential for female empowerment was ultimately sustained, as is evident in the celebrated instance of yet another Paston daughter, Margery Paston. Margery had contracted a clandestine marriage with the estate's bailiff, Richard Calle. Although Margery endured considerable abuse from her outraged relatives, she refused to disavow her union with Calle. Eventually, the Bishop, after examining Margery as to the actual words she exchanged with Richard, would uphold the union. Even at this juncture, however, Margery's brother was prepared to disrupt the marriage by fraud (a suggestion from which his mother, hard-boiled as she had been in her dealings with Margery, nevertheless recoiled, fearing lest he damn his soul).[18] In the end, the family was forced to accept the fact of the marriage – though they eschewed all further contact with the couple. Significantly, Calle remained as bailiff on the estate. Though disowning her in a legal sense, the family was probably not prepared to see their daughter entirely destitute.

The husband's authority and the 'feme covert'

From the time of her marriage, the wife was referred to as a *feme covert* – under the cover of her husband – a term which in English common law designated the wife's legal disabilities.[19] Accordingly, the husband had control of the wife's property during her lifetime, though he was required to seek her permission to sell it. Nor could the wife dispose of her property without her husband's permission. Indeed, the husband's authority over his wife and her property alike was considered sufficiently compelling that a widow could later recover her property by arguing that her former consent to the land's alienation during her husband's lifetime was invalid since she was 'under the rule of her husband' (*sub virga*: literally 'under the rod' or 'stick'). The main exception to this level of control occurred in the case of the independent business-woman, who, with her husband's permission, could set up as *feme sole* – implying that the husband would not be held responsible for her debts, and vice versa. Among wives, only the *feme sole* was permitted to represent herself in court, at least with regard to her business. But the wife was usually represented by her husband – the exception being when a woman had been raped or when matrons were called upon to determine delicate matters such as pregnancy, virginity, or even impotence.[20]

Patriarchal prerogative also affected the wife's making a will, which required the husband's permission, despite the fact that it was allegedly sinful to die intestate. The Church stipulated that the husband assign a dower for his wife at the time of the marriage for support during her widowhood – usually a third of his property at the time of the marriage – but this was the extent of her claims upon his estate. Although the clergy agitated to have wives automatically share in the common property which accrued during the course of the marriage (perhaps partially out of self-interest, since women were traditionally cast as the more generous almsgivers), this initiative was unsuccessful.[21] So far-reaching was the husband's governance over his wife that a murderous attack on the husband by his subject wife was considered treasonous rather than simply criminal.[22]

English common law pertained only to individuals who were free from the stigma of serfdom – primarily members of the nobility, gentry, or the bourgeoisie. But it has been argued that where the stakes were lower, a more rough and ready equality may have prevailed between spouses. Barbara Hanawalt posits that the rigours of the peasant economy necessitated the contribution of both husband and wife, and that this, in turn, created a mutual dependency that she characterizes as a partnership marriage. But it should be noted that, in theory, the peasant husband's power over his wife was as comprehensive as a man of more fortunate birth. Moreover, the work of Judith Bennett also indicates that the marital years correspond with the nadir of the woman's participation in the larger community in comparison with either her prenuptial years or her widowhood.[23]

The husband's authority transcended the temporal order, deeply affecting the wife's spiritual autonomy. This is already implicit with respect to his control over his wife's will and testament, since pious bequests were considered essential to a person's spiritual wellbeing and substantially affected her hopes for progress in the afterlife. But similar intrusions were also supported by canon law. Gratian's *Decretum* (c. 1140), arguably the most important canonical source for the entire Middle Ages, insists on the husband's right to revoke his wife's vow – a pivotal consideration when most important undertakings and relations were sealed by formal oaths. Even if he had formerly authorized the vow which he now abrogated, she was nevertheless bound to obey 'on account of her condition of servitude'. This seeming breach in justice is justified by recourse to a devastating series of texts meant to demonstrate that the husband's rule over his wife was divinely willed and apparent in the order of creation.[24]

These erosions of the wife's autonomy also appear in the various pastoral manuals that were produced to assist priests in hearing confession. On the one hand, the clergy expected wives to move their husbands to good. Indeed, Thomas of Chobham, writing c. 1216, even urges wives to be 'preachers' to their recalcitrant husbands.[25] On the other hand, the 'pulpit' she was assigned for this task was inauspicious in the extreme. Thomas reminds the prospective confessor that a wife is under the power of her husband: a married woman was not able to make any pious vow of abstinence, nor could the priest enjoin any special penance on her, as the husband could unilaterally dispense with it.[26] Ordinances of Church councils were likewise circulated to remind parish priests that a married woman could not vow without her husband's consent.[27] In the manner of an ideological see-saw, the woman's subordination became the essential lever for the man's ascendancy. Indeed, Raymond of Peñafort, the author of one of the most influential of the continental pastoral manuals, attempts to reconcile the husband's sinful revocation of his wife's previously authorized vow by arguing that in obeying her husband she is in fact obeying God.[28]

Echoes of these pressing issues reverberate throughout Chaucer's work. In *The Tale of Melibee*, Prudence becomes a preacher to her husband, assuaging her husband's anger at a recent outrage suffered by his household and urging forgiveness. The conundrum of the wife's vow is dramatically explored in *The Franklin's Tale*. Anxious over potential threats to her husband's safety at sea, the wife rashly vows to submit sexually to an admirer if he can perform an impossible task: namely, remove all the dangerous rocks from the coastline of Brittany. With the assistance of a conjurer, the suitor manages to create the illusion that the rocks have disappeared. Hence, Dorigen is theoretically obliged to commit adultery. Dorigen's husband could easily have revoked the ill-judged vow. But because their marriage is premised on equality, the condition on which she agreed to be his wife, he considers himself obliged to permit his sorrowing wife to keep her word, had the suitor not eventually waived his rights.

From an optimistic standpoint, the husband of *The Franklin's Tale* could be seen as prioritizing his wife's legal autonomy over her physical purity and his own rights to sexual exclusivity. The downside, of course, is the tale's eloquent demonstration of the havoc that results from granting legal autonomy to wives. Dorigen conforms with the stereotype articulated by canonist William Lyndwood (d. 1446), who cautions clerics against women 'who are accustomed to emit vows more readily than men, especially when they are placed in some sort of tribulation or distress'.[29]

Chaucer's *Clerk's Tale*, which sees an Italian despot take a peasant wife and subject her to extreme tests, explores the ecclesiastical assimilation of the husband and God. Viewed in the mode of secular hagiography, Griselda's dogged submission is constantly being tested by her husband – a procedure likened to the way gold is proved in a furnace. This biblical image is traditionally employed to signify God's probation of the just. In this case, however, the God who does the testing is a maniacal husband. And yet, in obeying him, Griselda clearly wins merit, thus valorizing her husband's abuse of power. It is not surprising that this tale first emerged in Italy, where the impact of Roman law, and the theoretical buttressing of the husband's authority, would be most acutely felt. The story was extremely popular and was even assimilated into the manual on behaviour that the kindly *Goodman of Paris* wrote for his wife to emphasize proper submission.[30]

Finally, the husband, as lord over his wife, was further authorized to enforce his will by force, since canonical authorities accorded him the right of correction, which might entail tying her up or depriving her of food.[31] There were limits to how this right might be exercised, but the husband was nevertheless accorded considerable disciplinary latitude. The canonist Panormitanus (d. 1445), though upholding the husband's right 'to castigate and imprison', stipulates that these disciplinary measures should be scaled in accordance with the offence and 'should not proceed to cruelty'.[32] From the standpoint of customary law, the *Norman Somma* states that a husband may not put out his wife's eye or break her arm as this behaviour exceeds the limits of correction.[33] An anecdote from *The Book of the Knight of the Tower*, a handbook of behaviour assembled (with the help of some local clerics) by a French knight for his daughters – one of the first works translated into English by William Caxton – is instructive on this score:

> A woman in no maner wyse ought to stryue ageynst her husbond/ ne answere hym so that he take therby displaysyre [displeasure]/ lyke as dyde the wyf of a burgeys whiche answerd to her husbond so noiously [vexatiously]. and shamefully to fore [in front of] the peple/ that he bicam angry and felle [fierce] to see hym self so rewlyd [overborne] to fore the peple/ that he had therof shame . . . [H]er husbond whiche was wrothe [angry] smote her with his fyste to the erthe. And smote her with his foote on the vysage [face] so that he brake her nose/ by whiche she was euer after al disfygured. And soo by her ryotte [quarrelling] and ennoye [troublesomeness] she gate her a croked nose moche evyll . . . [I]t is but honoure to a good woman to suffre and holde her in pees.[34]

Admittedly, the Knight shows an unfortunate tendency to teach by negative example – a didactic method that would seem to beget a certain amount of exaggeration. But the evidence of the ecclesiastical courts also attests to official tolerance for a high level of violence. Cruelty (*saevitia*) was one of only three grounds for a judicial separation (technically a *divortium a mensa et thoro* or 'divorce from bed and board') – the other two being adultery and 'spiritual fornication' (heresy or apostasy).[35] Although efforts to obtain such separations were rare in practice, the plea of cruelty was the most common suit for a legal separation.

Moreover, since the majority of these actions were unsuccessful, the abused wife might well imagine herself better off by remaining silent. In a case from York, for example, one Margaret Neffeld produced witnesses to show that her husband had attacked her with a knife, cutting her arm and breaking her knee. The husband pleaded correction and Margaret was ordered home.[36] On occasion, the courts used such cases as opportunities to reinforce woman's traditional subjection to lordship as occurred in Durham:

Thomas Kyrkehm; Isabell, wife of the same. The woman sought a divorce and separation from bed and board on account of the cruelty of the man. The man denied [it], and afterward, through the industry of the judge, the woman, on bended knees, humbly sought pardon from the man, and the man pardoned her for whatsoever earlier offence and he kissed her, and furthermore the man swore upon the book that he would not instill dread of mutilation of the members on the woman. [37]

Despite the enforced reconciliation, it is clear from the oath that Thomas was required to swear that the authorities did not dismiss Isabell's grievance as nugatory.

Coercion, consent, and correction: an exemplary case

A case before the ecclesiastical court of the Cistercian monastery of Whalley in Lancashire demonstrates the many ways in which the woman's ostensibly protected rights are hampered and occluded by the sheer magnitude of her husband's authority. In 1514 Agnes Houghton, alias Bulcok, petitioned for a separation *a mensa et thoro* from her husband John on the grounds of cruelty. John denied the charge, and a day was set for a hearing. Agnes, however, did not appear, having instead fled beyond the jurisdiction of the court of Whalley into York. John launched a countersuit for the restitution of conjugal rights – basically a claim intended to return the recalcitrant spouse back to the marital bed. A letter, claiming that Agnes 'refuse[d] to live with [John] and is vagabond everywhere' and requesting her return, went out to the officials of York.

Once apprehended and sent back from York, Agnes testified that she was terrified to live with John, claiming that the moment he had her alone he would kill her. A day was again set for proving her charges and this time Agnes appeared. Though making oblique references to an insurmountable impediment that invalidated her marriage, she produced no witnesses whatsoever. Agnes was ordered back to her husband under pain of excommunication. The couple were reunited 'at the instigation and urging of their kin', and were further enjoined to treat each other with marital affection.[38]

In less than a month, it came to the attention of the court that the couple were living apart. Both Agnes and John were thus summoned before the court and questioned. While both parties admitted that they were legally married with proper solemnization, Agnes asserted that she had never freely consented to accept John as her husband, rather having been compelled 'through the strength, and ordaining, and mediation of her friends'. Threatened with loss of friends and disinheritance, she submitted to the wedding. Moreover, 'she never slept with her aforesaid pretended husband unless compelled, nor did he know her except against her will and with her deeply dissenting, and struggling, and contradicting and compelled to it by force and blows'. Agnes also claimed to have run away from John at the first available opportunity. In other words, Agnes is now abandoning her original suit for a separation and is, instead, suing for an annulment. Six witnesses are adduced – all of whom could confirm that Agnes was weeping at the time of the ceremony, was threatened with loss of friends and wealth if she did not accept John, that she never inwardly consented to the match, and that John beat her. Other salient factors also emerge. On the basis of how long each witness claimed to have known the husband and wife, Agnes would seem to be around twenty, while John was at least forty at the time of the trial. Agnes's stepfather is described as *generosus*, signifying well or even nobly born, while John is characterized as 'an onest man and a Ryche'. Thus, the union was probably a classic January/May affair in which Agnes's youth and birth were traded for John's wealth.

Agnes's successive pleas each obscure the grounds by which she might have secured her freedom. According to her brother-in-law, to whose house she fled:

> On her arrival she said, Brother, I am com to you. And I ever told you that I never loved hym. And now he hathe gevene me cause more to hate hym then ever I did, ffor he hathe grevously beten me. And she showed the blows and the wounds to him as much on the arms as on the back. And he asked her the reason why he beat her, and she said because she did not wish to consent to lie [with him] both in action and in the use of the flesh and also because she clung to the home of Richard ffawcett.

The records, unfortunately, are mum on the subject of Richard ffawcett or the nature of their relationship. But Agnes's flight, nevertheless, undermined her petition for separation on the grounds of her husband's cruelty, as it would then become apparent that John's harsh 'correction' was warranted. And in fact, when a new date was set for her plea following her return from York, she could produce no witnesses to sustain her charge of cruelty.

Similarly, the plea for separation on the basis of cruelty obscures the potential invalidity of the union. But, once Agnes changed her plea, she was able to produce a number of witnesses who confirmed that she had not consented freely to the match. According to a Katherine Baxter, Agnes complained after her betrothal, 'Alas Katheryne, I am vndone, ffor myne ffrendes wole nedes compell me to haue John Bulcok, and by myne trouthe I had leuer dy then haue hym . . . And I pray you ber me record hir after.' Likewise, she expostulated with a neighbour who saluted her as 'Dame' in token of her married status.[39]

Clearly, Agnes was fully apprised of the potential invalidity of her union with John. Why, then, petition for a legal separation when grounds for an annulment existed? The probable answer is as simple as it is bleak: an annulment would have sent Agnes right back into the hands of her 'compelling' friends – a restraining factor which, presumably, had stopped her from launching a formal objection against John at the time of the wedding. A legal separation, however, would have enabled Agnes to retain the status of married woman, and possibly her own establishment. But, since the courts were generally intent on reuniting even the most hostile of couples, such a separation was always something of a vain hope.[40] The outcome of Agnes's suit is unknown. But whether her suit was upheld or denied, the circumstances attendant upon either ruling were extremely disadvantageous.

Married sexuality

The consensual definition of marriage had the effect of insulating the formation of the bond from the sex act. While Augustine acknowledged that offspring was marriage's main end and chief good, he particularly commended the marriage of Mary and Joseph for its chaste fecundity.[41] Considering this standard, it would not be surprising if sexual activity, even in the context of marriage, were fraught with ambivalence. Thomas of Chobham's pastoral manual is representative of the general discourse. Following Augustine, Thomas admits only three licit motives for sexual intercourse: in addition to the desire for offspring, a spouse should 'render the debt' of sexual intercourse if the other spouse requires it; likewise, a spouse tempted to extramarital fornication 'should cool himself' with his own partner.[42]

But the paths of sinful conjugal intercourse tended to outnumber their licit counterparts. In addition to the category of licit intercourse, Thomas further discerns 'fragile' coitus and 'impetuous' coitus. Fragile coitus occurs when a person approaches his or her spouse prompted simply by the 'fragility of incontinence'. Such a sex act is only venially sinful (which is to say that such an offence, if unconfessed, would cost you time in purgatory but not send you to hell). A third category, impetuous coitus, is subdivided into four subsets, all of which are mortally sinful. The first is 'coitus on account of the saturating lust of whorish embraces' – a state that is summarized in the patristic condemnation of the excessive lover of his own wife. The second stigmatizes all extra-vaginal forms of intercourse. The third involves prohibited times as stipulated by the Church calendar, while the fourth addresses the prohibitions pertaining to the wife's reproductive cycle. Thus pregnancy, menstruation, or the polluting presence of postpartum afterbirth rendered sexual contact mortally sinful. (Thomas also notes that some would add coitus in public, with people watching, as a possible fifth.)[43]

Even so, in the course of the high Middle Ages, these formerly implacable taboos gradually gave way to the obligation to render the conjugal debt – a concept of mutual sexual obligation ultimately deriving from St Paul (1 Corinthians 7: 3–5) and, as we have seen, one of the three licit motives for conjugal intercourse. Gratian had already set aside the obligation of sexual abstinence on these traditional feasts in the event that a spouse exacts the debt.[44] Thomas of Chobham will reluctantly follow suit. Pondering over the riddle of the spouse who threatens to sleep with another if the husband or wife will not render the debt on a feast day, Thomas initially compares such a sinful rendering with giving a sword to a madman. Eventually, however, he will determine that such a rendering is compulsory. Yet, if undertaken reluctantly, this obligatory sex act can be performed without sin.[45]

Pastoral authorities will likewise gradually dispense with the prohibitions surrounding the female body as well. Thomas of Chobham argues that a wife who has just given birth, and is nevertheless solicited by her husband for sex, should rise from her birthing bed to obtain purification in order to meet his sexual exaction. Continental authorities, particularly of the Dominican Order, would similarly waive prohibitions during pregnancy or menstruation.[46] Only a mutual vow of chastity could suspend a spouse's right to exact the debt. Indeed, so central was the debt to the medieval understanding of marriage, and so apprehensive was the medieval clergy about the propensities of the lay person forced to go without, that a suit for marital desertion was framed in terms of the restitution of conjugal rights, as is illustrated in the case brought against Agnes Bulcok by her putative husband, John.

From an ecclesiastical perspective, the debt is understood to be the one area of equality between husband and wife – a claim which modern scholars have too often accepted unchallenged. And yet it is clear from the above examples that a policy of sex on demand was prejudicial to the wife. On the most obvious level, women risked the considerable dangers of pregnancy. In addition, the mandatory rendering of the debt in defiance of the traditional taboos surrounding the woman's biological cycle must necessarily create a high degree of ambivalence not only from fears of potential sinfulness, but also for more concrete reasons as well. For example, it was widely believed that children conceived during menstruation would be leprous.[47]

The sexual double standard, already implicit in Church teaching on the conjugal debt, is especially apparent over the question of adultery. Gratian himself remarks on the injustice of society's differential attitude towards the adultery of the husband, which was generally tolerated, versus that of the wife, which was severely censured.[48] But, considering the patrilineal structuring of society, one need not look far to learn why this should be so. Robert of Courson (writing c. 1208–13) agonizes over what to advise the guilt-stricken female penitent who has confessed that she presented her husband with a spurious heir – a predicament with far-reaching implications that could lead to war and general devastation, if made known.[49] Not surprisingly, Isabel of Bavaria's spiteful revelations concerning the illegitimacy of her son, the future Charles VII, dealt a crushing blow to French morale in the Hundred Years' War. The anarchic potential of woman's adultery is symbolically imagined in Robert Mannyng of Brunne's *Handyling Synne*, wherein a dragon, which had been ravaging the countryside, is discovered in the rent skeleton of a female adulteress.[50] Literature's most famous adulterous lovers, such as Lancelot and Guinevere or Tristan and Isolde, are represented as sterile, suggesting that this is an area from which the masculine imagination would naturally recoil. Interestingly, a notable exception to the tacit rule of sterile adultery occurs in the twelfth-century Marie de France's *lai* of *Yonec*.

This double standard implicit in adultery is often hidden from view. Ecclesiastical courts, for example, harshly punished the offence in both sexes, often whipping offending parishioners through the streets in their underclothes, regardless of their sex.[51] But, as with the biblical woman taken in adultery, who was excused by Christ, women seem to be more frequently named before the ecclesiastical courts for this offence.[52] Moreover, we also find efforts to justify a differential treatment of men and women. Thomas Aquinas upholds the heightened severity towards adulterous women in terms of the integrity of the family. Others would argue that, even as Christ was married to the Synagogue before marrying the Church, so multiple sexual partners could be tolerated in the male, but not in the female (who must represent the virginal and monogamous Church).[53]

In addition, there are any number of ingenious attempts to blame the man's adultery on the wife. Particularly striking is the ever-pervasive bestiary lore, which has it that the viper copulates by the male thrusting its head into the female's mouth, spitting its semen therein. The female, however, annoyed by these sexual antics, bites his head off. As a result of his wife's noncompliant nature, the male viper frequently turns to an unnatural union with the murena or sea eel. The bestiarist is interested in how this pattern elucidates the marital *mœurs*. Thus to the wives, he alleges:

> Your husband, I admit, may be uncouth, undependable, disorderly, slippery and tipsy – but what is worse than the ill which the murena-mistress does not shun in him, once he has called her? *She* does not fail him. *She* embraces the slipperiness of the serpent with careful zeal. *She* puts up with your troubles

and offers the comfort of womanly good cheer. But you, O Woman, like the lady-snake who bites off his head, are not able to support your own man.

From this unlikely beginning, the bestiarist eventually swerves to the predictable condemnation of adultery.[54]

Clerical efforts to exculpate the husband and inculpate the wife nevertheless coexisted with an uncomfortable awareness of the wife's sexual vulnerability to the whims of her husband – a vulnerability that even extended to enforced adultery. Pastoral counsellors, such as Thomas of Chobham, denounce the husband who attempts to act as a pimp for his wife, even depriving him of communion on his deathbed.[55] In fact, conjugal units of pimps and bawds were commonplace in ecclesiastical courts, frequently entailing the explicit prostitution of the wife.[56]

Ecclesiastically sponsored resistance to the husband's rule

If the Church is to be faulted for the consolidation of the husband's power, it should also be credited for protecting women from this power's more brutal excesses. At times, the Church could even be considered an indirect sponsor of subversion. For instance, pastoral concerns frequently united with institutional self-interest over the question of alms. Thus authorities often encouraged the wife to go against the husband's explicit prohibition in this area. This even pertains to Raymond of Peñafort, who outstripped most of his clerical confrères in the promotion of the husband's authority.[57] In a similar vein, the English Church attempted to influence common law through securing wives the right to make binding wills regardless of the husband's permission – an initiative that was ultimately defeated.[58] One discerns a natural *quid pro quo* arising between the Church and its benefactresses. John Fisher's funeral oration for his pious penitent, Margaret Beaufort, for example, is informed by an ongoing desire to be generous with the woman who had always been generous with the Church.[59]

Finally, Church doctrine supported the initiative of women like Christina of Markyate, Margery Kempe, or Margaret Beaufort to convert their husbands to perpetual chastity – transitions that inevitably coincided with a relaxation of masculine rule. And yet, this tacit ecclesiastical support was, ironically, underwritten by the very disparagement of human sexuality that had cost women so much.

NOTES

1. For this patristic exegesis of Matthew 13: 8, see Jerome's *Against Jovinian* 1.3, trans. W. H. Fremantle, *The Principal Works of St Jerome*, A Select Library of

Nicene and Post-Nicene Fathers of the Christian Church, 2nd ser., vol. 6 (Grand Rapids: Eerdmans Publishing, 1893), p. 347.

2. C. H. Talbot, ed. and trans., *The Life of Christina of Markyate* (Oxford: Clarendon Press, 1987), pp. 62–3.

3. See John Noonan, 'Power to Choose', *Viator* 4 (1973): 413–34; Charles Donahue, 'The Policy of Alexander III's Consent Theory of Marriage', in *Proceedings of the Fourth International Congress of Canon Law*, ed. Stephan Kuttner, Monumenta Iuris Canonici, ser. C., Subsidia, vol. 5 (Vatican City: Biblioteca Apostolica Vaticana, 1976), pp. 251–81.

4. Penny Gold, 'The Marriage of Mary and Joseph in the Twelfth-Century Ideology of Marriage', in *Sexual Practices and the Medieval Church*, ed. Vern Bullough and James Brundage (Buffalo: Prometheus Books, 1982), pp. 102–17.

5. See Michael Sheehan, 'The Formation and Stability of Marriage in Fourteenth-Century England: Evidence of an Ely Register', *Mediaeval Studies* 33 (1071): 244–251, 253. Also see Christopher Brooke's discussion of the development of the ritual at the church door in *The Medieval Idea of Marriage* (Oxford University Press, 1989), pp. 248–54.

6. Donahue, 'The Policy of Alexander III', pp. 270 ff.; Noonan, 'Power to Choose', p. 433.

7. See esp. Jack Goody's *The Development of the Family and Marriage in Europe* (Cambridge University Press, 1983).

8. Talbot, ed., *The Life of Christina of Markyate*, pp. 46–7.

9. Ibid., pp. 50–3. On this model, see Dyan Elliott, *Spiritual Marriage: Sexual Abstinence in Medieval Wedlock* (Princeton University Press, 1993), esp. pp. 147, 208–9. Also see Jocelyn Wogan-Browne, 'Saints' Lives and the Female Reader', *Forum for Modern Language Studies* 4 (1991): 314–32, esp. 316–22.

10. Talbot, ed., *Life of Christina of Markyate*, pp. 58–9, 108–9; cf. pp. 60–1.

11. Elliott, *Spiritual Marriage*, pp. 143–4.

12. Talbot, ed., *Life of Christina*, pp. 64–5. See Thomas Head on Christina's plea of prior marriage to Christ in 'The Marriages of Christina of Markyate', *Viator* 21 (1990): 75–101.

13. Richard Helmholz, *Marriage Litigation in Medieval England* (Cambridge University Press, 1974), p. 91 and n. 60. Cf. Noonan, 'Power to Choose', p. 431.

14. Talbot, ed., *Life of Christina of Markyate*, pp. 58–9.

15. Norman Davis, ed., *The Paston Letters and Papers* (Oxford: Clarendon Press, 1976), no. 446, 2: 32. See Ann Haskell, 'The Paston Women on Marriage', *Viator* 4 (1973): 459–71, esp. 467–69.

16. Helmholz, *Marriage Litigation*, pp. 91, 25, 68, 74, 101; A. Esmein, *Le Mariage en droit canonique*, 2nd edn (Paris: Recueil Sirey, 1929), 1: 324 ff.; Sheehan, 'Formation and Stability', p. 258.

17. Sheehan, 'Formation and Stability', pp. 251, 263. Also see Helmholz, *Marriage Litigation*, pp. 27–31.

18. Margaret Paston to John Paston II, in Davis, ed., *Paston Letters*, no. 203, 1: 341–4.

19. See Frederick Pollock and Frederic W. Maitland, *The History of English Law*, 2nd edn (Cambridge University Press, 1952), 2: 407, 437.

20. Pollock and Maitland, *History of English Law*, 2: 399–436; on the *feme sole*, see ibid., 1:482. See Jacqueline Murray, 'On the Origins of "Wise Women" in

Cases for Annulment on the Grounds of Male Impotence', *Journal of Medieval History* 16 (1990): 235–49. Ruth Karras has since suggested that these female experts were often prostitutes (*Common Women: Prostitution and Sexuality in Medieval England* (New York: Oxford University Press, 1996), pp. 97–8), which would render woman's almost unique appearance in court somewhat ironic.

21. Sheehan, 'The Influence of Canon Law on the Property Rights of Married Women', *Mediaeval Studies* 25 (1963): 109–24.

22. Pollock and Maitland, *History of English Law*, 2: 485. See Paul Strohm's discussion of the 1352 statute on treason in 'Treason in the Household', *Hochon's Arrow: The Social Imagination of Fourteenth-Century Texts* (Princeton University Press, 1992), pp. 121–44.

23. See Barbara Hanawalt, *The Ties that Bound: Peasant Families in Medieval England* (New York: Oxford University Press, 1986), pp. 154–5, 218–19; Judith Bennett, *Women in the Medieval Countryside: Gender and Household in Brigstock Before the Plague* (Oxford University Press, 1987), pp. 129–41.

24. Gratian, *Decretum Magistri Gratiani* c. 33 q. 5 c. 11 dpc, c. 33 q. 5 c. 12–20 in vol. 1 of *Corpus Iuris Canonici*, ed. A. Friedberg (Leipzig: Bernhardus Tauchnitz, 1879), cols. 1254–6.

25. Thomas of Chobham, *Summa confessorum* 7.2.15, ed. F. Broomfield (Louvain: Nauwelaerts, 1968), p. 375. See Sharon Farmer, 'Persuasive Voices: Clerical Images of Medieval Wives', *Speculum* 61 (1986): 517, 530–4.

26. See, for example, Thomas of Chobham, *Summa confessorum* 4.2.7.11, p. 157; Elliott, *Spiritual Marriage*, pp. 155 ff.

27. See the Statutes of Salisbury I, c. 89 (1217–19), in *Councils and Synods with Other Documents Relating to the English Church*, ed. F. M. Powicke and C. R. Cheney (Oxford: Clarendon Press, 1964), 2,1: 89.

28. Raymond of Peñafort, *Summa sancti Raymundi de Peniafort de poenitentia, et matrimonio* 3.33.4 (Rome: Sumptibus Ioannis Tallini, 1603), p. 383.

29. William Lyndwood, *Provinciale (seu constitutiones Angliae)* (Oxford: H. Hall, 1679), bk 3, tit. 18, gloss e, p. 204.

30. Eileen Power, trans., *The Goodman of Paris*, 1.6 (New York: Harcourt and Brace, 1928), pp. 136–7; see further *Le Ménagier de Paris*, ed. Georgine E. Brereton and Janet M. Ferrier, with a foreword by Beryl Smalley (Oxford: Clarendon Press, 1981).

31. Gratian, *Decretum*, c. 33 q. 2 c. 10, in vol. 1 of *Corpus iuris canonici*, ed. Friedberg, cols. 1154–5; Esmein, *Le Mariage*, 2: 5–7.

32. Esmein, *Le Mariage*, 2: 5, n. 1.

33. Pollock and Maitland, *History of English Law*, 2: 456.

34. William Caxton, trans., *The Book of the Knight of the Tower* c. 17, ed. M. Y. Offord, EETS ss 2 (London: Oxford University Press, 1971), p. 35.

35. Esmein, *Le Mariage*, 2: 108–12.

36. Helmholz, *Marriage Litigation*, p. 105.

37. J. Raine, ed., *Depositions and Other Ecclesiastical Proceedings from the Courts of Durham Extending from 1311 to the Reign of Elizabeth*, Surtees Society 21 (London: J. B. Nichols, 1854), p. 57.

38. See Alice Cooke, ed., *Act Book of the Ecclesiastical Court of Whalley, 1510–38*, Chetham Society 44 (Manchester: Chetham Society, 1901), pp. 29–32. The

monastery's tribunal is known as a 'peculiar' court, signifying its special jurisdiction within Lancashire. See John Noonan, 'Marital Affection in the Canonists', *Studia Gratiana* 12 (1967): 481–509.

39. Cooke, ed., *Whalley*, pp. 36–44.

40. Helmholz, *Marriage Litigation*, pp. 100–4.

41. In addition to elevating the marriage of Mary and Joseph, Augustine introduced the three goods of marriage: faith (meaning sexual fidelity), offspring, and indissolubility (Elliott, *Spiritual Marriage*, pp. 46–8, 135).

42. Thomas of Chobham, *Summa confessorum* 7.2.2.1, p. 334.

43. Ibid., pp. 334–5.

44. Gratian, *Decretum* C. 33 q. 4 C. 11 dpc, in vol. 1 of *Corpus iuris canonici*, ed. Friedberg, col. 1254; James Brundage, *Law, Sex, and Christian Society in Medieval Europe* (University of Chicago Press, 1987), pp. 236–8, p. 242.

45. Thomas of Chobham, *Summa confessorum* 7.2.2.3, pp. 336–7.

46. Elliott, *Spiritual Marriage*, pp. 150–1; John of Freiburg, *Summa confessorum* 4.2.44 (Rome: s.n., 1518), fo. 220v.

47. Thomas of Chobham is very explicit on this score (*Summa confessorum* 7.2.10, pp. 365–6).

48. Gratian, *Decretum* C. 32 q. 5 C. 22 dpc, in vol. 1 of *Corpus iuris canonici*, ed. Friedberg, col. 1138.

49. See V. L. Kennedy's edition in 'Robert Courson on Penance', *Mediaeval Studies* 7 (1945): 320–1, C. 10.

50. Robert Mannyng of Brunne, *Handlyng Synne* lines 1741–1867, ed. Frederick James Furnivall, EETS os 119, 123 (London: Kegan Paul, Trench, Trübner, 1901, 1903), pp. 63–7.

51. See, for example, a number of instances at fourteenth-century Rochester in C. Johnson, ed., *Registrum Hamonis Hethe Diocesis Roffensis, AD 1319–1352*, Canterbury and York Society (Oxford University Press, 1948), 2: 925, 933, 948, 950, 957, 998–9.

52. In Rochester between 9 April 1347 and 4 November 1348, there were twenty-seven adultery charges. Although the marital status of the offenders is not always readily determinable, only eight of the cases clearly designate a married man (as opposed to a bachelor), while a full sixteen cases involved a married woman (see Johnson, ed., *Registrum Hamonis*). Likewise, in the thirty-three adultery cases at Buckingham, a preponderance of wives are cited (fourteen) versus husbands (four). See E. M. Elvey, ed., *The Courts of the Archdeaconry of Buckingham, 1483–1523*, *Buckingham Record Society* 19 (1975).

53. Eleanor McLaughlin, 'Equality of Souls, Inequality of Sexes: Woman in Medieval Theology', in *Religion and Sexism: Images of Woman in the Jewish and Christian Tradition*, ed. Rosemary Ruether (New York: Simon and Schuster, 1974), pp. 227–8.

54. T. H. White, trans., *The Bestiary: A Book of Beasts* (New York: Putnam, 1960), p. 171. This is a translation from the Latin of a twelfth-century English manuscript.

55. Thomas of Chobham, *Summa confessorum* 7.2.11, pp. 366–7.

56. In Buckingham, there were six conjugal teams over forty years. For the wife's prostitution, see Elvey, ed., *Buckingham*, nos. 46, 142a, 224; also see 153, 232,

292, 385. For the conjugal couple as procurers, see Karras, *Common Women*, pp. 62, 74.

57. Raymond of Peñafort, *Summa de poenitentia* 2.8.9, p. 252.

58. Sheehan, 'The Influence of Canon Law', pp. 119–20.

59. Brooke, *Medieval Idea of Marriage*, pp. 34–8; John Mayor, ed., *The English Works of John Fisher, Bishop of Rochester*, EETS ES 27, pt 1 (London: Trübner, 1876), pp. 289–310.

4

BARBARA A. HANAWALT

Widows

In a late medieval society in which young maidens were the ideal of beauty and desirability, the widow was not the most favoured subject among authors. Chaucer drew three notable portraits of widows – the Wife of Bath, Criseyde, and the poor peasant widow in *The Nun's Priest's Tale* – in addition to the widow in *The Friar's Tale*. Other widows appear in *The Canterbury Tales* but their status is not elaborated. Alisoun, despite outliving five husbands, is not called the Widow of Bath. For the fifteenth century, William Dunbar's poem, 'The Tretis of the Tua Mariit Wemen and the Wedo', provides a picture of a widow sharing some of the Wife of Bath's robust sexual views.[1] The literatures of France and Spain, and of course Italy, also feature lively widow stories.[2] Literary attitudes towards widows cover a wide range: January in *The Merchant's Tale* says he will marry a maid rather than a widow because widows can take property without producing heirs; in *The Prioress's Tale*, the mother of the young boy is described as a poor widow raising her son alone; and in *Troilus and Criseyde* the allure of a young widow's black clothes forms part of the temptation to romance. Historical backgrounds for all these perceptions of widows will form part of this chapter.

Widows were ubiquitous in medieval Europe. Contrary to the popular myth that the most common cause of death for adult women was childbirth and that, as a consequence, men outnumbered women, the majority of women survived their husbands. Some, like the Wife of Bath, outlived several. From fifteenth-century rural wills of adult males from Bedfordshire, we learn that 72 per cent had a surviving wife.[3] In London wills of the fourteenth and fifteenth centuries from the Husting Court (the supreme court of the city), 53 per cent of men's wills mention a surviving wife.[4] Although English records do not permit precise estimates of the percentage of widows in the population, the options available to widows, the roles they played in society, their decision to marry or remain in pure widowhood, their economic security, and the potential power they wielded are all of interest in this chapter. What strategies did women use and what avenues were open to them to function independently? Finally, were English widows any different from those on the continent?

To understand widows' options, we need to assess both lay and ecclesiastical regulations. The Wife of Bath could continue to manage her business as a widow, Chaucer's poor peasant widow was rearing two young daughters and tending her livestock alone, and the widow in *The Friar's Tale* was old and sick but of sound enough mind to challenge the summoner about the archdeacon's jurisdiction. English law offered such widows, for the first time in their lives, some measure of legal independence. As a maiden she had been under her father's protection; as a wife, control over her life had moved to her husband. A widow or adult single female, however, was on a par with men in private law and could make contracts, sue and be sued, own property, and plead in her own voice.[5]

In addition to these broad rights in private law, the law and custom of dower also protected widows. The dower was publicly announced at the church door at the time of the marriage (such an arrangement is often referred to in cases of subsequent dispute over dower). Thus when the Wife of Bath married five husbands 'at chirche dore' (1.460), she not only marrying in the usual location, but was also ensuring public proclamation of the agreed-upon dower. A husband might also make provisions after the marriage to take into account property acquired after the marriage.

Laws pertaining to women varied according to social status. Noble, knightly, and gentry women had dower by common law that provided a third of the husband's estate for the widow's life use. By the late Middle Ages other types of arrangements were also made, such as 'jointure and use' (which addressed wifely rights during and after the life of the husband). Borough custom (independent of common law) gave the widow a third of the estate for life use, while the testator had a third for the good of his soul and his children the remaining third. Remarriage did not remove the widow's accumulated dower rights; the Wife of Bath would thus have retained dower from each of her five husbands. In customary law applying to manors, the male serf did not own the land himself; instead, a man and his new wife took up their holding in both their names. As a widow, the wife might later enjoy the whole of the tenement for life use, or a half of it (depending on the custom of the manor). The poor peasant widow in *The Nun's Priest's Tale*, therefore, had a secure if not a luxurious livelihood. Dower was usually in the form of land or rights to rent land and houses. Thus women from all classes – noble, knightly, gentry, bourgeois, or peasant – could enjoy a life use of considerable property. At the very least, the widow had the right to 'freebench' (which included a place by the fire in the main room and perhaps a room to herself in the family tenement). Among the very poor, of course, begging would provide the only distance between the widow and death.

Like all medieval people, widows were governed not only by private law, but also by the Church. While wives could not make wills without their husband's consent, widows were free to do so. But the attitude of the Church towards widows was very ambiguous. On the one hand, the loss of a husband offered the opportunity for a woman to become more devout, spending her time in prayer and charity. On the other hand, widows were free, often young and wealthy, and could lead men into temptation.

Moralists thus had much to say about widows. Ideally speaking, a widow should bury her husband, see that his will was executed, and prepare to lead a chaste life (while rearing children and looking after her household). The Church even had a semi-religious role, that of vowess, for widows who chose to live in this world but who vowed to live a chaste life and not remarry. Vowesses registered with the bishop and took a vow before him to remain chaste and unmarried. Becoming a vowess gave a widow protection from fortune-hunters who wanted to force her into marriage, sometimes through abduction. These widows could also manage their estates and control the training and marriages of their children. Vowesses wore a distinctive mantle and ring. Margery Kempe (it seems) would much have liked this validation of her religious vocation: she did get permission to assume a distinctive dress, but never became a vowess, since her husband lived an inconveniently long time.

The Church did not prescribe a period of mourning for the widow and did not prevent her from entering quickly into another marriage: if the widow passed quickly from the oversight of one husband to another, at least a man was in control. An honourable reputation was the desired outcome whether a woman remained chaste or entered another marriage. The Church followed the lead of male scholars (and poets) who suggested that women's sexual appetites were voracious and, once unleashed, difficult to manage. Moralists worried, further, that well-dressed widows might wander abroad to tempt men:

> hit falleth to wedowes for to use symple and
> comune clothinge of mene colour and noght   [modest]
> gay ne starynge, ne of queynte and sotil schap,   [ostentatious]
> and take ensample of the holy wedowe Judith,
> of whom holy writ maketh mynde, that anone   [immediately]
> whan hir housbonde was deed sche lefte all hir
> gay attyre and apparaile . . .[6]

Some moralists, however, observed that black became the complexions of young widows (showing off the delicate tones of their skin and hair). Such vanity posed a threat to their chastity.

Such preacherly concerns may also be detected in medieval English and Scottish poetry. Criseyde looks very attractive in her 'blake wede' (1.169–77); her widowly beauty and vulnerability sets the tone for the whole poem. Scotsman William Dunbar's long satirical 'Tretis' sees a twice-married widow instructing two wives on how to entertain lovers while hoodwinking husbands: 'Weil couth I claw his cruke back', she says of one deceased and deceived spouse, 'and kemm his kewt noddill' (line 275: 'I knew well how to tickle his crooked back and to comb his cropped head').

The widow's challenge, then, was to exercise new-found freedom to her best advantage. She might choose to remain single, especially if there were children to help with tilling the ground or managing estates or businesses; she might (particularly if young) elect to enjoy the social benefits and material help of the married estate. Social class or estate conditioned available options: noble women had little choice in matters of marriage, since the king or her lord would decide for her; religious vocations, including that of vowess, were for the upper classes (not for peasants).

Peasant widows

Peasant widows were subject to customary law, although law alone did not dictate the comfort in which they might live. While they might receive from half to the whole of the joint tenement for life use, their comfort in widowhood depended on the size of the tenement. Cottars, such as the widow of Chaucer's *Nun's Priest's Tale*, had only a cottage and at most a few acres of land, but holdings could exceed 30 acres (13.5 ha). The greater the landholding the greater the comfort and the responsibilities of the widow; the land had to be cultivated. Other factors entered into provisions for widows. A widow with young children needed more resources to provide for them, but, if the children were grown and settled, a widow needed only provision for her old age. Studies show that about 14 per cent of village residents were widows.[7] And Bedfordshire wills suggest that rural widows had generous dowers; 63 per cent of the widows received the home tenement for life and the rest had other provisions for their survival including land and a house or at least a place in a son or daughter's house.[8] Husbands showed great confidence in their wives; 65 per cent made them executors of their wills. Wills, of course, tend to represent the upper end of the economic scale, but they do show that many widows were left well situated.

What options could a peasant widow consider? She could continue to farm the tenement either by hiring help or relying on her sons, if they were at least teenagers. One study shows that husbands leaving a widow with young children gave them the most generous provisions possible.[9] For instance, Agnes of the Land took over the family tenement and cultivated it for twenty years until her son Richard reached twenty-one. She then released the land to him and took her dower of a third of the property in both her name and his.[10] A widow could hire out the ploughing and harvesting, but remarriage was also a common solution to cultivating the land until the children were grown. If famine and disease made land readily available, young men would tend to marry young women, but if the land was scarce, they would marry a widow who had dower land for her life use.[11]

Older widows either received provision for their maintenance in the husband's will or manor court entry (record) or could make their own arrangements by purchasing land or by negotiating a retirement contract. Thus John Whytyng surrendered his tenement to another man with the provision that he supply John's widow with food, drink, and sixteen bushels of barley in addition to some livestock, an annual clothing and shoe allowance and the right to entry, a place by the fire, and a bed in her former husband's house.[12]

We must not assume that peasant widows lived lonely lives. Widows' wills reveal a great deal about the networks in which they participated (which included kin, servants, neighbours, and friends). Such women took great care in distributing their household goods, clothing, and other movables among those they held dear. One widow, who lived with her son, rewarded not only him but also the servant who took care of her; she also left bequests to two grandsons and three other relatives. Godchildren, close friends, local clergy, nieces and nephews were also beneficiaries of widows.[13]

Urban widows

Like rural widows, urban widows had dower property. The London wills recorded in the Court of Husting wills show that 86 per cent of testators left their wives with real property (lands, shops, gardens, tenements, rents, taverns, and breweries.) These wills represent the upper end of the social scale since this court required all men and women bequeathing real property to register their wills in the Husting Court.[14] Another court, that of the Archdeaconry of London, permits us to investigate the estates of the less prosperous. Only 18 per cent of the men leaving wills mention real property while 65 per cent simply refer to the residue of their estate.[15] Like rural testators, urban husbands trusted their wives as executors (86 per cent). In cases of disputed dower, London women went to court and were generally successful in gaining their rights.[16] The widows were as knowledgeable about London private law as was the widow in *The Friar's Tale* about procedures of ecclesiastical summoning.

What did the widows do with their dowers? Many were left with the equipment and apprentices from their former husband's craft or business. London did not prohibit women from carrying on businesses of their own and trading *feme sole* in the city, but few women did.[17] Even in the Brewers' Guild, which included more women than other guilds, only 7 per cent of the membership were widows in the early sixteenth century.[18] While some individual widows succeeded in pursuing their husband's craft, few are recorded.[19] In fourteenth-century Exeter, only three widows managed to carry on their husband's merchant activities.[20] The Wife of Bath might be invoked among these energetic widows, but she would have been in a small minority.

Continuing a craft or merchant enterprise required shrewdness and strength of character. A widow had to be prepared to take debtors to court, to make contracts for goods to produce, to train current apprentices and even to take on new ones. Apprentices complained about poor training.[21] Unscrupulous customers and lenders cheated widows. And strong social prohibitions against women travelling to foreign markets led some widows to abandon wine and wool trades. Many chose remarriage, usually to someone in a trade related to that of the husband, thus ensuring the success of the business.

Although in *The Merchant's Tale* January fantasizes that his wife might remain a widow after his death (4.2075–80), it was unusual for a London man to stipulate in his will that his wife should not remarry. Since a widow with children received a third of her former husband's estate for her life use (and a half if childless), a man looking for a wife might find her very attractive as a prospective partner. Not only would the new husband have the widow's dower for life use (often including the shop, apprentices, clientele, and merchandise). The market for widows in London was thus very competitive, as George's pursuit of a widow in the extensive Cely correspondence documents.[22]

Lest one think that the market benefited only men, consider the case of Thomasine Bonaventura. Born into a gentry family in Cornwall in the 1450s, her brother, a priest, had connections in London. Having entered a merchant tailor's household as an upper-class servant, she married her widowed master. He died in 1467, leaving her with a dower of half his property and a bequest of £100 in cloth from his shop, the terms of his apprentices, and £100 in cash. It appears that she had planned to take over the business, but instead married another tailor. He died in less than a year, leaving Thomasine half of his estate as dower. She then married John Percyvale, another tailor and a mayor of London. When he died in 1503, she apparently assumed the tailoring business of this last husband, including the training of apprentices.[23]

In addition to receiving the dower, the widow was appointed guardian of her children in 55 per cent of the cases coming into the mayor's court of orphans. While widows could administer their children's portion, the court favoured a male, usually a new husband, to take charge of these assets. Two thirds of the widows with children remarried between the time of their husband's death and the designation of guardians for their children.[24]

The economic advantages of marrying a widow with children were overwhelming. The new husband would be awarded the use of two thirds of the former husband's estate for the life of the widow and until the children reached the age of majority (twenty-one years of age or marriage). For instance, a fifteenth-century grocer married a widow with a dower of £764 and was appointed guardian of her six children with permission to trade with their patrimony (an equal amount) until they came of age.[25] While some have held that it was common for an apprentice to marry into the family of the master, including marrying his widow, I found very few cases in which this happened.[26] Perhaps the popularity of the idea of mistress/apprentice marriages comes from the Wife of Bath's marriage to Jankyn, her husband's apprentice. For the most part, these women married fellow guild brothers of their former husband.[27]

Like peasant women, urban widows had extensive networks of friends, kin, and clergy; their wills indicate generous charitable work. Widows belonged to parish guilds[28] and were active in the parish church. They left money for the poor or even more elaborate bequests for chapels or schools. Beneficiaries of personal bequests show that associates of their husband and these men's wives were close friends. Most widows, if they had children, kept in touch with them and even their grandchildren, godchildren, and nieces and nephews. Well-endowed urban women did have the option of becoming vowesses, thus preserving a religious life in addition to being active with family and friends.[29]

Royal, noble, and gentry widows

We think of elite widows as having the most freedom of all the classes, but we must remember that they had two lords to serve: their husband and their overlord or the king. Feudal law gave the overlord considerable power in deciding whether a noble or knightly widow would remarry and whether she would have wardship of her children and their property. A noble widow's powers of decision over her future life, therefore, were not as great as those of either peasant or urban women. Great wealth and estates did not automatically entail freedom of choice in widowhood.

The most pathetic of these widows were the royal ones. Joan of Kent was, perhaps, one of the most successful since she was able to help guide her son, the young Richard II, and to mediate between him and various factions. But Richard II's young widow, Isabel of France, was only six when her marriage was arranged and nine when her husband died. She had a very hard time getting her dowry back, even though the marriage to Richard had not been consummated. Joan of Navarre, widow of Henry IV, was accused of witchcraft. Katherine of Valois, briefly married to Henry V, was retired to Bermondsey Abbey; so too (as a poor dowager) was Elizabeth Woodville, a widow before and after her marriage to Edward IV.

The disturbed political times of the fifteenth century meant that many peeresses were widowed through the loss of husbands in battle or by execution. Of the forty-four who have been traced, twenty-one remarried at least once and some more than that. Some of these widows saw more than one of their husbands die a violent death for political causes. The Wars of the Roses left a pool of eligible widows for marriage.[30]

Noble widows, of course, always formed part of a larger political picture. Their marriages could bring about peaceful relations between feuding nobility, could be used to reward loyal henchmen of the king, or could be exploited as a money-raising scheme by the king either in arranging a marriage or in having the widow pay not to marry. Not only the king had designs on noble widows: fortune-hunters sought to abduct and marry them for wealth and title. Elizabeth de Burgh, Lady of Clare, is a good example. Her first husband died soon after her marriage. Since she was one of the heiresses of the vast Clare estates she proved particularly tempting. Theobald de Verdun abducted her from Bristol Castle and married her – he claimed that she had come out to meet him. When Theobald died shortly afterwards, the king married her to Roger Damory, but he died five years later in a rebellion against the king. She did not marry again, but became a vowess in the 1340s.[31]

Gentry women, although possessed of smaller estates, were also in demand as marriage partners. Alice de Bures's family made their fortunes in military and government service and had manors in East Anglia. She too married a man, Sir Guy Bryan, who pursued a military career. Following his death, Alice chose not to remarry, but to run the estates as she had when her husband was abroad.[32]

For noble widows, the network of friends and kin was vast. Their travels took them to their estates all over England so that they were forever visiting children and friends. Both London and the king's court were familiar to them. But many of these widows spent part of their disposable income on religious foundations or retired to them, as did Elizabeth de Burgh. While leaving chantries was common for merchant, gentry, and noble women, the peeresses in addition founded religious houses and colleges. Marie de Saint-Pol, widow of Aymer de Valence, Earl of Pembroke, founded a house of Minoresses at Denny in Cambridgeshire (later visited by Margery Kempe). She and Elizabeth de Burgh also founded Pembroke and Clare Colleges, Cambridge. Inspiration for widows who became vowesses, retired to nunnery precincts, or founded nunneries came, in part, from St Bridget of Sweden (see chapter 15, 'Margery Kempe', pp. 229–30). Her revelations, translated into English, were read by nuns and vowesses; Margery Kempe knew her work from memory and sought out her maidservant in Rome.

Widowhood in late medieval England, then, offered a number of options. Legally, widows could function as *femes soles*, farming their tenements on the manor, running crafts and businesses, and managing their estates. Whether in common law, borough law, or customary law, widows were left with a portion of their late husband's estate. Since they could bring this forward to another marriage, remarriage was common. For the most part in this chapter we have considered widows who had dowers substantial enough that they could live and leave some sort of legal record. There were also, of course, those who suffered in poor widowhood with barely enough to survive; there were those who could not survive at all.

The widow's position in England was, on the whole, different from that of widows on the continent. Ghent had generous dower provisions similar to London's, so that widows were very desirable marriage partners. But the widow did not have control over the wardship of her children or their inheritance and thus had to give up rearing her own children.[33] Elsewhere in the Low Countries there was a considerable shift in the legal status of marital property in the late Middle Ages. While initially property brought into marriage belonged jointly to the couple, by the mid-sixteenth century the husband had gained greater control over conjugal property.[34] In Florence in the late fourteenth and fifteenth centuries brides were typically in their early teens and husbands in their late thirties. This meant that Florence had a large population of widows who could choose to remain in their husband's home and not remarry, or return to their natal families and live there and perhaps remarry. But once they left the husband's home, they forfeited the rearing of their own children. In no case could these widows administer their conjugal property or their dowry.[35] While English widows' rights more closely resembled those of widows in the Low Countries, they too were beginning to see erosion of their freedom to exercise such rights at the dawn of the Renaissance.

NOTES

1. See 'The Tretis of the Tua Mariit Wemen and the Wedo', in *The Poems of William Dunbar*, ed. Priscilla Bawcutt, 2 vols. (Glasgow: Association for Scottish Literary Studies, 1998), 1: 41–55. Reference will be made to this edition.

2. See *Upon My Husband's Death: Widows in the Literature and Histories of Medieval Europe*, ed. Louise Mirrer (Ann Arbor: University of Michigan Press, 1992).

3. *Bedfordshire Wills, 1480–1519*, trans. Patricia Bell, Bedfordshire Historical Record Society 45 (1966). *Bedfordshire Wills Proved in the Prerogative Court of Canterbury, 1383–1548*, ed. Margaret McGregor, Bedfordshire Historical Record Society 58 (1979). *English Wills, 1498–1526*, ed. A. F. Cirket, Bedfordshire Historical Record Society 37 (1956).

4. *Calendar of Wills Proved and Enrolled in the Court of Husting, London, AD 1258–1688*, ed. Reginald R. Sharpe (London, 1889). Only medieval wills appear in this sample (until 1500).

5. Frederick Pollock and Frederic W. Maitland, *The History of English Law before the Time of Edward I*, vol. I, 2nd edn (Cambridge University Press, 1968), 1: 482.

6. G. R. Owst, *Literature and Pulpit in Medieval England* (Cambridge University Press, 1933), p. 119; see further pp. 388–9; Ruth Kelso, *Doctrine for the Lady of the Renaissance* (Urbana: University of Illinois Press, 1956), pp. 126–30; Chaucer, *Wife of Bath's Tale*, 3.348–54.

7. Judith M. Bennett, *Women in the Medieval English Countryside: Gender and Household in Brigstock before the Plague* (New York: Oxford University Press, 1987), pp. 143–4; see further J. Z. Titow, *English Rural Society, 1200–1350* (London: Allen and Unwin, 1969), p. 87; R. H. Hilton, *The English Peasantry in the Later Middle Ages: The Ford Lectures for 1973 and Related Studies* (Oxford: Clarendon Press, 1975), p. 99.

8. Barbara A. Hanawalt, *The Ties that Bound: Peasant Families in Medieval England* (New York: Oxford University Press, 1986), pp. 221–2.

9. Cicely Howell, 'Peasant Inheritance Customs in the Midlands, 1280–1700', in *Family and Inheritance: Rural Society in Western Europe, 1200–1800*, ed. Jack Goody, Joan Thirsk, and E. P. Thompson (Cambridge University Press, 1976), pp. 141–3.

10. Hanawalt, *Ties that Bound*, pp. 223, 225.

11. Zvi Razi, in *Life, Marriage, and Death in a Medieval Parish: Economy, Society and Demography in Halesowen, 1270–1400* (Cambridge University Press, 1980), pp. 63–136. Razi shows that six out of ten widows remarried before the Black Death but only 10 per cent married after it. See further Bennett, *Women in the Medieval English Countryside*, p. 146.

12. Hanawalt, *Ties that Bound*, pp. 228–36.

13. Ibid, pp. 238–9.

14. Barbara A. Hanawalt, 'The Widow's Mite: Provisions for Medieval London Widows', in *Upon My Husband's Death*, ed. Mirrer (Ann Arbor: University of Michigan Press), p. 25.

15. Guildhall Library: Archdeacon's Court, MS 9051/1 and 9051/2. The wills start in 1393 but are largely fifteenth-century. The Archdeacon's Court and the Consistory Court of London recorded wills in addition to the Husting Court.

16. Hanawalt, 'The Widow's Mite', pp. 26–35.

17. Maryanne Kowaleski and Judith M. Bennett, 'Crafts, Guilds, and Women in the Middle Ages: Fifty Years after Maryan K. Dale', *Signs* 14 (1989): 478–9.

18. Judith M. Bennett, *Ale, Beer, and the Brewsters in England: Women's Work in a Changing World, 1300–1600* (New York: Oxford University Press, 1996), p. 73.

19. See essays in *Medieval London Widows, 1300–1500*, ed. Caroline M. Barron and Anne F. Sutton (London: Hambledon Press, 1994).

20. Maryanne Kowaleski, 'Women's Work in a Market Town: Exeter in the Late Fourteenth Century', in *Women and Work in Preindustrial Europe*, ed. Barbara A. Hanawalt (Bloomington: Indiana University Press, 1986), pp. 155–7.

21. Barbara A. Hanawalt, *Growing Up in Medieval London: The Experience of Childhood in England* (New York: Oxford University Press, 1993), pp. 157–8.

22. Alison Hanham, *The Celys and their World; An English Merchant Family of the Fifteenth Century* (Cambridge University Press, 1985), pp. 309–15.

23. Mathew Davies, 'Dame Thomasine Percyvale, "The Maid of Week" (d. 1512)', in *Medieval London Widows, 1300–1500*, ed. Barron and Sutton, pp. 185–207.

24. Hanawalt, *Growing Up in Medieval London*, ch. 6.

25. Sylvia Thrupp, *The Merchant Class of Medieval London* (Ann Arbor: University of Michigan Press, 1948), p. 107.

26. Hanawalt, *Growing Up in Medieval London*, p. 171.

27. For a complete discussion see Barbara A. Hanawalt, 'Remarriage as an Option for Urban and Rural Widows in Late Medieval England', in *Wife and Widow in Medieval England*, ed. Sue Sheridan Walker (Ann Arbor: University of Michigan Press, 1993), pp. 109–40.

28. Katherine L. French, ' "To Free Them from Binding": Women in the Late Medieval English Parish', *Journal of Interdisciplinary History* 27 (1997): 387–412.

29. See Kay Lacey, 'Margaret Croke (d. 1491)', pp. 143–65 and Mary C. Erler, 'Three Fifteenth-Century Vowesses', in *Medieval London Widows*, ed. Barron and Sutton, pp. 165–84.

30. Joel T. Rosenthal, *Patriarchy and Families of Privilege in Fifteenth-Century England* (Philadelphia: University of Pennsylvania Press, 1991), pp. 171–245.

31. Jennifer C. Ward, 'Elizabeth de Burgh, Lady of Clare (d. 1360)', in *Medieval London Widows, 1300–1500*, ed. Barron and Sutton, pp. 29–46.

32. Ffiona Swabey, *Medieval Gentlewoman: Life in a Gentry Household in the Later Middle Ages* (London: Routledge, 1999).

33. Marianne Danneel, 'Orphanhood and Marriage in Fifteenth-Century Ghent', in W. Prevenier, ed., *Marriage and Social Mobility in the Late Middle Ages, Studia Historica Gandensia* 274 (Gent, 1989), 99–111.

34. Martha C. Howell, *The Marriage Exchange: Property, Social Place, and Gender in Cities of the Low Countries, 1300–1550* (University of Chicago Press, 1998).

This book is an excellent place to start looking at the complexities of medieval marriage contracts, dower, and dowry.

35. Christiane Klapisch-Zuber, *Women, Family, and Ritual in Renaissance Italy*, trans. Lydia G. Cochrane (Chicago, 1985). See also Anthony Molho, *Marriage Alliance in Late Medieval Florence* (Cambridge, MA: Harvard University Press, 1994).

5

KARMA LOCHRIE

Between women

The tripartite division of medieval women into the categories of virgin, wife, and widow screens out the very possibility of female fellowship, community, and even love. Under the system derived from patristic sources, women were classified by their sexual/marital status, and this medieval distinction had the effect of rendering relationships between women a meaningless or even illegible aspect of femininity. Female interactions simply did not register on the medieval radar screen, and as a result, they slip through scholarly studies as well. Where were the women who formed communities with each other, engaged in deep, abiding friendship together, and experienced sexual bonds with other women? The Middle Ages is positively verbose on the topics of male friendship and the dangers of sexual relations between men, and yet it was relatively silent about female friendship and love. One way of understanding this relative silence is to attribute it to the prevailing misogyny of the Middle Ages, which simply took female bonding and sexuality less seriously than it did male bonding and male sexuality. This explanation, however, falls into the trap of granting medieval misogyny hegemonic status in shaping and representing women's lives. Feminist scholars dealt with a similar problem when they first attempted to discern women and gender issues that the ideologies – past and present – obscured from historical record. What happens when readers and scholars similarly refuse to read medieval texts and study medieval history according to medieval taxonomies of women? Apart from the contexts of female religious communities and spirituality, where might we begin to look for the varied forms of female fellowship that medieval women might create together or that medieval texts might represent?

One way of thinking about female fellowship has been suggested by feminist historian Judith M. Bennett, who proposes a new category, 'lesbian-like', to resist medieval and modern habits of representing medieval women and to make more visible 'women whose lives might have particularly offered opportunities for same-sex love; women who resisted norms of feminine behavior based on heterosexual marriage; women who lived in circumstances that allowed them to nurture and support other women'.[1] Bennett's solution is not without its own problems, since there is considerable disagreement today about what constitutes a 'lesbian', and even more about what it means to apply this modern term to medieval women. Without invoking such problematic terminology as Bennett uses, however, one can attempt to look outside the medieval categories and those of modern scholarship to discern the variant – sometimes deviant – possibilities for relationships between women in a range of medieval texts, including explicitly misogynistic ones.

In the sections that follow, I pose a number of examples of what happens between women, according to sermon texts, *lais*, saints' lives, works by John Gower and Geoffrey Chaucer, a Lollard conclusion, and Heloise's critique of the Benedictine Rule as it applies to women. 'Between women' there was more going on than medieval categories or modern scholarship has so far recognized. From female friendship to female love, the Middle Ages did indeed imagine what occurred between women – sometimes in order to condemn it, sometimes to sponsor it, and sometimes to celebrate it as an alternative to heterosexual romantic love.

Two women talking

When women get together in deliberate acts of female fellowship, corruption ensues. That is, at least, the official view. Medieval anxiety about female affiliation can be found in the widespread representations of female gossip – the chattering of the renegade religious recluse, the debased advice of La Vieille, the Old Woman in the *Roman de la Rose*, or the recalcitrant whispers of women during Mass. Not only do these caricatures of female association distort and obscure the other kinds of female community that might have been possible in the Middle Ages but also they stigmatize all speech among women as gossip. One of the more hyperbolic expressions of the dangers of verbal transactions among women occurs in the late fourteenth-century Middle English translation of Aelred of Rievaulx's instruction for anchoresses, the *De institutione inclusarum*. Aelred laments the falling away of anchoresses from their practice of solitude, declaring that it is now commonplace to find a recluse seeking out the news and business of the world, instead of withdrawing from it. He imagines the following scenario:

> either tofore [before] the wyndowe shal sitte an olde womman fedynge hir with tales, or elles a new iangeler [gossiper] and teller of tidynges of that monke, or of that clerke, or of widowes dissolucion [widow's corruption], or of

maidens wantownes [wantonness], of the whiche arisith lawghyng, scornynge and vnclene thoughtes slepynge or wakynge, so that atte last the recluse is fulfilled with lust and likynge [desire], bakbitynge, sclaundre and hatrede and the tother [the other] with mete [meat] and drinke.[2]

Aelred imagines the slippery slope leading from solitary spiritual perfection to sexual and spiritual decadence through female gossip. The old woman interlocutor signals the scene of gossip, which seems to revolve exclusively around the sexual escapades of others – a widow's dissolute behaviour, a virgin's wantonness – until it enflames the recluse herself with lust, pleasure, anger, and slander in her waking and sleeping lives.

The anxiety that underlies this fantasy of Aelred's is not limited to his concern for the safety of the recluse; it extends to the nature of female social interaction itself. Numerous reverberations of this cautionary exemplum can be found throughout medieval misogynistic discourse. The early thirteenth-century guide for anchoresses, the *Ancrene Wisse*, for example, echoes Aelred's warning to recluses to refrain from social excesses with other women, particularly old women:

keep your ears far from all evil speech that is of this threefold kind, idle, foul and poisonous. It is said of anchoresses that almost every one of them has some old woman to feed her ears, a gossip who tells her all the local tidbits, a magpie who cackles about all that she sees and hears, so that the saying now runs, 'You can hear the news from a mill or a market, from a smithy or an anchorhouse.'[3]

A variety of medieval texts of vernacular religious instruction that addresses the subject of women's gossip situates its most flagrant abuses in the mass. Instead of listening to sermons or liturgy, according to this misogynist trope, women are seen whispering to each other and distracting the congregation. The church becomes a 'house of Daedalus' (that is, a labyrinth) filled with whispering, vain speech, and filth, according to the popular sermon anthology of John Mirk, the *Festial* (c. 1405). Likewise, Robert Mannyng of Brunne's *Handlyng Synne* (c. 1303), a treatise on vices and virtues, the sacraments, and articles of faith, and *The Book of the Knight of the Tower* (1484), a conduct text for women, both recount how the demon, Tutivillus, whose sole job seems to be to record women's gossip, takes notes as two women whisper during Mass. Their gossiping exceeds his skills of taking dictation, as he writes furiously, pulling his roll with his teeth and smacking his head against a wall as a consequence of the breakneck speed of his writing.

In the mid-fifteenth-century didactic treatise, *Peter Idley's Instructions to His Son*, the author invokes the language of sexual promiscuity, as Aelred did for gossiping recluses, to describe the outrage of women cackling like geese during Mass. Idley singles out their habit of gossiping about the men they ogle at church, especially about 'þe schort garmentes round all abouȝt / And how þe stuffyng off þe codpece berys ouȝt [the shortness of their garments, / and how the stuffing of the codpiece stands out]'.[4] Irreverence for the sanctity of the church and the ritual of the Mass is less Idley's chief concern than is the sexually voyeuristic character of women's furtive collaborations. Women's gossip with each other itself constitutes a sexual activity in misogynistic representations such as this one, not only in its preoccupation with men's bulging codpieces and wayward monks, widows, and virgins, but in its very excess.

In such representations, women's gossip, unlike male gossip, is nearly always erotic, since it tends towards sexual transgression, or alternatively, proceeds from a sexually promiscuous nature. Women speaking together, according to Aelred and others, incite each other sexually with their stories in a kind of homoerotic tale-swapping. The feminine propensity for slander is, in a sense, the homosocial corollary to women's propensity for heterosexual promiscuity. Women engaging in unbridled sex talk with their female gossips is, according to medieval misogynist logic, inextricably bound up with their unrestrained licentiousness. The two go hand-in-hand.

If the scene of gossip is common misogynist trope, it is also potentially a site of resistance. Chaucer's Wife of Bath is perhaps the most masterful exploiter of the gossip stereotype of female collaboration, working it to her own ends of tweaking masculine anxiety and bolstering her case for female sovereignty. Although she is primarily viewed as a spokeswoman for heterosexual sex and marriage, the Wife of Bath's closest relationship is with Alisoun, who not only conspires in the Wife's secret dalliance with Jankyn while her fourth husband still lives, but also occupies the privileged position of the Wife's confidant and gossip (a female friend who is given to idle talk):

> She knew myn herte, and eek my privetee,   [secrets]
> Bet than oure parisshe preest, so moot I thee!   [so might I thrive!]
> To hire biwreyed I my conseil al.   [revealed]
> For hadde myn housbonde pissed on a wal,
> Or doon a thyng that sholde han cost his lyf,
> To hire, and to another worthy wyf,
> And to my nece, which that I loved weel,
> I wolde han toold his conseil every deel.[5]   [secrets; every bit of it]

Not only does the Wife inhabit a speech community of her own outside clerical and spousal control, but she uses it to shame men, thereby provoking the anxiety that scaffolds much misogynist rhetoric on gossip. Her tale likewise invokes this female gossip community, which seems to possess the answer to the Queen's question that the Knight must find to save his life, discovering 'what thyng is it that wommen moost desiren' (3.905). The answer for husbands is one thing, but it is only part of the answer. The Wife of Bath's sovereignty rests, in fact, on her telling to other women the tales of her husband's and her own desires, for this act of telling is a form not only of power but of pleasure. Her refashioning of Ovid's tale of King Midas' secret condenses this aspect of the Wife's desire, for just as she takes real pleasure in revealing her husband's secrets to her female community of gossips, so too the wife in the story is 'inflamed in her heart' to reveal that her husband has ass's ears. By analogy, too, we see how female gossip becomes in the Wife's revision of Ovid as natural and uncontainable as the proverbial whispering of reeds.

Surpassing the love of men

Gossip in popular misogyny rendered the very notion of female friendship impossible except as a form of conspiracy. Although male friendship has been amply documented for the Middle Ages, scholars have yet to find evidence, theoretical or historical, for a concept or practice of female friendship. In spite of the apparent cultural illegibility of female friendship, however, it is still possible to discern expressions of passionate friendship and spiritual collaboration among women in medieval texts. In Chaucer's *Man of Law's Tale*, for example, passionate female friendship appears briefly in a narrative laden with masculine anxiety about female agency. Soon after Custance lands in Northumbria, she becomes so beloved of Hermengyld, the constable's wife, that 'Hermengyld loved hire right as hir lyf [Hermengyld loved her as much as her own life]' (2.535). Their friendship leads to Hermengyld's secret conversion to Christianity, which she conceals even from her husband, until the fateful day when they walk by the sea. Hermengyld is then approached by a blind man who begs her to restore his sight, but Hermengyld is afraid lest she be outed as a Christian and her husband have her put to death. Custance gives her the courage to perform the miracle, and the constable is converted by it. The friendship between Hermengyld and Custance continues for 'many winters', according to the Man of Law. In their final moments of friendship, the two lie in bed together, exhausted from praying. The friendship comes to an abrupt end when a lustful knight whom Custance has refused takes vengeance on her, killing Hermengyld and planting the evidence on Custance. Female friendship is finally subsumed under the Man of Law's larger project of representing female sanctity in terms of Custance's victimization at the hands of monstrous, masculinized women and her voluntary surrender to masculine governance. Such spiritual friendship among women, in conjunction with the Wife of Bath's more irreverent form of affectionate friendship with her gossip, represents the sole counter-voice to models of domestic and spiritual isolation of women found in most of the *Canterbury Tales*.

Historical and textual evidence suggests that the spiritual friendship represented in *The Man of Law's Tale* may have been more widely practised than is generally acknowledged. Felicity Riddy points to the evidence for female readerships dictating spiritual collections such as the Vernon Manuscript, to the social networks and reading communities within convents, and to mixing of religious and secular women in living communities such as Norman Tanner describes in Norwich.[6] In fifteenth-century Norwich, Tanner finds two groups calling themselves 'sisters living together' and 'sisters dedicated to chastity' that resembled the continental beguinages (communities of lay women).[7]

Margery Kempe provides a variety of glimpses into spiritual friendship among women in her *Book* (c. 1436), though none of the forms of friendship was institutionalized. The most famous of these is her visit to the anchoress, Julian of Norwich. The anchorite police might have seen in Kempe's visit precisely the dangers that Aelred described, but Kempe recounts a different scenario of 'holy dalyawns [conversation]' with Julian. Julian also urges Kempe to ignore the criticisms of others and to trust her tears as tokens of God's grace. In York Kempe visits another anchoress who 'had greatly loved her' only to find that she is denied access because of her own notoriety. She preaches to the women of Beverley from her place of detention, causing them to weep bitterly and sneak her some water. Kempe's charismatic appeal to English women leads the Mayor of Leicester to charge that 'I trowe þow art comyn hedyr to han a-wey owr wyuys fro us & ledyn hem with þe' [I believe you have come here to lure away our wives from us, and lead them off with you].[8]

Elsewhere Kempe receives comfort from female companionship, and she ministers to women in need. When she is in Rome and abandoned by her fellow pilgrims, she seeks help from Margaret Florentyne, who though she does not speak English accompanies her to Rome, invites her to eat with her every Sunday, and even serves Kempe her meal herself in a gesture of respect. Other ladies seek out Kempe's conversation. One such 'worshepful lady' ignores her own priest's excoriations of Kempe for her tears and 'louyd hir ryth wel [had great love for her]', desiring Kempe to remain with her. Even nuns 'desiryd to haue knowlach of þe creatur & þat þei xulde þe mor be steryd to deuocyon' [desired to have some knowledge of this creature, in order that they should be the more stirred to devotion]. The Abbess of Denney Abbey in particular 'oftyntymys [often] sent for þe sayd [said] creatur þat sche xulde [should] come to speke with hir & wyth hir sisterys'.⁹ Finally, she ministers to a woman in childbirth who seems to be afflicted with a postpartum madness that parallels Kempe's own preconversion condition. It is important to see in Kempe's book that she inhabits and is fostered by a female community that the narrative itself credits. It is not the only community of support Kempe enjoys, of course, but too much scholarly emphasis is placed on her reliance on male authority and too little attention has been paid to her crucial dependence on female companionship. Kempe's spirituality in the world depends crucially on her association with these spiritual and earthly female communities.

While Kempe offers glimpses of the kind of spiritual friendship between women that was possible in medieval culture, there was no fully elaborated theory of female friendship, such as there was for men in Aelred of Rievaulx's *De spirituali amicitia*. Letters between Hildegard of Bingen and Richardis (1151–2) are thought to provide a particularly eloquent expression of such spiritual friendship even in the absence of a clear tradition for women. Three centuries later Christine de Pizan attempted to provide a utopian vision – if not a theory – of female friendship in her monumental work, *The Book of the City of Ladies*. It must be noted that no scholar has so far identified such an allegory of female friendship in her work; in fact, the conservative heterosexism of her work has obscured the contribution it makes to imagining spiritual friendship between women in the Middle Ages. Not only does the book move from Christine's solitude as a reader of misogynist texts to her incorporation into a community of female readers, but it emphatically imagines Christine's intellectual and spiritual revitalization through the community of queens, classical figures, and martyrs that is lodged allegorically in the turrets, towers, and apartments built by Reason, Rectitude, and Justice. The urban feminine space, as Rectitude describes it, is a 'New Kingdom of Femininity':

> Now a New Kingdom of Femininity is begun, and it is far better than the earlier kingdom of the Amazons, for the ladies residing here will not need to leave their land in order to conceive or give birth to new heirs to maintain their possessions throughout the different ages, from one generation to another, for those whom we now place here will suffice quite adequately forever more.¹⁰

Instead of yielding to the pressure to provide a genealogical heritage such as the Amazons were compelled to do, this Kingdom of Femininity will rely on a self-sustaining community, both literally in the company of women who reside there and textually, in Christine's revision and compilation of their stories.

At the same time, Christine draws implicitly upon the Aristotelian ideal of 'ethical excellence' and Ciceronian notion of secular friendship as the 'love of virtue in another man'.[11] Christine makes only indirect use of these ideas in that she never explicitly addresses the subject of friendship between women. Her urban 'refuge', as she calls it, is nevertheless organized so that love of virtue is both exemplified by its feminine inhabitants and enacted through their civic unity and strength. In Christine's concluding speech, she warns the women of this urban refuge to seek out their own reflections in the virtuous materials out of which the city is constructed and to flee the false love of men for the true love of virtue. Christine offers more of an implicit model than an explicit example or a theory of female friendship in her book, but it follows in a tradition by which male friendship, too, is defined against false heterosexual love. Even though she continues to counsel women to obey their husbands, Christine invokes a higher love for virtue, and hence, virtuous women, that exceeds the marital love she endorses throughout the book.

Christine's allegorical city thus organizes without explicitly exemplifying a spiritual friendship between women that is forged from letters and from strength in numbers against masculine representation. Self-representation is one of the reigning principles of this communal ideal. As Reason tells Christine, 'now it is time for their [women's] cause to be taken from Pharaoh's hands'. That cause is women's self-representation, which provides not only the edifice of defence against masculine representation but also a community of women, past and present, and an enduring basis for feminine friendship, a source of spiritual and intellectual strength, and an 'ennobling love' that makes heterosexual love viable.

Desiring women

What about the viability of female same-sex desire in medieval culture? The records from secular courts are silent regarding medieval prosecution of women who engaged in sexual relations with other women.[12] The consensus of scholars of canon law and theology is that those cultural discourses were likewise relatively silent on the subject because canonists 'apparently did not perceive lesbian practices as a major problem or as a serious threat to the social order'.[13] Even if the Middle Ages wrote more about male sodomy than unnatural female sexual practices, however, it is important to recognize that it did include women in the category of sodomy. In the writings of the two great thirteenth-century theologians, Albertus Magnus defines sodomy as 'a sin against nature, man with man, or woman with woman', while Thomas Aquinas includes among the vices against nature copulation with an 'undue sex'. From the penitentials (manuals that listed appropriate punishments for the seven deadly sins) of Theodore in the seventh century and Bede in the eighth to the summae of Ivo of Chartres in the twelfth and Robert of Flamborough in the thirteenth (summae were manuals for confessors defining the sins and often suggesting ways of eliciting confessions about them), all include among the unnatural sexual sins a woman's fornication with another woman. Medieval theology, whether it took female same-sex desire seriously or not, did incorporate it in the categories of sodomy and unnatural sex acts.[14]

Others took female same-sex desire very seriously. Aelred of Rievaulx and the author of the *Rule for Anchoresses* did. The late fourteenth-century Middle English translation of Aelred's *De institutione inclusarum* delivers a cryptic warning to the recluse who thinks her chastity is safe as long as she avoids men:

> Bote I say not þis þat þu schuldest wene þat a man may not be defoyled witowte a wymman, ne a wumman wit-oute a man; vor in oþer wyse, moor cursed and abhominable, which schal not be sayd now ne ynemned, boþe in man and womman ofte chastete is lost.

> [But I do not say this, that you should suppose that a man may not be corrupted without a woman, nor a woman without a man; for in other ways more cursed and abominable, which shall not be said now nor named, both in man and woman chastity is often lost.][15]

Aelred here resorts to the primary code for unnatural sex acts by citing their abomination and their unspeakability. He is not being vague at all in this passage even though he does not name the corrupting acts or sin, for the very act of refusing to name the sin calls it into being: chastity is often lost, he warns, through the cursed relations of women with women and men with men.

The author of the *Ancrene Wisse* also frets about the dangers of the recluse's consorting with other women, since 'some have been tempted by their own sisters'. While this temptation by one's sisters could have taken many non-sexual forms, the author later addresses explicitly the dangers of unnatural sex. Having compared lechery to a scorpion, he attempts to issue a warning against acts that he refuses to name and even fears teaching to his readers:

> I dare not name the unnatural offspring of this devil's scorpion with its poisonous tail; but sorry she may be who, without a companion or with, has so fed the offspring of her lustfulness which I may not speak of for shame and dare not for fear, lest some learn more evil than they know and be tempted

by it. But let her consider the accursed inventions of her own lust . . . You who know nothing about such things, you need not wonder at or think about what I mean, but give thanks to God that you never came across such uncleanness; and have pity on those who are fallen into it.[16]

At least two acts seem to be alluded to in this warning, masturbation and sex with other women, although the 'accursed inventions of [women's] lust' suggests their endless resourcefulness. The author's fear of inciting the ignorant to indulge in this form of lechery echoes the discourse of sodomy, which is likewise anxious not to incite the very acts it means to condemn.

The concept of 'accursed inventions of women's lust' is, in fact, consistent with the misogynistic attribution of inordinate desire to women. Women's putative frailty makes them, in the discourse of misogyny, more susceptible to polymorphous perversity, rendering chastity a condition fraught with opportunity for those accursed inventions of women's lust to which the *Ancrene Wisse* author alludes. In the late fourteenth and early fifteenth centuries in England, celibacy became a contested site in the heretical critiques of clerical privilege by Lollards. In the 1395 manifesto, the *Twelve Conclusions*, posted on the doors of Westminster while Parliament was in session, the Lollards included among their attacks (on the priesthood, the doctrine of transubstantiation, and idolatrous religious practices) the following condemnation of the celibate life of nuns:

þe xi conclusiun is schamful for to speke, þat a uow of continence mad in oure chirche of wommen, þe qwiche ben fekil and vnperfyth in kynde, is cause of br[i]ngging of most horrible synne possible to mankynde. For þou sleyng of childrin or þei ben cristenid, aborcife and stroying of kynde be medicine ben ful sinful, ȝet knowing with hemself or irresonable beste or creature þat beris no lyf passith in worthinesse to ben punischid in peynis of helle. þe correlary is þat widuis, and qwiche as han takin þe mantil and þe ryng deliciousliche fed, we wolde þei were weddid, for we can nout excusin hem fro priue synnis.[17]

[The eleventh conclusion is shameful to speak of, that a vow of continence made in our church by women, who are fickle and imperfect by nature, is the cause of bringing the most horrible sin possible to mankind. For although slaying children before they are christened, abortion, and contraception by medicine are very sinful, yet having sex with themselves or irrational beast or creature that bears no life surpasses those sins in worthiness to be punished by the pains of hell. The corollary is that we would that widows, and those who have taken the mantle and the ring deliciously fed, were wedded, for we cannot excuse them from secret sins.]

Using the logic of medieval misogyny, the Lollard text argues that women's fickleness and imperfection incline them naturally to sexual perversions – 'the accursed inventions of women's lust'. Without the checks of male authority provided through marriage, monastic life only serves to foster this tendency towards sexual perversion in women. By failing to police the natural imperfection of women, the life apart among avowedly celibate women gives free rein to their nature, and this leads to 'the most horrible sin possible to mankind' – greater, presumably, even than the sodomy committed by the male religious addressed in the Third Conclusion. The Lollard text, like the *Ancrene Wisse*, ends up multiplying the abomination it first singles out, listing acts of increasing horror and taboo. Though abortion, infanticide, and contraception are the most terrible sins anyone can imagine women committing, the text implies, religious women commit sins worse than these: sex with themselves, sex with beasts, and sex with creatures bearing no life. 'Sex with themselves' incorporates two possibilities, masturbation and same-sex acts. A Latin version of this text from one of the manuscripts of Roger Dymmok's refutation of the Twelve Conclusions specifies same-sex acts rather than masturbation: 'coniunccio mutua feminarum contra naturam in actu carnali' ('intimacy between women in carnal acts against nature').[18] The worst of this abominable trinity of female sex-acts seems to be sex with 'creatures bearing no life'. This puzzling phrase might suggest dildos to the modern reader, but the language is peculiar. Whatever those creatures are, the conclusion as a whole advocates marriage as a way of reining in the perverse tendencies – the accursed inventions – of female lust.

The Lollards were not alone in using misogynist logic to imagine female sexual perversions to be greater and more frequent than those of men. One of the most overlooked suggestions that celibate women were in danger – in a way that celibate men were not – of succumbing to each other comes from Heloise, the famous ex-lover of Abelard. In her third letter to Abelard written in the 1130s arguing for the inadequacy of the Benedictine Rule for women, she addresses the regulations governing same-sex visitations to the monastery. After citing Ovid's *Art of Love* on 'what an opportunity for fornication is provided especially by banquets', Heloise goes on to question whether nuns should be allowed to entertain female visitors as are monks:

> And even if they admit to their table only women to whom they have given hospitality, is there no lurking danger there? Surely nothing is so conducive to a woman's seduction as woman's flattery, nor does a woman pass on the foulness of a corrupted mind so readily to any but another woman; which is why St Jerome particularly exhorts women of a sacred calling to avoid contact with women of the world.[19]

Heloise clearly alludes to the possibility of same-sex desire among women fed by the fornicating effects of banquets and by the natural tendencies of women to communicate corruption to each other. Heloise draws upon the same logic to which the Lollards appeal later, though she does not specify the wanton inventiveness of women. Unlike the Lollards, however, Heloise is not proposing that celibacy is impossible for women but that the rules governing women need to be gender-specific, that the spiritual life of women requires a different set of guidelines from those adopted by men – one that takes into account sexual, and even spiritual, differences.

The logic underlying both Heloise's warning against the dangers of female same-sex banqueting and the Lollard polemic against female celibacy points to a surprising conclusion regarding medieval sexual categories. The nature of women leans towards sexual perversion and corruption, not towards heterosexual ideals, making female celibacy a special case for both the Lollard and Heloise. Monks may share meals with secular men, as the Benedictine Rule permits (although the Lollards would later worry about the sodomitic consequences of monks' over-eating), but women are not safe with each other. The Eleventh Conclusion takes a more anxious and sinister view of the perversions that female celibates are given to, but it also argues against any reigning normative heterosexuality, at least where women are concerned. Marriage is the Lollard corrective to women's naturally perverse tendencies, making heterosexuality less normal than punitive and disciplinary in kind. If extravagant eating habits contribute to the wayward sexual tendencies of women, however, even marriage is no protection against it. Women 'deliciously fed' are a danger anywhere, in marriage or in the monastery.

Two very different literary texts take up the possibility of female same-sex desire without the misogynist scaffolding of the Lollard and Heloisian texts. The first text is John Gower's story of Iphis and Ianthe in the fourth book of his *Confessio amantis* (c. 1390). Drawing upon Ovid's tale in the *Metamorphoses* in which the girl, Iphis, is disguised as a boy and betrothed to another girl, Ianthe, Gower transforms what was a crisis of unnatural love in Ovid into a 'solein tale' [a singular/strange tale] of exemplary 'stable' love.[20] In Ovid's tale, Iphis is disguised as a boy by her mother because her father has threatened to kill a girl-child. Iphis' disguise proves so successful that her father arranges a marriage for her with Ianthe, whom Iphis had loved since they had first received instruction from the same teachers. Their love seems to arise naturally out of the sameness – of their ages, their loveliness, and their instruction – and this sameness produces an equal longing in the two girls. Ovid suggests that this same-sex love is both natural and stronger than most loves inasmuch as it proceeds from the equality and sameness between the two lovers.

Faced with her deep love for Iphis and the prospect of marriage to her, Iphis laments her 'strange and monstrous love' and prays for some shrewd art such as Pasiphae used in order to enjoy the love of a bull.[21] Iphis alone is deprived of hope because Nature forbids her love. The night before her wedding, Iphis' mother prays to Isis for help, and Iphis suddenly assumes the stride, musculature, and short hair of a man. The morphological resolution to Iphis' unnatural love appeases Nature's demands and removes the technical problems of fulfilling their marriage vows.

Gower's version of the Ovidian tale presents the love of Iphis and Ianthe not as monstrous but as natural. Gower's girls are also more precocious than Ovid's. In addition to enjoying the same instruction, this Iphis and Ianthe share the same bed 'sche and sche', where, prompted by Nature, they first begin experimenting in physical pleasure:

> and ofte abedde
> These children leien, sche and sche,
> Whiche of on age bothe be.   [the same age]
> So that withinne time of yeeres,
> Togedre as thei ben pleiefieres,   [playmates]
> Liggende abedde upon a nyht,   [lying]
> Nature, which doth every wiht
> Upon hire lawe forto muse,
> Constreigneth hem, so that thei use
> Thing which to hem was al unknowe.[22]

Interestingly, their morphological similarity does not constrain the two girls from practising that 'thing' that they had never known before, and Nature is the force behind their companionate embraces. In fact, it is the magnitude of their love that instils pity in Cupid and inspires him to transform Iphis into a man in the very act of making love. The two live a 'merie lif, / Which was to kinde non offence [merry life, / Which was no offence to nature]'. Although Gower's version admits of the offence to Nature that the love of Iphis for Ianthe might have given without the morphological adjustment, it does not present the unnaturalness of their love as an obstacle. Gower's text instead rewards the 'great love' of the two playmates with Iphis' sex change, a reward that they never seem to have needed in any case, since they were already practising that 'thing' with Nature's help. Genius provides the moral to Gower's tale, that love rewards those who are not slothful in serving her. Instead of lying in bed alone lamenting her love, as Ovid's Iphis does, Gower's Iphis demonstrates virtuous sexual industry in her playful embraces with Ianthe, and Cupid rewards sexual 'business' over slothful love – even in the case of 'sche and sche'.

In the second text, from the twelfth century, female same-sex desire is less the preliminary to heterosexual love than its final cause. Marie de France's

Eliduc is ostensibly about Eliduc's divided loyalties and loves, one conflict between his loyalty to a king who exiles him and his expatriate king, and the other, between his love for his wife, Guildeluec, and for his lover in exile, Guilliadon. However, Marie renames the *lai* after the women because, as she says, 'the adventure upon which the lai is based concerns the ladies'.[23] In the tale Eliduc's love seems to be determined by the shifting loyalties of the two kings, until he finally determines to run away with his lover, Guilliadon. His efforts, however, are spoiled when on their sea voyage away from Guilliadon's homeland, she learns that he is married and falls into a death-like swoon. When he arrives home, he takes her to a hermitage in the woods where he plans to have her buried and a monastery dedicated to her. Here the heterosexual romance becomes sidetracked. Guildeluec, concerned about her husband's strange withdrawal from her, has him followed, and then goes herself to the hermitage to find out the cause of his anguish. Her discovery of the seemingly dead Guilliadon morphs this tale into something other than a heterosexual romance:

> When she entered the chapel and saw the bed of the maiden who was like a new rose, she raised the coverlet and saw the body so slender, the long arms, the white hands, the fingers, slim, long, and full. Then she knew why her husband had grieved. She called the servant and showed him the marvel: 'Do you see this woman,' she said, 'who in beauty resembles a gem? This is my husband's beloved for whom he laments so, and in faith, it is no wonder when such a beautiful woman has perished. Either pity or love will prevent me from ever knowing joy again.' (p. 124)

Clearly, this love or pity that Guildeluec feels for Guilliadon differs from the sexual love of Iphis for Ianthe. Her love derives as much from an appreciation of Guilliadon's beauty as it does from a recognition of her nobility.

As the wife grieves over the dead Guilliadon, there is a strange weasel interlude. A weasel who enters the crypt is killed by the wife's servant, and the weasel's partner then attempts to revive the dead weasel. Unable to stir her, the second weasel goes out and returns with a rose, which it puts in the dead weasel's mouth. The animal comes back to life. Seeing this weasel pantomime, the wife takes the same rose and places it in Guilliadon's mouth, bringing her back to life. Whatever the medieval significance of swooning weasels turns out to be, the episode requires that we read the reviving of Guilliadon in terms of the revived weasel, that is, as part love and part miracle. Perhaps the weasel interlude functions as a way of diffusing and displacing the wife's desire for Guilliadon, rendering it less an imitation of weasel love than a symbolic expression of profound love. Taking the focus off Guildeluec's love for Guilliadon and rerouting it through a pair of weasels effectively contains and subsumes that love to the ends of Marie's story.

The wife ultimately sacrifices her own husband to Guilliadon, a gesture that curiously appropriates the trope of masculine sacrifice – the husband's release of his wife to another man, such as Arveragus performs in Chaucer's *Franklin's Tale* – which had many analogues in Latin literature. Guildeluec releases her husband out of love for Guilliadon (and secondarily, for Eliduc), and she exchanges her heterosexual love for spiritual love by founding a convent. Later, Guilliadon joins her in sororal fellowship after some years of 'perfect love' with Eliduc, and Guildeluec receives her 'as her sister and showed her great honour, urging her to serve God and teaching her the order' (pp. 125, 126).

The love between Guilliadon and Guildeluec is only briefly suggested in Marie's *lai*, but it represents a key divergence from the romance narrative and a transition from perfect heterosexual love to perfect spiritual love. It is the wife's love for Guilliadon that allows her to rise above her own love for Eliduc and, eventually, to embrace a spiritual community and love for God. Guilliadon's reunion with Guildeluec in her convent supersedes the heterosexual union that signals the fulfilment of the romance narrative.

Boy saints don't cry

Hagiography provides yet another configuration of female same-sex desire through the figure of the transvestite saint. The woman who cross-dresses as a man in order to achieve sanctity and deflect masculine desire became a common figure in the early Middle Ages. Over thirty legends with countless translations and retellings of the female cross-dressed saint compare with zero tales of male transvestite saints. The reason for the imbalance is, presumably, due to the masculine model of holiness whereby women renounce their femininity in order to achieve holiness, while men simply renounce sexuality. Yet there is more going on in the drama of the female saint who disguises herself as a man than mere passing, for in many cases her cross-dressing is eroticized. In the story of Euphrosyne, for example, the woman's disguise as a monk does not change her status as object of masculine desire, but actually provokes it in her fellow monks.

Jacobus de Voragine may be credited with establishing the transvestite saint in Western hagiography. His *Legenda aurea* [The Golden Legend, c. 1265] contains seven tales about cross-dressing that were translated into vernaculars between the thirteenth and fifteenth centuries, including the legends of Eugenia, Margaret, Marina, Natalia, Pelagia, Thecla, and Theodora of Alexandria. In the stories of Marina, Margaret/Pelagius, Theodora, and Eugenia, a crisis occurs when the cross-dressed saints are accused by women of seduction and paternity. In the stories of Eugenia and Theodora the accusations are made by women whom the transvestite monks have spurned. After being converted by the teachings of Paul and Christians singing psalms, Eugenia disguises herself as a man (Eugene) and presents herself to Helenus, abbot of a monastery. When she tells him she is a man, he replies, 'Rightly do you call yourself a man, because you act like a man though you are a woman.' Helenus accepts her into the monastery as a monk even though God has revealed to him that she is a woman. Later, a wealthy noblewoman whom Eugene has cured from an illness, 'seeing how elegantly youthful and personally attractive he was, fell heatedly in love with him'. Pretending to be sick again, she lures Eugene to her home, 'and she let him know how ardently she loved him and wanted him, begged him to come to her, then grasped him and kissed him, urging him to join her in bed'. Brother Eugene rebukes her, calling her the 'dark daughter of darkness'. Out of revenge, Melancia charges Eugene with trying to seduce her, and he/she is brought before the court of Philip, who happens to be the cross-dressed saint's father. There Eugene makes a public demonstration of her innocence by dramatically uncovering her breasts in the courtroom and identifying herself to her father.[24]

In contrast to Eugenia, Theodora cross-dresses partly out of penance for having committed adultery. She enters a monastery as Theodore and becomes known for her miracles and her holiness. A townswoman becomes enamoured of Theodore and commands him in no uncertain terms to 'sleep with me!' When Theodore refuses, the woman sleeps with another man, and when she becomes pregnant, accuses Theodore of being the father. Not only is Theodore expelled from the monastery, but he is given the baby delivered by the woman to raise. After seven years living outside the monastery, raising the child, and fending off the devil, Theodore is accepted back into the monastery. It is only at his death that his true sex is discovered.

These are just two examples of how the female transvestite saint adopts a masculine holiness at the same time that she incites a perverse desire in other women. One might read this desire of women for the cross-dressed Eugene and Theodore as evidence of the success of their masculine disguises, but the texts themselves do not urge such a reading. Melancia's lust for Eugene is inspired by his elegant youthfulness and personal attractiveness, qualities which are not necessarily gender-specific. At the same time, the legend assures us that she 'took for granted that Brother Eugene was a man'. But what kind of man is he? Melancia's hot love and attempted seduction of

Eugene not only pose the necessary crisis in Eugene's holy development, but they raise the possibility that lust is no respecter of gender. Who is it that Melancia loves, the boy Eugene or the woman Eugenia, or both? Is Melancia responding to the performance of masculinity and masculine holiness that Eugenia adopts? These are questions that the text permits, at least, and that are not completely laid to rest when Eugene exposes her breasts at her trial. 'To make sure that truth shall prevail over mendacity and wisdom conquer malice', Eugene 'opened her robe from the top to the waist, and was seen to be a woman.' At the same time, she is proved to be the judge's daughter. The transvestite body is made to signify the truth, yet the truth it tells is only a partial one: that Eugene could not have assaulted Melancia because Eugene is a woman. But this truth leaves unspoken the truth about desire raised in the legend: did Melancia desire Eugene precisely because she was a masculinized woman, a feminized monk, and/or an ambiguously elegant youth? Melancia does not say, for she is summarily destroyed by a fire from heaven when Eugene discloses her breasts. The truth of the transvestite saint's innocence – the truth that her body declares – is only meaningful in the context of the homoerotic desire directed at her. The story those breasts and disclosed body tell, paradoxically, is that Eugenia though a woman can act like a man, can signify truth, can repudiate female desire. In the end, however, what conditions Eugene's holiness and her truth but female homoerotic desire?

From phobic representations of female gossip, to anxious or utopian conceptions of female friendship and community, to misogynist fears of female same-sex desire, to redemptive visions of that same desire, the Middle Ages spoke its deepest fears and most sacred ideals through its figurations of relationships between women. The misogyny of medieval culture sometimes occluded the ways in which relationships between women were thought to signify, threaten, and redeem, but it did not completely silence them. Some of the silence has been the effect of the oversights and the disinterestedness of modern medieval scholarship. Only by reading between the women will the tracery of female relationships begin to emerge in medieval culture – those 'things' that she and she might have practised in the interstices of cultural formations of romantic and filial relationship, as well as those 'things' that signal cultural anxiety about female fellowship.

NOTES

1. Judith M. Bennett, '"Lesbian-like" and the Social History of Lesbianisms', *Journal of the History of Sexuality* 9.1–2 (Jan./April 2000): 10–11.
2. *Aelred of Rievaulx's De institutione inclusarum* MS Bodley 423, ed. John Ayto and Alexandra Barratt (London: Oxford University Press, 1984), p. 1.

3. *Anchoritic Spirituality: 'Ancrene Wisse' and Associated Works*, trans. Anne Savage and Nicholas Watson (New York: Paulist Press, 1991), p. 81.

4. See *Peter Idley's Instructions to His Son*, ed. Charlotte D'Evelyn (London: Oxford University Press, 1935), p. 210.

5. 3.531–8. Chaucer citations by fragment and line number appear in the text.

6. Felicity Riddy, '"Women Talking about the Things of God": a Late Medieval Sub-Culture', in *Women and Literature in Britain, 1150–1500*, ed. Carol M. Meale (Cambridge University Press, 1996), pp. 104–27.

7. Norman P. Tanner, *The Church in Late Medieval Norwich, 1370–1532* (Toronto: Pontifical Institute of Mediaeval Studies, 1984), pp. 64–82.

8. *The Book of Margery Kempe*, ed. Sanford B. Meech and Hope Emily Allen, EETS OS 212 (London: Oxford University Press, 1940; rpt 1961), pp. 42–3, 119, 130–1, and 116.

9. Ibid., pp. 79 and 93, 174–5, 200, and 202.

10. Christine de Pizan, *The Book of the City of Ladies*, trans. Earl Jeffrey Richards (New York: Persea Books, 1982), II.12.1.

11. Stephen Jaeger, *Ennobling Love: In Search of a Lost Sensibility* (Philadelphia: University of Pennsylvania Press, 1999), pp. 28–9.

12. For a summary of legal codes covering female same-sex desire and its persecution, see Jacqueline Murray, 'Twice Marginal and Twice Invisible: Lesbians in the Middle Ages', in *Handbook of Medieval Sexuality*, ed. Vern L. Bullough and James A. Brundage (New York: Garland, 2000), pp. 201–2.

13. James A. Brundage, *Law, Sex, and Christian Society in Medieval Europe* (University of Chicago Press, 1987), p. 400.

14. Albert the Great, *Opera omnia*, vol. 33, ed. Auguste Borgnet (Paris: Vivès, 1895), p. 400; St Thomas Aquinas, *Summa theologica*, II, II, Q. cliv, 11 and 12; Bede, *De remediis peccatorum, Patrologia Latina*, vol. 9, col. 570B; Ivo of Chartres, *Decretum, Patrologia Latina*, vol. 9, cols. 85, 87; and *Robert of Flamborough Liber poenitentialis*, ed. J. J. Francis Firth, Studies and Texts, vol. 28 (University of Toronto Press, 1971), pp. 229, 197.

15. *Aelred of Rievaulx's De institutione inclusarum*, ed. Ayto and Barratt, p. 27. This is the late fourteenth-century version in the Vernon Manuscript.

16. *Anchoritic Spirituality*, trans. Anne Savage and Nicholas Watson, p. 124. See also p. 71 for the earlier quotation from this work.

17. Anne Hudson, ed., *Selections from English Wycliffite Writings* (Cambridge University Press, 1978), p. 28.

18. H. S. Cronin, 'The Twelve Conclusions of the Lollards', *English Historical Review* 22 (1907): 303. In another Latin text, the corresponding phrase is 'communicatio cum seipsis' ('sex with each other'). See *Fasciculi zizaniorum*, ed. W. W. Shirley (Rolls Series, 1858), p. 368.

19. *The Letters of Abelard and Heloise*, trans. Betty Radice (New York: Penguin, 1974), p. 161. For the Latin text of the passage, see J. T. Muckle, 'The Letter of Heloise on Religious Life and Abelard's First Reply', *Mediaeval Studies* 17 (1955): 242–3.

20. *John Gower's English Works*, ed. G. C. Macaulay, vol. 1, EETS ES 81 (London: Oxford University Press, 1900; rpt 1957), 4.448, 444.

21. Ovid, *Metamorphoses*, ed. and trans. Frank Justus Miller, Loeb Classical Library (Cambridge, MA: Harvard University Press, 1984), p. 54.

22. *John Gower's English Works*, 4.478–87.
23. *The Lais of Marie de France*, trans. Glyn S. Burgess and Keith Busby (New York: Penguin, 1986), p. 111.
24. Jacobus de Voragine, *The Golden Legend: Readings on the Saints*, trans. William Granger Ryan, vol. 2 (Princeton University Press, 1993), p. 166.

II

TEXTS AND OTHER SPACES

6

JENNIFER SUMMIT

Women and authorship

Were there women authors in the Middle Ages? The answer depends on which term we consider to be in question, 'women' or 'author'. The burden of proof has long rested on the former, following the assumption that medieval authors were exclusively men. Accordingly, nearly every major work believed to have been written by a medieval woman – including the letters of Heloise, *The Book of Margery Kempe*, and many works by Christine de Pizan – has at various times been attributed to a male author. More recently, however, the term 'author' itself has come into question, as some scholars have asked whether authorship – at least in its familiar, modern sense – could be said to have existed in the Middle Ages at all. The author holds a privileged status in literary studies; more than simply a work's writer, the author carries an ideological function as the figure around whom ideas about literary tradition, authority, and creativity are organized. Yet what counts as an author has been historically variable.[1] The idea that authors were the sole originators of their texts is a relatively recent one, supplanting earlier models that invested those origins in divine or historically remote sources; likewise, the modern idea of the author as a single, creative individual holds limited relevance for medieval textual culture, in which many texts were collaborative, anonymous, or adopted as common property. Those who study literature by medieval women find themselves facing a critical quandary: is it possible to speak of medieval women authors if the 'author' did not exist in the Middle Ages?

This chapter will argue that it is, but not under modern definitions of the author as an original, self-expressive individual, which have limited application to the writings of medieval women. The often collaborative nature of medieval textual production makes it difficult to assign sole responsibility for a text or texts to individual women, while the notoriously unstable conventions of naming in medieval manuscripts belie modern efforts to identify female authors by name; the author we know as Marie de France, for example, never actually names herself as such, and it is unclear whether a single woman wrote all of the works attributed to her. Rather than indicating that there were no female authors, such conditions indicate the need for an understanding of authorship that can take into account the range of medieval women's authorial activities. To this end, it is first necessary to revise the question with which we began, to ask instead: in what sense was authorship understood to exist in the Middle Ages, and to what extent could the concept apply to women?

What is a medieval author?

Authorship held a variety of meanings in the Middle Ages within different institutional and cultural contexts. In scholastic settings, medieval grammarians employed the term *auctor* as a marker of doctrinal authority, signifying an ancient theologian or approved classical writer who commanded deference and obedience.[2] The *auctor*'s status emerged through a system that linked *auctoritas*, authority, to tradition, defined as a stream of continuous influence by its root *tradere*, to pass on. This is the understanding of the *auctor* to which Christine de Pizan refers in the well-known opening of *The Book of the City of Ladies*, when, reading in her study, she envisions 'a series of authors' ('moult grant foyson de autteur[s]') who appear to her 'like a gushing fountain' ('comme se fust une fontaine resourdant').[3] This fountain of authors derives its authority not from originality but from an affiliation with the past that renders individual authors virtually indistinct from one another. In medieval literature, the fountain has a long history representing tradition as an inexhaustible source that flows through individual writers.[4] But as well as offering a powerful image of *auctoritas*, the scene in Christine's study also marks the distance between the *auctor* and the living writer. For while the 'autteurs' in Christine's vision are joined through the force of tradition, no living writer could hope to attain equivalent status or authority. Chaucer, for example, frequently uses the term 'auctor' to refer to his sources, but he never applies it to himself, assuming instead the more humble role of the 'maker', or 'compiler'. So too Christine finds herself 'stupefied' ('comme personne en etargie') by the fountain of authors, but hardly inspired or invited to join their exalted ranks herself.

The contrast between the ancient *auctor* and the living writer is visible in the relation each bears to the actual, material practices of writing. The *auctor* as pictured in Christine's vision of the 'foyson de autteur[s]' is abstracted from the material realities of writing; his authority has no beginning or end and appears to stand outside of time. For living writers, in contrast, the act of writing was bound up in the wider social and historical networks of patronage, scribal reproduction and circulation. Those networks undermine the apparent autonomy of the *auctor*, by revealing that literary works owe their survival less to the continuous influence of a disembodied tradition than to the human acts and accidents that govern their reproduction and circulation at every stage of their history. By the same token, no medieval writer could unilaterally declare him- or herself to be an *auctor* without the support of the multiple agents and acts of textual transmission through which writing gained cultural authority.

Where a writer like Chaucer continually registers his distance from the *auctores* because he writes in the vernacular rather than Latin, the position of outsider is heightened for Christine because, as a woman, she is excluded from the scholastic institutions of literacy and learning through which the *auctores* emerged. Yet, as Christine's example shows, women could and did achieve high levels of literacy despite that exclusion. While Christine surpassed the literacy of most medieval women, a growing body of research indicates that female literacy in the Middle Ages was more common, and assumed a greater variety of forms, than has been previously imagined. The medieval definition of literacy measured only the ability to read Latin, and was therefore restricted to the clergy. Yet many medieval women could be considered 'quasi-literate': they may have known little Latin while attaining a high degree of facility in the vernacular.[5] The evidence for female literacy and literate practice, however, has been easy to overlook. At a time when the use of scribes or secretaries was a measure of social status, the fact that many women did not write in their own hands does not reflect their illiteracy or literary marginality. Indeed, women who did not compose texts in their own hands nonetheless had a variety of means at their disposal to register their creative influence on textual culture. The search for medieval women's writing unearths a range of literate forms and practices that existed outside the schools and their models of *auctoritas*, but held cultural significance nonetheless.

When we speak of medieval women and authorship, then, we need to draw a distinction between scholastic accounts of *auctoritas* and actual practices of medieval authorship, which fall outside the definitions of both the scholastic *auctor*, as rooted in a timeless tradition, and the modern 'author', as a self-expressive individual and original creator. While scholastic definitions of the *auctor* generally excluded women both ideologically and institutionally, medieval authorship, understood as a range of acts and cultural practices, extended more widely across social and gender boundaries than has been previously appreciated. Yet the very diffuseness of medieval literacy and its texts also makes the positive identification of female authors extremely challenging.

The problem of the signature

Medieval books themselves often impede the identification of individual authors, since the author's name – today taken to be the very marker of authorial identity and individuality – was commonly lost or ignored. Many texts circulated under authorial names that were patently false, often less through carelessness than through the efforts of scribes, translators, and compilers to establish a text's *auctoritas*. Vernacular texts showed particular vulnerability to being reassigned to the more authoritative *auctores* of the Latin past: for example, the work of Richard de Fournival appeared under the name Ovid, while that of Guillaume de Conches appeared as the work of the Venerable Bede.[6] Such false attributions show that the author's name was not seen as a 'signature' – if by this we understand a marker of individuality that stands outside the text and guarantees its authenticity by connecting it to a biographical person. Rather, it became a textual attribute that could be manipulated in order to support particular claims about works' social status. Gender was one of the attributes of authorship open to such manipulation. Christine de Pizan worried that her work would be reassigned to men, as indeed it was in early printed editions. But it is worth noting that while her name is erased from editions of her works on such masculine genres as politics and war, it is allowed to stand in contemporary editions of *The Treasure of the City of Ladies*, a work of advice for women, suggesting that literary topics elicited differing expectations about the author's gender, which in turn influenced the attribution of those works.[7] While modern literary criticism has prepared us to read the female signature as a marker of authenticity, the example of Christine de Pizan shows that signatures were liable to be treated like any other part of the text, and thus, like the title, illustrations, or chapter headings, were open to manipulation.

Even when it does survive, a female signature does not guarantee female authorship; rather, it can demonstrate how difficult it is to assign works to individual writers on the basis of textual evidence, as is the case with the lyric compilation known as the Findern Manuscript.[8] On its pages appear several female signatures which, together with the fact that numerous lyrics seem to issue from a female perspective, lend the impression of female authorship. Yet it has proved impossible to link the signatures with the lyrics as authors or even scribes: they might be the names of the manuscripts' readers, or even names left by others practising their handwriting in the books' margins. Like many medieval signatures, they raise more questions than they answer.

A related challenge is the fact that large numbers of medieval texts are anonymous, circulating with no name at all. Many of these, like the Findern lyrics, appear to issue from a female perspective or 'voice': such is the case with the longstanding genre of *Frauenlieder*, women's songs, which include Anglo-Saxon works like *The Wife's Lament* and *Wulf and Eadwacer* and lyrics like 'Ich was ein chint so wolgetan' ('I was a maiden so lovely') in the well-known collection, *Carmina Burana*. We can only speculate about whether or not these texts may have been written by women, as several readers have done to highly suggestive ends. But despite our modern desire to assign texts to single, named authors, it is also important to recognize that medieval anonymity was seen not as a lack of authorship, but as a form of authorship with cultural value in its own right. Anonymous female-voiced texts demonstrate that in the Middle Ages, the indeterminacy of authorial gender was not seen as a problem to be definitively solved – rather, it was part of a sophisticated literary game. To describe this condition, Laurie Finke coins a useful term, 'epicene writers', in order to describe 'a third term which is not a category or sex in itself, but a space of possibility that puts sexual identity into play'.[9] An example of such 'epicene writing' might be glimpsed in a poem preserved in Cambridge University Library, a love lament that is recorded in both male and female pronouns, encouraging its reader to explore how its meaning changes when gender is reversed.[10] The literary culture responsible for such a poem reveals itself to be highly self-aware of the problems that anonymous authorship raises for interpretation, particularly around questions of gender. In anonymous texts such as these, the act of writing is not an expression of individual identity or selfhood, the hallmarks of modern authorship; to the contrary, it produces a space where identity and selfhood – along with the signs of gender that they carry – are suspended.

Visionary women: authors by negation

The most dramatic examples of writing as a suspension, rather than assertion, of selfhood come in the work of medieval women visionaries. Faced with the challenge of expressing divine messages, the visionary writer establishes her authority on the basis of her self-effacement, in order to show that her writing issues not from her individual consciousness but from a heavenly source. The twelfth-century German visionary and abbess Hildegard of Bingen develops a metaphorical language for expunging the signs of her selfhood from her writing, picturing herself as a passive instrument through which God's message could sound, 'like a trumpet, which only returns a sound but does not function unassisted, for it is Another who breathes into it that it might give forth a sound'.[11] Just as Hildegard attempted to write herself out of her work, later visionaries called on a similar language of self-negation: the French visionary Marguerite Porete sought what she called a 'vie adnientie', or the 'annihilated life', while the Swedish visionary St Bridget is described by her spiritual director as 'alyenat fro hir self rapt in spirit'.[12] Such self-annihilation became a common idiom for visionary writers and was used even by men like Richard Rolle and Meister Eckhart. But for women writers, a culturally available language of female humility and debasement adapted itself readily to this selflessness, as Rolle and Eckhart acknowledge by borrowing feminine language and gestures to describe their own visionary experience.[13] For the German beguine writer Mechthild von Magdeburg, femininity became proof of divine inspiration: the very improbability that 'a frail woman [would] write this book out of God's heart and mouth' establishes that 'this book has come lovingly from God and does not have its origins in human thought'.[14] Thus Mechthild stresses her femininity in order to disclaim any literary agency at all: 'I do not know how to write, nor can I, unless I see with the eyes of my soul and hear with the ears of my eternal spirit and feel in all the parts of my body the power of the Holy Spirit.'[15] The thirteenth-century French visionary Margaret of Oingt prefaces her work with a similar disclaimer: 'I ask all those who read this text not to think badly [of me] because I had the presumption to write this, since you must believe that I have no sense or learning with which I would know how to take these things from my heart, nor could I write this down without any model than the Grace of God which is working within me.'[16] But such feminine humility also offered a powerful strategy for self-authorization; when the English anchoress Julian of Norwich insists, 'I am a woman: leued [uneducated], febille and freyll', she transforms the position of 'woman' into both a model of Christian humility and an extraordinary figure of miraculous inspiration. There are significant historical and doctrinal differences between these female visionaries that should give us pause before we group them together simply on the basis of their common status as visionaries or women; yet together they show how women's perceived weakness, humility, and unlearnedness were thought to make them into privileged conduits of God's word.

If women were excluded from many of the official channels of theological learning, visionary writing gave them special access to divine knowledge that transcended, and revealed the insufficiency of, that learning. This is the point that Porete makes when she insists that only those who 'abase [their] knowledge' can understand her message of divine simplicity:

Theologians and other clerks,
You will not have the intellect for it,
No matter how brilliant your abilities,
If you do not proceed humbly.
And may Love and Faith, together,
Cause you to rise above Reason,
[Since] they are the ladies of the house.[17]

The struggle – explicit or implicit – between the female visionary and the 'theologians and other clerks' whom Porete targets above comprised a multilayered conflict over the meanings and institutional uses of religious authorship. The visionary 'author' pictures writing as a space of self-dissolution that guarantees the expression of divine will without human intervention. Yet that very effort to disclaim intervention was easily read as an attack on the traditional, mediating role of the clergy. Following Porete's execution for heresy in 1310, in part due to her model of the 'annihilated self', a contemporary English theologian, John Baconthorpe, identified her offence as having 'published a book against the clergy'.[18] Porete may have invited suspicion because she wrote her book herself, without the usual textual mediation of a scribe or other representatives of institutional literacy. But as visionaries were subject to greater levels of suspicion and attack, such mediation became increasingly necessary and visible.

By virtue of its self-conscious marginality to ecclesiastical institutions of literacy, women's visionary writing found political uses during historical moments when those institutions were contested. In the fourteenth century, the female visionaries St Bridget and St Catherine of Siena were outspoken in their critique of the Avignon papacy, when the pope resided in France. At a time when ecclesiastical power seemed in disarray, the words of women visionaries carried authority precisely because they claimed to issue from beyond the fray. To those whose causes they supported, like Pope Urban VI, the visionary women's messages were welcome. On the other hand, Jean Gerson, the famous Chancellor of the University of Paris who supported the French papacy, found women visionaries to be less than credible, and he warned that 'every teaching of women, especially that expressed in solemn word or writing, is to be held suspect, unless it has been diligently examined'.[19] By stressing the need to examine the writing of women visionaries, Gerson bolstered the importance of textual mediaries like scribes, spiritual directors, confessors, and other figures who represented clerical institutions of literacy and authority. In medieval women's visionary writings, the scribe was a constant feature, such as Hildegard's scribe, Volmar, Bridget of Sweden's spiritual director and editor, Alfonso of Jaën, and the scribes who feature

while disclaiming originality or inspiration, nonetheless bears the mark of his shaping hand. While the process of writing by compiling pays homage to a system of *auctoritas* based on citation and *traditio*, it would be wrong to assume that compilation was necessarily a non-creative act. To the contrary, its uses in literary culture reveal that medieval authorship did not require a modern concept of originality in order to produce new cultural forms. The point is worth stressing because compilation proved an available form of authorship for women writers.

As might be expected, Christine de Pizan offers one of the most articulate and complex meditations on medieval authorship by compilation. In her *Book of Deeds of Arms and of Chivalry* (c. 1410), Christine draws on the work of two medieval authorities on the arts of war: Honoré Bouvet, the author of *L'Arbre des batailles* [The Tree of Battles], and the fourth-century Roman Vegetius, author of *De re militari*. In the book's third part, Christine describes a visit by 'a solemn man in clerical garb', representing Bouvet himself, who authorizes her to take his work as a source:

> It is good for you to gather from the Tree of Battles in my garden some fruit that will be of use to you, so that vigor and strength may grow within you to continue work on the weighty book. In order to build an edifice that reflects the writings of Vegetius and of other authors who have been helpful to you, you must cut some branches of this tree, taking only the best, and with this timber you shall set the foundation of this edifice. To do this, I as master will undertake to help you as disciple.[29]

The metaphors of collection that Christine uses – the gathering of fruit from the garden, the selection of branches from a tree – echo Gower's distinction between the *auctor* who is the work's originator and source and the writer who compiles extracts, *auctoritates*, into a new work. But Christine also suggests that compilation is more than an act of textual subservience. In response to Christine's narrator's questions, Bouvet affirms that compilation bolsters the authority of both parties, the *auctor* as well as the compiler:

> Dear friend, in this matter I reply that the more a work is seen and approved by people, the more authentic it becomes . . . It is therefore not a rebuke, but a lawful and praiseworthy matter when material is suitably applied, wherein is the mastery of the material, for therein is the indication of having seen and read many books.[30]

Here authority becomes the product of a reciprocal relationship between *auctor* and compiler, thus making the compiler a vital key in medieval authorship.

Christine describes her own authorial practice as compilation not only in the *Deeds of Arms* but also in her better-known works. In *The City of Ladies* Christine discusses the example of Proba, a Roman Christian matron who compiled selections of classical literature to form a new work, the *Centos* – which literally means a patchwork, or a work made up through literary borrowings:

> Now she would run through the Eclogues, then the Georgics, and the Aeneid of Vergil – that is, she would skim as she read – and on one part she would take several entire verses unchanged and in another borrow small snatches of verse and, through marvelous craftsmanship and conceptual subtlety, she was able to construct entire lines of orderly verse.

The resulting work retells the stories of the Old and New Testaments by 'adapting Vergil's works to fit all this in so orderly a way that someone who only knew this work would have thought that Vergil had been both a prophet and evangelist'.[31]

The historical female poet to whom Christine refers, Faltonis Betitia Proba, was the author of *Cento Vergilianus de laudibus Christi*, which was admired by Boccaccio, Christine's immediate source. Proba was not the only early woman poet to turn compilation into a Christian form of authorship: the Byzantine Empress Eudocia of Constantinople (c. 400–466) composed a similar work entitled the *Homerocentoes*, which compiled verses from *The Iliad* and *The Odyssey* to retell the story of the Old and New Testaments, recasting Zeus as God the Father and Jesus as Odysseus, while the Virgin Mary at the annunciation is arrestingly described, using fragments of *The Odyssey*, as 'sitting by the fireside with her attendant women / turning sea-purple yarn on a distaff' (*Odyssey* 6.52–3).[32] Like Proba, Eudocia turns compilation into an art of transformation and conversion that, by selecting passages from pagan authors, transforms their meaning to support Christian history. The process is endorsed by the later historical writer Ranulph Higden, who describes his own *Polychronicon* as a work made by gathering together from authors ('ex variis auctorum decerptum'), many of whom are not Christian: yet he defends his use of pagan authors by comparing himself to the biblical Ruth who gathered corn after men (Ruth 2), thus feminizing the act of compilation even as he Christianizes it.[33]

Like Proba, Christine de Pizan herself employs careful selection to transform her sources in *The City of Ladies*, as she does in retelling Proba's own story. Christine's source, Boccaccio, takes Proba as an exceptional model of feminine virtue and uses her story to deride women more than to praise them; Christine, by contrast, ends her own account by selectively citing Boccaccio in order to make Proba an example to women:

'Boccaccio observes that it should be a great pleasure for women to hear about her.'[34] Thus the process of citing an *auctor*, Christine shows, can be a way of remaking and converting the sources of antifeminism into a history of women.

A related authorial model is offered by Marie de France, who describes her authorship of her well-known *Lais* as a work less of original composition than of assemblage: 'des lais assembler'.[35] Her use of the term 'assembler' has prompted a long-running debate over the nature of Marie's work: to what extent is she an original creator herself, or is she 'merely' gathering together works – most likely oral ones – that she presents in her collection? But such efforts to differentiate original creation from the assembly of earlier sources are challenged by Marie's description of her own authorial practice, in which the gathering of old works and the production of new ones are perfectly intertwined. In the Prologue to the *Lais* Marie explains:

> The custom among the ancients –
> as Priscian testifies –
> was to speak quite obscurely
> in the books they wrote,
> so that those who were to come after
> and study them
> might gloss the letter   [gloser la lettre]
> and supply its significance from their own   [E le dur sen le surplus mettre]
> wisdom.[36]

Marie's terms here – 'gloser la lettre' and 'surplus' – describe acts of writing instigated by acts of reading, in turn producing new texts out of old. This view of authorship follows Isidore of Seville's etymology of 'author' as 'he who augments' ('Auctor ab augendo dictus').[37] Authorship by this model is less an act of origination than one that, through reading and 'glossing', augments – and thus fulfils the latent promise of – the texts of the literary past.

Consuming authors: medieval women as readers and patrons

If, as Marie de France indicates, medieval 'authorship' could embrace acts of reading as well as writing, it is difficult to know where to draw the distinction between author and reader – or indeed, how many readerly activities in the Middle Ages could also be considered 'authorial' ones. As readers, medieval women registered a powerful influence on literary and textual cultures. One of the avenues through which they did so was patronage. Since medieval book production was a bespoke trade – largely driven by the direct demand of individual patrons and readers – the production of many important manuscripts was instigated by women. The *St Albans Psalter*, created in the early twelfth century for Christina of Markyate, reflects her influence: it contains texts upholding the principles of chastity by which she lived, while its illustrations prominently feature scenes of the Virgin Mary reading, reflecting the growing cultural influence of female literacy.[38] Similarly, the medieval Czech abbess known as Lady Kunigunde commissioned the *Passionale of the Abbess Kunigunde*, a collection of mystical works that includes a text specially written for her, 'The Prayer of Lady Kunigunde', which makes Lady Kunigunde not only the work's patron and reader but also its imagined speaker.[39] Both books use texts and images to produce a kind of semi-autobiographical work in which the female patron and reader could see herself reflected. The same could be observed of deluxe manuscripts like the famous Book of Hours of Mary of Burgundy, which features an illumination of its female patron engaged in devout reading that literally makes her a part of the book. If these female patrons are not technically the 'authors' of the books with which they are associated, they nonetheless substantiate D. F. McKenzie's insistence that no text is the product of a single author.[40] Women like Lady Kunigunde and Christina of Markyate share responsibility for their books' creation in a way that requires us to expand our notion of medieval authorship beyond the expectation of solitary creation to recognize the network of relationships that underlies the production of manuscripts and that gives the patron an exceptional degree of textual agency.

As patrons not only of individual books but also of writers, women played a foundational role in the shaping of vernacular literature from its earliest stages. The Anglo-Saxon poet Caedmon was celebrated by Bede for his songs of divine praise; subsequently, he has been considered the first English poet. Yet Caedmon's poetry would not have been possible without the support of a female patron, the formidable Abbess Hild, who deserves recognition in the same literary–historical narrative that has adopted Caedmon as origin.[41] Her example demonstrates that even inspired poetry does not spring into being through the agency of the poet alone but depends on a material substratum of support; once we grant its existence, we are able to recover women into important, even foundational, roles in medieval literary history. Eleanor of Aquitaine played a significant role in the spread of Arthurian literature, which was continued by her daughter, Marie de Champagne, the well-known patron of Chrétien de Troyes. Chrétien acknowledges that Marie's active patronage bordered on collaboration, as she provided him the material (*matière*) and interpretation (*sens*) that he elaborated in his work.[42]

Because they were generally excluded from institutions of literacy that favoured Latin, women became the privileged addressees of vernacular writing, and in the history especially of vernacular religious writing, women are legion as addressees. Some of these women are known by name: Richard Rolle, for example, addressed some of his most important vernacular writing to Margaret Kirkeby, whose influence is registered in Rolle's English works such as *The Form of Living*. The Middle English Vernon Manuscript, which contains Rolle's *Form of Living* as well as works such as the *Ancrene Wisse* and *The Abbey of the Holy Ghost*, is believed to have been compiled especially for religious women, perhaps living in a community.[43] Similarly, *The Scale of Perfection* and Nicholas Love's *Mirror of the Blessed Life of Jesus Christ* are specifically addressed to religious women readers in their prologues. Whether or not their authors had specific, historical women in mind, like Margaret Kirkeby, these works helped to make the figure of the pious female reader into an icon of vernacular literacy, requiring even male readers of these works to imagine themselves in female positions.

Devotional reading was an active process that enlisted the reader as the co-creator of meaning. Indeed, in many instances devotional reading is conceived as a form of writing: thus the late fourteenth-century English *Book to a Mother* instructs its female addressee, 'thou maist lerne aftir thi samplerie [exemplar] to write a feir trewe bok', by which it imagines that the reader herself will become a fresh 'book' in which she herself can 'write withinne and withoute' the lessons of humility, poverty, and chastity.[44] Devotional works addressed to women break down distinctions between literary production and consumption by challenging modern assumptions that production is necessarily active and primary, and consumption contrastingly passive and secondary. Rather, works commissioned by or otherwise written for women reveal the myriad ways in which consumption directly instigated production and thus became a creative force in medieval textual culture.

Reading and writing clearly bear a mutually productive relationship with one another in letters, a form of textual production in which women actively participated; however, this participation has likewise stood outside the limits of modern definitions of authorship. St Jerome maintained a wide and active correspondence with women, largely on matters of theological importance. His most frequent correspondent was Marcella, who was as active a writer of her own letters as she was a reader of Jerome's; as Jerome observes, 'our letters always crossed, outvied in courtesies, anticipated in greetings'.[45] Their letters manifest a degree of intellectual collaboration that ultimately erases distinction between the two writers, Jerome admits: 'all that I had gathered together by long study, and by constant meditation made part of my nature, she first sipped, then learned, and finally took for her own'.[46] The crossing of self and other, reader and writer, that is made possible in the exchange of letters reveals the production of gendered authorial positions to be a process of mutual formation and negotiation. Heloise demonstrates how letters create gender identity through such negotiations in the subscription to her first letter: 'to her master, or rather her father, husband, or rather brother; his handmaid, or rather his daughter, wife, or rather sister; to Abelard, Heloise'.[47] Rather than manifesting a stable, gendered authorial identity, letters reveal that identity to be a sophisticated fiction that is created through reciprocal and collaborative textual relations.

Letters have an unstable status in literary history. While long favoured by women as a literary form, they have been taken to confirm women's marginality to authorship rather than their participation in it. Yet if letters do not have authors, as Foucault insists, they offer an opportunity to challenge the assumptions that underlie modern theories of authorship, which erect divisions between creative authors and passive readers, as well as between the authorship of literary and non-literary texts.[48] The medieval letter recalls the broader conditions of medieval textual culture, in which texts were shaped through communal structures, and in which the act of transmission was also an act of making meaning. As such, it offers a cogent example of how the specific historical and textual conditions of medieval literary culture demand new definitions of authorship, definitions that will allow us to appreciate the full range of women's authorial activities.

NOTES

1. The insight that the author is a figment of the history of writing, rather than a transhistorical phenomenon, was most influentially formulated by Michel Foucault's essay, 'What is an Author?' trans. Josué V. Harari, in *The Foucault Reader*, ed. Paul Rabinow (New York: Pantheon Books, 1984); for an exploration of the broader implications for the study of early literature, see the essays collected in *The Construction of Authorship: Textual Appropriation in Law and Literature*, ed. Martha Woodmansee and Peter Jaszi (Durham, NC: Duke University Press, 1994).
2. This discussion draws from A. J. Minnis's now-classic study, *Medieval Theory of Authorship*, 2nd edn (Philadelphia: University of Pennsylvania Press, 1988); for a discussion of the meaning of the term 'author' in the Middle Ages, see Marie-Dominique Chenu, OP, 'Auctor, Actor, Autor', *Bulletin Du Cange: Archivium Latinitas Medii Aevi* 3 (1927): 81–6.
3. Christine de Pizan, *The Book of the City of Ladies*, trans. Earl Jeffrey Richards (New York: Persea Books, 1982), pp. 4–5. The French text is from Maureen Curnow, ed., 'The Livre de la Cité des Dames of Christine de Pizan: a Critical Edition' (PhD diss., Vanderbilt University, 1975), 619.
4. Roger Dragonetti, *Le Mirage des sources: l'art du faux dans le roman médiéval* (Paris: Seuil, 1987), p. 41.

5. The term 'quasi-literate' is developed by Franz H. Bäuml, 'Varieties and Consequences of Medieval Literacy and Illiteracy', *Speculum* 55 (1980): 246.

6. E. Ph. Goldschmidt, *Medieval Texts and their First Appearance in Print*, Bibliographical Society Transactions Suppl. 16 (London: Oxford University Press, 1943), pp. 86–7.

7. For a discussion of these and other early editions, see Cynthia J. Brown, 'The Reconstruction of an Author in Print: Christine de Pizan in the Fifteenth and Sixteenth Centuries', in *Christine de Pizan and the Categories of Difference*, ed. Marilynn Desmond (Minneapolis: University of Minnesota Press, 1998).

8. A facsimile of the manuscript exists: *The Findern Manuscript: Cambridge University Library MS. Ff. I. 6*, introduction by Richard Beadle and A. E. B. Owen (London: The Scolar Press, 1977). For further discussion of the possible significance of female signatures in the Findern Manuscript, see Sarah McNamer, chapter 13 'Lyrics and Romances', pp. 197–201 in this volume.

9. Laurie A. Finke, *Women's Writing in English: Medieval England* (New York: Longman, 1999), p. 95.

10. The poem is preserved as Cambridge University Library MS Add. 5943, fo. 178v; it is reproduced as 'A Carol', in *Women's Writing in Middle English*, ed. Alexandra Barratt (London: Longman, 1992), p. 287.

11. *The Letters of Hildegard of Bingen*, trans. Joseph L. Baird and Radd K. Ehrman, 2 vols. (New York: Oxford University Press, 1998), 2: 181.

12. Marguerite Porete, *The Mirror of Simple Souls*, trans. Ellen L. Babinsky (New York: Paulist Press, 1993); see chapter 5, 'Of the Life which is called the Peace of the Annihilated Life', pp. 82–4. Alfonso of Jaén, 'Epistola solitarii ad reges', edited as an appendix to Rosalynn Voaden, *God's Words, Women's Voices: The Discernment of Spirits in the Writing of Late-Medieval Women Visionaries* (York Medieval Press, 1999), p. 171.

13. For Meister Eckhart, see Amy Hollywood, *The Soul as Virgin Wife: Mechthild of Magdeburg, Marguerite Porete, and Meister Eckhart* (University of Notre Dame Press, 1995); for Rolle, see Felicity Riddy, ' "Women Talking About the Things of God": A Late Medieval Sub-Culture', in *Women and Literature in Britain, 1150–1500*, ed. Carol M. Meale, 2nd edn (Cambridge University Press, 1996), p. 107.

14. Mechthild of Magdeburg, *The Flowing Light of the Godhead*, trans. Frank Tobin (New York: Paulist Press, 1998), p. 144.

15. Ibid., p. 156.

16. *The Writings of Margaret of Oingt, Medieval Prioress and Mystic*, trans. Renate Blumenfeld-Kosinski, The Focus Library of Medieval Women (Newburyport: Focus Information Group, 1990), p. 26.

17. Porete, *Mirror of Simple Souls*, p. 79.

18. Cited by Michael G. Sargent, 'The Annihilation of Marguerite Porete', *Viator* 28 (1997): 257.

19. Jean Gerson, *Œuvres complètes*, ed. P. Glorieux, 10 vols. (Paris: Desclée, 1960–73), 9: 468. Translation from D. Catherine Brown, *Pastor and Laity in the Theology of Jean Gerson* (Cambridge University Press, 1987), p. 223.

20. See Voaden, *God's Words, Women's Voices*, p. 57.

21. *The Book of Margery Kempe*, ed. S. B. Meech and H. E. Allen, EETS OS 212 (Oxford University Press, 1940), pp. 152, 153–4.

22. John C. Hirsch, 'Author and Scribe in *The Book of Margery Kempe*', *Medium Aevum* 44 (1975): 150. Lynn Staley, *Margery Kempe's Dissenting Fictions* (University Park: Pennsylvania State University Press, 1994), p. 36.

23. Edmund Colledge and Romana Guarnieri, 'The Glosses by "M. N." and Richard Methley to "The Mirror of Simple Souls"', *Archivio Italiano per la Storia della Pietà* 5 (1968): 357–82.

24. Jacques de Vitry, *Life of Marie d'Oignies*, trans. Margot H. King (Toronto: Peregrina Publishing, 1989), 18.

25. Dyan Elliott, 'Authorizing a Life: the Collaboration of Dorothea of Montau and John Marienwarder', in *Gendered Voices: Medieval Saints and their Interpreters*, ed. Catherine M. Mooney (Philadelphia: University of Pennsylvania Press, 1999), p. 168.

26. *The Book of Margery Kempe*, p. 71.

27. John Gower, *Vox clamantis*, in *The Complete Works of John Gower: The Latin Works*, ed. G. C. Macauley (Oxford: Clarendon, 1902), II prol. 7–8; pp. 77–82; English translation, *The Voice of One Crying*, in *The Major Latin Works of John Gower*, trans. Eric W. Stockton (Seattle: University of Washington Press, 1962).

28. Minnis, *Medieval Theory of Authorship*, p. 173.

29. Christine de Pizan, *The Book of Deeds of Arms and of Chivalry*, trans. Sumner Willard, ed. Charity Cannon Willard (University Park: Pennsylvania State University Press, 1999), p. 144.

30. Ibid.

31. Christine de Pizan, *The Book of the City of Ladies*, pp. 65–6.

32. Cited by Kenneth G. Holum, *Theodosian Empresses: Women and Imperial Dominion in Late Antiquity* (Berkeley: University of California Press, 1982), pp. 220–1. For a short biography of Eudocia and a selection of her other work, a life of St Cyrian, see Marcelle Thiébaux, *The Writings of Medieval Women: An Anthology*, 2nd edn (New York: Garland, 1994), pp. 49–69.

33. *Polychronicon Ranulphi Higden monachi cestrensis*, ed. Joseph Rawson Lumby, Rerum britannicarum medii aevi scriptores 41, 9 vols. (London: Longman, 1865), 1: 6. See Minnis, *Medieval Theory of Authorship*, p. 113.

34. Christine de Pizan, *Book of the City of Ladies*, pp. 66–7.

35. *Les Lais de Marie de France*, ed. Jean Rychner (Paris: Librairie Honoré Champion, 1983), Prologue, line 47.

36. Marie de France, Prologue, *The Lais of Marie de France*, trans. Robert Hanning and Joan Ferrante (1978; reprint, Durham, NC: Labyrinth Press, 1982), 28, lines 9–22. The French is from *Les Lais de Marie de France*, ed. Rychner, lines 15 and 16.

37. Andre Leupin, 'The Impossible Task of Manifesting "Literature" on Marie de France's Obscurity', *Exemplaria* 3 (1991): 221–42, at 227.

38. See *The St Albans Psalter*, ed. Otto Pächt, C. R. Dodwell and Francis Wormald Millett, Studies of the Warburg Institute 25 (London: The Warburg Institute, 1960); Millett, 'Women in No Man's Land: English Recluses and the Development of Vernacular Literature in the Twelfth and Thirteenth Centuries', in *Women and Literature in Britain, 1150–1500*, ed. Meale, pp. 91–2.

39. Alfred Thomas, *Anne's Bohemia: Czech Literature and Society, 1310–1420* (Minneapolis: University of Minnesota Press, 1998), pp. 35–40.

40. See D. F. McKenzie, *Bibliography and the Sociology of Texts*, 2nd edn (Cambridge University Press, 1999).

41. Clare A. Lees and Gilliam R. Overing, 'Birthing Bishops and Fathering Poets: Bede, Hild, and the Relations of Cultural Production', *Exemplaria* 6 (1994): 35–65.

42. June Hall McCash, 'The Cultural Patronage of Medieval Women: An Overview', *The Cultural Patronage of Medieval Women*, ed. McCash (Athens: University of Georgia Press, 1996), pp. 15, 18–19. But see also Joan M. Ferrante, *To the Glory of Her Sex: Women's Roles in the Composition of Medieval Texts* (Bloomington: Indiana University Press, 1997), who stresses the ambivalence of Chrétien's regard for his female patron (pp. 118–20).

43. See N. F. Blake, 'The Vernon Manuscript: Contents and Organisation', in *Studies in the Vernon Manuscript*, ed. Derek Pearsall (Cambridge: D. S. Brewer, 1990).

44. This remarkable example is cited by Nicholas Watson in 'Fashioning the Puritan Gentry-Woman: Devotion and Dissent in Book to a Mother', in *Medieval Women: Texts and Contexts in Late Medieval Britain. Essays for Felicity Riddy*, ed. Jocelyn Wogan-Browne et al. (Turnhout, Belgium: Brepols, 2000), p. 177.

45. *Select Letters of St Jerome*, trans. F. A. Wright, Loeb Classical Library (New York: G. P. Putnam's Sons, 1933), p. 457; see also Appendix I, 'Of Jerome's Correspondence with Roman Women'.

46. Ibid., p. 455.

47. *The Letters of Abelard and Heloise*, trans. Betty Radice (Baltimore: Penguin, 1974), p. 109. See Martin Irvine, 'Heloise and the Gendering of the Literate Subject', in *Criticism and Dissent in the Middle Ages*, ed. Rita Copeland (Cambridge University Press, 1996), p. 107.

48. As Foucault writes, 'A private letter may well have a signer – it does not have an author' ('What is an Author?' pp. 107–8).

7

CHRISTOPHER CANNON

Enclosure

Where the view is held that a body contains something – as it is now and was in the Middle Ages – every person lives in an enclosure. But a particular form of medieval devotion also elaborated this structural metaphor as an entire way of life, arranging a person's every daily thought and activity so as to limit even the body's contact with the world, enclosing that person permanently within the protections of a dwelling. Because the defining gesture of such devotion was complete withdrawal from social encounters, enclosed men and women were called 'anchorites' after the Greek *anachorein*, meaning 'to retire, retreat'.[1] Since such isolation was, by its nature, a piety of strict discipline, an anchorite also tried to leave behind all physical comfort, and the anchoritic dwelling was itself often painfully small, sometimes no more than eight feet (2.4 m) square. It was commonly attached to the north side of a church so that the anchorite's main outward view would be through a window which faced the altar (but even this opening was sometimes no more than twenty-one inches (53 cm) square). The dwelling could also have two other windows, one for obtaining food and other necessities, the other for communicating with priests or visitors, but, even here, communication was limited; these windows were mostly kept closed, and when opened were still to be covered with a curtain.[2] Although the dwelling had to have a door for the anchorite to enter in the first place, it was blocked up as part of the ceremony of enclosure, at which point the Office for the Dead and prayers for the dying were said. Once enclosed, in other words, the anchorite was only meant to leave his or her dwelling in death, and its narrow confine was therefore, in principle as well as practice, not so much a house as a tomb.[3]

Thirteen rules written in England which describe and recommend such a life survive, the earliest dating from c. 1080 (the *Liber confortatorius*), the last written in the second half of the fourteenth century (Walter Hilton's *Epistola ad quendam solitarium*).[4] Although not itself a rule, the *Life of Christina of Markyate* (c. 1156–66) is also a crucial piece of English anchoritic writing: at root an accurate biography (shaped by the conventions of saint's life) it gives an extremely rich account of the cultural forces which drove one particular woman to choose enclosure. In fact, while most anchoritic rules were written by men, this form of life was particularly popular among women in medieval England, and the majority of surviving rules are specifically addressed to women.[5]

Since most educated women in this period were only taught to read in the vernacular, such rules were also written in English from a comparatively early date, and they therefore also play a central role in the growth of English as literary language. *Ancrene Wisse* (c. 1215–24), a 'guide for anchorites', exemplifies all of these phenomena: it was written in English, when other religious writing was typically written in Latin, for 'three sisters', who were enjoined to read from it each day, and it was subsequently copied and up-dated so frequently (for an ever wider group of readers) that it alone helped to ensure the 'continuity of English prose' for a century and a half.[6] When English prose of this sort became the common coin of devotional writing – in rules such as Richard Rolle's *Form of Living* (1348) and *The Scale of Perfection* by Walter Hilton (d. 1397) – anchoritic instruction itself began to shift its focus from the particular person to the entire Christian community. It is as a culmination of these later developments that the anchorite Julian of Norwich produced her *Showings* (c. 1393), a meditation on the experience of one woman's enclosure designed as a general guide for spiritual improvement.[7]

The enclosed life and the rules recommending it remain of interest because of the detailed account they give of some medieval lives (particularly the lives of some medieval women) but, also, because they point and confront a paradox constituted by all forms of medieval Christian devotion: the injunction to separate oneself from worldly things the better to devote oneself to God was itself a means to denying those connections with other people (that 'community') which a better spirituality was itself meant to perfect. This is true of the anchoritic life in the most practical sense: even though the anchorite withdrew from the common life of the town or village where she had lived, she was still at its physical centre (because attached to its church) and, precisely because she could not move, she both required contact with others (in order to obtain food) and had no means to escape anyone who sought her out. The constant pressure of such contradictory circumstances and demands was not, however, grounds for enclosure's failure, but the material of its success. The anchoritic life was difficult because it was an attempt to discover new social and spiritual possibilities, to resolve the conflicts inherent in the Christian imagining of goodness by living out its implications. Such a way of life may also be understood then as a kind of thoughtfulness wherein the implications of a metaphor – that a life *can* be enclosed – are tested, stretched, and refined. We are therefore also interested in such lives and their texts because they are a very early attempt – perhaps the earliest in English – to extend human possibility by cultivating and exploring, even as they set limits to, an individual mind. They make a profound contribution to intellectual history by fashioning, as a response to the Christian demand that a person live both entirely 'within' but also for others, what we now call the 'self'.

Ascesis

A crucial premise of anchoritic devotion is, as *Ancrene Wisse* puts it, that 'they are right who live according to a rule' (p. 1), that is, that a life is well lived to the extent that it is regulated.[8] Such a method for human improvement may be traced back to Aristotle who believed that 'like activities produce like dispositions', and, therefore, that goodness could be instilled in people simply by shaping their actions. Good people are, in this view, well-made things (like the 'neatest shoes' as Aristotle puts it), and 'ethics' is a kind of craft whereby training people in good 'customs' (*ethos*) necessarily improves their 'character' (*ēthos*).[9] Since the enclosed life exists by virtue of such regulations, it might therefore also be described as an *ethics*. Of course the fundamental principles of that ethics were themselves determined by the behaviour of earlier and exemplary Christians, in particular by the habits of early recluses such as St Anthony (often described as the first anchorite) who, in the third and fourth centuries, rid himself of all 'oppressive obligations and abrasive relationships' by retreating into the desert.[10] St Anthony's actions had still deeper roots in the Gospels, where Jesus tells his disciples to leave everything that they have so that they might 'receive an hundredfold and possess life everlasting' (Matthew 19: 29).

It is also the case that an ethics entirely based on regulation will tend to equate adherence to rules with moral excellence no matter what those rules happen to be, with the predictable result that recommended activities grow increasingly difficult, the better to demonstrate that rules are being followed (it is the resulting discomfort which proves that a person would not have done a particular thing in the absence of a rule). The term generally used to refer to such a commitment to hardship is *ascesis*, which simply means 'exercise' or 'training', but it has come to refer to any system of obstacles and injuries which renders the exercise of rule-following particularly visible. As the *Life of Christina of Markyate* makes clear, enclosure is ascetic simply because it is so very uncomfortable:

The confined space would not allow her to wear even the necessary clothing when she was cold. The airless little enclosure became stifling when she was hot. Through long fasting, her bowels became contracted and dried up. There was a time when her burning thirst caused little clots of blood to bubble up from her nostrils.[11]

Christina's situation here is aggravated by the fact that she is also in hiding (and therefore unable to make a sound), but this further restriction only helps to make clear how ascesis is a principle whereby the most horrific physical suffering will be redescribed as ethical success: 'she bore all these daily anxieties and troubles with the calm sweetness of divine love' (p. 105). Similarly, although the author of *Ancrene Wisse* is aware of the real dangers of such an ethics, and often acknowledges its severity by worrying that asceticism will do damage to anchorites unless they are 'healthy and completely strong' (p. 191), even he urges anchorites to 'mortification of the flesh with fasts, with vigils, with scourgings, with hard clothing, a hard bed, with sickness, with great labours' (p. 169).

As it attempts to define every aspect of an anchorite's world through regulation, anchoritic ascesis may also be understood as a *formal principle*. A rule which described what an anchorite could eat, drilled her in her every waking activity, told her what she could and could not enjoy, not only shaped her character but finally determined her very thoughts. As Nietzsche later observed, ascesis is the principle which produces an 'inner world', for in the same measure that it inhibits 'outward discharge' it turns a person back on herself, expanding and extending an inner space, giving it the 'depth, breadth, and height' that person has been denied in the physical world.[12] The resulting imaginary shape has become so familiar that we tend to regard it as both natural and necessary: like the author of *Ancrene Wisse* we tend to believe that each person is, in some measure, 'of two parts, of body and of soul', that our flesh is a containing and protecting 'vessel' with something 'inside' it (p. 129). And anchoritic rules are already so committed to this principle that they are themselves divided into 'inner' and 'outer' parts,[13] with *Ancrene Wisse* following this 'body model' so closely that its 'inner rule' (Books 2–7) is also physically surrounded by its 'outer rule' (Books 1 and 8).[14] The very fact that a text can be built to conform to such a shape is itself enough to show, however, that it is not given, but imagined. To the extent that any inside is produced as a 'complex coproduct' of any outside (that no inside exists without an outside to surround it), such an imagining is also particularly fragile where it becomes difficult to specify what actually resides 'inside' or 'outside'.[15] *Ancrene Wisse* demonstrates this fragility in all those places where it finds the boundaries of the body impossible to maintain (in Book 4, for example, 'inner temptations' come from outside even as an 'outer temptations' are experienced 'inside' (p. 87)). But all anchoritic devotion recognizes that the body is a construct in its very demand for enclosure: the body is thereby provided with a second outside to shore up those bodily limits which are themselves so hard to specify.

Enclosure is therefore not only a form of life built according to the same principles as the medieval body, it is a *tool* for securing that body's imaginative boundaries, providing a set of images whereby the anchorite can orient and understand an individual human's shape in the context of a larger world. Thus, in *Ancrene Wisse*, the anchorhouse is described as a fortification or 'castle' (p. 32) so that the fragility of the anchorite's body can be imaginatively secured as a 'castle of earth' (p. 179). This image also explains why the anchorite continues to experience temptations because, as *Ancrene Wisse* also argues, it is only the strong fortification which needs to be attacked (p. 107). Enclosure also helps the anchorite to understand herself as Christ-like, since as Aelred of Rievaulx points out in the anchoritic rule called the *De institutione inclusarum* (c. 1160–2), Christ first took on human form enclosed 'within the womb of a maiden' (p. 80). *Ancrene Wisse*, which takes the *De institutione* as its main source, further develops this image by describing Christ as the first 'recluse' because he was so enclosed (p. 173).[16]

It is also the case, however, that the anchorhouse reproduces the body model of the anchorite so well that it can also reproduce the body's problems: not only is it also subject to invasion, but, by duplicating the sites from which the body can be invaded, the anchorhouse actually multiplies the points of the body's vulnerability. Thus, in *Ancrene Wisse* the anchorite must not simply 'guard her eyes well' from the temptations which might greet them (p. 32), but she must 'shut her window firmly' since it is through this gap in the protective dwelling that she might also 'receive a hand and a foolish word' (p. 34). As the tool of an ethics committed to regulation, enclosure works so well that it finally also exposes the violence coiled within ascesis as an ethical principle. It is only in the context of anchoritic devotion that looking out a window could constitute spiritual death, that simply by 'peeping' an anchorite could somehow allow the 'claws of hooded and sharp temptation' to enter her dwelling at the cost of her soul ('deprived at one stroke of earth and also of heaven') (p. 51). It is only in the enclosed life that most natural and simple human action could become the means by which an anchorite might actually lose 'all the good that [she has] begotten' (p. 36).

Community

In seeking to live a life of pure devotion, the anchorite enclosed herself at the cost of removing herself from a community, that form of life in which most Christian devotion actually occurred. As every Christian is enjoined in the gospels (Luke 10: 27), the anchorite is told in *Ancrene Wisse* to do everything 'either for love of God alone or for the good of another and his advantage' (p. 178), but she will find it difficult to do the latter, since the very terms of her enclosure prohibit her from even having neighbours. As Aelred of Rievaulx formulates the problem in the *De institutione*, the anchorite is enclosed as if 'dead to the world' (p. 62) but she leaves that world 'in order to love [her] neighbour perfectly' (p. 78), and he therefore also wonders: 'what good then will you be able to do to your neighbour?' (p. 77). His answer seems to ring hollow even to himself (her 'offering', he says, must be limited to her 'good will'), and even the more imaginative solution of *Ancrene Wisse*, that 'during the day some time, or the night' the anchorite 'gather in [her] heart all the sick and sorrowful who endure misery', is in deep conflict with the very logic of enclosure (p. 16): should the anchorite perform such an act of meditation she will live her solitary life through the imaginative recreation of the very people she is supposed to define her solitude against.

This doctrinal problem is intensified by the more fundamental problem of a world which will not go away no matter how strong separating boundaries are made. Although *Ancrene Wisse* treats the anchorite's five senses as protective devices, 'guardians', filtering contact with the outside world in order to protect what lies within (p. 27), these senses can only protect to the extent that they are always in contact with the world, and they are therefore also vehicles for pursuing 'the flesh's pleasure according to the will's desire' (p. 59). It is, in fact, the protective shell of the anchorite's body which will defeat her spirituality the most quickly. As Marx wryly observed, the person who seeks holiness through solitude has only created the opportunity to discover that his or her stomach is 'profane': every attempt at 'self-seeking' quickly falls foul of physical needs (particularly for food and water), needs which can only be satisfied through a 'seeking for other things and human beings'.[17] Thus *Ancrene Wisse* is forced to acknowledge that 'an anchor[ite] who does not have her food to hand needs two women' (p. 196). But it also recognizes the dangers of such need: while even the 'good anchorite' devoted to spiritual things must 'come down to the ground of her body and eat, drink, sleep, work, speak and hear', it is precisely 'flesh's need' that is the 'devil's snare' which threatens to lead her to sin (pp. 66–7).

A still larger version of this paradox is manifest in the way in which the well-lived anchoritic life always seemed to form communities around itself.

The *Life of Christina of Markyate* describes a local landscape dotted with anchorites who were clearly in regular communication (p. 16), and, as was the case for Markyate Abbey itself, a very large number of nunneries 'evolved from a community of recluses'.[18] Such a process can also be traced through the various surviving texts of *Ancrene Wisse*, for the earliest version of this rule is addressed to three sisters, but a later version is addressed to 'twenty or more' women, who the author actually refers to as a 'community' (p. 119).[19] Of course anchoritic life was never as solitary as the rules sometimes want to pretend: in addition to other anchorites and servants, an anchorhouse typically, if only occasionally, hosted guests (this is clear enough from the warning in *Ancrene Wisse* that 'two nights is enough for anyone to stay, and that should very seldom be' (p. 199)). It was also the case that because the anchorite stood apart from others, but was always surrounded by a world of people, her very liminality actually tended to draw her into a community's affairs.[20] We learn in the *De institutione* that 'it is not unknown for a recluse to take up teaching' (p. 49), and *Ancrene Wisse* makes clear that many an anchorite served as the town gossip (pp. 44–6). It is also clear in *Ancrene Wisse* that, in times of war or unrest, an anchorhouse could be used as a secure hiding-place for 'livestock, or clothes, or boxes or charters' (p. 193).

And yet, the deep and inherent conflict between community and isolation in the anchoritic life also amounts to a resolution of the problem, for it is precisely because the pressure of others is so constant that a solitary anchorite will have to care about them. Fundamental to this achievement is the injunction to prize the 'love of God', since no matter how dead to the world she succeeds in becoming, an anchorite begins her isolation, as it is described in the *De institutione*, 'buried with Christ in his tomb' (p. 62). It is initially surprising that anchoritic rules stress the amorous nature of this relationship rather than its spirituality: even as she is enjoined to prize her chastity above all other things, Christ 'woos' the anchorite ('grant me your love, which I long for so much' (p. 183)), 'spreads out his arms' to her, and 'bows down his head as if to offer a kiss' (p. 185). The love of God is carefully differentiated from lust in this same context ('the burning of God's love drives the burning of foul love out of the heart' (p. 185)), but it is still human desire which is identified as a crucial component of the anchorite's life.

This is not unlike the 'cure by love' described by Freud in which a person procures an identity by seeking those qualities which she understands herself to lack in another, loving that person as a method of psychic formation (as Freud puts it, the endangered 'ego' loves 'what possesses the excellence which the ego lacks for making it an ideal').[21] But Jacques Lacan provides the most detailed description of why another, once sought and encountered, should provide such safety: it is when our attraction to another is most intense –

when we feel that a foreign identity will absorb us because we desire it so much – that, according to Lacan, we are forced to secure our *own* identity, building 'armor' very like the anchorite's 'castle' around ourselves ('on the mental plane . . . realized [as] the structures of fortified works'). It is precisely because the passionate embrace of the other also involves such a paralysing fear of absorption that it is *dangerous* – in other words, that the anchorite is finally able to remain separate, to constitute a separate identity as a 'rigid structure'.[22] It is as he also understands this truth that Aelred of Rievaulx begins his discussion of the 'inner man' by envisioning an amorous encounter between Christ and the anchorite: Aelred knows that it is only as she imagines Christ as her 'Bridegroom' or makes him her 'friend' that she will be able to 'prefer solitude' (pp. 62–3). And *Ancrene Wisse* devotes most of the last and most important book of its inner rule (part 7) to elaborating the romance between a lover (who is both a knight and Christ) and a 'lady' (who is both every soul and the anchorite) because its author believes that it is only the love of another which will 'set [the anchorite] free from all her enemies' (p. 180), that it is only by yielding to some love that the soul (or any anchorite) can remain safely enclosed within a 'castle' (either the shell of the body or the anchorhouse itself) (pp. 179–80). Community is therefore equivalent to solitude in anchoritic devotion because the presence of the other actually *secures* the boundaries which separate the anchorite from the world, which secures her autonomy as a person.

Subjection

Safe and independent as she finally succeeds in being, however, the anchorite always suffers. This is not only because suffering is a property of the ascetic life (because, as it is put in *Ancrene Wisse*, 'two things pertain to an anchorite, confinedness and bitterness' (p. 173)), but because trials are themselves a crucial part of a medieval Christianity which demanded an *imitatio Christi*, an imitation of Christ's suffering by which every Christian could claim his or her share in the redemption this suffering had earned. It is possible to relate this common Christian equation between suffering and salvation to the subservience always demanded of medieval women, thereby claiming that certain kinds of suffering were actually a mode of female empowerment: according to Caroline Walker Bynum, it was through the very injuries women were asked to inflict on themselves that they could merge their own 'humiliating and painful flesh' with the tortured body of Christ, producing out of such intense 'physicality' a 'lifting up' or 'redemption'.[23] This is certainly a presumption governing *Ancrene Wisse*, where an audience is trained in practices of ruthless denial and told that 'God shed his blood for all, but it only has value for those who flee the flesh's pleasure and torment themselves' (p. 166).

But it is equally well the case, as Nietzsche long ago also observed, that there is a serious ethical problem when 'will and desire are abolished altogether', when people who are suffering are trained to think that neither complaint nor relief is warranted: principles which could make human beings so passive before their own destruction are simply 'narcotics' and it may simply be wrong to describe such a result as an achievement.[24] Where such a critique has been directed at the work of Bynum it notes that an eagerness for self-torment is a very odd sort of empowerment and might be better described as a procedure for *furthering* social domination, either of women in particular (if we remember that it was always men who encouraged women to adopt such forms of life), or of all Christians (if we note that it was an institutionalized Church which subdued its followers by means of such orthodoxies).[25] A broader view might be, as Jacques Derrida has it, that all Western philosophy, even the pre-Christian, is based upon an equation between suffering and self-determination to the extent that it presumes there is some origin for all human existence: in this sense the anchorite is only an extreme version of the way that we still ennoble death or its precursors (injury, pain, hardship) because we think we *are* insofar as we owe a 'gift of death' to some creator or act of creation.[26] However broadly true this may be, it is certainly according to this logic that Julian of Norwich describes herself in her *Showings* as 'right nowte' (p. 13). As she says later, to be nothing is to be good because it is to be like Christ: 'our lord Iesus nawted for us,' and so 'we stond al in this manner nowtid with him' (p. 29). And it is as the enclosed life was a mode of living committed to the necessity of sacrifice that it can only allow the anchorite to come into being as she is willing to sacrifice that being altogether.

The two meanings inherent in the term 'subjection' – either 'coming to be a subject' or 'being subject to another's power' – apply very precisely then to the procedures an anchorite employed to imagine herself, to become, as we can now also call it, a 'subject'. It is, of course, God to whom the anchorite is subjected, and, in anchoritic writings, even when God's power is described as 'love', that love is a form of domination since it demands reciprocation: indeed, at the culmination of his 'wooing' of the anchorite in *Ancrene Wisse*, the 'lover' Christ points out that he holds 'a cruel sword' over the anchorite's head, which he will use to 'part [her] life and [her] soul and sink them both into the fire' if she should actually refuse him (p. 184). As Sarah Beckwith puts it, 'the anchor[ite] must come to love her own subjection, to desire it more than life itself'.[27] It is also the case that *Ancrene Wisse* sits on the cusp of a new instrument of power employed by the Church after the Fourth Lateran

Council (1215) which mandated that every Christian be confessed yearly.[28] Insofar as *Ancrene Wisse* devotes an entire book to careful elaboration of the procedures and importance of confession (part 5) and the answering punishments of penance (part 6), it is one of the earliest English texts to begin what Michel Foucault has called that 'immense labor' whereby the modern subject was given its characteristic contours through confession, where a space which had not actually existed prior to confession's demands was first posited, and then brought into being, by the need to describe it.[29] Thus, when *Ancrene Wisse* uses the image of the vessel to imagine how confession will reveal what is hidden within the 'pot' of the self, it is not simply accusing the anchorite of having sinful thoughts, but telling her that she *has* thoughts ('facts', however 'outrageous') hidden within her body:

> But let her pour all the pot out to her own father confessor, or to some man of holy life, if she can get him – spew out there all the outrageous facts, there, with foul words, ill-treat that filth quite outrageously, in accordance with what it is, so that she is afraid of hurting the ears of the person listening to her sins.
>
> (p. 159)

These defining procedures of self-examination can themselves be related to yet another way in which the term 'subjection' is appropriate to the practices recommended by anchoritic rules, for insofar as confession is spoken, it is a procedure whereby a person makes him- or herself the 'subject of [a] statement', a *grammatical subject* with its own fixed positions and possibilities in those rules that already govern language.[30] *Ancrene Wisse* illustrates this procedure particularly well when it scripts the very words the confessing anchorite must use when she approaches her confessor: she is made a subject in language simply as she is told to say, 'I am an anchor[ite]' (p. 147), and her subjectivity is sculpted by linguistic possibility when she is told not to describe failures of chastity in one set of statements ('"I have had a lover"' or '"I have been foolish about myself"', (p. 146)) but, instead, in another ('"Sir, God's mercy, I am a foul stud mare, a stinking whore"' (p. 147)).

And, however sinful, the psychological and grammatical subject position created in early rules such as *Ancrene Wisse* becomes the position from which anchoritic writings such as the *Showings* of Julian of Norwich finally emerge. There, in sixteen visions and lengthy meditations upon their meaning over two decades, Julian founds her inner life on the physical demands of ascesis, a 'bodily sekeness' and 'wounds' which are sought as 'gifts from God' (p. 2). And like every anchorite, Julian wishes to suffer because Christ did ('I would that his peynes were my peynes' (p. 5)), although her self-description turns quickly from the importance of pain to definitions of a 'privy inward syte', a perceptual acuity which she says she has gained from her sacrifice (p. 89). As I have noted, Julian describes herself as worthless, but her *Showings* are, in sum, the discovery of an identity – an 'I', endlessly generating further self-description – and the strong authorial presence of Julian is a further demonstration of the productive possibilities of subjection: the *Showings* are not only the earliest English text we know to have been written by a woman, but we know this because this text so fully produces 'Julian' and links that subject to this text. Moreover, if, as Judith Butler has argued, 'there is no formation of the subject without a passionate attachment to subjection' – if every subject emerges in subjection – then the *Showings* are also the culmination of a literature in which enclosure is the paradigm of the making of any self.[31] As Julian of Norwich shows herself at work creating her own inner life – as the enclosed life creates the subjectivity of each anchorite – she shows us how each one of us will go to work creating our own.

It is in this sense, then, that enclosed life and its literature are the crucial arenas in which the modern self was first defined and mapped. The work of Nietzsche, Freud, Lacan, Foucault, Derrida, Butler and other philosophers of the subject bears directly upon anchoritic texts because the subject under discussion in all this writing is precisely the same. Further securing the connection between these modern and medieval theories is the surprising parallel between the description of subject formation in the *Showings* and Hegel's *Phenomenology of Perception* (1807), a text itself foundational for all the modern thinkers I have just mentioned. Just as Hegel uses images of lordship and servitude to describe the formation of what he calls 'independent consciousness' in the *Phenomenology*, Julian uses this image in an equally famous section of the *Showings* to describe the importance of suffering:

And thus in the servant was shewid the mischefe and	
blyndehede of Adams fallyng; and in the servant was shewid	[blindness]
the wisdam and godenes of God Son. And in the lord was	
shewid the ruth and pite of Adams wo; and in the lord	[compassion]
was shewid the hey noblyth and the endles worship that	[high nobility]
mankynde is cum to be the vertue of the passion and the	[by]
deth of his derworthy Son; and therefore mytyly he enioyeth	[dearly beloved]
in his fallyng, for the hey reysing and the fullhede of bliss	[fullness]
that mankynde is cum to, overpassing that we shuld have	
had if he had not fallen; and thus to se this overpassing	[see]
nobleth was myn understondyng led into God in the same	[nobility; at]
tyme that I saw the servant fallen. (pp. 82–3)	

Julian makes 'fallyng' equivalent to 'understondyng' because sacrifice is equivalent to 'wisdam and godeness' in medieval Christian doctrine. The image of the lord and servant explains the role of powerlessness in self-determination by showing how the former leads to the latter: the splitting of the divine and the human self (whether it be 'Adam' or 'God Son') into both the powerful lord and the dependent servant demonstrates that the subject's autonomy (its 'overpassing understondyng') requires the *acceptance* of dependence; it is only by recognizing the capacity of a divine power to define one's self that a person becomes *self*-conscious, aware of one's mind as a separate and powerful entity.

Hegel's discussion of the relationship between a 'lord' and 'bondsman' repeats this explanation but generalizes it, separating it from Christian doctrine and thereby showing how, even in the absence of some divinity, the self always gains its own power from a powerful other. His 'bondsman' is subject to another's 'lordship', not because of that lord's prior sacrifice or inherent strength, but simply because that 'lord' is *already* a subject: the first thing a mind trying to imagine itself in the world must discover is that there are other minds who have imagined *it* better than it has yet been able to imagine itself. In this initial awareness of another's defining power the new subject is 'seized with dread', but this simple terror is actually the foundation of its success, for it leads to 'an absolute melting-away of everything stable', ridding the forming subject 'of [its] attachment to natural existence in every single detail', leaving it aware of nothing other than its own existence.[32] For Hegel the result of this confrontation between the new subject (as 'bondsman') and the prior subject (as 'lord') is 'self-consciousness' simply because the self has nothing left to know but what it is.[33] Julian calls such an achievement being 'right noght' because it results from embracing one's own weakness, but inasmuch as it finally blocks out all the world in *favour* of the self, it can constitute a powerful mind. In both the anchoritic and Hegelian models the subject is *enclosed* by the process of subjection, and, as a result, enclosure is the method a subject must always use not only to describe and articulate but, finally, to *assert* itself. Hegel did not base his imagery or explanation on Julian's, but the similarities are inevitable. The *Showings* describe something very like the modern subject because the enclosed life is the social, ethical, and metaphorical space in which that subject is still thought to find its footing. Medieval readers therefore looked to anchoritic writings for that account of subjectivity which modern philosophy might now seek in Hegel's *Phenomenology*. It is for this reason above all others that we still care about medieval enclosure too: for it is there that we find a history of the self we now each feel we are, and it is there that we learn how what we are first came to be.

NOTES

1. Greek *anachorein* is comprised of *ana-*, 'back' + *chorein*, 'to give place, withdraw'. See *OED*, s.v. 'anchorite'.
2. The measurements I give are for an anchorhouse excavated at Leatherhead church in Surrey. On this and on living arrangements in anchorhouses generally see Anne K. Warren, *Anchorites and their Patrons in Medieval England* (Berkeley: University of California Press, 1985), pp. 29–41.
3. For an example of such a ceremony see the *Servicium recludendi* in London, BL, MS Cotton Vespasian D. xv, fos. 61v.–65r., as edited in Henry A. Wilson, *The Pontifical of Magdalen College*, Henry Bradshaw Society 39 (London, 1910), pp. 243–4. This service is summarized in English in Warren, *Anchorites and their Patrons*, pp. 97–8.
4. For an annotated list of these rules see Warren, *Anchorites and their Patrons*, pp. 294–8.
5. Warren, *Anchorites and their Patrons*, pp. 18–29. There is a rich appendix detailing the evidence we have for anchorites in England (750 have left some trace) in Rotha Mary Clay, *The Hermits and Anchorites of England* (London: Methuen, 1914), pp. 203–63.
6. The most readily accessible version of this text is *Ancrene Wisse: Guide for Anchoresses*, trans. Hugh White (Harmondsworth, Middlesex: Penguin, 1993), and all quotations here will be taken from this translation and cited by page number in my text. Another excellent translation is provided in *Anchoritic Spirituality: Ancrene Wisse and Associated Works*, trans. and intro. Anne Savage and Nicholas Watson (New York: Paulist Press, 1991), pp. 41–207. There is as yet no modern edition of the whole of the Middle English text, but a useful point of entry into its language is provided by *Ancrene Wisse, Parts Six and Seven*, ed. Geoffrey Shepherd (Exeter: Short Run Press, 1985; first published, 1959) and the parallel text and translation of parts 7 and 8 in Bella Millett and Jocelyn Wogan-Browne, *Medieval English Prose for Women: The Katherine Group and Ancrene Wisse* (Oxford: Clarendon Press, 1990), pp. 110–49. All of these translations and editions are versions of the later, revised, text of *Ancrene Wisse* (generally called 'Corpus', after Corpus Christi College, Cambridge MS 402, the manuscript in which this text is found), but several earlier versions of the rule also survive.
7. Julian of Norwich, *A Revelation of Love*, ed. Marion Glasscoe (University of Exeter Press, 1976; rev. edn 1986). Quotations from Julian will be taken from this edition and cited by page number in my text. Julian refers to both 'revelations' (p. 1) and 'shewings' (p. 8) but editions traditionally choose one of these words for the work's title.
8. On 'self and religious rules' see Linda Georgianna, *The Solitary Self: Individuality in the Ancrene Wisse* (Cambridge, MA: Harvard University Press, 1981), pp. 8–31. See also Elizabeth Robertson, *Early English Devotional Prose and the Female Audience* (Knoxville: University of Tennessee Press, 1990), pp. 44–76.
9. See Books 1 and 2 in *The Ethics of Aristotle: The Nichomachean Ethics*, trans. J. A. K. Thomson, rev. Hugh Tredennick (Harmondsworth, Middlesex: Penguin, 1976), esp. pp. 83–4 and 91–2 (from which the quoted phrases are taken).
10. Peter Brown, *The Making of Late Antiquity* (Cambridge, MA: Harvard University Press, 1978), p. 86.

11. *The Life of Christina of Markyate: A Twelfth-Century Recluse*, ed. and trans. C. H. Talbot (Oxford: Clarendon Press, 1959; reprinted 1987), also reprinted as Medieval Academy Reprints for Teaching 39 (University of Toronto Press, 1998), pp. 103–5. Subsequent references to the *Life* are given by page number in the text.

12. Friedrich Nietzsche, *On the Genealogy of Morals*, pp. 449–599 in *Basic Writings of Nietzsche*, ed. and trans. Walter Kaufmann (New York: Random House, 1968), pp. 520–1.

13. Warren, *Anchorites and their Patrons*, p. 104.

14. Jocelyn Wogan-Browne, 'Chaste Bodies: Frames and Experiences', in *Framing Medieval Bodies*, ed. Sarah Kay and Miri Rubin (Manchester University Press, 1994), pp. 24–42 (p. 27).

15. Sarah Beckwith, 'Passionate Regulation: Enclosure, Ascesis, and the Feminist Imaginary', *South Atlantic Quarterly* 93 (1994): 803–24, at 808. In this important article, Beckwith shows how the body is 'psychically projected' in *Ancrene Wisse* through the very rules which attempt to control it (pp. 807–11).

16. Aelred of Rievaulx, 'A Rule of Life for a Recluse', trans. Mary Paul Macpherson, in *Treatises and the Pastoral Prayer*, Cistercian Fathers series 2 (Kalamazoo: Western Michigan University, Medieval Institute Publications, 1971; 2nd printing: 1982), pp. 41–102 (p. 80). Hereafter citations to this text will be from this translation and cited by page number in my text.

17. Karl Marx, *The Holy Family*, trans. R. Dixon (Moscow: Foreign Languages Publishing House, 1956), p. 162.

18. Sally Thompson, *Women Religious: The Founding of the English Nunneries after the Norman Conquest* (Oxford: Clarendon Press, 1991), p. 30. See also the whole of the chapter on 'Hermits and Anchoresses' (pp. 16–37).

19. For the early reference to 'three sisters' see *The English Text of Ancrene Riwle (Cotton Nero A.xiv)*, ed. Mabel Day, EETS os 225 (1952), p. 85, and, for a translation of the relevant passage, see E. J. Dobson, *The Origins of Ancrene Wisse* (Oxford: Clarendon Press, 1976), pp. 1–2.

20. See Christopher Holdsworth, 'Hermits and the Powers of the Frontier', *Reading Medieval Studies* 16 (1990): 55–76.

21. Sigmund Freud, 'On Narcissism: an Introduction', pp. 59–97 in *The Penguin Freud Library*, vol. 2 (*On Metapsychology: The Theory of Psychoanalysis*), trans. James Strachey (Harmondsworth, Middlesex: Penguin, 1984; reprinted 1991), p. 96.

22. See Jacques Lacan, 'The Mirror Stage as Formative of the Function of the "I" as Revealed in Psychoanalytic Experience', pp. 1–7 in *Ecrits: A Selection*, trans. Alan Sheridan (New York: W. W. Norton, 1977), p. 5.

23. Caroline Walker Bynum, *Holy Feast and Holy Fast: The Religious Significance of Food to Medieval Women* (Berkeley: University of California Press, 1987), p. 246.

24. Nietzsche, *On the Genealogy of Morals*, pp. 566–7; and for 'The Meaning of Ascetic Ideals' generally, see the whole of the 'Third Essay' of this work (pp. 533–99).

25. See David Aers, 'The Humanity of Christ: Reflections on Orthodox Late Medieval Representations', in David Aers and Lynn Staley, *The Powers of the Holy: Religion, Politics and Gender in Late Medieval English Culture*

(University Park: Pennsylvania State University Press, 1996), pp. 15–42, esp. pp. 30–8.

26. Jacques Derrida, *The Gift of Death*, trans. David Wills (University of Chicago Press, 1992).

27. Beckwith, 'Passionate Regulation', p. 808.

28. On confession and penance in *Ancrene Wisse* see Georgianna, *Solitary Self*, pp. 79–119.

29. Michel Foucault, *The History of Sexuality*, vol. 1 (An Introduction), trans. Robert Hurley (New York: Random House, 1978), p. 60. On Foucault, confession as productive of self-knowledge, and *Ancrene Wisse* see also Beckwith, 'Passionate Regulation', pp. 813–16.

30. Foucault, *History of Sexuality*, p. 61.

31. Judith Butler, *The Psychic Life of Power: Theories in Subjection* (Stanford University Press, 1997), p. 67.

32. G. W. F. Hegel, *Phenomenology of Spirit*, trans. A. V. Miller (Oxford University Press, 1977), p. 117.

33. Hegel, *Phenomenology of Spirit*, pp. 118–19.

8

SARAH SALIH

At home; out of the house

And a-noon þe creature was stabelyd in hir wyttys & in her reson as wel as euyr sche was be-forn, and preyd hir husbond as so soon as he cam to hir þat sche myght haue þe keys of þe botery [buttery] to takyn hir mete & drynke as sche had don be-forn. Hyr maydens & hir kepars cownseld hym he xulde [should] delyuyr hir no keys, for þei seyd sche wold but ȝeue [give] away swech [such] good as þer was, for sche wyst not what sche seyde as þei wende [thought]. Neuyr-þe-les, hir husbond, euyr hauyng tendyrnes & compassyon of hir, comawndyd þei xulde delyuyr to hyr þe keyys.[1]

That delivery of the household keys marks Margery Kempe's recovery from the madness which had kept her confined to her bed for eight months following the birth of her first child. The keys embody the circumscribed, but real, authority over her household, its resources and its servants which, as a married woman of the urban elite, she might normally expect. Her servants, perhaps aware of the sometimes inconvenient consequences of religious conversion, fear that Margery, like other urban holy women, will engage in excessive charity, but at this stage her vocation takes less dramatic forms, and she is content to resume her former role in the household. Margery does not tell us what she did with the keys once she had regained them. Her *Book* is interested in housewifery only when it can be shown to have spiritual significance, as when Margery undertakes the nursing of her aged husband as a penance for her earlier sins (p. 181). Margery and her amanuenses assume that she is of interest only insofar as she is not a housewife, and her later spiritual career demands that she leave the house and her duties there. This chapter is about the life she refused, and about everything symbolized by her keys.

We are concerned here, paradoxically in a companion to medieval women writers, with the vast majority of medieval women who wrote nothing more than family letters and household accounts, if that; who were not mystics; who apparently accepted the roles prescribed for them. There are too many variables to attempt here a full-scale survey of the lives of medieval laywomen in their households. Class, location, and life-cycle all intersect with gender: general statements about the experience of medieval women almost invariably need qualification. P. J. P. Goldberg's study of the records of York's ecclesiastical court finds fluctuations in women's circumstances over relatively short periods of time and within relatively minor differences of status: urban young women in the late fourteenth century had more autonomy than their rural sisters in their choice of husbands.[2] One version of the didactic poem, 'The Good Wife Taught her Daughter', assumes that a housewife will routinely sell goods in the market place, and warns her only not to get drunk on the proceeds; yet John Paston III wrote of his sister's marriage to the family's steward: 'he shold neuer haue my good wyll for to make my sustyr to selle kandyll and mustard in Framlyngham'.[3] Entirely proper wifely behaviour in the one case is a shocking breach of class status in the other, perhaps all the more so because of the Pastons' relatively recent rise to gentility.[4] Even 'lay women' is not as clear-cut a category as it initially appears: many vowesses continued to live in the world, combining the management of property with religious observance, and nuns in this period increasingly withdrew from the communal life to form households within convents.[5] Lay women and nuns visited each other, and set down in one another's spaces both groups probably felt quite at home.

Nevertheless, it is possible to identify some persistent themes by concentrating on depictions of women within and without their households, and the kinds of behaviour considered appropriate to each location, focusing both on historical evidence of household-based activity and on the literary and didactic texts in which these activities were prescribed, imagined, and policed. Sources of all kinds confirm that the house is *the* privileged locus for medieval women: notionally, this is where the good woman can be found, busy about her domestic duties. The Book of Proverbs defines female virtue and female vice with reference to domestic space. In a passage containing the germ of the medieval conduct book, the good woman is placed in the household, and valued for her work there, particularly the provision of food and clothing to household members.[6] This biblical ideal evidently remained relevant, for Christine de Pizan paraphrased it as advice to women of the urban elite.[7] The harlot, conversely, is 'talkative and wandering, not bearing to be quiet, not able to abide still at home, now abroad, now in the streets, now lying in wait near the corners'.[8] The opposition between the good woman in the household and the bad woman in the street continues to inform medieval texts of all genres, which write gendered morality in spatial terms. 'Wandrynge by the weye', in *The Canterbury Tales*, is a transparent euphemism for female sexual transgression, an activity automatically suspected of any woman in the wrong place.[9] It is perhaps unsurprising that the anchoritic readership of *Ancrene Wisse* should be warned of the dangers of leaving the anchorhold by the example of Dina, and yet the same exemplum is apparently equally relevant to the non-enclosed aristocratic secular women addressed some two hundred years later by *The Book of the Knight of the Tower*.[10] Both texts acknowledge that Dina was the victim of rape, which, nevertheless, she is held to have invited by the act of leaving the house: as the Knight explains, 'by a foolysshe woman cometh many euyllis & domages'.[11] A woman outside of her proper location is by definition 'a foolysshe woman'. This perception can be shown to have influenced practice: Goldberg argues that Thomas Nesfeld of York relied on Proverbs when opposing his wife Margery's petition for a separation on the grounds of cruelty.[12] Thomas's witnesses successfully claimed that his violence against Margery was provoked and justified by her refusal to stay within the household: 'the said Margery left her home in the parish of Bishophill and went to a house, the which this witness does not remember, in the city of York without and contrary to the said Thomas, her husband's mandate and precept, and stayed there from noon of that day until the darkness of night'.[13] The court's rejection of Margery's petition testifies to its disapproval of such behaviour. Even Christine de Pizan's celebration of both the domestic and non-domestic achievements of women, often identified as protofeminist, locates them firmly in an architecture, a City of Ladies conceptualized as a household headed by the Virgin Mary.[14]

Women were found in the medieval household as its permanent or temporary head, as wives, daughters, boarders, servants, and apprentices, all categories with differing privileges and responsibilities. They were always in a minority in elite households, which were staffed largely by men who performed many of the tasks usually classified as female today, such as cooking and cleaning, leaving only laundry and sewing as female preserves.[15] Sewing, however, was so strongly associated with women that the Virgin Mary herself miraculously appeared to Thomas Becket to help him to mend his hairbreeches.[16] The lists of the household of Sir John Howard in 1455 and 1467 confirm men's numerical dominance: in the first list Howard's mother, wife, and four daughters are attended by five gentlewomen, and the only other woman in the entire household is the wife of one of the yeomen. There are thirty-four gentlemen and yeomen servants. In the 1467 list the number of gentlewomen has risen to seven, and 'Margery Alpha and her dawter' appear among the grooms; meanwhile the household has expanded considerably, now maintaining ninety-one gentlemen, yeomen, and grooms.[17] A woman would usually have headed a household only in widowhood, though this was not an uncommon occurrence.[18] However, as we will see, women of gentry level and above might temporarily head the household while their husbands were absent: thus all such wives had to have the necessary skills to run the household. The medieval household was typically based around a nuclear family but also frequently included more distant relatives as well as unrelated people in various capacities. Adolescent or young adult children might move into other households as servants, boarders or apprentices, depending on the relative status of the two households. Margaret Paston, for example, asked her son to find a gentlewoman prepared to take his sister as a boarder, 'for we be eythere of vs wery of othere' (1, no. 201). These younger women were presumably trained to run their own future households by observing the senior lady, their mother, hostess, or employer: as Agnes Paston reminded her daughter Elizabeth when she paid for her to stay with Lady Pole, 'che must vse hyr-selfe to werke redyly as other jentylwomen don' (1, no. 28). Such work surely included learning household management. While in others' households, such young women were under their authority and protection: employers might, for example, take on the familial responsibility of arranging servants' marriages.[19]

What did women do within households? As we would expect, they did domestic labour, but the division between domestic and non-domestic does not match the modern one. The virtuous housewife of Proverbs, whose labour is entirely within and for the benefit of her household, is, in the context of medieval England, an idealized figure. The household was not only conceived of as a private sphere: it was both family dwelling and workplace. Although the actual activities which took place in the household obviously varied considerably across social levels, women were routinely found as active partners of their male relatives running the family business, whether that was a small farm, an urban workshop, or a great estate. Female apprentices learnt a trade as well as domestic skills within the household, and it was entirely usual for artisans in some crafts to train their wives and daughters to assist them.[20] Rural women brewed ale primarily to provide for their households but also sold the surplus to neighbours: domestic labour here led readily to commercial enterprise.[21] Margery Kempe's business ventures began with brewing, a traditionally female occupation. Although Margery was well enough informed about the technicalities of the work to identify its problems – 'þe berm [barm] wold fallyn down þat alle þe ale was lost' – she did not brew herself, but funded the enterprise and employed servants (pp. 9–10). In this instance a woman's household task was transformed into a large-scale commercial concern, so that she became 'on of þe grettest brewers in þe town N. a iij ʒer or iiij' (p. 9). Her next venture, into milling, perhaps shows her using the confidence gained from the first to branch out into commercial activities not usually associated with women, but she still, tactically, identified the enterprise as domestic, 'a newe huswyfre' (p. 10).

Farther down the social scale there is evidence of the variety of women's activities within the household. The 'Ballad of the Tyrannical Husband' lists the duties of a ploughman's wife with no servant: milking, making butter and cheese, caring for children, tending poultry, brewing, baking, cooking, cleaning, making linen and woollen cloth.[22] The list thus includes many activities that would be performed in elite households by male servants. While the husband is identified with just one job, ploughing, which is located outside the household, the wife is envisaged as being centred in the household, but not entirely confined to it: she goes to the green to see to her geese, for example. The ballad thus imagines a fairly strict gendered division of labour, and its lost conclusion would presumably have mocked the husband's inability to cope with his wife's tasks. Its picture of women's labour is to some degree idealized: Barbara Hanawalt finds that 'medieval peasant women did not spend much of their time producing from scratch the basic necessities for their families' and relied in part on specialists for activities such as weaving and brewing.[23] The 'Anonymous Husbandry' is less rigid in its gendered allocation of tasks on a large estate: the dairy may be supervised by a man or a woman, although this is evidently normally a woman's job: 'if it were a man he ought to do the same things a dairymaid would do', perhaps because a woman is cheaper to employ than a man.[24] The dairymaid's duties include winnowing corn with a female assistant, caring for 'small stock' such as poultry and piglets, as well as preparing butter and cheese from the milk of the cows and sheep (pp. 424, 428). Rural women might also work alongside men doing the same jobs: the 'Husbandry' counts such women as, administratively, men: 'you should engage the reapers in a team, that is to say five men or women (hommes ou femmes), whichever you wish, and whom you term "men" (ke hom appelle des hommes), make one team' (p. 445).

Paradoxically, the private life of nobility and gentry almost always had a public aspect. Noblewomen and gentlewomen frequently ran estates in the temporary or permanent absence of their husbands, who were frequently called away to court, to war, or to deal with business or litigation. Robert Grosseteste's Household Rules for the Countess of Lincoln write indifferently of 'how lord or lady can examine their demesne estate': lordship is the same activity whether performed by lord or lady.[25] Rowena E. Archer identifies numerous examples of noblewomen administering their estates.[26] Philippa Maddern argues that the Paston family's definition of honourable behaviour included many activities, such as maintaining relationships with clients, patrons, and friends, which were as likely to be done by women as by men even when the men were at home. The women of the Paston family were central to the family's project, and many of their activities were not gender-specific.[27]

The activities of Margaret, wife of John Paston I, offer a convenient example. The Paston Letters typically show Margaret located in one of the Paston households in Norwich and Norfolk – she only once visited London – while John was absent, usually in London. How they shared responsibilities when he was at home is unclear, as there are of course no letters covering these periods. The letters covering their separations show Margaret tirelessly representing the Paston interests: collecting rents, ordering woods felled, selling wool, involving herself in marriage negotiations, and both reporting on and participating in the shifting networks of friendship, affinity, and clientage so essential to the maintenance of the family's position and property.[28] In a letter of 1449 she apologizes for moving from one Paston household to another for fear of kidnapping: 'be-seching ʒou þat ʒe be not displesyd þow I be com fro þat place þat ʒe left me in' (I, no. 132). Her rhetoric of having been placed in a household by her husband writes her as far more passive than her actions suggest that she actually was: the letter is itself a performance of good wifeliness as well as a report on events. Despite her apology, she had assessed the situation and made the decision to move: she exercised effective autonomy within a fictive framework of deference and passivity. The threat of kidnapping was to be taken seriously: a year earlier, anticipating the need to defend their manor of Gresham, she famously wrote to John with a shopping list of crossbows, almonds, sugar, and cloth for the children's gowns. In this letter Margaret made the military judgment that the manor of Gresham could not be defended with longbows and so crossbows would be needed. She also, presumably, planned to spend the quieter moments of the siege seeing to the family's clothing and food supplies (I, no. 130). Although she was later to complain to her son that soldiers 'set not be [would not take orders from] a woman as thei shuld set be a man', it is clear from John Paston's petition to the Chancellor, complaining that 'riotous peple brake, dispoiled, and drew doun the place of your seid besecher in the seid toun and drafe out his wiff and seruauntes there beyng', that she remained in residence at Gresham to oversee its defence in person (I, nos. 199, 38). Margaret's own term for this aspect of her role was 'captenesse', a word otherwise unrecorded in Middle English and so perhaps showing a gap between the expected and the actual household duties of women (I, no. 180). The Paston household was an economic and political as well as a domestic unit, and Margaret's responsibilities as its housewife correspondingly various.

Women's notional placement within the household may thus include activities for its benefit which take place elsewhere: the household is as much a metaphorical concept as a concrete location. Even when inside her household, a woman is not necessarily in private in the sense of being free from observation: Karma Lochrie argues that though women may represent the private sphere for men, this function exposes women themselves to scrutiny.[29] The household can be imagined as a theatre in which all members perform their assigned roles, observed by the others. Although duties are often shared, roles are gendered: women must perform as good women. Even within the household, values attach to different spaces, and how a woman's presence registers varies. It is possible that the few women in an elite household such as Sir John Howard's would have been confined to certain parts of the building. Roberta Gilchrist argues that the architecture of high-status households constructs a series of consistent binary divisions between public and private, male and female, hall and chamber.[30] The Ménagier de Paris emphasizes Lucretia's chastity by locating her not only at home, but also in the inaccessible heart of her household 'within and in the innermost part of her house [dedans et ou plus parfont de son hostel], in a great chamber far from the road'.[31] Mark Girouard assembles evidence that it was common practice for women to feast alone in chambers while the masculine household ate in the hall.[32] A tale in *The Book of the Knight of the Tower* confirms the practice, and also raises the possibility that these different spaces might produce different gendered perspectives. In this exemplum, 'it happed at a feste that thre grete ladyes satte in a Closette / and spaken of theyr good auentures', discovering in the course of this conversation that they have all been courted by the same man, Boucicaut, 'a wyse man / and wel bespoken amonge alle other knyghtes' (p. 43). They send for him – presumably he is summoned from the hall, although his location is not specified in the text – and proceed to oppose the perception they have together developed in the feminine space of the closet to that of the masculine-dominated hall: 'we supposed that ye had ben feithfull and trewe / And ye are not but a trompeur [deceiver] and a mockar of ladyes' (p. 44). The text hastens to close down the subversive potential of the closet, having Boucicaut storm out in a temper leaving the ladies 'more abasshed than he was', but nevertheless, surely unintentionally, leaves open the possibility – or the fear – that gendered spaces may produce gendered values, and that female seclusion might also function as freedom from observation.

However, the gendered association of women with the private and men with the public parts of the household is not necessarily a full representation of medieval practice. The picture is complicated by the general retreat of the elite, both men and women, from hall to chambers during the later Middle Ages: relative privacy speaks of status as well as gender.[33] Other evidence suggests that gender segregation within the household was not always total. Women who headed households certainly could not be entirely secluded. Christine de Pizan's *Treasure* instructs the wise princess to dine in hall 'ordinarily, and especially on solemn days and feast days' (p. 61). Bishop

Grosseteste's rules for the Countess of Lincoln have a gender-neutral conception of lordship, in which a lord who happens to be a lady is instructed to take a formal meal in the hall as a statement of status: 'you yourself be seated at all times in the middle of the high table, that your presence as lord or lady [seignur ou dame] is made manifest to all and that you may plainly see on either side all the service and all the faults'.[34] Women other than the head of household might also dine in hall: a fifteenth-century treatise places gentlewomen on the second table in an earl's hall.[35] Another version of the Grosseteste rules adds to the discussion of eating in hall: 'Streytly for-bede ȝe that no wyfe be at ȝoure mete', presumably envisaging a clerical household.[36] Margery Kempe, however, reports dining as the guest of monks and bishops with some regularity: 'sche was set to mete wyth many worthy clerkys & prestys & swyers [squires] of þe Bysshoppys, and þe Bysshop hym-self sent hir ful gentylly of hys own mees [portion]' (pp. 34–5; cf. pp. 26, 109).

Women, therefore, might in some circumstances appear in the hall, and men likewise in the chamber. Kim Phillips critiques Gilchrist's analysis, citing literary and historical evidence that suggests that although noblewomen might usually have slept, worshipped, and given birth in all-female company, at other times they mingled with men.[37] As the same rooms were used for different purposes at different times of the day – a chamber might function as dining-room, reception-room, and bedroom – it is only for limited periods of time that any space could have been designated as unambiguously private. Certainly, the lord and his intimates would have access to the chambers, and even in their absence, male attendants would serve the women. Eleanor de Montfort employed one Roger of the Chamber to organize her baths.[38] Christine de Pizan's *Treasure* advises princesses to employ married men for service in chambers, and warns against men who visit 'to play and divert themselves in the apartments of the ladies and maidens' (pp. 86, 117). The ladies in the Knight's exemplum do not hesitate to invite Boucicaut into their closet, and in another of his stories, a knight's wife is punished for eating privately in her 'garderobe' with her husband's clerk and servants: in this space, 'the men and wymmen iaped [played, fooled around] to geder eche with other' (p. 18). As with the Boucicaut story, an enclosed space to which women are confined can be reinterpreted as a secluded space within which women's contact with men is invisible and thus unregulated.

If a woman's invisibility in her chamber is troublesome, so too is her visibility at her window. The writings of moralists and poets use the window as the paradigm of the dangerous threshold, through which unregulated contact, threatening female chastity, may occur. Scenes of women coming to grief through the symbolic penetration of looking through windows recur in medieval writing, scenes in which reader and writer observe the woman framed in her window as she simultaneously observes or is observed by the outside world. Christine de Pizan is in a minority in imagining a window scene in which a woman displays her exemplary performance of her household responsibilities: her wise gentlewoman in the *Treasure* supervises her estate workers from her window (p. 131). More typically, in men's writing, such looking is dangerous. The Knight of the Tower retells the biblical story of David and Bathsheba as a warning to women against visibility: 'This Bersabee ones kembed & wesshed her heer at a wyndowe where as kyng dauid myght wel see her' (p. 107). The erotic potential of windows is such that the old woman in the *Romance of the Rose* satirically advises girls to admit their lovers through the window even if the door would be more convenient.[39] The Ménagier de Paris translates this sense of danger into practical instruction when he advises his wife to ensure that their younger maidservants are lodged well away from the windows of the house (pp. 219–20). The window scenes in Chaucer's *Troilus and Criseyde* are full of erotic disturbance, which is then moralized in John Lydgate's retelling of the story. The conventional misogyny of Lydgate's *Troy Book* writes sexual transgression in spatial terms, but assumes also that *any* space can be problematic:

(As seith Guydo), yit al day men may se	
It shewed oute at large fenestrallis,	[windows]
On chaumbres hiye, & lowe doun in hallis,	[high]
And in wyndowes eke in euery strete;	[also]
And also eke men may with hem mete	[meet with them]
At pilgrymages and oblaciounes,	[thanksgivings]
At spectacles in cytes and in townys	[cities]
(As seith Guydo), and al is for to selle.[40]	[everything]

The focus on the 'fenestrallis' both admits outsiders to the chambers and halls of the household and also seems to allow the women to emerge into public. The very existence of windows dissolves the demarcation of spaces by gender: suddenly women are everywhere, overflowing the boundaries of their households, their visibility implying their availability.

The evidence for women's enclosure in inner spaces of their households is thus ambiguous, and their enclosure within the household itself does not amount to a literal, physical imprisonment. The enclosure may have been as nominal as the enclosure of nuns can be shown to be.[41] Margery Kempe was asked whether she had her husband's permission to make a pilgrimage away from home, but her response to the question: 'Why fare ȝe þus wyth me mor þan ȝe don wyth oþer pilgrimys þat ben her, wheche han no lettyr no mor þan I haue?' suggests that the requirement was a technicality

(p. 122). Like nuns, secular women may be visible outside their households so long as the purpose and manner of their public appearance is properly regulated, and for the details of such regulation, we turn to the conduct book.

Conduct literature works on at least two levels to produce the apparently voluntary containment of women within their households.[42] It works to contain women literally, but also to produce women who have so interiorized the values of the household that they will carry them with them even when elsewhere. Peter Stallybrass outlines the threefold and mutually implicated enclosure of the chaste body, the silent mouth, and the closed door, which makes women 'patriarchal territories'.[43] All these layers are relevant here, but none are unqualified. Conduct literature directed to secular women does not order silence, enclosure, and perpetual virginity: total segregation may be recommended to nuns – and then as the statement of an ideal rather than a description of practice – but is never practicable for other women. For secular women, the body, the mouth, and the door cannot remain shut for ever. Nevertheless, their behaviour is still subject to gender-specific regulation. Conduct literature proposes an ideal of sober speech – in Christine de Pizan's words, 'controlled speech and sensible eloquence' – faithful marital sexuality and journeys outside of the house to a limited set of places.[44] *The Book of the Knight of the Tower* is, as Cynthia Ho argues, extremely anxious about the dangers of allowing women to speak, but even this text must allow women to advise and reprove their husbands in the privacy of marriage and the home: the Knight represents himself as being defeated in argument by his own wife's superior sense and morality.[45]

Conduct books typically offer their women readers a mixture of piety, instructions for self-formation, and practical advice on the running of households: they aim to produce a woman obedient to and yet also the trustworthy deputy of her husband, a regular churchgoer and astute negotiator, who can kill fleas, clean linen, order feasts, and keep her servants in order. The housewife is to be formed both within and alongside her household: keeping the two ordered are parallel processes. The opening of the Ménagier de Paris's treatise on household management locates the production of a good woman in the private space of the marital bedchamber, where the elderly Ménagier recalls his fifteen-year-old bride offering herself as a blank slate to be formed as wife and housewife:

> beseeching me humbly in our bed [en moy priant humblement en nostre lit], as I remember, for the love of God not to correct you harshly before strangers nor before our own folk, but rather each night, or from day to day, in our

chamber, to remind you of the unseemly or foolish things [les descontenances ou simplesses] done in the day or days past, and chastise you, if it pleased me, and then you would strive to amend yourself according to my teaching and correction.[46]

In conduct literature, the regulation of the self and of the household are complementary activities, the feminine version of the self-control required of elite men as a prerequisite to control of others.

Thus the state of the household may be read from the state of the housewife. Her demeanour when abroad identifies her with the household of which she is the embodiment. The Ménagier cites the negative example of 'certain drunken, foolish, or ignorant women [d'aucunes yvrongnes, foles, ou non sachans], who have no regard for their honour, nor for the honesty of their estate or of their husbands, and go with roving eyes and head horribly reared up like a lion [les yeux ouvers, la teste espoventablement levee comme un lion], their hair straying out of their wimples and the collars of their shifts and robes one upon the other'.[47] His own wife is to demonstrate her perfect discipline, which speaks of the perfect discipline of her household: her neat dress and sober demeanour testify to her contented husband, obedient maids, clean house, and generous hospitality. Eyes, as the windows of the individual, giving access to the interior, come in for as much attention as the windows of the household, with the Ménagier, the Knight, and the Good Wife all contributing their comments on the subject. The Knight, like the Ménagier, recognizes the discipline of the body as a symbol of the respectability of the household: a woman 'stedfast in lokyng' 'shalle ye holde you in youre estate more ferme and sure' (p. 25). The management of eyes is class- as well as gender-specific: as Phillips shows, the medieval lady looked ahead with a steady gaze, while downcast eyes signified social inferiority.[48]

In conduct literature generally, women may go to certain defined places outside the household without compromising their reputations: it is indiscriminate wandering 'fram house to house' which is forbidden.[49] The Knight assumes that his daughters will need to know how to conduct themselves in public situations: they may dance and sing at the feasts to which ladies of their status are properly invited, but should 'haue alwey by ye somme of youre frendes or of youre seruauntes'.[50] They should, that is, remain literally surrounded by, within, their households, even when physically elsewhere. When outside, the good woman is to adopt a demeanour which exemplifies her control over her speech and sexuality, thus defining the nature of her interaction with the outside world. Conversely, prostitutes in many cities were ordered to wear distinctive articles of clothing: the need to distinguish them visually indicates that they shared public space with non-prostitute women.[51] In 'The Good Wife Taught her Daughter', modest conduct is a sign that a woman carries the protection of the household with her.

> Aquinte noȝt with ilk a man þou metest in þe strete; [every]
> þou he ȝiue him to þe, schortli þou him grete.
> Lat him go bi þe wai, bi him þou ne stonde,
> þat he þoruȝ no uilenie þin herte noþing chonge. [through]
>
> (p. 162)

The poem's ideal is not segregation, but self-discipline: it envisages a daughter who will be in the street, who will speak to men in public, and who will have to use her own judgment in striking the proper balance of being polite without being flirtatious. She is not signalling her unavailability, exactly, but the severely restricted terms of her availability: she must demonstrate by her dress and behaviour that she is neither a 'genttyll woman, or a callot'.[52] A young woman visible in public must expect constant scrutiny, but the poem wants to train her to be a subject as well as an object: she must speak, look, and act. The Good Wife also tells her daughter how to deal with an offer of marriage: 'Scheu hit to þine frendes, no forhele [conceal] hit noȝt. / Sit noȝt bi him, no stond, þar sunne [sin] mai be wroȝt' (p. 158). Instruction is necessary precisely because the young woman is assumed to have enough mobility and autonomy to meet a suitor in private, should she so choose, and to make her own decision about whether to accept an offer of marriage. In attempting to limit her autonomy, the poem also shows its potential extent. Felicity Riddy argues that the intended audience of the poem would have included urban women working as servants, a group which included women who certainly made their own decisions about offers of marriage, as matrimonial cases show.[53] Not all followed the Good Wife's advice to discuss offers with their friends and many can be shown to have taken the initiative in courtship.

Ann Rosalind Jones defines the fundamental paradox of the conduct book: its investment in the conscious production of what it also claims to be natural behaviour.[54] It is an idealistic genre: an aristocratic conduct book such as *The Book of the Knight of the Tower* ignores the responsibilities of estate management that the Knight's daughters would surely have had to deal with, and substitutes the management of personal, especially marital, relationships and the development of individual self-discipline. It suggests that to become a lady is in itself a project. It is firmly gendered: where general treatises on estate management ignore gender, the conduct book as a rule confines itself to gender-specific instructions. The Knight's daughters are offered advice on motherhood as well as general deportment, but nothing is said about the duties they would have expected to share with their husbands. The genre is open to analysis from the perspective of the performative construction of gender, because it explicitly demands the production of gendered identities in culturally specific actions. 'The goode wif thaught hir doughter fele [many] tyme and ofte gode woman for to be': being a good woman does not come naturally, but is the product of intense training, which the Good Wife can provide because she herself has been so trained (pp. 159, 170). Everything is legible and significant: dress, gesture, speech, and place all embody the discipline of which the individual is both subject and performer.

With performativity comes the potential for instability. The self formed in compliance with the conduct book's instructions need not be regarded as inauthentic if the self is imagined as being formed from the outside in, or if the importance of the surface is emphasized, but the process certainly has the potential to go awry. Christine de Pizan openly acknowledges that being a successful princess demands self-conscious dissimulation: 'she should be so wise and circumspect that no one can perceive that she does it calculatingly'.[55] Shame lies in being caught out in such dissimulation: the stress on outward demeanour almost inevitably produces the figure of a woman who, if she chooses, could be other than her dutiful performance of good womanhood. The very existence of conduct books implies the presence of women who need their instruction because they are not already obedient to it. Their addresses and instructions to women readers unintentionally but unavoidably present different models of behaviour, different ways of being a woman: an alluring vista of flirtation, fine clothes, and trips to wrestling matches and taverns. The parents of Christina of Markyate, hoping to persuade their daughter to marry rather than enter a convent, quite logically reversed the instructions that would later be codified in conduct literature: they took her to feasts, encouraging her to dress well, drink wine, and converse freely.[56] We have already seen how the story of the three ladies at a feast can yield a counter-reading: conduct books offer rich opportunities to the resisting reader. 'Doutter, ȝif þou wilt ben a wif', the Good Wife begins: thus assuming that the reader does wish to become a wife, but also, with that 'if', opening up other possibilities and other disciplinary programmes.[57] Conduct books address the reader as dutiful daughter, willing learner, promising to induct her into womanhood. In so doing they produce excess, in the possibility that once so interpellated into subjecthood, she will become an agent and will have the option not to perform her womanhood in the recommended manner. The alternatives to good womanhood include the saint as well as the harlot. To return to the starting point of this chapter, *The Book of Margery Kempe* represents a medieval woman whose saintliness is marked precisely by its distance from the secular model of good womanhood to which she had initially been trained.

NOTES

I am grateful to John Arnold, Anke Bernau, Charlie Dickinson, Samantha Riches and especially to the editors of this volume for their comments on drafts of this chapter: any remaining errors are of course my own. I am grateful to Dr Kim M. Phillips for sending me a copy of a section of her unpublished work, 'The Medieval Maiden: Young Womanhood in Late Medieval England'.

1. *The Book of Margery Kempe*, ed. Sanford Brown Meech and Hope Emily Allen, EETS OS 212 (Oxford University Press, 1940), p. 8. All references are to this edition.

2. P. J. P. Goldberg, '"For Better, For Worse": Marriage and Economic Opportunity for Women in Town and Country', *Women in Medieval English Society*, ed. Goldberg (Stroud: Sutton, 1997), pp. 112–13.

3. *The Good Wife Taught Her Daughter; The Good Wyfe Wold a Pylgremage; The Thewis of Gud Women*, ed. Tauno F. Mustanoja, Annales Academiae Scientiarum Fennicae BLXI 2 (Helsinki, 1948), p. 199; note that the other versions forbid selling altogether: see Felicity Riddy, 'Mother Knows Best: Reading Social Change in a Courtesy Text', *Speculum* 71 (1996): 75 for further discussion; *Paston Letters and Papers of the Fifteenth Century: Part 1*, ed. Norman Davis (Oxford: Clarendon Press, 1971), no. 332.

4. Colin Richmond, *The Paston Family in the Fifteenth Century: The First Phase* (Cambridge University Press, 1990), pp. 1–22.

5. For vowesses, see P. H. Cullum, 'Vowesses and Female Lay Piety in the Province of York, 1300–1530', *Northern History* 32 (1996): 21–41; Mary C. Erler, 'English Vowed Women at the End of the Middle Ages', *Mediaeval Studies* 57 (1995): 155–203; for nuns' households, Roberta Gilchrist, 'Medieval Bodies in the Material World: Gender, Stigma and the Body', in *Framing Medieval Bodies*, ed. Sarah Kay and Miri Rubin (Manchester University Press, 1994), p. 58; and for an example, *Visitations of Religious Houses in the Diocese of Lincoln, Vol. II: Records of Visitations held by William Alnwick, Bishop of Lincoln 1436–1449 Part 1*, ed. A. Hamilton Thompson (London: William Dawson and Sons, 1969), pp. 46–53.

6. Douay Bible: Proverbs 31: 10–31.

7. Christine de Pizan, *The Treasure of the City of Ladies or the Book of the Three Virtues*, trans. Sarah Lawson (Harmondsworth: Penguin, 1985), pp. 147–8. All references in the text are to this edition.

8. Proverbs 7: 10–12.

9. *Canterbury Tales* fragment 1 (A), line 467. See Barbara A. Hanawalt, 'At the Margins of Women's Space in Medieval Europe', Hanawalt, *'Of Good and Ill Repute': Gender and Social Control in Medieval England* (Oxford University Press, 1998) for further discussion.

10. *The Ancrene Riwle, from MS Corpus Christi College, Cambridge 402*, ed. and trans. Mary Salu (University of Exeter Press, 1990), p. 24; cf. Genesis 34: 1–2.

11. *Caxton's Book of the Knight of the Tower*, ed. M. Y. Offord, EETS ss 2 (Oxford University Press, 1971), p. 82.

12. P. J. P. Goldberg, 'Fiction in the Archives: the York Cause Papers as a Source for Later Medieval Social History', *Continuity and Change* 12 (1997): 439.

13. *Women in England c. 1275–1525: Documentary Sources*, ed. P. J. P. Goldberg (Manchester University Press, 1995), pp. 141–2.

14. Christine de Pizan, *The Book of the City of Ladies*, trans. Rosalind Brown-Grant (Harmondsworth: Penguin, 1999), p. 201.

15. Kate Mertes, *The English Noble Household 1250–1600: Good Governance and Politic Rule* (Oxford: Basil Blackwell, 1988), pp. 57–9; C. M. Woolgar, *The Great Household in Later Medieval England* (New Haven and London: Yale University Press, 1999), p. 96.

16. *Materials for the History of Thomas Becket, Archbishop of Canterbury*, ed. James Craigie Robertson, Rolls Series 67, 7 vols. (London: Longman, 1876), 2: 293.

17. *The Household Books of John Howard, Duke of Norfolk, 1462–1471, 1481–1483*, ed. Anne Crawford (Stroud: Alan Sutton, 1992), pp. xxxviii–xl, xl–xlii.

18. Mertes, *English Noble Household*, p. 54. Frances Underhill's study of Elizabeth de Burgh shows the considerable power that could be wielded by a wealthy widow: Frances Underhill, *For Her Good Estate* (London: Palgrave, 1999).

19. Goldberg ed., *Women in England*, pp. 110–14.

20. Maryanne Kowaleski and Judith M. Bennett, 'Crafts, Gilds and Women in the Middle Ages: Fifty Years After Marian K. Dale', in *Sisters and Workers in the Middle Ages*, ed. Bennett, Elizabeth A. Clark, Joan F. O'Barr, B. Anne Viten, and Sarah Westphal-Wihl (University of Chicago Press, 1989), pp. 16–17.

21. Judith M. Bennett, 'The Village Ale-Wife: Women and Brewing in Fourteenth-Century England', in *Women and Work in Pre-Industrial Europe*, ed. Barbara A. Hanawalt (Bloomington: Indiana University Press, 1986), p. 23.

22. *Reliquiae Antiquae: Songs and Carols*, 2, ed. Thomas Wright and James O. Halliwell (London: Percy Society, 1841), pp. 196–9.

23. Barbara A. Hanawalt, 'Peasant Women's Contribution to the Home Economy in Late Medieval England', in *Women and Work in Pre-Industrial Europe*, ed. Hanawalt, p. 8.

24. *Walter of Henley and Other Treatises on Estate Management and Accounting*, ed. Dorothea Oschinsky (Oxford: Clarendon Press, 1971), pp. 424–7.

25. Ibid., p. 391.

26. Rowena E. Archer, '"How Ladies . . . who Live on their Manors Ought to Manage their Households and Estates": Women as Landholders and Administrators in the Later Middle Ages', in *Women in Medieval English Society*, ed. P. J. P. Goldberg (Stroud: Sutton, 1997).

27. Philippa Maddern, 'Honour among the Pastons: Gender and Integrity in Fifteenth-Century English Provincial Society', *Journal of Medieval History* 14 (1988): 365.

28. *Paston Letters I*, for example, nos. 136, 150, 154.

29. Karma Lochrie, *Covert Operations: The Medieval Uses of Secrecy* (Philadelphia: University of Pennsylvania Press, 1999), p. 137.

30. Mark Girouard, *Life in the English Country House: A Social and Architectural History* (New Haven and London: Yale University Press, 1978), p. 56.

31. *Le Ménagier de Paris*, ed. Georgine E. Brereton and Janet M. Ferrier (Oxford: Clarendon Press, 1981), p. 53; *The Goodman of Paris (Le Ménagier de Paris): A Treatise on Moral and Domestic Economy by a Citizen of Paris (c. 1393)*, trans. Eileen Power (London: George Routledge and Sons, 1928), p. 102.

32. Girouard, *Life in the English Country House*, pp. 45–6.

33. Woolgar, *Great Household*, pp. 162–4; Girouard, *Life in the English Country House*, pp. 46–54.

34. *Walter of Henley*, p. 403.

35. Woolgar, *Great Household*, p. 161.

36. *The Babees Book*, ed. Frederick J. Furnivall, EETS os 32 (London: Trübner, 1868), p. 329; the provenance of this manuscript is unknown: *Walter of Henley*, p. 21.

37. Gilchrist, 'Medieval Bodies in the Material World', p. 51. Kim M. Phillips, 'The Medieval Maiden: Young Womanhood in Late Medieval England', PhD thesis, University of York, 1997, pp. 86–100.

38. Woolgar, *Great Household*, p. 167.

39. Guillaume de Lorris and Jean de Meun, *Romance of the Rose*, trans. Frances Horgan (Oxford University Press, 1994), p. 213.

40. John Lydgate, *Troy Book*, Chadwyck-Healey (Literature Online) Book III, lines 4322–9.

41. Penelope Johnson describes convent walls as 'permeable membranes', *Equal in Monastic Profession: Religious Women in Medieval France* (University of Chicago Press, 1991), p. 152, an assessment confirmed by my own work on English nuns: *Versions of Virginity in Late Medieval England* (Woodbridge: Brewer, 2001), pp. 127–51; see also Nancy Bradley Warren, *Spiritual Economies: Female Monasticism in Later Medieval England* (Philadelphia: University of Pennsylvania Press), 2001, esp. pp. 55–69.

42. Claire Sponsler, *Drama and Resistance: Bodies, Goods and Theatricality in Late Medieval England* (Minneapolis: University of Minnesota Press, 1997), pp. 68–72, stresses the extent to which the conduct book seeks to make discipline desirable.

43. Peter Stallybrass, 'Patriarchal Territories: the Body Enclosed', in *Rewriting the Renaissance: The Discourses of Sexual Difference in Early Modern Europe*, ed. Margaret W. Ferguson, Maureen Quilligan, Nancy Vickers (University of Chicago Press, 1986), p. 127.

44. Christine de Pizan, *Treasure of the City of Ladies*, p. 57.

45. Cynthia Ho, 'As Good as her Word: Women's Language in *The Knight of the Tour d'Landry*', in *The Rusted Hauberk: Feudal Ideals of Order and their Decline*, ed. Liam O. Purdon and Cindy L. Vitto (Gainesville: University Press of Florida, 1994), p. 106; *Knight of the Tower*, pp. 163–76.

46. *Ménagier de Paris*, p. 1; *Goodman of Paris*, p. 41.

47. *Ménagier de Paris*, p. 9; *Goodman of Paris*, p. 50.

48. Kim M. Phillips, 'Bodily Walls, Windows and Doors: the Politics of Gesture in Late Fifteenth-Century English Books for Women', in *Medieval Women: Texts and Contexts in Late Medieval Britain: Essays for Felicity Riddy*, ed. Jocelyn Wogan-Browne, Rosalynn Voaden, Arlyn Diamond, Ann Hutchinson, Carol M. Meale, Lesley Johnson (Turnhout: Brepols, 2000), p. 190.

49. *The Good Wife Taught her Daughter*, p. 160.

50. *Knight of the Tower*, p. 45.

51. Ruth Mazo Karras, *Common Women: Prostitution and Sexuality in Medieval England* (Oxford University Press, 1996), pp. 20–2.

52. *The Good Wife Taught her Daughter*, p. 173.

53. Riddy, 'Mother Knows Best', p. 83; Goldberg, 'For Better, For Worse'.

54. Ann Rosalind Jones, 'Nets and Bridles: Early Modern Conduct Books and Sixteenth-Century Women's Lyrics', in *The Ideology of Conduct: Essays on Literature and the History of Sexuality*, ed. Nancy Armstrong and Leonard Tennenhouse (London: Methuen, 1987), pp. 40–1.

55. Christine de Pizan, *Treasure of the City of Ladies*, p. 69.

56. *The Life of Christina of Markyate: A Twelfth-Century Recluse*, ed. and trans. C. H. Talbot (Oxford: Clarendon Press, 1959), p. 49.

57. *The Good Wife Taught her Daughter*, p. 158.

9

ALCUIN BLAMIRES

Beneath the pulpit

A sharp impression of medieval women's role 'beneath the pulpit' in the sense 'subjected to the institutional power of the Church' is first implied, and then defied, in Chaucer's *Friar's Tale*. This tale criticizes the abuse of ecclesiastical law to extort money from a woman. It is introduced by the Friar after he has ostensibly complimented the Wife of Bath on her learning, but urged her to leave discussion of serious moral matters to expert preachers and religious educators (male, university-trained, such as himself). Following this reassertion of masculine control of the theological domain the Friar proceeds to a tale expressly concerned with contested jurisdiction in which, however, an old woman unexpectedly has the final say. It will be useful to dwell on this tale by way of introduction to a chapter devoted to the rights, limitations, rituals, and contributions of women in relation to Mother Church.

The layered ironies of *The Friar's Tale* converge on *jurisdiccioun*. There is an archdeacon who has jurisdiction delegated from the bishop to punish offences against the Church's laws in the sexual, financial, doctrinal, and sacramental domain (3.1319–20). Part of this jurisdiction is delegated by the archdeacon to a summoner whose task is to track down offenders and issue summonses on pain of fine or excommunication ('Cristes curs', line 1347). Chaucer's pilgrim Friar hates summoners, and gloats that he himself is outside their remit: summoners have 'no jurisdiccioun' over his order (line 1330). The summoner in his tale, operating an extortion racket even as he embodies the long arm of the Church's terrestrial power, unthinkingly assumes self-exemption from any spiritual reckoning whatever. He fails, that is, to imagine himself 'beneath' that ultimate authority of which the pulpit is mediator.

Chaucer assigns to an old widow named Mabel the right – the spiritual jurisdiction – to precipitate the nemesis courted by the summoner. The summoner boasts to the devil whom he befriends in the tale that though Mabel is no easy prey he will exact twelve pence from her or summons her. In response to his bullying her replies are at first gracious, but when she protests poverty and innocence, the summoner threatens her over an alleged previous conviction for adultery. Incensed, Mabel swears on her own salvation that the allegations are false, and formally curses the summoner into the power of the devil unless he repents.

While the frankly uncontrite attitude of the summoner confirms the devil's right to take him, it is the woman's curse, something like an extra-legal lay excommunication, that has initiated this.[1] The widow's own earnest will, her maverick jurisdiction, overcomes corrupt ecclesiastical practice and even helps dispatch a flawed soul to hell. This means that the tale engages, on an interestingly democratized and gendered basis, with a controversy that the Wyclifites were promoting about the episcopal power of 'cursing'.[2] The tale affirms a spiritual power in cursing, but de-institutionalizes it, allows a mere lay woman to administer it.

Mabel becomes the commanding figure in the story. Although there may be a secondary option to read 'widow' as 'church', and although we are aware of the pull of the folktale formula assigning notable acts of redress to ostensibly weak victims, she recalls a long line of Christian heroines defying alien institutions; she is a latter-day St Katherine of Alexandria trouncing her oppressors. There is a distinct impression that women of the shire could tell bishops a thing or two.

It is a narrative that helps us to focus salient aspects of medieval woman 'beneath the pulpit'. First, it is consistent with the Friar's implied and on the whole orthodox distaste for intellectually ambitious 'preaching' women. It replaces that spectre with the safer prospect of a staunch champion of morality able to expose ecclesiastical fraud from a position of temporary unauthorized independence. Second, the tale ascribes strong piety to a lay woman, a traditional attribution, as we shall see. Third, the tale recalls, though it does not support, two negative pulpit stereotypes about women, one alleging their unstable sexual mores and the other their gullibility: these had been thought to justify women's disenfranchisement from ecclesiastical office. Fourth, in a more venerable sense the Friar nevertheless inscribes the possibility that women, particularly widows, are not spiritually unsuited to exercise a kind of sacerdotal function, notably when the encompassing male ecclesiastical establishment is corrupt. But the tale does all these things, of course, without actually presuming to alter institutional gender arrangements.

A more routine if fleeting impression of women beneath the pulpit (to stay for a moment with Chaucer's writing) is provided by the Sunday visit of a carpenter's wife to church in The Miller's Tale. Here Alisoun goes, face washed to a formidable brightness, 'Cristes owene werkes for to wirche' (1.3307–11). This may seem to invite the reader's condescension. For whom is that brightness, does superficiality lurk in that jingling of 'works to work', and is her mind on her importunate lodger Nicholas, whom she has agreed to satisfy? Yet she eludes satire here, her ordinary piety surviving even amidst the aromatic courting rituals of Absolon the parish clerk whose own mind is certainly not on Christ's works as he censes her assiduously among the other parish wives.

It is interesting that her husband apparently does not go with her to the church. Medieval writers provide incidental evidence to suggest that women's reputation for piety in this respect much exceeded men's. One feasible generalization about women beneath the pulpit, therefore, is that they attended church (and other places, where sermons were preached) in conspicuous numbers. A thirteenth-century German preacher, Berthold of Regensburg, declares: 'You women, you go more readily to church than men do; speak your prayers more readily than men; go to sermons more readily than men.' Peter Biller detects fact behind such rhetoric. Evidence appears, he suggests, in European inquisition trials concerning Catharism, for they disclose a deep penetration of Catholic Christianity into the lives of ordinary women – their presence at vigils, their orthodox conversations about basic doctrine.[3]

The very pressures that kept many women sequestered from the public eye doubtless enhanced the social attraction for them of church attendance. Their zeal in this is somewhat substantiated by misogynous insinuations about it. Women were alleged to frequent churches in order to be seen there, and to ogle men. Hence Dunbar imagines a merry widow man-hunting at 'kirk' with illuminated book wide open on knee and cloak drawn about her face to shield her roving eyes.[4] This sort of cheap satire is indignantly repudiated in Christine de Pizan's *City of Ladies* at one point. When Reason states that 'it's well known that women flock to churches in great numbers to listen to sermons, to make their confessions and to say their daily prayers', Christine mentions the insinuations of 'some writers' that women go there all dressed up, 'to show themselves off to men'. Reason retorts that 'pretty young girls' are heavily outnumbered in church by older women in plain clothing.[5]

In this passage Christine refrains from retaliatory satire, though satirists occasionally claimed that the chief oglers in church were male (as in a sardonic passage on flesh-hunting gallants in Gower's *Confessio amantis*).[6] Christine also refrains from asserting outright that women's churchgoing exceeds that of men, but she nevertheless gives that impression. There is no reason to doubt medieval women's conspicuous presence in churches and chapels.

Within, they might be segregated, like Bertilak's wife and her ladies in *Sir Gawain and the Green Knight*.[7] They might also, in certain conspicuous church rituals, be very pointedly distinguished from men. Thus, as Karma Lochrie reminds us, a woman's position was physically differentiated when making confession in the church. Prior to the introduction of the confessional box in the late sixteenth century, confession often took place in public with the confessee at the front of the congregation, facing the priest if male, but if female, preferably with her back to the priest. This was supposed to prevent the woman from becoming subject to, or prompting, the sexual attentions of the priest.[8]

Of course, the chief differentiation of women in church lay in the stark fact that they could not officiate there. In orthodox medieval Catholic doctrine they were absolutely excluded from the sacerdotal office. They were not to be ordained; they were not to administer sacraments – except baptism in an emergency; and they were not to preach – except in the case of abbesses preaching to nuns. Yet these were not uncontested matters. Since the debates about them – especially about preaching – are now little known, they are worth pausing over here.

An underlying obstacle was men's presumption that women could not generally attain or sustain the necessary authority to preach. We come back to a question of jurisdiction. In a vernacular religious handbook widely used in Britain in the fourteenth century, known as the *Speculum Christiani*, there is a definition of preaching that distinguishes it from more casual forms of teaching, partly in terms of the formality of assembly for the purpose, but more importantly in terms of persons to whom it is delegated: 'it longeth [belongs] to hem that been ordeynede ther-to, the whych haue iurediccion and auctorite, and to noon othyr'.[9] Any claim for women to have such jurisdiction and authority was hampered by notorious and formidable statements in the Bible: first, the Genesis declaration that Eve, after the Fall, was to be in the power of her husband; and second, St Paul's declarations that women should not teach, should remain silent in church, should have no authority over men, and should confine their questions to their husbands at home.

These routine justifications of a male monopoly over public speaking and preaching were characteristically buttressed by ascribing chronic instability to the feminine temperament. The same justification was trotted out to explain women's exclusion from judicial office. In a Middle English version of an encyclopaedic work, the reader is told that women's brains are characterized by 'lightnes' (frivolity) rather than 'sadnesse' (gravity). Women could be appointed as judges if it were not that 'Lyghtly they trowe þat men hem say [they readily believe whatever men tell them] / And as soone hit is away [just as quickly forget it].'[10] The English poet John Gower produced a variation on this conventional insult when in a passage elaborating the claim that God did not make women to lead, he wrote that women are like sieves: the 'record of their memory' is 'written in the wind'.[11] A millennium earlier, Ambrose was already alleging lack of mental consistency as a reason why the evangelical profession was assigned to men, even though Mary Magdalene was the first person to announce the news of Christ's resurrection to the male disciples.[12] To these claims that women were credulous and lacked intellectual staying-power and authoritative status, there was added sheer sexual paranoia. It was suggested that women instructing men in public were always going to incite desire in their auditors, however little they meant to.[13]

The case against women preaching was elaborated in the University of Paris in the later thirteenth century, in the long wake of scares about the activities of women in the Waldensian and other heterodox movements. The case was refurbished when the Lollard movement raised the spectre of lay ministry again in late fourteenth-century England. Readers who find the negative arguments numbingly predictable might be interested to learn that the theologians who rehearsed them also reckoned with serious contrary views.

The 'authority' argument was challenged in three ways. One was to interrogate the detail of St Paul's strictures against women 'teaching'. The extent of the *inclusiveness* intended by Paul had evidently been queried early in the history of the Church, to the alarm of the Greek exegete, Origen. In a commentary on Corinthians (c. AD 250) Origen saw fit to combat the public activity of the Montanist prophetesses Priscilla and Maximilla, not only by insisting on the non-'public' nature of the biblical precedents they cited (such as Deborah and Huldah in the Old Testament, Anna in the Gospels, and the four daughters of Philip whose prophesying is mentioned in the Acts of the Apostles), but also by promoting an inclusive reading of St Paul's injunction against women speaking out in church; 'if they will learn anything, let them ask their husbands at home: for it is a shame for women to speak in the church' (1 Corinthians 14: 35). Origen thought that the text here could not be referring only to women with 'husbands'. 'If it did, virgins would either be speaking out in an assembly, or be without anyone to teach them, and the same would be true of widows.' Could not 'husbands' therefore 'also include brother, kinsman, son'?[14]

The ambiguity remained, a chink in St Paul's prohibition and a cue for debate. Hence, in a discussion of women and preaching in the 1260s, the Franciscan Parisian master Eustache d'Arras concludes (contrary to the line taken by Origen) that St Paul means to speak of married women (*mulieribus nuptis*), those who are 'of the common status of women'; 'he does not speak of women specially picked out and privileged [to preach]'.[15] Eustache mainly intends to safeguard the preaching reputation of certain female saints, which we shall consider in a moment. But the negotiability of the Pauline position is apparent and continues to be an option for those challenging its blanket application. A Lollard called Walter Brut who was tried before the Bishop of Hereford for heresy in 1391–3 is reported to have argued that 'Paul does *not* state that women are *not able* to teach or to exercise authority over men – nor do I presume to affirm it, since women, devout virgins, have steadfastly preached the word of God and have converted many people while priests dared not speak a word.'[16]

The second way in which the 'authority' argument could be challenged was to appeal to an authorization higher than that of the Church. Unlicensed preaching was customarily denounced on the basis of a line in Paul's Epistle to the Romans, 'How shall they preach, unless they are sent?' (Romans 10: 15). An Oxford preaching manual of the fourteenth century declares that no unauthorized lay men, and no woman whatever, may preach; 'nor will it suffice for a person to say that he has been sent by God, unless he clearly proves this (for heretics customarily make this claim)'.[17]

Of course 'heretics' made this claim. The Waldensians made it. The Lollards made it. Among the Lollards, women therefore knew of it: at least, the Norfolk Lollard Margery Baxter is recorded to have believed that the sect leader in the area, William White, was 'ordained and sent by God'.[18] Doubtless this controversial fomulaic justification was rather widely known – not confined (as the debate about St Paul's exact meaning may have been) to university or sectarian circles. Orthodoxy itself paradoxically had recourse to the same justification in order to explain away the preaching powers associated with some of its own female role-models – since they constituted an awkward precedent on behalf of women's preaching authority. Notable examples of this would be the sister saints, Mary Magdalene and Martha, as well as St Katherine of Alexandria. The lives of these saints, as established in the time of the creation of the thirteenth-century *Golden Legend*, attributed great efficacy to their preaching. Eustache d'Arras confirms the belief – zealously held by many 'to the praise and glory of all women saints', he says – that holy women such as Mary Magdalene and Katherine 'merit celestial crowns, because even if they were not sent by a man (as by a prelate having that power), yet they preached both by instigation of the Holy Spirit and as sent by the Holy Spirit'. Theirs was a special, direct, spiritual authority.[19]

The preaching exploits associated with these and some other women saints are unambiguously spelled out in the medieval legends about them.[20] Women of all sorts, even if they could not read, had access to the legends and therefore to the saints' reputation for preaching, through sermons and of course through visual hagiography, especially if they worshipped in a church dedicated to one of the relevant saints. Women as a group might in fact find themselves particularly regaled with stories of biblical women and female saints. The *Meditations on the Life of Christ*, which became hugely popular by the end of the fourteenth century, was written for a woman. One famous Italian manuscript version of it provides elaborate narrative illustrations for episodes concerning, for example, the Samaritan woman and Mary Magdalene. The Samaritan woman, whose appeals to the citizens brought the people of a whole city out to hear Jesus, is another 'public-speaking' exemplar. Some male commentators, for instance Chrysostom and Abelard, enthused about her as a preacher and *magistra* ('professor'); others tried to disempower her, claiming that she just reported to the citizens what she had seen and heard.[21]

Established devices for limiting the impact of such female precedents included slogans. Irregular women heroes such as these were 'to be admired, not imitated'; and their exploits were to be regarded as exceptional necessities in the fledgling Church, at a time when (in the biblical idiom) 'the harvest was large, but the reapers few'. It is evident that, depending on the anxiety levels within the Church and the region at the time, women 'beneath the pulpit' might be made aware, sometimes enthusiastically and sometimes grudgingly, that legendary holy women had been *in* the pulpit. Abbesses, preaching to nuns in their convents, remained a 'live' reminder of that possibility. One or two very exceptional women (such as Hildegard of Bingen) managed to get official permission to preach publicly.[22] Otherwise, within the bounds of orthodoxy, the prohibition enshrined in canon law prevailed, and women's capacity to exercise intellectual, vocational, and leadership powers remained curtailed.

One symptom of a certain frustration was the eagerness with which women who were converted to Wyclifite or 'Lollard' faith involved themselves in the vernacular Bible readings and discussion groups that characterized this movement in the late fourteenth and early fifteenth centuries. Records of persecution make clear that initiatives within such groups were often taken by women, even though not many of them could read.[23] Margery Baxter, one of the Norfolk Lollards charged with heresy during a purge in 1428–31, referred to another Lollard woman, Hawisia Mone, as 'profoundly learned' in the doctrine of the regional sect leader.[24] The attraction of Lollardy for women doubtless lay substantially in its promise of direct access to knowledge and study of forbidden scripture in their own language. (Orthodoxy only conceded the Psalms as suitable for the laity's verbatim consumption, and this I believe explains why it was acceptable for a woman, Eleanor Hull, to translate a learned commentary on the Seven Penitential Psalms in the fifteenth century.)[25] At the same time the Lollard movement was implicitly hospitable to female aspiration in its elaboration of the idea that all faithful lay persons, of either sex, were effectively 'good priests', with as much power as any ordained priest of whatever rank.

A further sign of challenge to gender doctrines in Lollardy, following on from that opening up of the concept of 'priesthood', was surely its adherents' hostility to clerical celibacy. Many of the Norfolk Lollards were alleged to have believed that it was more meritorious for priests and nuns to marry and procreate than remain celibate.[26] Celibacy distanced the priesthood and it had little relevance to the household religious fellowship that was characteristically – and expediently – developed among Lollard communities. Opposition to celibacy had been among the tenets proclaimed in a Lollard manifesto of 'Twelve Conclusions' audaciously attached to the doors of Westminster Hall and St Paul's in 1395. However, there was a further corollary. Not only (the third Conclusion) ought those in orders to marry, but (the eleventh Conclusion) widows too should marry rather than take unnatural vows of continence – as, with great formality, they sometimes did.[27]

There is an interesting possibility that Chaucer engages with some of these 'hot' issues in *The Wife of Bath's Prologue*.[28] The two factors in the Wife of Bath's discourse that beg to be viewed in the context of Lollard argument are her invasion of the domain of biblical interpretation and her defence of marriage as against virginity or widowhood. In the first case, she seems to embody the energy and the aspiration of the Lollard women studied by Claire Cross – women who knew parts of the Bible by heart from household oral readings of it. With whatever exegetical shortcomings, the Wife strikes out as a 'reasoner in scripture'. In the process, her repeated appeal to the unadorned text, to what the Bible 'expressly' says (3.27–8, 59–62, 719–20), aligns her vocabulary with that of the Lollards, who were intent on repudiating the interpretative encrustations of theological commentary. Simultaneously, she takes more or less the Lollards' line on marriage. While she stops short of declaring that celibacy is not, as they would say, commendable or meritorious, she conspicuously justifies the remarriage rather than the continence of widows.

It is not that the Wife of Bath 'is' a Lollard. She is far from that, for example, in her participation in pilgrimages, which were anathema to the Lollards. But Chaucer, I believe, has caught the pulse of the moment: his Wife's borrowings from Jerome are brought to a focus on two issues that were part of the incipient Lollard movement's agenda – women's access to scripture, and the newly contentious matter of marriage versus celibacy. However, the *Wife's Prologue* is also of course a juggling act with misogyny, and that is another 'pulpit' subject to which we should now turn.

Through sermons in and out of church and through confessional instruction, women encountered a construction of themselves that was often routinely misogynous, or (to our eyes) subtly misogynous even when it modelled them in ostensibly complimentary ways. Exhortations about marriage incessantly urged women to a proper subjection to husbands. Wives were left in no doubt of the responsibility to perform their part in the 'mutual debt' of marital sex. It has always seemed to me that the 'mutual' debt was a convenient way of providing a theory of marital 'equality', which in practice was likely to reinforce a right to marital rape of wives. Nevertheless, many sermons dealt even-handedly with questions about marriage, and some even developed a view of tolerance and mutual respect between partners that makes the arrangement attempted between Dorigen and Arveragus in Chaucer's *The Franklin's Tale* seem less idiosyncratic. 'There is a kind of love founded on partnership [*dilectio socialis*]', writes Gilbert of Tours in a mid-thirteenth-century sermon addressed to wives, 'and this is the love which husband and wife owe to each other, because they are equal and partners.' In such a marriage 'there should also be freedom to correct each other, so that a husband may be free to criticize his wife, and she accept it for the love she bears him, and vice versa'.[29] It is a fine sentiment, but it is differentiated from normative partisan insistence on wifely obedience only by the somewhat slender mechanism of that 'vice-versa'.

In the sermons, criticism of female instability, credulity, vanity, and sexual incitement was ubiquitous. Women were endlessly reminded of the 'foolish' credulity of Eve – that Eve was 'seduced' by the serpent but that Adam was not. Consolations were found, admittedly. One was that Adam disgraced himself more than Eve since she had greater temptation than he. Another was that a second woman, the Virgin Mary, was the agent of salvation cancelling Eve's role as agent of sin. Less well known to medievalists now are the 'privileges' that were ascribed to women, on the basis that Eve was created from a superior substance, strong bone, but Adam only of muck; that Eve was created in Paradise, but Adam outside it; and that she was created last, as if the climax of God's handiwork. Woman's other 'privileges' were to have conceived Christ; to have seen Christ first at the resurrection; and (in the person of the Virgin Mary) to outrank all angels in the celestial hierarchy.[30] These 'privileges' have sometimes been derided as some sort of scholastic joke, but they appear extensively in perfectly serious sermon and other contexts. It can be argued that they do not *do* anything for women – indeed they locate women's 'advantages' only in relation to males, Adam and Christ. Nevertheless, they must have been gratifying to female auditors as a palliative at worst, or as a gratifying counter-propaganda to misogyny at best.

More fundamentally (in terms of impact on daily living and perceptions of the body) women were discreetly reminded from the pulpit that menstruation, though a 'natural infirmity' not technically to be ashamed of, was a latent sign of their corruptive status. Sex during menstruation was particularly vilified in sermons. Churchgoing during menstruation was, shall we say, allowable but a matter for the scrupulosity of the individual (in other words, a potential for pollution could not be eliminated).[31]

Women also knew that there was something 'impure' about parturition. The rite of purification following birthing evolved quite early in the Middle Ages into 'a full-blown penitential ritual involving the complete prostration of the mother while reciting the penitential psalm *Miserere mei*'.[32] During the later Middle Ages mothers seem to have undertaken versions of the ritual (as a celebration of female solidarity) enthusiastically.[33] Yet the nuance of pollution attaching to childbirth can be judged from difficulties that theologians had in reconciling the 'virgin birth' with birth through the vagina. Even Hildegard wondered whether the Virgin Mary gave birth 'through her side' and not through the vagina, where 'there would have been corruption'.[34]

Along with men, women were instructed through confession and in sermons addressed to married folk that, apart from menstrual periods, there was a complicated timetable of holy days on which sexual intercourse was to be eschewed. One of Boccaccio's stories in the *Decameron* (2.10) mischievously draws attention to the accumulation of days of continence thus made theoretically advisable. Donna Bartolomea finds her puny husband's punctiliousness on this matter life-denying, and goes off with a robust pirate who is less devoted to the chaste observance of all manner of saints' days.[35] The jest will seem less outlandish when it is remembered that the faithful were supposed to abstain from intercourse during Advent and Lent, before Whitsun, on all major feast days and their vigils, on the quarterly ember days, on Sundays, some Wednesdays and Fridays, and three days before receiving communion.[36]

Doubtless the minutiae of abstinence were more often breached than observed, but women and men could not escape the fact that the monthly calendar was organized by fast and feast days. In fact women might be the more obliged to be vigilant about this, in the light of their responsibility for household and meals. *The Book of the Knight of the Tower* gives us a vignette of a model widow who observed a rule of abstinence on Wednesdays and Fridays (she was a real woman called Cecyle de Balleuylle, who had died when the knight himself was ten) and whose last daily routine was to summon her steward, to check what meat should be provided next day.[37] In such a household, and for such a woman, the implications of the calendar of fast and feast must have been no small matter.

Feast days for saints, and other holy days, were of course also public occasions; they were community events. The Wife of Bath lists 'vigilies' and 'processiouns' alongside sermons, miracle plays, marriages, and pilgrimages as social occasions that give pretext for dressing up. A *vigilia* meant the offering of prayers either individually or communally on the day or night before a religious festival. It is all very well for Chaucer and other satirists to insinuate that they are suspect occasions for assignations and for female displays of urban wealth,[38] but we should read also against that grain and try to imagine the positive dynamic of vigils and processions. They may have been rather important for women, for whom opportunities for public appearance were not generally encouraged.

At the same time it is to be remembered that the focused public nature of holy days provided formal contexts for ideologically manipulative acts of individual punishment. It may be amusing to read the hortatory story of a fornicator who, for his prolonged sexual intercourse under the altar (on the Vigil of Our Lady!), is sentenced to 'goo al about the Chirche al naked on thre sondayes betyng hym self'. It is more awesome to read the formal sentencing of the Lollard Margery Baxter to four floggings around the parish church of Martham in Norfolk in the presence of the solemn parish procession on four separate Sundays.[39]

One further way in which the Church influenced women's lives socially was through the religious fraternities or guilds. Women could become members of these. Margery Kempe was admitted to membership of the Guild of the Holy Trinity at Lynn shortly before she died.[40] The 'Guildsmen' of Chaucer's *General Prologue* probably belong to such a fraternity. Within the guilds, which had influential civic roles, there was some measure of equality between male and female members. However, as Swanson reminds us, wives could not 'aspire to governance'.[41] Again they came up against a bar to authority – and had to attain it vicariously, for example through the advancement of their husbands within the guild hierarchy.

Earlier, we saw that the Church both celebrated and tried to limit the impact of certain 'preaching' women saints. Of course, women saints (and the Virgin Mary) had various functions for women, some of them very pragmatic. A local church might be named after St Margaret of Antioch: miraculously released from the belly of a fiendish dragon, she was immensely popular as a patron saint of childbirth. Ways of thanking her or supplicating her ran from the inexpensive to the lavish – from lighting a lamp to her, or bequeathing some personal object (jewellery, even a kerchief) to her shrine in a church, to funding the decoration of a chapel for her, or endowing a new chapel.[42] Propitiatory acts when someone in the family was ill were endemic in that culture. The fifteenth-century Paston Letters disclose how John Paston's mother ordered a wax image, of the same weight as her son, for the famous shrine of the Virgin at Walsingham. John's wife also went there in person to pray for him.[43]

This is a reminder of one dominant role into which women were socialized in the Middle Ages – the role of solicitude for the sick. Just after Christine de

Pizan's passage about the piety of women, quoted earlier, comes a series of rhetorical questions, attributing the performance of Acts of Corporeal Mercy largely to women. 'Who is it that visits the sick and attends to their needs? Who gives aid to the poor? Who goes to the hospitals? Who helps bury the dead? To my mind, these are the tasks that women perform', observes Reason.[44] Relentlessly, the medieval Church conditioned women to be the forerunners of Jane Austen's Emma, looking after the needy Miss Bates of the locality.

More exceptionally, women might be exhorted that however busy their day became with charitable or household concerns, they should make space and time for their own personal devotions. One of Gilbert of Tournai's sermons for wives quotes a passage from a letter mistakenly ascribed to St Jerome at this period, recommending that a wife should leave herself some 'private' time. She should choose a 'place on her own' (a *remotus locus*) to compose her thoughts and devotions in tranquillity.[45] The fact that Jerome's name was attached to this recommendation must have given it a circulation greater than Gilbert's sermons – though that was quite extensive – in the Middle Ages.

What might a medieval woman properly ponder in 'a room of her own'? Before concluding, it will be important to take a look at the particular direction which the Church began to foster in personal devotion during the Middle Ages. In England, this direction, usually designated by the expression 'affective piety', was given official backing through the medium of Nicholas Love's *Mirour of the Blessed Life of Jesus Christ*, written in 1407–9.

Affective meditation on the infancy of Christ and especially on his suffering at the crucifixion had been increasingly commended and practised. By the fourteenth century it dominated the lay religious imagination. In one sense, in that it invited any individual into an empathic relation with Christ's human family and with his human suffering, it could be said to allow a 'democratization' of religion. In another sense it could be termed a condescending instrument of the clerical elite to deflect the religious concentration of the laity from areas of the faith in which their intervention was not welcome. The element of condescension is plain in the way affective piety, a piety that dwells on the bodily dimension of Christ's life, was represented as a type of elementary practice suitable for those – including *de facto* most women since they were barred from universities – whose educational limitations disqualified them from more sophisticated forms of contemplation. Nicholas Watson sums it up as 'a tradition which associates devotion to Christ's humanity primarily with women and which at the same time claims such devotion to be inferior to contemplation of the godhead, being suitable mainly for beginners'.[46] Nicholas Love introduced his book of meditation with an argument that concentration on the 'manhood' of Christ befits 'simple souls' who, unable to think except in bodily ways, nevertheless ought to have something appropriate to 'feed and stir their devotion'.[47]

Enactments of biblical story both as part of the Church's liturgy and in the civic religious plays were one channel for the spread of affective piety.[48] Visual art (for example the 'Pièta', and Christ as 'Man of Sorrows') was another. Franciscan preachers especially disseminated it. A Franciscan Good Friday sermon preached in 1431 in Newcastle specifically urges the women who are present to think of the Virgin's distress on seeing her son's body hanging on the cross and on hearing his cries:

> Think how, hearing these, his grieving mother said 'Lord what misery is mine! My child cries out that his father has forsaken him. I wish I could die on the cross with him. [. . .] Oh Gabriel, why did you say I was "full of grace?" I am full of misery, among all women full of sorrow. My son is dying, ah, me!'[49]

This is a mild example. Meditations ran to technicolour extremes, preoccupied with the lacerations left on Christ's body by his scourging, and with the blood gushing from numerous gashes once he was nailed on the cross.

What women might have *gained* from cultivating devotions such as these has recently become a contentious matter. According to one school of thought, here lay an empowerment of women, both because the period's cultural description of their bodies was preoccupied with blood and lactation and with nourishing in ways that implied a convergence between women and the salvific life-giving body of Christ (pouring out Eucharistic blood on the cross), and secondly because women were so constituted by their culture as subjected, powerless, suffering beings that they could 'represent' with particular force the suffering humanity of Christ.

According to a contrary school of thought, there lay not empowerment but disempowerment in the late-medieval promotion of affective piety. In this view the women and men who practised it were in effect taking a kind of drug (affective ecstasy, so to speak) which kept them fixated on a particular sentimental construction of the 'humanity' of Christ, and diverted attention from aspects of his ministry which could pose serious problems for the medieval Church. The argument is that alternative, more challenging, and hence institutionally marginalized delineation of what was important in Christ's 'humanity' and ministry remained visible in heterodox contexts, or lurked in otherwise orthodox writing such as Langland's.[50]

In this latter view affective piety was less a 'natural' phenomenon than an instrument of control, one that subtly absorbed the religious energies of women in particular. This is a conspiracy theory that is not easy to disprove. We might qualify it somewhat by recalling what we earlier noticed

in relation to women and preaching: namely, that certain female saints acquired runaway reputations for preaching that were a little embarrassing
to some theologions and therefore necessitated damage-limitation clauses.
This suggests that the prelatical elite did not so much engineer trends of
belief affecting women, as struggle (sometimes) to accommodate trends as
they arose.

Nevertheless, cumulative strategies and habits of thought did conspire to
keep women generally 'beneath' the pulpit. Just one story, that of 'Pope Joan',
circulated in the Middle Ages that credited a woman with reaching the pin-
nacle of power in the Church (allegedly in the ninth century), becoming pope
by intellectual talent and by dint of male disguise: but it was a disparaging
story. In Boccaccio's version, a gifted woman named Giliberta follows her
lover to England and adopts a male disguise in order to study there with him.
When he dies she remains committed to advancing her intellect, lectures in
Rome, and eventually so impresses the cardinals with virtue and knowledge
that she/he mounts the papal throne as Pope John. Subsequently (because, in
Boccaccio's view, 'merciful' God would not 'allow a woman to hold so lofty
a place') this pope is stricken with gender stereotype in the form of rampant
sexual desire. Later she suddenly gives birth during a formal procession in
Rome, disclosing her biological gender and flouting the celibacy of the office
in one sensational act.[51]

It is a teasing story because at first it plainly recognizes that women might
qualify in talent and saintliness for the highest ecclesiastical office – but
then squashes this recognition under the heel of crude misogynous insult.[52] I
wonder how many medieval readers would have noted, though, how heavily the story depends on the 'infamy' of public childbirth. It is the biology
of unpredictable parturition and not the sin of lust, the subtext might be
thought to assert, that would differentiate a transgressive female pope from
a transgressive male one.

Women had little opportunity to achieve high office in the Church. Yet as
we conclude this chapter it is worth pointing out that they would sometimes
have been encouraged to see a woman as the very epitome of the Church.
This woman was 'Ecclesia' and she was a commonplace of early medieval
crucifixion iconography, though later her role was assimilated into that of
the Virgin Mary, standing next to the cross.[53] Ecclesia appears next to the
crucified Christ with a chalice or cup, sometimes catching Christ's blood
in it. She collects and ministers the blood of Christ for the faithful. By a
stunning paradox, the very sex that was forbidden by canon law to touch
the sacred vessels of the Mass could be viewed holding a Eucharistic chalice
at the originary moment of the shedding of Christ's blood.

In the iconography, Ecclesia is balanced on the other side of the cross by 'Synagoga', another woman, representing unbelief – a reminder of the positive/negative ambivalence surrounding women in medieval ecclesiastical culture. But Synagoga does not obliterate Ecclesia, rather the reverse. Perhaps, as has been suggested, the female Ecclesia was no mere grammatical abstraction but a latent model of authority for women, even a subtly subversive model if some women who saw her chose to read in her an authorization for direct female connection to Christ and to the sacrament, unmediated by male clerical control.[54] But if that is so we have come full circle to the widow of Chaucer's *Friar's Tale*. We come back to a side of medieval culture which concedes that women might on occasion spectacularly ignore their lowly prescribed relation to 'the pulpit', might cut the red tape, and assume powers that were institutionally denied them. The mutterings of conventional masculine authority about such phenomena, that they were 'to be admired, but not imitated', were beside the point. The fundamentals of belief were nurtured around miracles. While the miracles of female saints and visionaries – even of rural widows – might be open to anxious scrutiny, everyone knew that the grace of miracle could burst forth through any woman or man. The medieval church could not do without its female luminaries.

NOTES

1. Her curse (1624) is implicitly juxtaposed with the bishop's (1587). Of course, excommunication only indirectly jeopardized salvation, by denying participation in the sacraments.
2. See, e.g., Norman P. Tanner, ed., *Heresy Trials in the Diocese of Norwich, 1428–31*, Camden Society, 4th ser., 20 (1977), p. 160.
3. Peter Biller, 'The Common Woman in the Western Church in the Thirteenth and Early Fourteenth Centuries', in *Women in the Church*, Studies in Church History, 27, ed. W. J. Sheils and D. Wood (Oxford: Blackwell, 1990), pp. 127–57 (pp. 139, 144).
4. 'The Tua Mariit Wemen and the Wedo', 422–35, in W. Mackay Mackenzie, ed., *The Poems of William Dunbar* (London: Faber, 1932).
5. Christine de Pizan, *The Book of the City of Ladies*, trans. Rosalind Brown-Grant (Harmondsworth: Penguin, 1999), I. 10 (p. 25).
6. v. 7059–90; G. C. Macaulay, ed., *The English Works of John Gower*, EETS ES 81–2 (London: Oxford University Press, 1900–1).
7. Malcolm Andrew and Ronald Waldron, eds., *The Poems of the Pearl Manuscript* (London: Arnold, 1981), line 942.
8. Karma Lochrie, *Covert Operations: The Medieval Uses of Secrecy* (Philadelphia: University of Pennsylvania Press, 1999), p. 30. Nevertheless, visual evidence suggests that in the later Middle Ages the woman knelt by the confessor's knees with her head slightly turned aside.

9. Gustaf Holmstedt, *Speculum Christiani*, EETS OS 182 (London: Oxford University Press, 1933), p. 2.

10. *Sidrak and Bokkus*, ed. T. L. Burton, 2 vols., EETS OS 312 (Oxford University Press, 1999), Laud MS, 9163–82 (2: 564).

11. John Gower, *Mirour de l'Omme*, trans. William Burton Wilson (East Lansing: Colleagues Press, 1992), lines 17, 593–654.

12. *Commentary on Luke*, trans. in Alcuin Blamires (ed.), *Woman Defamed and Woman Defended: An Anthology of Medieval Texts* (Oxford: Clarendon Press, 1992), p. 62.

13. Thus 1 Timothy 2: 12 (against women teaching) is glossed, 'If a woman speaks, she incites the more to lust, and is herself incited', in the *Ordinary Gloss* to the Vulgate Bible.

14. J. Kevin Coyle, 'The Fathers on Women and Women's Ordination', *Église et Théologie* 9 (1978): 51–101, at 73–4. In the medieval Latin Vulgate Bible the locution *viros suos* is indeed open to interpretation, though Origen himself cites the Bible in Greek.

15. Alcuin Blamires, 'Women and Preaching in Medieval Orthodoxy, Heresy, and Saints' Lives', *Viator* 26 (1995): 135–52, at 148.

16. Blamires, 'Women and Preaching', pp. 136–7. For further discussion of the Brut case, see Margaret Aston, 'Lollard Women Priests?' in her *Lollards and Reformers* (London: Hambledon Press, 1984), pp. 49–70 (pp. 52–9); for an edition of the formal repudiation of Brut's views, see Alcuin Blamires and C. W. Marx, 'Woman Not to Preach: A Disputation in British Library MS Harley 31', *Journal of Medieval Latin* 3 (1993): 34–63.

17. Robert of Basevorn, *Forma praedicandi*, quoted from Blamires, 'Women and Preaching', p. 149.

18. Tanner, ed., *Heresy Trials*, p. 47.

19. From 'Utrum mulier praedicando et docendo mereatur aureolam.' Text in Jean Leclercq, 'Le Magistère du Prédicateur au xiiie siècle', *Archives d'Histoire Doctrinale et Littéraire du Moyen Age* 21 (1946): 105–47, at 120.

20. 'Women and Preaching', pp. 142–5.

21. Alcuin Blamires, *The Case for Women in Medieval Culture* (Oxford: Clarendon Press, 1997), pp. 195–7.

22. Barbara Newman, *Sister of Wisdom: St Hildegard's Theology of the Feminine* (Berkeley and Los Angeles: University of California Press, 1987), pp. 11–12; nevertheless Hildegard assented to the exclusion of women from ecclesiastical office (p. 247).

23. Claire Cross, '"Great Reasoners in Scripture": the Activities of Women Lollards 1380–1530', in *Medieval Women*, Studies in Church History, Subsidia 1, ed. Derek Baker (Oxford: Clarendon Press, 1978), pp. 359–80; Shannon McSheffrey, 'Literacy and the Gender Gap in the Late Middle Ages: Women and Reading in Lollard Communities', in *Women, the Book and the Godly*, ed. Lesley Smith and Jane H. M. Taylor (Cambridge: D. S. Brewer, 1995), pp. 157–70.

24. Tanner, ed., *Heresy Trials*, p. 47.

25. See Alexandra Barratt, ed., *Women's Writing in Middle English* (London: Longman, 1992), pp. 219–23. On women's access to the Bible, see Alcuin Blamires,

'The Limits of Bible Study for Medieval Women', in *Women, the Book*, ed. Smith and Taylor, pp. 1–12.

26. Tanner, ed., *Heresy Trials*, pp. 17 and 166.

27. Anne Hudson, ed., *Selections from English Wycliffite Writings* (Cambridge University Press, 1978), pp. 24–9.

28. Alcuin Blamires, 'The Wife of Bath and Lollardy', *Medium Aevum* 58 (1989): 224–42; and 'Crisis and Dissent', *A Companion to Chaucer*, ed. Peter Brown, (Oxford: Blackwell, 2000), pp. 133–48 (pp. 139–43).

29. David D'Avray and M. Tausche, 'Marriage Sermons in *Ad status* Collections of the Central Middle Ages', *Archives d'Histoire Doctrinale et Littéraire du Moyen Age* 47 (1980): 71–119, at 114–16.

30. See the chapter, 'Eve and the Privileges of Women', in Blamires, *Case for Women*, pp. 96–125.

31. A doublethink noted by Dyan Elliott, *Fallen Bodies: Pollution, Sexuality, and Demonology in the Middle Ages* (Philadelphia: University of Pennsylvania Press, 1999), pp. 2–7.

32. Elliott, *Fallen Bodies*, p. 5.

33. Gail McMurray Gibson, 'Blessing from Sun and Moon: Church as Women's Theatre', in *Bodies and Disciplines: Intersections of Literature and History in Fifteenth-Century England*, ed. Barbara Hanawalt and David Wallace (Minneapolis: University of Minnesota Press, 1996), pp. 139–54.

34. See Newman, *Sister of Wisdom*, p. 176.

35. Giovanni Boccaccio, *The Decameron*, trans. G. H. McWilliam (Harmondsworth: Penguin, 1972), pp. 220–7.

36. J. A. Brundage, *Law, Sex, and Christian Society in Medieval Europe* (Chicago University Press, 1987), pp. 154–64.

37. William Caxton, trans., *The Book of the Knight of the Tower*, ed. M. Y. Offord, EETS ss 2 (London: Oxford University Press, 1971), ch. 135 (p. 182).

38. *General Prologue*, 1.377–78; and see Blamires, *Case for Women*, p. 149.

39. Respectively Caxton, *Book of the Knight of the Tower*, ch. 35 (p. 59); and Tanner, ed., *Heresy Trials*, p. 43, and pp. 22–3 of his Introduction.

40. Clarissa Atkinson, *Mystic and Pilgrim: The 'Book' and the World of Margery Kempe* (Ithaca: Cornell University Press, 1983), p. 76.

41. Robert Swanson, 'Social Structures', in *Companion to Chaucer*, ed. Brown, pp. 397–413 (pp. 406–7).

42. Katherine J. Lewis, '"Lete Me Suffre": Reading the Torture of St Margaret of Antioch in Late Medieval England', in *Medieval Women: Texts and Contexts in Late Medieval Britain*, ed. Jocelyn Wogan-Browne et al. (Turnhout: Brepols, 2000), pp. 69–82 (pp. 79–80).

43. Norman Davis, ed., *Paston Letters and Papers of the Fifteenth Century* (Oxford: Clarendon Press, 1971), Pt 1, p. 218.

44. *City of Ladies*, trans. Brown-Grant, 1. 10 (p. 25).

45. D'Avray and Tausche, 'Marriage Sermons', p. 110 and n. 97; and (pseudo-) Jerome, Letter 148, *Patrologia Latina*, 22. 1216.

46. Nicholas Watson, '"Yf wommen be double naturelly": Remaking "Woman" in Julian of Norwich's *Revelation of Love*', *Exemplaria* 8 (1996): 1–34, at 6.

47. Michael G. Sargent, ed., *Nicholas Love's 'Mirror of the Blessed Life of Jesus Christ'* (New York: Garland, 1992), p. 10 (my translation).

48. Carol M. Meale, '"This is a Deed Bok, the Tother a Quick": Theatre and the Drama of Salvation in the *Book* of Margery Kempe', in *Medieval Women*, ed. Wogan-Browne et al., pp. 49–67.

49. A. G. Little, *Franciscan Papers, Lists, and Documents* (Manchester University Press, 1943), pp. 244–56 (p. 255; my translation).

50. Empowerment is argued in Caroline Bynum's books, esp. *Holy Feast and Holy Fast*; disempowerment in David Aers, 'The Humanity of Christ: Reflections on Orthodox Late Medieval Representations', in David Aers and Lynn Staley, *The Powers of the Holy: Religion, Politics, and Gender in Late Medieval English Culture* (University Park: Pennsylvania State University Press, 1996), pp. 15–42.

51. For a comprehensive study, see Alain Boureau, *The Myth of Pope Joan* (University of Chicago Press, 2001); Giovanni Boccaccio, *Concerning Famous Women*, trans. Guido A. Guarino (London: Allen and Unwin, 1964), ch. 99, pp. 231–3.

52. Wyclif fleetingly considers the validity of Pope Joan's papacy in *De Potestate Pape*, and the Lollard Brut also invokes her; Aston, 'Lollard Women Priests?', pp. 68, 57–8. Near the end of the thirteenth century the Guglielmite sect in Italy had its own female pope; Barbara Newman, 'Woman Spirit, Woman Pope', *From Virile Woman to Woman Christ* (Philadelphia: University of Pennsylvania Press, 1995), pp. 182–223.

53. Emile Mâle, *The Gothic Image*, trans. Dora Nussey (New York: Harper and Row, 1958), pp. 186–92.

54. Jo Spreadbury, 'The Gender of the Church: the Female Image of *Ecclesia* in the Middle Ages', in *Gender and Christian Religion*, Studies in Church History, ed. R. N. Swanson, 34 (Woodbridge: Boydell and Brewer, 1998), pp. 93–103. Barbara Newman affirms the gender importance of female personifications in 'God and the Goddesses: Vision, Poetry, and Belief in the Middle Ages', in *Poetry and Philosophy in the Middle Ages: A Festschrift for Peter Dronke*, ed. John Marenbon (Leiden: Brill, 2000), pp. 173–96.

III

MEDIEVAL WOMEN

10

CHRISTOPHER BASWELL

Heloise

A visitor to the Cemetery of Père Lachaise, east of Paris, may come across the canopied Gothic Revival tomb of Heloise and Abelard. They are a much-visited couple in that crowded suburb of the dead – though less than Jim Morrison, less than Colette – and were among the first there, moved with the permission of Napoleon in 1804. For Père Lachaise was a commercial venture and needed some famous bodies to attract the monied corpses of the Second Empire. Thus was Heloise written into the emerging romance of capital.

It was not the first time Heloise had been cast into romance, not to speak of other genres, at the beck of masculine power. In her own youth she had heard herself written by Abelard into heartfelt lyrics of their passion, and in the early 1130s she encountered his narrative of the subsequent castration and fall from ecclesiastical pride, the *Historia calamitatum*. In the late 1270s Heloise was recast (in that part of the *Romance of the Rose* by Jean de Meun) as an instance of womanly virtue within an otherwise misogynist diatribe by a jealous husband;[1] and later a treatise on courtly love was posthumously written under her (explicitly learned) authorship.[2] Heloise's own writings, however, record a profound and persistent will to *choose* her role, often in conflict with the men and institutional expectations around her, including Abelard, and their efforts to inscribe and circumscribe her. What she some-times willed, and how she expressed that will in her letters, remain shocking. That shock at the core of Heloise's choices – the scandal of her will – is the cultural irritant which has provoked the many versions of her identity from her own day until now. These pages explore the profound and unresolved spiritual crises, crises of secular and religious conversion, that characterized Heloise's choice and will in the relatively small body of her surviving letters.

Let us begin with perhaps the only text by Heloise whose authenticity has always lain beyond dispute, and probably the last that survives; all Heloise's other writings have at various times been attributed to third parties, among them Abelard himself.[3] This is a brief, almost business-like letter of the mid-1140s, fairly soon after Abelard's death, written to the influential Abbot of Cluny, Peter the Venerable, Abelard's friend and final protector. As Abbess of the nuns of the Paraclete, Heloise thanks Peter for a recent visit, in terms at once fulsome and observant of ecclesiastical hierarchy ('your greatness has descended to our lowliness'), though no more so than is typical of such letters.[4] She thanks him for the Mass he conducted, for a sermon he delivered, and especially for bringing the nuns 'the body of our master' and founder of the Abbey, Abelard himself. She then turns to the main purposes of her rhetorical humility, reminding Peter of the promises he made during that visit 'to your sister, or I should say, to your servant': a series of Masses to be said on her behalf at Cluny after her death, for which she now requests written confirmation, as well as the official document of Abelard's papal absolution from charges of heresy, 'to be hung on his tomb'. Almost as a postscript, she also asks Peter to look about for a Church appointment for Astralabe, the son she and Abelard had conceived during their affair of 1116–17.

This is an accomplished letter. It makes restrained use of anaphora and prose rhythm, even rhyme, and moves effectively between the first-person plural of Heloise's voice as abbess, and the singular of her role as recipient of Peter's promised Masses and as mother of Astralabe. It suggests a writer in calm control of contemporary epistolary style, who knows her way around the ecclesiastical structure of her day and how to effect her own and her convent's needs within it. Peter Dronke suggests that Heloise's epistolary style was actually avant-garde, reflecting Italian models that were new to her region, in which case she may have been Abelard's teacher in this arena (as in others).[5] It is only one of many occasions when this highly literate abbess successfully elicited documentary proofs of the rights and status of her convent.[6] If Heloise had once found herself written into Abelard's works, in this letter she arranges for Abelard to be written officially into the institutional history of the Paraclete, a story largely of her own successes.

Heloise had been abbess at the Paraclete, in Champagne, for well over a decade by the time of this letter, as she would be for about another twenty years. She and a group of nuns had come there at Abelard's suggestion in 1129 when Abbot Suger of St Denis evicted the nuns from Argenteuil, the convent where Heloise had received her early education and in which she had become a nun, with at least initial despair, after the birth of her son and Abelard's castration. By this time, further, she had overseen the production of the unique liturgy of the Paraclete and a series of other religious texts written for the nuns by Abelard at her request; and she had supervised at least the first of six daughter houses founded in her lifetime. Whatever the interior life of the woman who wrote this letter, she is politically astute, alert to her own position and secure in it.

There is no hint here, though, of the explosive passions, the persistent bodily memories, the spiritual struggle and the dense verbal counterpoint of mutually committed but debating wills, which we encounter when we move back in Heloise's textual life to the highly charged letters she exchanged with Abelard from the Paraclete in the 1130s. For the private history preceding that exchange we have but two significant witnesses. First, there is Abelard's own highly self-interested account of the young Heloise and their affair in his *Historia calamitatum*. Equally important, though, is the narrative of Abelard's last days which Peter the Venerable had sent the Abbess Heloise in a letter written at least a year after Abelard's death (21 April 1142) but before the visit to the Paraclete, just discussed, in which he brought Abelard's body there.

Peter the Venerable actually devotes two thirds of this letter to Heloise herself. It is a letter of great delicacy, discreet about her past, with a restrained but clear agenda for her future. Peter (c. 1094–1156) was probably closer to Heloise's age (of which we remain uncertain) than he was to Abelard's. He opens his letter by recalling the reports ('fama') he had heard, when barely past his own adolescence, of a young woman whose learning in the secular arts 'surpassed all women' and 'almost every man' – a point Abelard had made in his *Historia calamitatum*, saying that her learning, supreme among women, 'had won her renown throughout the realm'.[7] Clearly Heloises's accomplishments and fame preceded her affair with Abelard. Peter's entire letter is full of literary allusions and flattering references to Heloise's learning and her current teaching among the nuns of the Paraclete. He also seems to acknowledge her long period of doubt and resentment, of (at best) mixed commitment to the holy life. Now, though, he encourages her to fashion herself as a mother, teacher, and warrior for her nuns, comparing her to the biblical Deborah and the classical Penthesilea. He offers a letter both of consolation and of heroic religious calling and resolve. As we will see, this dialogue between spiritual struggle and heavenly praise echoes a key thematic strand in the earlier letters between Heloise and Abelard themselves.

The textual core of the relationship of Heloise and Abelard, now almost universally accepted as authentic, consists of an exchange of three pairs of letters, initiated by Heloise but sparked by Abelard's 'consolatory' and self-vindicating *Historia calamitatum* (c. 1132).[8] This long letter to an unidentified man focuses on three interwoven crises of his adulthood: his constantly embattled position in the schools; his affair and marriage with Heloise, subsequent castration, and entry into monastic life; and the condemnation his theological positions suffered at the Council of Soissons (1121). Heloise is important here, but less important than Abelard's almost constant public struggles with academic and ecclesiastical authority.

If Abelard's letter provoked the exchange, it was Heloise who initiated the intense dialogue between the two of them. She moves herself from the third person object of male narrative into a participant, inscribing her own role in history, in letters which she might reasonably expect would be edited – as medieval letter collections often were – and circulated. Probably an editorial hand intervened at some point, as was common among letters meant to circulate; this was possibly a third party, possibly Abelard himself, but just as possibly the learned Heloise, who had as much as thirty years to collect and amend the letters. The interplay among intimate memories of an erotic past, a fierce but private current struggle, the semi-public status of medieval letters, and the very public notoriety of their affair, is never far from the surface of their exchange. And the charged negotiation between these two keen minds results in letters of almost choral echo and response.

The formal salutation of Heloise's first letter suggests, at once, the variety of identities in which she imagines herself, and the extent to which they all remain kinds of relation with Abelard: 'To her master, or rather father, husband, or rather brother; his handmaid, or rather his daughter, wife, or rather sister; to Abelard, Heloise'.[9] There is a metastasis of identity here, a focus on one other person so intense as to populate Heloise's universe. Heloise repeatedly will balance this multiplicity of roles against Abelard's uniqueness: 'solus', 'unice'. Indeed, her insistence that 'you after God are the sole founder of this place [Tu post deum solus]' approaches – no doubt self-consciously – an almost blasphemous worship of another mortal.[10]

The letter begins with a revisionary summary of the *Historia calamitatum*, focusing on their affair and its conclusion in the violent spectacle of Abelard's castration, the 'supreme treachery [summa proditio]' which will become a key phrase in the correspondence. At the heart of the letter's eloquence is Heloise's plea for Abelard to be once again present to her, if no longer erotically, then verbally, as a spiritual guide and consoler through a re-newed correspondence. The letter gains much of its tense rhetorical strength from the conflicting strategies of this plea, as Heloise alternately insists on Abelard's obligations and begs for his comfort:

> Yet you must know that you are bound to me by an obligation which is all the greater for the further close tie of the marriage sacrament uniting us, and are the deeper in my debt because of the love I have always borne you, as everyone knows, a love which is beyond all bounds. You know, beloved, as the whole world knows, how much I have lost in you, how at one wretched stroke of fortune that supreme act of flagrant treachery [summa et ubique nota proditio] robbed me of my very self in robbing me of you . . . Surely the greater the cause for grief the greater the need for the help of consolation . . . I looked for no

marriage bond, no marriage portion . . . The name of wife may seem more sacred or more binding, but sweeter for me will always be the word mistress, or, if you will permit me, that of concubine or whore.[11]

There is at once glory and abjection in Heloise's swift movement among the roles and demands of wife, mistress, and whore; even as she explores a socially humiliating and self-abnegating identity, she enacts a powerful choice and reminds Abelard of her history of complex resistance and obedience.

The paradoxical tone of the letter has perhaps its most intense expression in the word by which she at once begs and demands a return of Abelard's textual presence: 'obsecro'. It is a term she uses both in her first person plural voice as Abbess of the Paraclete, and in the singular voice of her private sense of abandonment. Yet at the same time, Heloise insists on Abelard's obligations towards one who has so fully given up her selfhood at his command; and this claim upon his debt informs her resentment at the long silence that followed their separation and entry into holy orders, even perhaps Abelard's unwillingness to speak with her privately when he visited the Paraclete.

The second half of Heloise's first letter revisits the love affair that Abelard had narrated in the *Historia calamitatum*. What he reported as (at least initially) a largely private passion, though, Heloise recalls as flagrantly public. Abelard's looks and charm were desired by all women, she writes, and the streets of Paris rang with the songs he wrote about their love: 'queens and great ladies envied me my joys and my bed'.[12] This memory of almost ecstatic exposure, however, is now replaced by an equally widespread and humiliating knowledge: 'It was desire, not affection which bound you to me, the flame of lust rather than love . . . This is not merely my own opinion, beloved, it is everyone's.'[13] The excruciating interjection 'beloved [dilectissime]' in the midst of this assertion is followed by Heloise's insistence that she became a nun only upon Abelard's order, not from any religious devotion. She can expect no grace from God, only from Abelard in the form of his letters; yet this insistently secular comfort, Heloise finally suggests, might still engender a higher grace. 'How much more rightly might you now rouse me to God than you did, then, to desire?'[14]

It is in response to this faint and final hint that Abelard frames his reply, which is at once austere yet dense with transformative echoes of Heloise's language and imagery. Abelard's salutation ('To Heloise, his dearly beloved sister in Christ, Abelard her brother in Christ') restricts the range of identities in which he will now encounter her and uses epistolary convention, placing her name first, to suggest Heloise (an abbess) is now his superior. He invokes Heloise's own vocabulary with 'obsecro': 'Listen, I beg you, with the ear of your heart' – a listening that is associated with spiritual understanding – to a catalogue of citations about wifely virtue;[15] and it is in soliciting the corporate prayers of her convent that he then echoes Heloise's earlier 'beloved', 'dilectissima'.[16] Finally, should he die, Abelard asks to be buried at the Paraclete; yet even this prospective burial links him to Heloise only institutionally, at a 'burial-ground, where our daughters, or rather our sisters in Christ may see my tomb more often', and offer more frequent prayers.[17] Even the memory of their marriage and parenthood, then, is pulled into the transformed orbit of conversion and an institutional relationship.

Heloise's second letter is one of the great expressions of private emotion of the Middle Ages, eloquently resisting Abelard's somewhat chilly gestures and dismissals of worldly experience. The letter does begin and end, significantly, in dialogue with Abelard's call to a converted relationship, but its core cries out in an agonized language of secular desire, heat, and bodily memory, all juxtaposed with an insistently and self-accusingly externalized appearance of holiness. Indeed, it is only within the stylized conventions of the salutation that Heloise can openly embrace the altered identity that Abelard's letter had proposed: 'To her only one after Christ, she who is his alone in Christ'.[18]

The imagery of wounds, largely restricted to Abelard's castration in the first letter, now shifts metaphorically to herself. If Fortune 'still had a single arrow', Heloise writes, 'she could find no place in me to take a wound'.[19] Fortune has reversed not only Heloise's fate, but 'all the laws of equity in our case'. They were spared during their affair but punished once they married; and worse, 'you alone [solus] paid the penalty in your body for a sin we had both committed'.[20] This bodily memory pulls the letter away from its reproach of a personified Fortune and into an extraordinary statement of direct 'rage against God': 'I can find no penitence to appease God, whom I always accuse of the greatest cruelty in regard to this outrage.'[21] Heloise's own bodily memory is insistently present in this rage:

> Even during the celebration of the Mass . . . lewd visions of those pleasures take such a hold upon my unhappy soul that my thoughts are on their wantonness instead of on prayers . . . Sometimes my thoughts are betrayed in a movement of my body, or they break out in an unguarded word.[22]

Heloise's spiritual anguish and self-accusation (she calls herself a religious hypocrite) also participate, however, in a tradition of spiritual struggle already implicit in the earlier references to Fortune, whose most famous source is the questing dialogue of Boethius' *Consolation of Philosophy*. Heloise begins to close her letter by again invoking that text, asking Abelard to be her doctor and bring her the grace of healing, 'medicaminis . . . gratiam'.[23] The memories of romantic intimacy and the call for spiritual guidance remain indissolubly linked in this letter.

Abelard's reply is schematic, almost testy. It lists the elements of 'your old perpetual complaint' and responds to each in turn. He explicitly resists Heloise's emotional appeal, and turns instead to doctrine and (like Boethius' interlocutor Lady Philosophy) to reason. He insistently approaches Heloise's position in the context of her convent community, addressing her as a bride of God, and head of her order. He beseeches Heloise, again with the term 'obsecro', to cease her complaints. Abelard here invokes Heloise's imagery of the loving body, but again converts it to the argument of spiritual love. He warns her to abandon her bitterness against God, using the argument that it will cut her off from bliss after death, and thereby separate her from him: it is his most daunting threat.

Finally, Abelard circles back to Heloise's first letter and its memory of their bodily passion. He echoes her phrase about 'supreme betrayal [summam proditionem]'[24] but now applies it to himself as betrayer of her uncle, in whose house he had seduced her; further, he converts Heloise's earlier language of violence against his own body into an admission of the violence he practised upon hers, forcing her to have sex in the convent to which she had retreated, on forbidden days. This in turn recalls Abelard's memories of erotic, though socially accepted, violence in the fusion of blows and caresses with which he engaged Heloise when she was his student.[25] The torment of her persistent desires will lead, he promises, to a heavenly crown.

These are letters of negotiation between two powerful and still stubborn personalities, but they are equally the record of Heloise's private spiritual crisis. Abelard provides warily limited consolation, and a certain guidance in the process. Nevertheless it is Heloise who defines the intensity of bodily memory, emotional striving, and spiritual self-loathing with which the letters open. Abelard urges her towards spiritual resolution, but does so within parameters of vocabulary, imagery, and epistolary style that Heloise increasingly sets. Even at the end of the exchange, she remains in verbal control, though spiritually unresolved. Abelard, always the brilliant debater, may constantly pull Heloise's vocabulary towards a scenario of achieved spiritual conversion, but their later letters simply cap off and veer away from their private striving, rather than resolve it.

Heloise never returns to her body's erotic memory, but the corporate female bodies of the Paraclete nuns persist in the three further letters in this group, one from Heloise and two replies from Abelard. The letters take a far more discursive, institutional turn, and are less intense and stylistically engaging; yet they still have important links to the earlier letters of complaint and consolation. Heloise's third letter asks Abelard to describe the origins of nuns and compose a conventual rule for the Paraclete. The public voice and institutional perspective she uses here might suggest a capitulation to

Abelard's earlier urgings, but that should not be confused with resolution. In her earlier letters, writing had been an unhappy substitute for Abelard's double absence, imposed by his castration and by his institutional struggles elsewhere; she longed for his 'words which would picture for me the reality I have lost'.[26] Here, her own writing is an equally frustrated substitute, but now for the repressed speeches which may all too likely burst ('prorumpant') from Heloise's own body. She can restrain her written words, though, and moves to different topics, both as an act of obedience and, it seems, as a distraction from private emotions and bodily memories that are unabated. Instead, Heloise invokes the bodily difference of her whole order to insist on a rule written specifically for nuns.

The rule that Abelard provided urged the nuns to study scripture, and it was this practice that elicited Heloise's very final surviving letter to him, perhaps from the mid-1130s, which briefly prefaces forty-two questions ('Problemata') about biblical reading and particular passages, each followed by Abelard's response.[27] Heloise's prefatory letter is intimate, but on behalf of the whole order; she calls Abelard 'dear to many, but dearest to us'. In asking Abelard's help, she returns to the language of debt and obligation that was so dense in her first letter; yet the yearning private needs are absent, converted into an obligation between teacher and students, founder and convent. The love by which the nuns are seized ('correptae') is a love of letters.[28] Heloise writes here with the kind of control and restraint seen in the still later letter to Peter the Venerable.

Letters that combine such great passion, learning, and stylistic brilliance do not burst out of nowhere. How did Heloise learn to harness rhetoric, prose rhythm, and verbal counterpoint to achieve the eloquence we have seen above? Large fragments of some hundred and thirteen love letters between a teacher and his female student, only recently coming to wide scholarly attention, may provide an answer.[29] The letters trace a charged, often strained romantic and finally sexual connection between the teacher and student, who write increasingly as equals. The teacher disappoints his student romantically at several points, especially with his sometimes bookish and stilted, Ovidian notions of their love. The student repeatedly presses them towards a more sustaining love that could include the spiritual; ultimately, he responds badly to her expression of 'great exultation of mind' and she cuts off their correspondence.

Are these letters by Abelard and Heloise? A growing number of scholars agree with Constant Mews's arguments that they indeed are. Our uncertainty of Heloise's age complicates the question: traditionally she has been thought to be sixteen or seventeen at the time of the affair, which makes letters filled with such learned references as these unlikely. But the term 'adolescentula', by which Abelard first names her, could mean a young woman as old as twenty-eight years.[30] Certainly the level of learning and range of quotations fit them, as does the implicit story of a secret affair, and the trenchantly independent spirit of the young woman. Abelard mentions an exchange of letters as part of his plan of seduction in the *Historia calamitatum*.[31] Mews points to key terms in the vocabulary of both letter-writers that suggest contact with Abelard's teaching or its immediate arena; to this I would add the woman's tendency to formulate even abstract notions through concrete and bodily imagery, perhaps a prelude to the insistent bodied presence in Heloise's later letters. Mews's arguments, taken all together, do inspire at least a hesitant confidence that the letters were indeed written by Abelard and Heloise during their affair.

I do not, however, find in them the kind of accomplished and quite elevated eloquence seen by Mews and some others.[32] Rather, many of the letters seem authentic exactly because they do have a tone of the schoolroom exercise, with (for instance) the woman's careful distinction of categories of love ('caritas', 'dilectio', 'amor') or the man's almost pedantic addendum to one letter, noting how he had thrown himself on his bed in frustration after writing it.[33] One can easily imagine a playful (or even a cynical) flirtation that grew into complicated love in the context of epistolary set-pieces. Whether or not these letters are finally accepted as 'authentic', they offer the best window we have had on how a woman like Heloise could have acquired the unparalleled combination of passion and rhetorical resource she displays in her later correspondence.

Even harder to identify certainly with the hand of Heloise, yet indissolubly linked to her influence, is the body of sermons and liturgical poetry that Abelard produced for the Paraclete, in a final blossoming of creativity in his last years.[34] Not 'by' Heloise, they are nonetheless authentic traces of her continuing impact on her aging and ill lover. Heloise's textual presence spread across her order in other ways as well: in the grants and charters she elicited for the house, in the twelfth-century poems and epitaphs about their affair,[35] in the abbey's cartulary (a permanent copy of its charters and other documents) and necrology (the record of deaths among its members and patrons). Her letters have gained her other inspired followers across the centuries, who have produced further texts in Heloise's name if not her voice. Dead by 1164, Heloise is not done writing.

NOTES

1. Lines 8729–8956. It was also Jean who 'discovered' the letters for the later Middle Ages, and translated them into French: *La Vie et les epistres Pierres Abaelart et Heloys sa fame*, ed. Eric Hicks (Paris: H. Champion, 1991).

2. *Two Late Medieval Love Treatises*, ed. Leslie C. Brook (Oxford: Society for the Study of Mediaeval Languages and Literature, 1993).

3. For a review and powerful refutation, see Barbara Newman, 'Authority, Authenticity, and the Repression of Heloise', *Journal of Medieval and Renaissance Studies* 22 (1992): 121–57.

4. Unless noted, all translations of Heloise's and Abelard's Latin are from Betty Radice, *The Letters of Abelard and Heloise* (London: Penguin, 1974). The original is edited by Giles Constable, *The Letters of Peter the Venerable* (Cambridge, MA: Harvard University Press, 1967), 2 vols., 1: 400–1.

5. See Giles Constable, *Letters and Letter-Collections* (Turnhout: Brepols, 1976); Peter Dronke, *Women Writers of the Middle Ages* (Cambridge University Press, 1984), pp. 110–12.

6. Heloise also obtained charters of lands and other grants, and letters of privilege for the Paraclete from powerful authorities: see Julia Barrow, Charles Burnett, David Luscombe, 'A Checklist of the Manuscripts', *Revue d'Histoire des Textes* 14–15 (1984–5): 287–92.

7. Radice, *Letters of Abelard and Heloise*, p. 278; Constable, *Letters of Peter*, 1: 304; Radice, *Letters of Abelard and Heloise*, p. 66.

8. The Latin text, and that of all the letters with Heloise, are most accessible in editions by J. T. Muckle in *Mediaeval Studies* 12 (1950): 163–213; 15 (1953): 47–94; 17 (1955): 240–81; and (edited by T. P. McLaughlin) 18 (1956): 241–92. The Latin letters with Heloise are also in Hicks (note 1 above).

9. Radice, *Letters of Abelard and Heloise*, p. 109, Muckle, *Mediaeval Studies* 15 (1953): 68.

10. Radice, *Letters of Abelard and Heloise*, p. 111, Muckle, *Mediaeval Studies* 15 (1953): 69.

11. Radice, *Letters of Abelard and Heloise*, p. 112–13; Muckle, *Mediaeval Studies* 15 (1953): 70–1.

12. Radice, *Letters of Abelard and Heloise*, p. 115; Muckle, *Mediaeval Studies* 15 (1953): 71.

13. Radice, *Letters of Abelard and Heloise*, p. 116; Muckle, *Mediaeval Studies* 15 (1953): 72.

14. My translation; Radice, *Letters of Abelard and Heloise*, p. 118; 'Quanto autem rectius me nunc in Deum quam tunc in libidinem excitares?' Muckle, *Mediaeval Studies* 15 (1953): 73.

15. Radice, *Letters of Abelard and Heloise*, p. 123; Muckle, *Mediaeval Studies* 15 (1953): 75.

16. Radice, *Letters of Abelard and Heloise*, p. 124; Muckle, *Mediaeval Studies* (1953): 76. Heloise, naturally, also echoes the language of her former tutor, especially the terminology of Abelard's ethics and theology.

17. Radice, *Letters of Abelard and Heloise*, p. 125; Muckle, *Mediaeval Studies* 15 (1953): 76–7.

18. Radice, *Letters of Abelard and Heloise*, p. 127; Muckle, *Mediaeval Studies* 15 (1953): 77.

19. Radice, *Letters of Abelard and Heloise*, p. 129; Muckle, *Mediaeval Studies* 15 (1953): 78.

20. Radice, *Letters of Abelard and Heloise*, p. 130; Muckle, *Mediaeval Studies* 15 (1953): 79.

21. Radice, *Letters of Abelard and Heloise*, pp. 128, 133; Muckle, *Mediaeval Studies* 15 (1953): 78, 80.
22. Radice, *Letters of Abelard and Heloise*, p. 133; Muckle, *Mediaeval Studies* 15 (1953): 80–1. The passage exploits the sibilant alliteration of the dramatic setting: 'Inter ipsa missarum solemnia . . .' (81).
23. Radice, *Letters of Abelard and Heloise*, p. 134; Muckle, *Mediaeval Studies* 15 (1953): 81.
24. Radice, *Letters of Abelard and Heloise*, p. 146; Muckle, *Mediaeval Studies* 15 (1953): 88.
25. Radice, *Letters of Abelard and Heloise*, p. 67; Muckle, *Mediaeval Studies* 12 (1950): 183. Abelard had some kinky edges.
26. Radice, *Letters of Abelard and Heloise*, p. 109; Muckle, *Mediaeval Studies* 15 (1953): 68.
27. *Patrologia Latina*, vol. 178, cols. 677–730. Discussed in Dronke 1984, pp. 134–9. There is a translation (not always reliable) by Elizabeth Mary McNamer, in *The Education of Heloise: Methods, Content, and Purpose of Learning in the Twelfth-Century* (sic) (Lewiston: Edwin Mellen Press, 1991), pp. 111–83.
28. *Patrologia Latina*, vol. 178, col. 678.
29. The letters were first edited in 1974, with a suggestion they might be by Abelard and Heloise. A new book now offers a translation and powerful claim that these are indeed the authors: Constant Mews (with Neville Chiavaroli), *The Lost Love Letters of Heloise and Abelard* (New York: St Martin's Press, 1999).
30. Mews, *Lost Love Letters*, p. 32.
31. Radice, *Letters of Abelard and Heloise*, p. 66–7.
32. C. Stephen Jaeger, *Ennobling Love: In Search of a Lost Sensibility* (Philadelphia: University of Pennsylvania Press, 1999), pp. 160–64.
33. Mews, *Lost Love Letters*, letters 23, 37.
34. Joan M. Ferrante, *To the Glory of Her Sex* (Bloomington: Indiana University Press, 1997), pp. 56–67.
35. Peter Dronke, *Abelard and Heloise in Mediaeval Testimonies* (University of Glasgow Press, 1976), pp. 19–22.

11

ROBERTA L. KRUEGER

Marie de France

In the 1160s, an author who identifies herself as 'Marie' dedicated a collection of Breton stories or *lais* to a 'noble reis', most likely Henry II Plantagenet. Some time later, a 'Marie' who announces that she is 'de France' penned the *Fables*, which she says she translates from King Alfred's English translation of Aesopic tales; these she dedicated to 'le cunte Willame'. Finally, the *Espurgatoire seint Patriz*, an account of an Irish knight's voyage to the underworld, was translated from a religious text of monastic origin into the vernacular for the benefit of a lay audience by one 'Marie', probably around 1190. During the course of her career, 'Marie de France' thus produced works in three different genres – Breton tale, animal fable, spiritual voyage – each of which blends literary traditions and linguistic registers and whose topics progress from a tapestry of marvellous love stories, to a shrewd observation of animal and human social behaviour, and finally, to a vision of sin and redemption.

We know nothing for certain about the historical Marie de France. Some critics have even doubted that a single author penned these three disparate works or that they were necessarily written by a woman.[1] It is true that no manuscript contains all three works together, and Marie's twelve *Lais* appear together in only one manuscript, which also contains the *Fables*. Nonetheless, a strong authorial presence throughout this varied corpus leads most critics to agree that the same 'Marie' composed the *Lais*, the *Fables*, and the *Espurgatoire*. Whether or not these works portray a gendered authorial identity, and whether that gender be 'feminine' or 'androgynous', is one of the many interpretive questions raised by this provocative corpus.[2]

Literary culture flourished among elite men and women in monasteries, convents, and courts in England and France during the so-called 'renaissance' of the twelfth century. Although the vast majority of medieval texts were male-authored, women participated actively in the production of culture as audiences and patrons and, sometimes, as authors, first of Latin texts and, increasingly, of French writings.[3] In England, royal patrons included Matilda

I and her daughter, the Empress Matilda, who succeeded in placing her son, Henry II, on the English throne. Perhaps the most remarkable literary patron was Henry II's wife, Eleanor of Aquitaine, granddaughter of William of Poitiers, the first troubadour. Eleanor had divorced the French King Louis VII before marrying Henry; she has been credited with helping to disseminate the discourse of 'courtly love' within courts in northern France and England. She has been considered the dedicatee of the *Roman de Troyes* and Wace's *Brut*, among other works, and her daughter, Marie de Champagne, inspired Chrétien de Troyes' *Le Chevalier de la Charrete*, or *Lancelot*. In religious houses, women may have played an even more active role not only as patrons and readers but also as writers. Three female-authored saints' lives were produced in twelfth-century England, among them the moving Anglo-Norman *Life of St Katherine* by Clemence of Barking.[4]

During the first bloom of vernacular production, with women situated strategically in English courts and convents, it is not surprising that a single talented woman composed texts as diverse as the *Lais*, the *Fables*, and the *Espurgatoire*. Marie's works stand as an eloquent testimony to the vitality and variety of medieval women's literary voices and to the dynamic intersection of French, Latin, Breton, English, Arabic, and Irish cultures in the Middle Ages.

The *Lais*

The Prologue to the twelve *Lais,* which are collected in Harley MS 978, announces an ambitious project.[5] In a dense series of epigrams – any one of which could have stood alone to introduce such a collection – the narrator acknowledges her duty to impart knowledge, the generative effects of good works, the practice of the Ancients who wrote obscurely so that their successors could 'gloser la letre' [gloss the word] and add the 'surplus de leur sens' [the addition of their understanding] and, finally, the necessity of undertaking a 'grevose oevre' [serious work] in order to avoid sin and free oneself from suffering (1–27).

The speaker then describes her own unique enterprise: she has decided not to undertake translation from Latin into 'Romanz' (vernacular French), as so many others have done. Rather, she turns to the *lais* (narrative songs or brief tales that recall adventures) which she has heard and will commemorate. The author then dedicates her work to the noble king in whom all 'biens' take root and asks that he not think her 'surquidiee' – presumptuous – in daring to make him such a 'present' [gift] (54–5).

As she skilfully weaves together introductory topics, the author primes the audience for her complex poetic and hermeneutic project. Like the ancients, she can be expected to write 'obscurement', enigmatically, so that her readers will add their own 'sens'. Speaker and reader are involved in an interactive process that commemorates good works, so that memory may flower and engender moral transformation.

Yet the optimistic mode of the General Prologue is countered by the Prologue to the collection's first tale, *Guigemar*, where the author finally names herself as Marie, 'not forgotten in her time'. Here we learn that success can engender not only fame but also envy and slander. The speaker sharply chastises 'bad dogs, cowards and traitors', 'jongleurs' and 'losengiers', saying that she will speak in spite of them (*Guigemar*, 1–18).

These paired Prologues present a vexed pair of narrative stances: the first, a formal voice, boldly announces an ambitious programme and presents it in a royal court; the second, a more defensive voice, is painfully aware of wagging tongues within a community formed by language, where one can all too easily be victim of 'vilenie'. Such ambivalence can be traced through the collection: the formal authoritative voice remains masterfully in control of the aesthetic project, especially in Prologues and Epilogues. The more private voice, who names herself 'Marie' [which can also mean 'marie', 'unfortunate'] as she voices her suffering, seems to ally herself at various moments with characters in the collection who are ostracized or calumniated, beginning with the hero of the first story, *Guigemar*, who is 'péri', ostracized for his failure to love.

All of the *Lais* are about men and women who suffer in love, but there is no simple lesson in this mosaic of tales. Rather, in diverse ways, each tale inscribes social and sexual transgression, the fusion of animal and human natures, real and otherworld settings in a way that encourages readers to 'gloss', or interpret, for themselves.

Marie sets the stage for interpretative activity in *Guigemar*, the first *lai*. The eponymous hero, who has shunned love, is wounded in the thigh by his own arrow, which rebounds from an androgynous hind (a doe with stag's antlers). The hind prophesies that Guigemar will be cured only when he meets a woman who suffers in love as much for him as he does for her. Transported in a marvellous ship, Guigemar comes to a land where an unhappily married lady languishes, locked up by her jealous old husband. At this point, the narrator pauses to describe the room where the lady is imprisoned: its walls are painted with an image of Venus, goddess of love, who teaches how lovers must love loyally and who casts into the fire a book about love by Ovid. This intriguing description of a work of art (technically known as an ekphrasis) intrudes strikingly into the otherworld landscape of a Breton tale. By portraying Venus casting a book by one of the great authorities on love into the flames, Marie announces both her mastery of classical tradition and her break with it: she suggests that she will portray desire in a different guise.

If we observe this intriguing scene more closely, we see that the oppositions it seems to set up between male and female versions of love are not as clear-cut as they may at first appear to be. Questions of agency and source arise. Who painted the incendiary scene in this chamber (or who ordered it to be painted) – the jealous husband or the unhappy wife? Which one of Ovid's books does Venus burn – the *Ars amatoria*, in which the rules for seduction are spelled out, or the *Remedia amoris*, in which love is rejected? As Marie calls attention to her distinctive authority by reviving classical figures within a marvellous landscape, she complicates the straightforward identification of genders and moral positions and so launches the collection's interrogation of eros. In this and other critical moments, Marie also helps to inaugurate a debate about gender issues that will continue within many courtly French narratives.[6]

No easy 'rules' of love emerge from the ensuing stories. The lovers in *Guigemar* are adulterers, yet the marvellous elements of the *lai* – a talking hind, a marvellous ship, and knots that can be untied only by the lovers – serve to promote and maintain their passion, which is reciprocal and loyal. These faithful lovers are followed in the next *lai*, *Equitan*, by a shrewdly calculating pair of adulterers who plot the murder of the husband (a faithful, unsuspecting seneschal) and receive their due – a double death in a boiling bath – in a *fabliau*-like conclusion.

The love situations in the *lais* are rendered more complex and their psychological intensity deepened by the author's fusion of the real world and the other world, of human and bestial natures. The eponymous hero in *Bisclavret* is a werewolf whose occasional transformations into a wolf horrify his wife.[7] She steals her husband's clothes so that he will remain a beast, while she herself, behaving in a beastly fashion, consorts with another knight. The werewolf displays courtesy before the King and is adopted at court, where he behaves impeccably until his wife and her lover appear there. Taking just revenge against her treachery, Bisclavret snaps off his wife's nose. He reverts to his human nature, but some of her descendants are born nose-less. The marvellous mark of 'bestiality' has thus been passed from husband to wife, upon whose body it evokes various possible 'meanings' – castration, betrayal, shame, sexual transgression.

Animal and human nature, real world and otherworld domains also fuse in a trilogy of successive *lais* – *Yonec*, *Laustic*, and *Milon* – that feature birds in tales of transgression and transformation. Muldumarec in *Yonec* is a marvellous bird who transforms himself into a man to respond to the desire of an unhappily married lady, a *mal mariée*, who longs for an adventure to befall her like those that she has heard sung or told. Her lover is killed by her jealous husband, but the adulterous couple's son, Yonec, eventually avenges his father's death. In *Laustic,* a jealous husband cruelly kills a nightingale, whose song served as an excuse for his wife's frequent visits to a windowsill from which she would speak to her neighbour, a handsome knight. No longer able to go to the window, the lady wraps the dead bird in an embroidered cloth that recounts the story and sends it to her lover, who preserves it in a beautiful reliquary. This transformation, which creates a poetic object to commemorate loss, seems emblematic of many of the *Lais* themselves. The most positive transformation occurs in *Milon,* where a swan has borne messages between Milon and his lady for twenty years, until the son recognizes his father in battle and reunites his biological parents in marriage. Since *Yonec, Laustic,* and *Milon* succeed each other in the Harley manuscript, the narrator's 'assemblage' of these tales invites comparison of their inscription of desire, loss, and poetic and moral transformations.

In contrast to much chivalric literature where women are often passive objects or marginalized temptresses, Marie's female characters are central figures who exhibit courage and ingenuity. It is often women's speech – *paroles de femme* – that launches the story and women's actions that attempt to resolve the crisis.[8] An abandoned orphan in *Fresne* recovers her birth-family and marries her beloved, thanks to her own resilience and generosity. A resourceful maiden in *Deux amants* writes a letter to her aunt and procures a potion to strengthen her lover, but she is unable to make him drink it during the test in which he expires. As she dies of sorrow, she scatters the potion on the mountainside where it flowers into 'meinte bone herbe' [many good herbs/plants] that commemorate her love and valour (*Deux Amants,* 225–9).

The otherworldly settings of the *lais* allow the narrator to critique feudal society and to imagine alternatives to courtly values. *Lanval* depicts a knight who has been passed over by King Arthur in the latest distributions of lands and women. After falling asleep near a river beyond the town, Lanval is visited by a beautiful fairy lady who has sought him out for her pleasure: she bestows her love and all the wealth that he could desire, provided that he keep their love a secret. The fairy lady's generosity and loyalty contrast with Arthur's injustice and with Guenevere's manipulative behaviour in the ensuing narrative. When, at the end, the fairy lady ravishes Lanval away with her on horseback to Avalon, Marie's seems to reject feudal courtly values and to dramatize the subversive idea that loyal love cannot survive easily in a world ruled by men.[9]

Many characters in the *Lais* are depicted as readers, writers, or storytellers. Instances of literary activity within the *Lais* invite the audience to reflect on Marie's literary artifice and on the uses of language and fiction.[10] In some *lais*, Marie dramatizes the link between writing and desire (as in *Chievrefueil*, where Tristan enigmatically inscribes a message on a branch that only Iseult can read) or between writing and death (as in *Chaitivel*, where the death of three knights and the thigh-wound of a fourth are at the origin of the fiction). As she portrays the desire, transgression, and transformation of characters who read and write, Marie invites her readers to reflect upon their own activity as readers and interpreters and their investment in the making of fiction.

The *Fables*

The self-reflexivity and meta-critical framework of the *Lais* guarantee Marie's survival with modern readers well into the twenty-first century. Yet, if we judge from the ample number of extant manuscripts (twenty-five), her most popular work with medieval audiences was her collection of *Fables*. Aesopic fables – short tales with a moral, often but not always featuring talking animals – were important texts in medieval education and were an integral part of the curriculum throughout the European Middle Ages.[11] By translating the *Fables* into witty octosyllabic verse, Marie brought a key curricular text in the first extant translation to a vernacular audience, where these stories could be enjoyed by women as well as men, by lay people as well as clerics.

Even more forcefully than in the *Lais*, Marie asserts her authority as a teacher and insinuates a female voice into a tradition that she explicitly describes as male and patrilineal, that of 'li ancïen pere' (line 11).[12] In the Prologue, Marie informs us that the fables were translated from Greek to Latin by Aesop at the behest of King Romulus, who wrote for the moral edification of his son. In the Epilogue, we learn that Marie, like Aesop, translates for a patron, 'le cunte Willame', this time 'en romanz' (the French vernacular) from the English translation made from the Latin by 'li reis Alvrez' (lines 9–18). Aesop and Romulus, as Marie describes them, are legendary figures, far removed from the prose translation of a fourth-century Latin work that appears to be her closest source (the so-called *Romulus Nilantinus*). This particular King Alfred remains a conundrum, and if he made an English translation, it has disappeared. But Marie's inscription of eminent male authors and rulers valorizes her authorship and her engagement in *translatio studii* (the transmission of learning from Greece to Rome, and then to Europe). She also interrupts, as a female teacher, a masculine line of textual transmission that includes a father and son, a master and clerk, two kings, and a count, and thus cleverly inserts herself as an agent into paternal, clerical, and feudal relationships.

As in the *Lais*, a deceptively simple framework enfolds a complex mosaic of interlacing themes, colourful characterizations, sharp insights, and penetrating – and sometimes contradictory – morals. The first forty stories of these are from the *Romulus Nilantilus*; the remaining sixty-two are from a variety of other sources, including Arabic story collections, and may be compiled for the first time by Marie.[13] Scholars who have compared Marie's version with sources and analogues note Marie's distinctive features.[14] Marie is not indifferent to the gender of her animals, and often seems to pay special attention to the characterization of female animals – a pregnant sow, a bear who is raped.[15] On several occasions, she appeals specifically to women in the audience. Sometimes, she pointedly diminishes the antifeminist bent of a fable (as when she shows some sympathy for the Widow of Ephesus, who is traditionally an example of female inconstancy) or a tradition (as in her retelling of Adam's fall, which is exemplified by the curiosity of a male peasant).[16] She also repeatedly draws analogies to medieval society and life at court by her use of feudal terminology and dramatizes (through the protective cover of beast fiction) the perils of bad governance.[17]

The social world of the *Fables* is shaped by forces that divide the powerful from the weak, men and beasts, rich and poor, clever and stupid, proud and humble, wise and foolish. Yet the interplay of animals within the fables does not always support such easy distinctions. If the lion is powerful in a number of fables, he is by no means always just; in Fable 11, the hunter lion never shares his prey. The lion is portrayed as weak and sickly in Fable 14, having learned, to his dismay, that when adversity strikes the mighty they lose their power. The clever fox – who 'wins' the game in a great number of fables – is outsmarted in the end by the cat, who has only one trick (Fable 98). Marie is careful not to condemn all women, and she often defends them, but she does not shrink from blaming 'many' women who may offer bad advice to their husbands and from warning 'sage home' not to listen to 'fole feme'. No species, neither gender can hide from the moralist's critical eye.

In contrast to the *Lais*, where the marvellous register allows Marie to effect several positive social and moral transformations, the natural setting of the *Fables* provides few truly happy endings or positive examples – the mouse aiding the lion who spares his life being one of the rare exceptions. If some animals and men escape unharmed from their brush with ridicule, treachery, or danger, many more become dupes or victims – often of their own folly or corruption turned upon themselves.

Little wonder, then, that the moralist promotes scepticism and teaches strategies of self-protection. Foremost among these are circumspection and quick intelligence, often deployed in verbal manipulations. Many creatures preserve their 'bien' or save their skins by linguistic ruse. In Fable 47, a peasant who argues that a one-eyed man would only value a horse for half of its worth manages to sell the animal at a good price; clever women in two successive fabliau-like tales use their wits to fend off charges of adultery (Fables 44 and 45); the cock made careless by the fox's flattery saves his feathers by flattering the fox, in turn, in Fable 60 (which is a source of Chaucer's *Nun's Priest's Tale*).

Throughout the collection, Marie casts an observant eye on the use and abuse of language. She also questions the ability of humans to learn from fictions like her own. The collection is framed by two tales that illustrate creatures' failure to reap the benefits bestowed on them: a cock disdains a precious stone that he finds in a barnyard in Fable 1, and in Fable 102, the 'Woman and the Hen', a hen disparages the nourishment offered by a woman, because the hen's nature cannot prevent her from scratching.

Amid their profusion of proverbs and moral endings, the fables pointedly do *not* offer a simple formula for living. If, as has been suggested, the collection might have served as a 'mirror for princes', instructing rulers on the principles of government,[18] the *Fables'* most profound lesson may have been to encourage the reader's reflection and self-knowledge. Marie invites her readers to develop, sharpen, and eventually deploy their wits – not in the shadow of a master or by the doctrine of a book, but on their own, as in the fable of 'The Crow and Her Young' (Fable 92), where the mother tells her youngster to go forth and fend for itself, so that she may attend to others.

What emerges above all from Marie's collection is the wit of the fabulist, who displays her talents artfully but prudently. Suspicious of the tendency of other clerks to claim authorship (as the author of so many tales of verbal trickery might well be), Marie reinforces her signature in the Epilogue with a final proverb: 'cil fet que fol ki sei ublie' [he who allows himself to be forgotten is a fool] (line 8). At first, in her Prologue, Marie had distanced herself from her project, saying it was not appropriate that she write such tales and that she did so only at the behest of a courtly patron, 'ki flurs est de chevalerie' (line 31). By the end of the *Fables*, she seeks to claim and to protect the work as uniquely her own. With the *Fables*, Marie has shrewdly placed her work in the mainstream of clerkly and courtly cultures, adapting an ancient form into the vernacular in a way that would ensure its appeal to readers and adapters throughout the European Middle Ages and early modern period.

The *Espurgatoire seint Patriz*

The *Espurgatoire seint Patriz* (St Patrick's Purgatory), probably written around 1190, is regarded as Marie's last work and, by many critics, as her least original. At first glance, Marie appears to follow closely the narrative of her Latin sources, the long and short versions of H. of Saltrey's *Tractatus de Purgatorio sancti Patricii* (c. 1179–85), which recounts the sensational voyage of the Irish knight Owein down into and back from Purgatory.

Although the spiritual vision of the *Espurgatoire* seems far removed from the *Lais* and the *Fables*, Marie's last work is no less an accomplishment. She brings the important new concept of Purgatory out of monastic circles to a lay audience. The idea that sins might be alleviated through intercessors' prayers and the suffering of sinners in a liminal space between Heaven and Hell was an invention of the high Middle Ages, as the historian Jacques Le Goff has described it.[19] The Latin *Tractatus* located Purgatory in a particular geographical location, near the famous Irish pilgrimage site on Lough Dough in County Donegal, and described the lower world in trenchant detail. By bringing this fantastic yet allegedly 'real' vision to an audience of 'laie gent' and 'simple gent' in a vernacular verse translation, Marie made an important contribution to the European imagination and helped prepare the terrain for Dante's *Divine Comedy*.

As Marie translates her source, she cleverly steps to the forefront of an august literary genealogy, placing herself directly after God and St Patrick: she states that she translates 'al nun de Dieu' (line 1) at the behest of 'uns prosdom' [a worthy man] (line 9). As the text's French editor points out, Marie makes the Prologue her own through the use of feminine participles and intervenes throughout the tale, assuming the stance of author rather than mere translator.[20]

Like Patrick and Owein, Marie seeks to 'aovrir ceste escriture e descovrir' (lines 29–30) – to open and uncover writing about a place that is hidden, removed, and 'oscure' (a word that occurs repeatedly in the *Espurgatoire* and, as we recall, in the *Lais*). This realm is not only 'obscure' because it is far removed geographically, in distant Ireland; it is also difficult as a theological concept. Marie's arduous task in her final work is thus to reveal and make concrete the occult divine world through the opening of her own 'escriture'.

The narrator exclaims frequently – in interventions not in her source – to marvel at or empathize with Owein's sufferings. As Marie recounts Owein's voyage deeper and deeper into a world where moral failings are embodied as corporeal torments, she conjures up visions of organs and body parts – mouth, ears, genitals, arms – that are nailed and burning, and of the horrendous sights, smells, and sounds of suffering. These are counterbalanced by a final bright vision of the sensual and spiritual delights of paradise replete with 'herbes . . . de bone odur' (line 1589) (a leitmotif, we recall, from the *Lais*).

As the final proof of the 'truth' of her lesson, Marie adopts the long version of her sources to append several brief tales recounted by a hermit to the Abbot Florencien (intervening, again, as female narrator in the male transmission of religious teaching). The last of these stories tells how two devils attempt to waylay an honest priest and trap him into sin by placing a lovely young girl – a foundling child – in his path. After raising the girl (who recalls both Fresne and the maiden in *Deux amants*), the priest curbs his urge to rape her (induced by the devils) by cutting off the instrument of his passion. His castration recalls the corporeal suffering of Purgatory (see line 1089, 'genitailles'). Unlike Owein's horrifying vision, this painful act is not followed by an image of Paradise and salvation. Marie closes her text rather abruptly, stating that the priest then placed the young girl in the service of God. Was he therefore redeemed? The reader can only wonder. A complex knot of emotions, motivations, and intentions – transgression, violent desire, self-mutilation, divine service – forms the final resting-place of Marie's literary journey.

As she has done in both the *Lais* and the *Fables*, Marie has created a literary account whose ultimate 'truths' are difficult to grasp and whose lessons remain, at some level, dark and enigmatic. Marie's narrator makes clear that such 'obscurities' are not the exclusive purview of theologians, monks, or hermits. Just as she has insisted at several points in the journey that Owein chooses to remain a knight rather than enter religious orders (lines 1923–32; 1971–80), so Marie promotes the 'active' life by asserting, in both Prologue and Epilogue, that she has made her story memorable and suitable for lay people.

It might be tempting to see in the progression of the *Lais*, the *Fables*, and the *Espurgatoire* the story of a teacher and the changing relations over a lifetime between a woman writer and her audience. The *Lais* present an ambitious writer at the royal court who blends classical and fairy-tale elements to recount tales of young women and men in love. In the *Fables*, a mature writer translates a key curricular text for widespread vernacular circulation and addresses broader ethical, social, and political concerns. Finally, at the end of her life, Marie might seem to venture on a spiritual journey that serves as a kind of *summa*, probing deeper into the terrain of moral flaws and failings present in her earlier work and offering the hope of salvation.

Such a biography, however, arises less from Marie's words than from the will of readers who would seek to impose an authorial identity upon writing that remains, in many ways, fragmentary, enigmatic, and 'obscure'. If there is coherence and continuity in the narrative voices of the *Lais*, the *Fables*, and the *Espurgatoire*, it is because these texts lead the reader, at every turn, to reflect upon their interpretative questions.

We might conclude that Marie's works, in commemorating the 'granz bien' of the past, encourage their readers to amend their lives and to live wisely in undertaking serious work and attending closely to the truth. But these texts also tell another story about irretrievable loss, about the prevalence of human folly, the fragmentation of the self, and the difficulty of redemption. What kind of narrative do readers shape as they 'gloss' the text and add the 'surplus de leur sens'? How may the meanings readers glean from these texts serve to transform their lives? These questions arise in different ways in each of Marie's works as they continue to engage readers in reflection upon their *sens* and their transformative poetics.

As we began with the question of Marie's identity and of women's place in medieval culture, it is fitting to end with questions that keep us from erecting too hastily simple categories through which to apprehend the works of the past. The works signed by 'Marie' offer eloquent testimony to the strong female voices that characterize French vernacular culture from its earliest manifestations. The body of Marie de France's works reminds readers not only that women's intellectual communities thrived in medieval France and England, but also that medieval society was far more diverse, multilingual, multicultural, and self-reflective than some have construed it to be. Through their complex literary, cultural, and moral transformations, Marie's writings continue to offer 'meintes bone herbe' to readers today who would undertake the 'grevose oevre' of seeking meaning in her words.

NOTES

1. Single authorship has been contested by Richard Baum, *Recherches sur les œuvres attribuées à Marie de France* (Heidelberg: C. Winter, 1968). The case that the feminine narrative voice of the *Lais* is not necessarily the production of a woman author has been advanced by Jean-Charles Huchet, 'Nom de femme et écriture féminine au Moyen Age: Les *Lais* de Marie de France', *Poétique* 48 (1981): 407–30.

2. Questions of gender identity in Marie have been debated for some time. For a range of views, see Michelle Freeman, 'Marie de France's Poetics of Silence: the Implications for a Feminine *translatio*', *PMLA* 99 (1984), 860–83; Rupert Pickens, 'The Poetics of Androgyny in the *Lais* of Marie de France: *Yonec, Milun*, and the General *Prologue*', in *Literary Aspects of Courtly Culture: Selected Papers from the Seventh Triennial Congress of the International Courtly Literature Society*, ed. Donald Maddox and Sara Sturm-Maddox (Cambridge: D. S. Brewer, 1994), pp. 211–19; and, most recently, Miranda Griffin, 'Gender and Authority in the Medieval French Lai', *Forum for Modern Language Studies* 35 (1999), 42–56.

3. For an overview of women's writing in French from the sixth to the fifteenth century, see my 'Female Voices in Convents, Courts and Households: the French Middle Ages', in *A History of Women's Writing in France*, ed. Sonya Stephens (Cambridge University Press, 2000), pp. 10–40.

4. A translation of Clemence's masterful *Life of St Katherine* is provided by *Virgin Lives and Holy Deaths: Two Exemplary Biographies for Anglo-Norman Women*, trans. Jocelyn Wogan-Browne and Glyn S. Burgess (London: J. M. Dent, 1996), pp. 4–43. The other female-authored lives are an anonymous *Life of St Edward the Confessor* and a *Life of St Audrey* by a 'Marie' whose link to Marie de France is generally not accepted.

5. Marie de France, *Lais de Marie de France*, ed. Karl Warnke, trans. Laurence Harf-Lancner (Paris: Librairie Générale Française, 1990).

6. See my 'Beyond Debate: Gender Play in Old French Courtly Fiction', in *Debating Gender in Medieval Literature*, ed. Thelma Fenster and Clare Lees (New York: St Martin's Press, forthcoming).

7. For a fine reading of the interplay of human and animal natures in this *lai*, see Matilda Bruckner, 'Of Men and Beasts in *Bisclavret*', *Romanic Review* 82 (1991): 251–69.

8. See Anne Paupert, 'Les Femmes et la parole dans les *Lais* de Marie de France', in *Amour et merveille: Les 'Lais' de Marie de France*, ed. Jean Dufournet (Paris: Champion, 1995), pp. 169–87.

9. A reading of *Lanval* as a 'feminist' critique of courtly society has been offered by Sharon Kinoshita, 'Cherchez la femme: Feminist Criticism and Marie de France's *Lanval*', *Romance Notes* 34 (1994): 263–73.

10. Robert Sturges, 'Texts and Readers in Marie de France's *Lais*', *Romanic Review* 71 (1980): 244–64; Diana M. Faust, 'Women Narrators in the *Lais* of Marie de France', *Stanford French and Italian Studies* 58 (1988): 17–28.

11. See Edward Wheatley, *Mastering Aesop: Medieval Education, Chaucer, and His Followers* (Gainesville: University of Florida, 2000).

12. *Les Fables*, ed. and trans. Charles Brucker, 2nd edn (Louvain: Peeters, 1998).

13. On the way that Marie's knowledge of Arabic tales influenced her literary strategies in the *Fables*, see Sahar Amer, *Esope au féminin: Marie de France et la politique de l'interculturalité* (Atlanta: Rodopoi, 1999).

14. See the discussion by the *Fables*' editor, Charles Brucker, in his French edition of Marie de France, *Fables*, pp. 11–18.

15. Harriet Spiegel, 'The Woman's Voice in the *Fables* of Marie de France', in *In Quest of Marie de France, A Twelfth-Century Poet*, ed. Chantal A. Maréchal (Lewiston: Edwin Mellen Press, 1992), pp. 45–58.

16. Sahar Amer discusses Marie's distinctive treatment of women in *Esope au féminin*. Amer also emphasizes the complex morality of the *Fables* and my analysis is indebted to her study.

17. Karen Jambeck, 'The *Fables* of Marie de France: a Mirror of Princes', in *In Quest of Marie de France, a Twelfth-Century Poet*, ed. Maréchal, pp. 59–106.

18. As argued by Jambeck, 'The *Fables* of Marie de France'.

19. See Jacques Le Goff, *The Birth of Purgatory*, trans. Arthur Goldhammer (University of Chicago Press, 1981), particularly pp. 193–201.

20. Yolande de Pontfarcy, 'Introduction', *Espurgatoire seint Patriz*, ed. Yolande de Pontfarcy (Louvain: Peeters, 1995), pp. 38–45. Discussion of Marie's poem is also provided by Michael J. Curley in his translation of Marie de France, *Saint Patrick's Purgatory: A Poem by Marie de France* (Binghamton, NY: Medieval and Renaissance Texts and Studies, 1993).

12

DAVID F. HULT

The *Roman de la Rose*, Christine de Pizan, and the *querelle des femmes*

In 1402, Christine de Pizan, one of the first and most illustrious women of letters in the French tradition, was gradually establishing a reputation as a serious writer. Her talents up to that point had been devoted predominantly to the composition of conventional courtly lyric for the enjoyment of her royal and noble patrons, who were already sufficiently impressed by her poetic skills to acquire and exchange manuscripts of her work. On 1 February of that year, Christine put the finishing touches on a small collection of documents which she addressed to Isabeau de Bavière, Queen of France, and Guillaume de Tignonville, Provost of Paris, for their scrutiny and, it was hoped, favourable judgment. This dossier, labelled as the 'Epistles of the Debate over the *Romance of the Rose* between certain persons of note', represented a brief exchange of letters that, the previous year, had grown out of a discussion between Christine and Jean de Montreuil, Provost of Lille, concerning the dubious merits of the famous allegorical poem. Featured prominently was a letter written by Christine which took issue, point by point, with a laudatory treatise on the *Rose* that Jean de Montreuil was circulating among his acquaintances. Jean de Montreuil had himself been introduced recently to the *Rose* by a colleague, Gontier Col, a secretary of the royal chancery, and, in his zeal, wanted to convince reticent colleagues of the work's value. Christine's intention, according to the introductory epistle addressed to the Queen of France, was to 'take a stand, based upon arguments grounded in truth, against certain opinions contrary to pious behavior, and also contrary to the honor and praise of women'. The debate did not end there, however. Over the following nine months, none other than Jean Gerson, the pre-eminent theologian and influential Chancellor of the University of Paris, sided with Christine and contributed his own lengthy document to the debate; Gontier Col's brother, Pierre, reiterated the defence of the *Romance of the Rose* and Christine added still another response which virtually put an end to the exchange. The importance that Christine accorded to the *querelle des femmes*, as contained in this collection of letters, the first vernacular literary quarrel in the French tradition, can be inferred not only from her ceremonious presentation of it to the Queen, but also from her inclusion of it in manuscripts of her collected works that she compiled as early as the summer of 1402.

Christine de Pizan's cavils with the *Romance of the Rose* were certainly not random, nor were they without significance for the direction and success of her future career. At the turn of the fourteenth century, the *Rose* was quite simply the most admired and most sought-after work composed in French, a fact which is all the more striking because of the work's convoluted genesis. Some 170 years previously, in the second quarter of the thirteenth century, an otherwise undocumented author named Guillaume de Lorris had the brilliant idea of composing the story of a young man's initiation into love in the form of a first-person allegorical dream narrative. In the dream, the young man comes upon an earthly paradise, a garden built by the personified character Pleasure and peopled by such other personifications as Youth, Beauty, and Courtliness, as well as the God of Love himself (portrayed as a winged youth with bow and arrows). In one of the hidden corners of the garden, the narrator finds the rose-bush covered with rosebuds and falls hopelessly in love with one of them after having been struck by the God of Love's arrows. The balance of Guillaume de Lorris's narrative recounts the Narrator/Lover's attempts to get close to the rosebud, which is guarded by a further set of personifications antithetical to the love quest: Jealousy, Evil Tongue, Shame, and Fear. The latter build a formidable castle to protect the rosebud and the pining lover is left outside. The fragmentary narrative ends in mid-sentence, leaving the fictional dream unresolved.

Guillaume de Lorris's account dramatizes the myriad psychological and social elements we now associate with the term 'courtly love': submission of the timid lover to his beloved; distanced longing and prayers for the lady's mercy; the importance of beauty and youth; concern for the lady's reputation; refinement of manners and speech. As an 'art of love', Guillaume de Lorris's *Romance of the Rose* provided a blueprint for all subsequent accounts of male desire and the psychological dimensions of female response as circumscribed within courtly society.

The unfinished work might have drifted into obscurity were it not for the fact that some forty years later, around 1270, a second author, Jean de Meun, undertook a continuation that would bring the work to narrative completion. To Guillaume's initial 4,000 lines of rhyming octosyllabic couplets, Jean added a massive 17,000-line continuation, replete with numerous digressions and encased discourses drawing upon a wide range of classical Latin authors as well as medieval sources: Ovid, Juvenal, Abelard, Alan of Lille, Boethius. In satirically unmasking the solipsistic and disingenuous tactics of the courtly tradition, Jean de Meun compiled an encyclopaedic array of discourses focusing upon love as a universal human predicament, delving into such topics as procreation, celibacy, friendship, marriage, prostitution, homosexuality, and obscene language. The conclusion of the work recounted an outrageously obscene and blasphemous scene of sexual intercourse, couched beneath flimsy allegorical language that portrayed the narrator as a pilgrim who penetrates an orifice in the castle wall with his staff in order to gain access to the sacred relics protected therein. Distanced adoration of the rose had turned into its metaphorical rape. The combined ribaldry and erudition of Jean's text constituted a provocative and authoritative summation of commonplaces from the student milieu of Paris in the latter half of the thirteenth century. It would also become one of the most notorious compendia of misogynist lore available in the vernacular, branding women with the vices of unfaithfulness, deceptive behaviour, vanity, loquaciousness, and lubricity.

Within scarcely a generation, the composite *Romance of the Rose* had become a bestseller and maintained its position as the most renowned work written in the vernacular over the following two centuries. The work circulated widely beyond the borders of France, exercising considerable influence both in England and in Italy. Whether a result of its licentious images, its cutting satire, or quite simply the access it provided, as a *florilegium* (a gathering of the flowers of literature, an anthology), to a large number of hitherto unavailable texts translated from Latin into the vernacular, the work soon acquired a cult following. Every library, it seems, sought to possess a copy, a fact attested by the nearly three hundred manuscripts that have survived, a figure that dwarfs that for any other medieval work in a European vernacular with the exception of Dante's *Divine Comedy*. Patrons for the manuscripts ranged from secular and regular clergy, to wealthy bourgeois, to the highest nobility, who commissioned lavishly illustrated copies on fine quality vellum.

At the time Christine de Pizan launched her debate, the *Rose* was thus a text of towering importance and Jean de Meun was lionized as a great poet and a model of clerkly brilliance. Christine took issue with essentially three interrelated aspects of the work: its verbal obscenity and the indecency of the concluding allegorical description of sexual intercourse; the negative portrayals of women, which tended to treat them as a group and not as individuals, thereby making their 'vices' natural and universal; the work's ambiguity, the absence of a clear authorial voice and intention which would serve as a moral guide to susceptible or ignorant readers. Thus, while a good portion of the polemic involved matters of content that Christine judged morally or socially unacceptable, considerable attention was paid by both sides in the debate to issues of interpretation and readerly competence. According to the principle behind Christine's argument, which she was perhaps the first to formulate and which remains current in contemporary debates over obscenity and pornography, if a certain readership (be it children, women, or jealous husbands) risks being harmed or urged to violence by such a work, it should be banned. This was in fact what Christine recommended in her first letter: '[The *Rose*] merits being blanketed in fire rather than being crowned with laurel.'[1] Gerson echoed this thought in a sermon of late 1402 critiquing the *Rose*: 'If I possessed the only copy of the *Romance of the Rose*, even if it was worth a thousand *livres*, I would burn it rather than sell it for publication' (*Débat*, p. 182).

Understandable as Christine's disgust and frustration with certain portions of the *Romance of the Rose* might have been, her attack on the book and its author, when viewed against the backdrop of her entire career, appears conflicted. After all, many of her favourite rhetorical strategies – the figurative vocabulary of love, the dream vision as narrative structuring device, the use of allegorical personifications as authority figures – derived from the tradition of which the *Rose* was the pioneering text. Jean de Meun's other celebrated accomplishment was his important translation into French of Boethius' *Consolation of Philosophy*, the single work that perhaps most influenced Christine's thought. Furthermore, Jean de Meun was not the only illustrious representative of misogynistic discourse, Ovid and a certain Matheolus, presumptive author of the *Lamentations* of a vituperatively woman-hating and long-suffering husband, being other prominent examples. He was, however, as a relatively near contemporary (Jean de Meun died in Paris c. 1305), the prime model for the exclusively male clerkly establishment of Christine's time, and so to attack him was to attack a private club of which Christine was manifestly an outsider. It was also the perfect means, through a strategy of provocation requiring some sort of response, by which to establish a dialogue. To understand fully the place of this debate in the context of Christine's career as an author thus requires not solely seeing it as a move to censure a noxious misogynistic discourse or to express moral indignation (which it certainly was!) but also as a strategic step in the construction of a career and the public establishment of an 'other' voice.

Born in Italy, Christine came to France at a very young age when her father, a renowned physician and astrologer named Tommaso da Pizzano, was summoned to the court of Charles V (reigned 1364–80). Married at the age of fifteen, Christine was left a widow with three children by the time she was twenty-five, around 1389–90. Much of what we know about Christine's life at this time comes from autobiographical moments in her writings, which speak about the personal and professional difficulties involved in her need to make a living by her pen in order to support herself and her family. In a later prose work which intriguingly combines personal reminiscences with political and philosophical commentary, *Christine's Vision* (1405), she provides precious information about her transition from grieving widow to author/publisher and helps fill in some of the gaps in the period leading from her earliest poetic publications to a point at which her prominence had led to important commissions of serious works from the highest nobility. Christine describes an apprenticeship devoted to frothy poetic compositions, which she calls 'pretty things'.[2] Christine's earliest output, which included hundreds of popular fixed-form poems of various genres (ballads, rondeaux, virelais) dating to the period 1393–1400, the poetic collection entitled *One Hundred Ballads* (c. 1399), *The God of Love's Letter* (1399), and the *Debate of Two Lovers* (1400), predominantly falls into the category of conventional courtly poetry. The 'nobler subject matter' to which *Christine's Vision* refers is undoubtedly related to a dual evolution in her writing that would begin to appear in the following years and that would predominate after 1405: a move towards didactic matter of a political, social, or moral bent; and, formally speaking, the adoption of prose. The first of these new works betokening a seriousness of purpose hitherto absent was the *Letter of Othea* (1400–1), a compendium of exemplary mythological tales in alternating verse and prose aimed at the instruction of young princes, completed precisely at the time Christine sent her first letter to Jean de Montreuil.

Christine's interest in the *Romance of the Rose* was not limited to her participation in the debate with Jean de Montreuil and the brothers Col. In fact, references to the *Rose* or to the debate occur sporadically in her writings through the period 1399–1405. In one of her first longer poems, the 1399 *The God of Love's Letter*, she placed a harangue against the *Rose* in the mouth of the god of Love, Cupid (*Selected Writings*, p. 22). While this critique was undoubtedly not intended to launch a debate, it does contain the kernel of a preoccupation which will last for several years and guide Christine's career, especially when one considers Cupid's later remark that misogynistic attacks turn up so frequently because 'women did not write the books'. One response to such misogynistic content is represented by the epistolary debate. Another response, this one of a social and cultural nature, is Christine's very career as a writer, the ultimate step of which, perhaps, was her composition of a revisionary book celebrating the famous women of legend and history, *The Book of the City of Ladies* (1405).

Christine's decision to inveigh against Jean de Meun and the *Rose* in the debate of 1401–2 does not therefore reflect a new discovery so much as an amplification of issues with which she had already been grappling for some time. The very context of the debate, a lone woman pitted against several lofty representatives of the male intelligentsia of the time, formally trained in classical Latin literature and Catholic theology, itself suggests a first instance of the symbolic drama Christine never ceased to rehearse throughout her writings of this period. Here as elsewhere, Christine's use of the diminutive *-ette* to refer to herself (*femmelette*, *seulette*, and so on), her straightforward and consistent deprecation of her own abilities, as in her reference to 'my meagre wit' in the dedicatory letter to Guillaume de Tignonville in the first *Rose* dossier of 1402, turns her weakness to a strategic advantage. These frequent rhetorical moves are not lost on the most clever of her interlocutors in the debate, Pierre Col, who will, contrariwise, call attention to Christine's vigorous arguments (certainly with a modicum of irony) as well as to the public successes Christine had already had by 1402 and admonish her by glossing his remarks with the fable of the fox and the crow:

> So I beg you, oh woman of such great intellect, to uphold the honour you have acquired on account of the loftiness of your intelligence and of your carefully articulated language; likewise, I beseech you not to try your hand at hitting the moon with a heavy iron shaft, even though you have received praise for the cannon ball you shot over the towers of Notre Dame. Beware lest you resemble the crow, who, because he was flattered on account of his song, began to sing louder than was his custom and lost his mouthful.   (*Débat*, pp. 109–10)

This warning did not fail to evoke a sharp response from Christine, directly in defence of her budding career, but, once again, couched rhetorically in terms of her inferiority:

> You give me orders, even accuse me, as though I were presumptuous about myself . . . I consider my situation and my knowledge something of scant importance: all that matters, and here I'm being truthful about it, is that I love study and the solitary life. Moreover, by spending a lot of time in such solitude, it is quite possible that I gathered lowly little flowers [*fleurettes*] from this delicious garden, rather than climbing upon those high trees to pick the tasty, sweet-smelling fruit (not because my appetite and desire to do so are not great, but because the weakness of my understanding does not permit it); and even so, on account of the fragrance of the little flowers, from which I have made slender garlands, those who wanted to have them – people to whom I dare not refuse them – were astounded by my labour, not for any greatness, but because of its very novelty, to which they are unaccustomed. Furthermore, they have not kept quiet about it (even though it was hidden for a long time), but I assure you that this did not occur at my request.   (*Débat*, pp. 148–9)

Christine specifies the nature of her work's novelty in her later *Vision*: 'My aforementioned volumes had brought me renown because they had been sent as presents to many princes of foreign lands, not by me, but by others who considered my work a novelty originating in a woman's sensibility'[3] (*Lavision*, p. 166).

As far as Christine's self-effacing depictions of her scrawny literary garlands are concerned, they do not square well with one of the most remarkable of Christine's bookish achievements: her professional commitment to the book as a vehicle for authorial success, which led her to establish a workshop in which she had manuscripts of her works executed for noble patrons. Her constitution of the first *Rose* dossier in a presentation copy to the Queen is undoubtedly similar to her earliest confections of manuscript copies of individual works, most of which have not survived. Starting in 1402, however, and continuing through to 1410, the year Christine compiled what remains her most famous manuscript, the lavishly illustrated BL Harley 4431, she specialized in collected editions of her complete works. All in all, Christine's position as an author, a scribe, a publisher, is totally striking in the literary milieu of the early fifteenth century and it is probably not before the sixteenth century that we find author/publisher figures, male *or* female, as enterprising as she. In this regard, it is important to note that, as an editor, Christine knew how to present matters in her favour. The version of the *Rose* dossier contained in Christine's manuscript collections is highly selective, omitting what were undoubtedly the two most elaborate texts written by the *Rose* defenders, Jean de Montreuil's initial treatise, of which no copy has survived, and Pierre Col's letter, cited above, which was transcribed by chance in a much fuller manuscript collection executed separately from Christine's. To put it in other terms, Christine, as publisher, engineered the shape, and consequent reception, of the debate.

Christine's precocious interest in women and their place in society, for which she is most admired today, is not without its contradictions. The profession to which she was called, which allowed her, essentially, to earn her living after the death of all her male protectors (King Charles V, her father, her husband), was unambiguously gendered masculine. In an early description of her personal and professional transition following the death of her husband, contained in *Fortune's Transformation* (1400–3), Christine elaborates an eerily physical description of her bodily change, at the end of which she concludes: 'I am still a man and I have been for a total of more than thirteen full years, but it would please me much more to be a woman ... but since Fortune has transformed me so that I shall never again be lodged in a woman's body, I shall remain a man' (*Selected Writings*, pp. 106–7). The transformation from female to male betokens the overwhelming importance that the social symbolism of masculinity held for her. Learning itself was considered to be the province of men, who alone had access to official places of education such as the University, to such an extent that Lady Opinion reveals to the narrator in *Christine's Vision*, 'some people say that clerics or priests forge those works for you, and that they could not come from a woman's sensibility'. And yet whereas 'becoming a man' was essential to her ability to function in society as a widow, her comments about her own novelty as an author suggest that her success was precisely due to her identification as a woman. It was, in fact, by masquerading as a woman that Christine was able to be taken seriously as a man, that is, as an author. How indeed do we reconcile Christine's constant reminders of her feminine nature – uses of the diminutive, assertions of her inferiority of style and content – with the masculine enterprise in which she knowingly and actively took part? How do we, contrariwise, understand Christine's radically gender-bending view of her own position in the context of her opinions of contemporary femininity, such as we find outlined in the staunchly conservative *Treasure of the City of Ladies* (1405), in which she advocates the most conventional social roles of women as wives and mothers?

Christine's professional and intellectual achievements were extraordinary for her time, as was her awareness of the constructedness of social categories of gender as it applied to her own case. Nonetheless, her social vision of women in general – her staunch advocacy of duty to husband, modesty, and chastity, as well as of the Christian virtues – followed the most conventional attitudes of her time, thus creating interesting shifts across her career. It is in this regard helpful to take a cue from Christine and delineate the three major phases of her professional career. The first phase extends from the death of her husband to the point, 1399, demarcated in *Christine's Vision*, at which she started gravitating towards more serious topics and began to monumentalize her work in manuscript form. The second and most prolific phase, 1399–1405, covers that sketched out in *Christine's Vision*, a period distinguished by her various encounters with the *Romance of the Rose*, her most outspoken pro-woman statements, and her most detailed autobiographical musings – the period for which she is best known today. The third phase follows 1405 to the time of her death (probably around 1430), a period during which she virtually abandoned verse composition, concentrated on political and moral treatises, while relegating autobiographical material to the margins of her writing. This is not to say that there is no overlap. Many of Christine's lyrics from the 1390s are autobiographical in nature, lamenting her solitude and her grief as a widow, and even in the most austere treatises of her later period, Christine makes it clear that hers is a female voice. To be sure, one of her most skilful and moving ballad collections, *One Hundred Ballads of a Lover and a Lady*, dates to this period (1407–10), but Christine makes it clear in the Prologue that she wrote it solely because it had been commissioned by a noble patron: 'my inspiration now lies elsewhere . . . I'd rather occupy myself with other business, with more learning' (*Selected Writings*, p. 217). *Christine's Vision* narrates a crucial shift in the author's public persona and in her feeling about herself as an intellectual, to the extent that, as the last significant autobiographical moment in Christine's corpus, it functions as a sort of palinode to her previous writings.

In the *Vision*, Christine seems to reconfigure the various notions of gender that were so important in her earlier works. In her opening account of how individuals are conceived, in the baking oven of Chaos, sex is added by Nature, independently of the fusion of spirit and matter:

> My spirit approached this place, intent on witnessing this marvel. Then the breath of this great figure [Chaos] pulled my spirit toward him until it fell into the hands of the crowned lady [Nature]. When she had put the mold with all the materials into the oven, she took my spirit and stuck it in, and exactly in the way she usually gave form to human bodies she mixed everything together. And like this she let me bake for a time until a little human body was made for me. But according to the wishes of her who had made the mixture I received the female sex – because of her and not because of the mold.
>
> (*Selected Writings*, p. 177)

Fortune's Transformation, completed only two years earlier, is doubly contradicted in the later work: the Goddess Opinion, philosophical authority of the central portion of the *Vision*, directly criticizes Christine for having attributed to Fortune what is properly her domain, the determination of events in the history of humanity. More important, Philosophy, in the final section, reproaches her for having wanted to change her gender, to which Christine replies: '"Why are you asking me this? Don't you know that covetousness has not so overwhelmed me that I might wish to change my very being for that of another, for all Fortune's goods and for all possible riches?"' (*Lavision*, pp. 180–1). In personal terms, whereas Christine had bemoaned her husband's death in her earlier writings, the *Vision* lends this event a positive valence, as the means of access to her own solitary life of study surrounded by books. Indeed, as Philosophy will express it, Christine's loss of her husband was a necessary condition for her being able to enter into such a life: 'If your husband had lasted up to the present moment, you would not have been able to indulge yourself in study as you have, for household duties would not have permitted it' (*Lavision*, p. 175).

Whereas the *Vision* celebrates solitude and study as Christine's principal goals, it also advocates a hermeneutic stance that takes a distance from her convictions in the *Rose* debate. In this regard, both the *Vision* and the work immediately preceding it, *The Book of the City of Ladies*, show in distinct ways either that Christine had made peace with the massively popular allegorical poem, or quite simply that public opposition served no further purpose. The moral certainty expressed in Christine's letters turns into an intellectual relativism in the *Vision*. Lady Opinion, the very principle of intellectual inquiry, or, as Christine puts it, 'the cause which leads people to attain truth through study and understanding', is, we are told, the daughter of Ignorance. All intellectual formulations, including, we are told, both sides in the debate of the *Rose*, are motivated by Opinion. In a similarly revised position, in reference to the misogyny of Jean de Meun and Matheolus, Lady Reason consoles Christine at the beginning of the *Book of the City of Ladies*:

> 'And as for the poets of whom you speak, don't you know that they have spoken of many things in fables, and that many times they mean the opposite of what their texts seem to say? And one can approach them through the grammatical figure of *antiphrasis*, which means, as you know, that if someone says this is bad, it actually means it is good and vice versa. I therefore advise you to profit from their texts and that you interpret the passages where they speak ill of women that way, no matter what their intention was.'
>
> (*Selected Writings*, p. 122)

The manipulative play between intention, surface meaning, and the reader's interpretation, which Reason recommends here as an antidote to the oppression of misogynistic texts, had been explicitly disallowed by Christine in her letters on the *Rose*.

Christine's championing of woman's cause in society was certainly deeply felt, yet one has the impression from the two major works completed in 1405, the *Book of the City of Ladies* and the *Vision*, that a chapter in her intellectual life had been closed. The *City of Ladies* provides the final response to the concerns expressed early in her career by the God of Love: not only does a woman finally 'write the books', but the architectural construct of the city physically erases the harmful implications of Jean de Meun's fortifications. What the *Vision* adds to this, however, is somewhat of a de-sexualization of Christine's self-image, an assertion that the contemplative life, leading to a communion with God and the Trinity, ultimately rejects material wealth as well as physical particularities. Lest we be tempted to see in Christine's ruminations on her life a precocious example of modern autobiography, an account of one's life for its own sake, she makes it perfectly clear that the major events and reversals of her life are meant to provide exemplary instruction for her readers: following upon the example of Boethius, perhaps her most important intellectual and spiritual predecessor, she ends the *Vision* with Philosophy's instructions, the injunction to seek fulfilment inside rather than in external things.

In this regard, Christine's devotion to books and libraries, as a space of solitude and inner perfectioning, becomes itself a metaphor for interior self-satisfaction:

> I began to realize that the world is full of dangerous snares and that there is only one single good, and that is the way of truth; I therefore embarked on the path to which nature and the stars inclined me, that is the love of learning. Then I closed my doors, that is my senses, so that they would no longer wander around external things and snapped up your beautiful books . . .
>
> (*Selected Writings*, p. 193)

When Christine closes the door of the study she likewise closes her eyes to the outside world as a space of personal fulfilment. It would be incorrect, however, to say that 1405 marks an end to her engagement with society. It simply marks a different kind of engagement, born of France's political sorrows in its continuing war with England and the debilitating madness of King Charles VI, an engagement characterized by the austerity of a discourse in prose pointed towards military, political, and moral issues. The most noteworthy books of this period include *The Book of the Body Politic* (1407), *The Book of the Deeds of Arms and Chivalry* (1410), *The Book of Peace* (1412), and *The Book of the Prison of Human Life* (1418). After 1418, Christine maintained a silence for eleven years, broken only by her last, remarkable work, which itself assembles the various threads of her artistic life: the *Tale of Joan of Arc* (1429). Joan of Arc, contemporary counterpart of the great ladies Christine had monumentalized in *The City of Ladies*, provides an incomparable synthesis of the themes most dear to Christine: patriotism, virtue, female power, and the miracle of divine intervention. The fact that Christine returned to verse composition for the first time in twenty years in order to tell this tale further accentuates her personal investment in one of the very first literary celebrations of the Maid of Orleans.

NOTES

Note: Except for the passages from *Selected Writings*, all translations are my own.

1. *Le Débat sur le Roman de la Rose*, ed. Eric Hicks, Bibliothèque du XVe siècle, vol. 43 (Paris: Honoré Champion, 1977), p. 21. Henceforth cited parenthetically as *Débat*.
2. *The Selected Writings of Christine de Pizan*, ed. Renate Blumenfeld-Kosinski (New York: W.W. Norton, 1997), p. 194. Henceforth cited parenthetically as *Selected Writings*.
3. *Lavision-Christine*, ed. Sister Mary Louise Towner (Washington, DC: The Catholic University of America, 1932), p. 166. Henceforth cited parenthetically as *Lavision*.

13

SARAH McNAMER

Lyrics and romances

Lyrics

Only three late Middle English lyrics are explicitly attributed to women in the surviving manuscripts: a poem in praise of Venus by 'Queen Elizabeth', almost certainly Elizabeth Woodville, the wife of Edward IV; a hymn to the Virgin attributed to 'a holy ankaresse of Maunsffeld'; and another hymn in praise of the Virgin by Eleanor Percy.[1] Stylistically, each of these lyrics is highly accomplished and self-consciously literary, differing little from the elevated verse produced by professional male poets during this period. The form of Woodville's hymn to Venus is a complex elaboration of the sestina (a complicated continental verse form of six-line stanzas and an envoy); the anchoress's poem is an excellent imitation of Lydgate's fashionable aureate style; and Percy's prayer is a sophisticated macaronic poem, a poem that mixes two languages, each Middle English stanza ending with a Latin line which rhymes with that of the previous stanza. It may be that the ability of these women to produce lyrics so similar to those by the period's celebrated male poets led to their being credited with authorship. But if these women did gain some measure of recognition because of their ability to write like men, it is nonetheless interesting that, in all three cases, the subject matter is the praise of a powerful female figure.

If these three poems constituted the only evidence of women's involvement in the production of Middle English lyrics, any further discussion of the subject would quickly come to an end. Fortunately, however, the story is far more complex and interesting – and continually unfolding – thanks to that ubiquitous and mysterious figure, 'anonymous'. Anonymity is the fundamental condition of the Middle English lyric as genre: while certain lyrics – defined here simply as short poems – are attributed to authors such as Chaucer, Charles d'Orléans, Lydgate, and Dunbar, the vast majority are silent on the matter of their origins. In the face of this silence, scholars have developed strategies for determining whether or not a particular poem is

likely to have been written by a woman – with the result that over thirty
lyrics have emerged which lay strong claim to our attention as we chart the
contours of women's literary production in England.[2]

At the outset, it is worth focusing on the strategies used to recover anonymous lyrics by women, for they reveal as much about past and present assumptions about women's writing as they do about the content of the lyrics
themselves. Where the secular lyric is concerned, the chief strategy has been
to look for poems which make use of a woman's voice or express a woman's
point of view. While this approach may seem obvious, it must be used with
caution: male authors, after all, have always been capable of adopting female
personae, and indeed the dominant forms of continental female-voiced lyric
in the Middle Ages – the *cantigas de amigo* (songs of a friend), the *chan-
sons de toile* (songs at the loom), the *pastorela* (shepherdess's song), and
the *alba* (dawn song) – were produced primarily if not exclusively by men.[3]
Determining whether the gender of the author and the speaker are the same
is thus a serious challenge. But a brief look at the most common type of
female-voiced lyric in Middle English, the 'popular woman's song', can illu-
minate some basic criteria for separating lyrics by women from those that
only purport to be so. This type of poem usually takes the form of a carol
(a lyric with a refrain) in which a young woman laments the absence of her
lover or, more frequently, her seduction and abandonment by him. Because
the carol itself was originally a dance song, it was once assumed that the
female-voiced versions were genuinely popular in origin, reflecting an oral
tradition of dance songs composed by women. While it is widely accepted
that such a tradition may have existed, however, two recurrent features of
most of the surviving carols suggest that they do not belong to it. First, they
are ironic: one can detect a presence behind the poem, manipulating the lyric
voice in such as way as to satirize the speaker. Such satire is clearly evident
in poems which function as confessions of sexual adventure and consequent
downfall, the maiden who yields to her seducer being not only betrayed in
the end, but left pregnant:

> qwan he and me browt un us þe schete, [when]
> Of all hys wyll I hym lete;
> Now wyll not my gyrdyll met – [my belt will not meet]
> a, dere god, qwat xal I sayn?[4] [what shall I say?]

Second, the background situation and the female voice itself are often overdramatized: the woman's voice issues from a fully developed female persona,
one whose femaleness is often foregrounded through references to her body
and what her virile lover does to it ('he gafe my mayden-hed a spurne'; 'he
prikede & he pransede, nolde he neuer lynne [he would not cease]').[5] Such

bold signals that it is a woman who speaks are, in themselves, grounds for suspecting that the source of that voice is a wry male author. But by the same token, these criteria for ruling *out* certain lyrics as products of women writers can provide grounds for ruling *in*: if a lyric written in a woman's voice is free of self-mocking irony and not overdramatized, the possibility that it was written by a woman is quite plausible.

On the basis of internal evidence alone, a number of lyrics have gradually gained admission – if only on a provisional and tentative basis – into the expanding canon of medieval women's writing. But an equally productive strategy has been to look for external evidence of female authorship – above all, the evidence presented by manuscripts. One in particular, the Findern Manuscript (Cambridge University Library MS Ff. i.vi), vividly illustrates the value of such evidence for the project of recovering lyrics by women. One of the striking features of this manuscript is the presence of several women's names, names which appear to be signatures and can be traced to provincial families living at or in the vicinity of the Findern estate in Derbyshire in the late fifteenth and early sixteenth centuries. Close examination of the physical features of the volume has led scholars to conclude that women of the Derbyshire gentry were heavily involved in the production of the manuscript, which is primarily a collection of secular verse by the period's renowned authors (Chaucer, Gower, Lydgate, and others). Twenty-nine anonymous lyrics appear in the volume, and while none of these are directly attributed to the women whose names appear in the manuscript, the palaeographical evidence, combined with a close reading of the poems themselves, strongly suggests that women composed at least fifteen of them.[6]

Most of the anonymous poems that have been proposed as candidates for inclusion in the corpus of medieval women's writing are love lyrics. They vary considerably, as we might expect; for not only were their authors writing from outside the kinds of literary circles that tended to favour particular styles of composition among established male poets; they also lacked a visible tradition of literary foremothers that might supply models of a woman's love poem. Thus, while some of these poems are quite naive, others are technically complex, making use of anagrams, metrical innovations, experimental rhyme schemes, and so on. Different as they may be in degree of poetic sophistication, however, the women's love lyrics from this period are often united in one important respect: they tend to include a specificity of detail which lends them a distinctive *personal* quality. Their authors, in other words, seem to have viewed the lyric as a self-expressive genre, as a medium for communicating the private thoughts and feelings arising from lived experience. This is one of the features which distinguishes the women's poems from the dominant tradition of medieval love lyric, in which the passionate 'I' who speaks is typically a poetic fiction, the sentiments expressed are general enough to have broad applicability, and the poem itself is intended to be widely circulated or publicly performed.

This tendency to personalize and privatize the genre is evident in the use women make of a particular lyric form: the verse letter. By the late fourteenth century, it is not uncommon for love poems written by men to present themselves as 'little bills' to be delivered to the beloved. But the proportion of verse letters among women's lyrics is especially high, no doubt in part because the personal letter itself was perceived as a genre open to women at this time: the fifteenth century is the age when private correspondence first flourished in secular English society and, as collections such as the Paston letters illustrate, women often engaged in letter-writing to express intimate thoughts and desires as well as to communicate matters of practical import. Moreover, the notion of the lyric-as-letter seems to have been particularly inviting to women, who tend to exploit the analogy between the two genres at the deep level of function. Epistolary formulas are not used merely to add rhetorical flourish, but to underscore the lyric's status as a private communication between one person and another.

One of the clearest examples of this is a poem beginning 'Ensamples fayre ye fynde in nature'.[7] Dating from the late fourteenth century, the lyric seems to have been composed by a lady of the court engaged in a secret liaison with a man of royal birth, perhaps even Henry V before he became king. As the author enjoins her lover to keep the affair secret, preserve her good reputation, and endure their separation patiently, she makes no attempt to craft a poem with wide applicability or public appeal; indeed, the fact that the lyric is often confusing, alluding to various aspects of the affair in quite elliptical ways, appears to confirm that it was composed as a private communication to the lover (who would have no need for a clear exposition of the background scenario). Four of the seven women's lyrics preserved in a manuscript from the early sixteenth century, Oxford, Bodleian MS Rawlinson C. 813, are also verse letters bearing a distinctly personal stamp.[8] Indeed, one of these takes the gap between empty conventional sentiment and the reality of a particular love affair as its explicit theme. It is composed as a response to a lover's letter or poem, in which he has portrayed his beloved as the stereotypical mistress of poetic convention: the hard-hearted, fickle woman whose beauty has wounded and ensnared him. With subtle wit, the author responds to his poetic conceits with appeals to reality. Her beauty cannot be causing him such distress, she asserts, for she is in fact rather plain: 'I knowe right well I was never soo bewtiouse / That I shuld you constren to be soo amerous.'[9] As for the charge of inconstancy, she reminds him in the most direct of terms that she will continue to be faithful:

> Truly, unconstant you shall me never fynde,
> But ever to be trewe, faithffull and kinde,
> And to you beire my trewe harte withouten vareance,
> Desiring you to make me noo dyssemblance.

The author goes on to associate 'dissembling' with poetic 'fantasy', which she sees as an obstacle to true love. Her final plea is that they strive 'all fantasyez to exclude / Off love fayned, and the contrarye to attaine'. By writing this down-to-earth verse letter as a corrective to her lover's indiscriminate deployment of poetic conventions, she has initiated just this kind of project.

The poems in the Findern manuscript also exhibit this tendency to personalize the conventional, not only in their letter-like intimacy of address, but also in their transmutation of standard poetic topoi.[10] Superficially, many of these poems seem to fit within the tradition of the male-authored courtly love lyric – a tradition which includes, of course, the depiction of the beloved as distant, an elaboration of the suffering caused by this 'merciless' beloved, and the lover's vows of undying fidelity (which take the playful form of the feudal pledge of perpetual service and obedience). But while the authors of the Findern lyrics borrow some of the terms of courtly love, they do so with a twist: they adapt them to the circumstances of their own lives as provincial women – circumstances which can be reconstructed from the evidence we have of the Derbyshire gentry in the fifteenth century as well as from contemporary letters by provincial women such as the Pastons and Stonors.[11] The most striking feature of such adaptation is the way that the conventional pledge of service and fidelity is transformed in these poems. At first glance, the pledges in the Findern lyrics seem to be just like the exaggerated, flirtatious feudal vows of the standard courtly lyric. One speaker vows 'Yow to sarue [serve] watt ʒe commaund me'; another asserts, 'You to serue and trwly plese / Is my desyr and hertus esse [ease]'; another promises 'To lefe and dure [endure] in yowre seruyce / Wytoute faynyng of my hert / Thow I fele neuer soo grete smerte'.[12] But on closer inspection, these pledges appear to be iterations of an altogether more serious kind of promise, one directly applicable to the authors of the lyrics: the marriage vow. In the standard marriage rites of the period, the bride is asked to obey and serve her spouse, for better or for worse, until death. The authors of the Findern lyrics thus appear to have intended the poems to function as serious assurances

of their marital fidelity in the face of extended separations from their
husbands:

> Thus Y am sette
> Neuer to lette,   [cease]
> For well nor woo
> You to serue,
> Tyll that Y starue   [die]
> Where-euer ye goo.

Stanzas such as these have a sincere and intimate tone. The self-expressive
quality of the lyrics, however, need not imply that the authors of the Findern
lyrics lacked poetic self-consciousness. Indeed, the fact that the lyrics express
similar sentiments in similar ways strongly suggests that their authors crafted
the poems with the help of each other – thus making up for the lack of an
established tradition of women's love poetry by creating a living tradition of
their own.

The preponderance of what appear to be personal, self-expressive love
poems by women is significant, in part because private poetry is so rare in
the Middle Ages – or indeed in the lyric as a genre before the Romantic
period. But not all women's love poetry is private or serious in character;
a small number of comic love poems are likely to have been written by
women. Presumably intended for public performance, these lyrics playfully
mock men, exposing their shortcomings as lovers – their physical defects,
lack of manners, and their 'dowbilnys' or insincerity in love. The opening
stanzas of this lyric from the Findern manuscript exemplify women's capacity
for composing in the comic mode:

> What-so men seyn,
> Love is no peyn
> To them, serteyn,   [certainly]
>   But varians.
> For they constreyn
> Ther hertis to feyn
> Ther mowthis to pleyn   [lament]
>   Ther displesaunce.[13]

Since men do nothing but beguile, this poem concludes, they ought to be
'Begelid, parde, / Withowtyn grace'. It is easy to imagine the entertainment
value of such a poem to a group of women – or its flirtatious effects in mixed
company.

In the attempt to identify anonymous lyrics by women, then, the scholarly
focus on poems written from a woman's point of view has been productive, particularly when internal clues to female authorship are supported by

manuscript evidence. But there are limits to the usefulness of this approach. It is no accident that virtually all of the lyrics it has yielded are love poems: for this method requires female authors to write *as women* in order to be identified as such – and love poems foreground gender in a uniquely prominent way. The implicit assumption that women necessarily write in a woman's voice has thus had the unhappy consequence of inhibiting investigation of other kinds of anonymous lyrics which are written from a gender-neutral point of view or which feature dramatic personae (including male personae) as speakers. Such lyrics include philosophical poems, poems of instruction, proverbs, verse recipes, charms, lyrics on nature, occasional verses, and – most significantly – religious lyrics, which outnumber all other kinds of Middle English lyric by far. To date, no anonymous lyrics belonging to these categories have been attributed to female authors. But potentially fruitful avenues for investigation include further manuscript research, particularly in the case of religious lyrics; attending to the social contexts in which lyrics such as verse recipes or poems for the instruction of children are likely to have been used; or considering the possibility that certain kinds of lyrics, such as the lullabies and laments of the Virgin, were modelled on traditions of oral poetry by women even if they were written in final form by men.[14]

The question of women's role as *consumers* of the Middle English lyric has, to date, received scant attention.[15] As we turn now to the genre of romance, however, we shall see that consumption, rather than production, has been the dominant issue where women are concerned.

Romances

Precisely how to define romance as a genre has generated significant controversy. Attempts to define it according to subject matter or form have often failed to capture the capaciousness and elasticity of the genre as it evolved in England from the twelfth through the fifteenth centuries. For while many insular romances – that is, romances circulating in England – feature an adventure-seeking knight as hero, explore the themes of love and chivalry, celebrate the world of the aristocracy and its values, and contain elements of the supernatural, many do not conform to this image of the classic French romance: their themes, heroes, and plots are far more varied, incorporating elements from hagiography, history, folktale, and local legend. Formal boundaries which would distinguish the romance from other genres are also difficult to demarcate. In recent years, there has thus been increasing acceptance of a broad, practical definition, one which focuses on the genre's primary function rather than its matter or form. Romance, according to this line of thinking, is a secular narrative designed chiefly for purposes of entertainment.[16] Defined thus, surviving insular romances include fourteen written in Anglo-Norman and over one hundred in Middle English; the circulation of French romances in England during the fourteenth and fifteenth centuries brings the tally even higher.[17] Late medieval England was thus rich in romances, and they form a significant leavening element in a literary culture largely dominated by religious and didactic writing. The overtly recreational character of the genre, however, does not mean that it performed no serious cultural work. Many romances clearly served powerful ideological interests: they not only reflected but possessed the potential to perpetuate certain beliefs, values, and behaviours, including – crucially – those related to gender. Much recent scholarship has thus emphasized romance's ideological dimensions when considering women's relationship to the genre.

The vast majority of romances were written by anonymous authors. Curiously, however, the possibility that women may have written some of the surviving romances has never been seriously investigated, even though there are ample grounds here, too, for questioning the persistent tendency to assign all anonymous literature to men. Women evidently possessed the creative capacity to compose romances: given Marie de France's exquisite mastery of the *lai*, surely other women could have imagined compelling stories of love and adventure. Moreover, the dominant metrical forms of romance – chiefly couplets and tail-rhymes – required no formal schooling; and as we have seen in the case of the lyric, women could prove quite skilled at metrical composition. It may well be that more substantive cultural factors inhibited women from trying their hand at this genre. In any case, it is important to recognize that this question has yet to receive critical scrutiny; if there were any female authors of insular romances, they remain invisible.

In another sense, however, women have been very visible participants in the production of romance: they have often been credited as the genre's ideal readers. Romance is overtly marked as a woman's genre in a number of medieval texts, most famously in Chaucer's *Nun's Priest's Tale*, in which the narrator makes this mocking claim:

> This storie is also trewe, I undertake,
> As is the book of Launcelot de Lake,
> That wommen holde in ful greet reverence.[18]

In his *Troilus and Criseyde*, Chaucer again implies that women – particularly aristocratic women – form the ideal reading community for romance when he depicts Criseyde and her female companions enjoying a 'romaunce . . . of Thebes' read aloud to them by a maiden in an enclosed, feminized space.[19] The thirteenth-century Middle English romance *Sir Tristrem* portrays Ysoude as a reader of romance, and one of the Harley lyrics lists the beloved's habit of reading romances among the decidedly feminine attributes which make her so attractive:

> Heo haþ a mury mouht to mele   [She has a pleasing mouth for speaking]
> wiþ lefly rede lippes lele   [with lovely red lips well-suited]
> romaunȝ forte rede.[20]   [for reading romances]

Such scenes of women reading romances might, in themselves, give the impression that the genre evolved in medieval England primarily in response to audiences of women, continuing a trajectory initiated by female patrons and readers at the courts of Eleanor of Aquitaine and Marie de Champagne. But there is an immediate reason to be sceptical of these images of women readers, or at least to refrain from extrapolating from them to broad conclusions about the readership of romance in general. In more than a few romances, the inscribed audience is one of men. 'Lordingis', begins the narrator in one; 'All werthy men', hails another; 'worshipfull sirres', another; and so on.[21] Addresses to mixed audiences are equally prevalent. It is widely acknowledged, of course, that inscribed audiences are often fictional conventions; they cannot be taken as unproblematic evidence of a work's actual readers. But they do serve to put into question the historical status of the image of the romance-reading woman – and the necessity of looking to external evidence in order to determine the extent of women's participation as consumers of romance.

Recent research on book ownership among women, based largely on the evidence of manuscripts and wills, has begun to yield a more reliable picture of women's relationship to romance as readers.[22] This research has not been comprehensive, but enough evidence has accumulated to suggest that, after works of religious devotion, romance is the genre that women owned most frequently in late medieval England. Moreover, certain patterns have emerged within this general framework. Evidence of female ownership of Middle English romances is surprisingly rare. It can be demonstrated that women owned copies of *The Four Sons of Aymon*, *Sir Degrevaunt*, *Generydes*, *The Chronicles of Jerusalem*, the prose *Merlin*, *The Holy Grail*, Chaucer's *Troilus and Criseyde*, and Lydgate's *Troy Book* and his *Siege of Thebes*;[23] manuscripts containing *King Horn*, *Floris and Blauncheflur*, *Robert of Sicily*, *The King of Tars*, *Joseph of Arimathea*, and *King Ponthus and the Fair Sidone* are also thought to have been produced for women.[24] But this list represents a very small fraction of the total number of Middle English romances. In contrast, the abundant evidence for women's ownership of French romances during the fourteenth and fifteenth centuries is striking. Aristocratic women in particular appear to have had a decided taste for French Arthurian romances circulating under titles such as *Launcelot, Tristrem, Artur de Britaigne, Merlyn, Guiron le Courtois,* and *Mort Artu.*[25] Thus, while it may not be possible to take the pronouncement in the *Nun's Priest's Tale* as an accurate reflection of the readership of romance in general, evidence of book ownership strongly suggests that the more precise generic subcategory – *Lancelot de Lake* as French Arthurian romance – may well be a fitting description of what aristocratic women of late medieval England did 'holde in full greet reverence'.

Another approach to the question of women's relationship to romances as consumers has considered how women are depicted in them – the assumption being that the more sympathetically an author has attempted to portray women's desires, values, inner lives, and social circumstances, the more appealing a given romance is likely to have been to female members of the audience. There are limits to the validity of this assumption, of course. Cross-gender identification is certainly possible: female readers need not always identify with female characters, and indeed, identifying with the male hero of romance may have enabled many women imaginatively to experience a kind of freedom of action that they were denied in their own lives. Nonetheless, a brief look at how images of women change over time in insular romance suggests certain patterns that correlate to some degree with the external evidence of book ownership.

Early insular romances include fourteen written in Anglo-Norman between about 1150 and 1230 and eight composed in Middle English during the thirteenth century. Most of the Middle English texts derive from Anglo-Norman sources, and while there are significant differences between the two in some respects, they are quite similar in their depiction of women. Compared to the Old French romances which preceded them, for instance, the early insular romances exhibit relatively little interest in delineating the complex psychological states of women in love. Moreover, while two versions of the Tristan legend figure among the early romances, most are less risky in their moral stance, eschewing the theme of adulterous passion and presenting the woman in love as one for whom socially profitable marriage is the ultimate goal. At the same time, however, the early romances as a whole tend to promote the view that women should have an active role in attaining their emotional and sexual desires. The figure of the 'wooing woman', for instance, figures prominently in both the Anglo-Norman and early Middle English corpus, where she is typically free of the negative associations accruing to the lustful woman in the broad tradition of medieval misogyny. No censure is attached to Rymenhild in *King Horn* when she falls passionately in love with Horn, invites him into her chamber, leads him to her bed, gives him wine, initiates embraces and kisses, and proposes marriage.[26]

Blauncheflur in *Floris and Blauncheflur*, Ysoude in *Sir Tristrem*, Belisaunt in *Amis and Amiloun*, and Josiane in *Bevis of Hampton* are further examples of the positively portrayed wooing woman who actively seeks union with her beloved and persists in pursuing that goal, despite numerous obstacles. The chief impediment to a woman's happiness in most of these romances is the threat of being married off to one she does not love – a threat which clearly had social parallels at the time these texts were written, despite the insistence of the Church from the twelfth century on that the consent of both parties was necessary to the formation of a valid marriage. The early romances often register resistance to the practice of pressuring women into arranged marriages, treating female characters in such a plight with sympathy and exposing the political and economic motives of those who trade women like chattel in the marriage market. These sympathetic portrayals of women may not be enough to suggest that women commissioned the romances or formed the primary audience for them; but they do seem to be deliberate attempts to appeal to female members of the audience.

Middle English romances of the fourteenth century are, on the whole, less interested in exploring aspects of women's experience in the drama of desire. In part, this shift reflects the expansion of romance itself as a genre: not only does it become more popular in character, catering to audiences other than the elite; it also encompasses a far wider range of subject matter, so that the courtship plot which had been so central to the genre in its earlier manifestations becomes diluted or displaced.[27] Even in the romances that retain the classic pairing of chivalry and courtship, scenes involving love and women tend to be greatly compressed while scenes of fighting and demonstrations of the hero's prowess are amplified. Indeed, women are often portrayed as dangerous obstacles to the hero's success in proving himself. The treatment of the wooing woman in fourteenth-century romance fits within this general pattern. Positive renderings of women who initiate liaisons all but disappear; when wooing women do surface, they are generally far less bold than their thirteenth-century counterparts, or, in the case of the lady in *Sir Gawain and the Green Knight*, depicted as perilous to the hero.

If the image of woman as lover receives less favourable or extensive treatment in the fourteenth-century romances, however, female characters do receive significant attention in a type of romance that comes into its own during this period: the 'family' romance in which family members are separated, endure various trials and tribulations, and are eventually reunited and reconciled. Influenced by hagiographical narratives, these romances emphasize the virtues of patience and trust in providence and seek to elicit sympathy for those suffering misfortune. They present women as especially vulnerable, and especially good at suffering; female protagonists thus figure prominently in this type of romance – often, like the eponymous heroine in *Emaré*, in the role of the 'calumniated wife' who is unjustly accused of wrongdoing. Whatever the ideological implications of presenting the patient endurance of suffering as a feat for which women have a special aptitude, it remains true that this body of romances at least attempts to define heroism as a condition open to women – and one that is not dependent on violent displays of physical prowess.

The fourteenth century is the period when Middle English romances begin to address themselves to a company of men – the 'worshipfull sirres' and 'lordingis' mentioned above. But it is in the fifteenth century that the genre appears to undergo a more thorough masculinization: in addition to increasing evidence of male ownership of romances during this period, the content of many romances seems designed to appeal particularly to men. Malory's *Morte d'Arthur* is the most significant example of this trend. Comparison of Malory's text with his sources reveals an often stark abridgement of scenes involving women – particularly those which, in his originals, credit women with complex inner lives – and the retention or expansion of episodes having to do with the masculine world of martial exploits. More striking still is the pronounced emphasis on bonds between men and the explicit valuation of such homosocial connections above the heterosexual unions celebrated in traditional Arthurian romance. This is nowhere more evident than in the famous concluding scene of the *Morte*, in which Arthur, having lost Guinevere and the Round Table, laments, 'And much more I am soryar for my good knyghtes losse than for the losse of my fayre quene; for quenys I myght have inow, but such a felyship of good knyghtes shal never be togydirs in no company.'[28]

If late Middle English romance seems to have been directed increasingly towards male readers, however, there are indications that women were sometimes able to counter this trend by exercising their power as consumers. Such power is evident, for instance, in the fact that aristocratic women continued to seek out – and often to bequeath to their daughters – French versions of Arthurian romances even after the publication of Malory's celebrated rendition.[29] But it is perhaps fitting to conclude this overview of the genre with a return to a homegrown English production, the Findern manuscript, for it offers an especially compelling example of such power. As we have noted, women were actively involved in the compilation of this manuscript. One of the clearest signs of this involvement is the presence of two women's names – Elizabet Koton and Elisabet Frauncys – at the conclusion of the romance of *Sir Degrevaunt*. Since these names appear where scribal signatures usually do, it is likely that the two women copied out the romance themselves; but even if they did not, the romance is clearly 'signed' under their names in a way that grants them a special possession of it.

Significantly, *Sir Degrevaunt* is one of the most female-friendly romances in the entire Middle English corpus. Not only does it feature attractive, re-sourceful, intelligent female characters who wield influence over men; it also stages a debate between the world of men and that of women – and finds the former wanting. As the dual plot progresses – the love affair between De-grevaunt and Melidor developing even as the conflict between Degrevaunt and Melidor's father escalates – the romance exposes the limits of the mas-culine values of physical prowess, decisive action, and fighting for justice, asserting that these must be tempered and complemented by a set of values associated with women – hospitality, conversation, compromise, and recon-ciliation. Moreover, female desire is vindicated in the end, triumphing even over patriarchal authority as Melidor, having engaged in an affair with her father's enemy, ultimately weds her beloved and enjoys a long and happy life with him. So sympathetic to a woman's point of view is *Sir Degrevaunt*, in fact, that serious consideration of the possibility that it was written by a woman would not be unreasonable. But at the very least, the presence of this text in the Findern manuscript testifies to the capacity of women to procure the kind of romance in which they could see their gender celebrated – even, in an era of romance's masculinization, against the odds.

NOTES

1. The three lyrics are printed in Alexandra Barratt, ed., *Women's Writing in Middle English* (London: Longman, 1992), pp. 275–7 and 279–81.
2. The anonymous lyrics that have been proposed as products of women writers can be found in the following anthologies and articles: Barratt, *Women's Writing*, pp. 264–90; Sarah McNamer, 'Female Authors, Provincial Setting: the Re-versing of Courtly Love in the Findern Manuscript', *Viator* 22 (1991): 303–10; Linne R. Mooney, '"A Woman's Reply to Her Lover" and Four Other New Courtly Love Lyrics in Cambridge, Trinity College MS R. 3. 19', *Medium Aevum* 67:2 (1997): 250–1; Anne F. Sutton and Livia Visser-Fuchs, 'The Cult of Angels in Late Fifteenth-Century England: an Hours of the Guardian Angel Presented to Queen Elizabeth Woodville', in *Women and the Book: Assessing the Visual Evidence*, eds. Lesley Smith and Jane H. M. Taylor (London: British Library 1997), pp. 234–5; and F. M. Padelford, 'Liedersammlungen des XVI Jahrunderts besonders auf der Zeit Heinrichs VIII. IV. 7. The Songs in Manuscript Rawlinson c. 813', *Anglia* 31 (1908): nos. 7, 19, 36, 37, 46, 51.
3. See Peter Dronke, *The Medieval Lyric*, 3rd edn (Cambridge: D. S. Brewer, 1996), pp. 86–108 and 167–85.
4. Rossell Hope Robbins, ed., *Secular Lyrics of the XIVth and XVth Centuries* (Oxford: Clarendon Press, 1952), p. 18.
5. Ibid., pp. 23, 19.

6. See McNamer, 'Female Authors'.

7. See Mooney, '"A Woman's Reply"'.

8. Three of the Rawlinson lyrics are printed in Barratt, *Women's Writing*, pp. 264–8. All are printed in Padelford, 'Liedersammlungen'; see note 2 above.

9. Barratt, *Women's Writing*, p. 266.

10. The Findern lyrics likely to have been written by women are printed in McNamer, 'Female Authors', pp. 303–10. Three appear in Barratt, *Women's Writing*, pp. 268–74.

11. See McNamer, 'Female Authors', for a historical contextualization of the Findern lyrics.

12. McNamer, 'Female Authors', pp. 303, 306, 307.

13. Ibid., 304; Barratt, *Women's Writing*, pp. 268–70. Other humorous poems possibly by women include 'He that wil be a lover in every wise', Barratt, *Women's Writing*, p. 290, and perhaps 'Vnto you, most froward, þis lettre I write', Robbins, *Secular Lyrics*, pp. 219–20.

14. For an array of these other kinds of lyrics, see Robbins, *Secular Lyrics*, and Carleton Brown, ed., *English Lyrics of the XIIIth Century* (Oxford: Clarendon Press, 1932), *Religious Lyrics of the XIVth Century* (Oxford: Clarendon Press, 1924), and *Religious Lyrics of the XVth Century* (Oxford: Clarendon Press, 1939).

15. Many secular and religious lyrics are addressed to women, but with rare exceptions – such as the celebrated 'Love Ron' of Thomas of Hales, which the manuscript tells us was written at the request of a young woman – it is difficult to distinguish between fictive and historical addressees. For the 'Love Ron', see Brown, *English Lyrics of the XIIIth Century*, pp. 68–74.

16. Derek Pearsall's simple definition, 'secular narratives, with a hero, designed for entertainment' has been influential (Derek Pearsall, *Old English and Middle English*, *The Routledge History of English Poetry*, vol. 1 (London: Routledge, 1977), p. 113); see Rosalind Field, 'Romance in England, 1066–1400', in *The Cambridge History of Medieval English Literature*, ed. David Wallace (Cambridge University Press, 1999), p. 152. The definition advanced in *A Manual of the Writings in Middle English* – 'a narrative about knightly prowess and adventure, in verse or in prose, intended primarily for the entertainment of a listening audience' (Helaine Newstead, 'Romances: General', in *A Manual of the Writings in Middle English 1050–1500*, Fascicule 1: Romances, ed. J. B. Severs (New Haven: Connecticut Academy of Arts and Sciences, 1967), p. 11) – is more restrictive but still places the emphasis on entertainment.

17. A descriptive list and bibliography of the Middle English romances can be found in Severs, *Manual*, Fascicule 1. The Anglo-Norman romances are discussed by Susan Crane, *Insular Romance: Politics, Faith, and Culture in Anglo-Norman and Middle English Literature* (Berkeley: University of California Press, 1986). For a partial list of the French romances circulating in England in the fourteenth and fifteenth centuries, see Carol M. Meale, '". . . Alle the Bokes that I Haue of Latyn, Englisch, and Frensch": Laywomen and their Books in Late Medieval England', in *Women and Literature in Britain, 1150–1500*, ed. Carol M. Meale, 2nd edn (Cambridge University Press, 1996), pp. 139–41.

18. *The Riverside Chaucer*, 7.4401–3, p. 258.

19. Ibid, 2.100, p. 490.

20. George P. McNeill, ed., *Sir Tristrem*, Scottish Text Society 8 (1886), lines 1257–8; G. L. Brook, ed., *The Harley Lyrics: The Middle English Lyrics of Ms. Harley 2253*, 4th edn (Manchester University Press, 1968), p. 38.

21. Carol M. Meale, '"Good Men / Wiues Maydens and Alle Men": Romance and its Audiences', in *Readings in Medieval English Romance*, ed. Carol M. Meale (Cambridge: D. S. Brewer, 1994), p. 209, n. 3.

22. See Meale, '". . . Alle the Bokes that I Haue"', for a discussion of both method and evidence.

23. Ibid., pp. 140–2.

24. *King Horn* and *Floris and Blauncheflur* appear in Cambridge University Library MS Gg.iv.27; *King Ponthus*, in Oxford, Bodleian Library MS Digby 181; and the other three in the Vernon Manuscript, Oxford, Bodley MS eng. poet.a.1. Each of these manuscripts is believed to have been compiled for women.

25. Meale, '". . . Alle the Bokes that I Haue"', pp. 139–40.

26. See esp. lines 252–66; 307–12; 403–14, in Donald B. Sands, ed., *Middle English Verse Romances* (University of Exeter Press, 1986).

27. See Severs, *Manual*, Fascicule 1, for an overview of the various kinds of Middle English romance.

28. Eugène Vinaver, ed., *Malory: Works*, 2nd edn (London: Oxford University Press, 1971), Book xx: ii, p. 685.

29. Meale, '". . . Alle the Bokes that I Haue"', pp. 139–40.

14

NICHOLAS WATSON

Julian of Norwich

'Take it generally'

Julian of Norwich's *Revelation of Love* is the earliest work in English we are sure is by a woman. It is also one of the most ambitious Middle English texts we have, straining the resources of the vernacular in which it was written, as it strains the understanding of readers today. The work grew out of a visionary episode it dates to 1373, when Julian was thirty, and was completed over a period that may have reached into the fifteenth century. It exists in two versions which I call here by their manuscript titles: *A Vision schewed [. . .] to a devoute woman* (the Short Text) and *A Revelacion of Love* (the Long Text). Powerful though they are, neither was widely read in the Middle Ages. *A Vision* survives in one fifteenth-century manuscript in a northern dialect (London, BL Additional 37790), while the earliest copies of *A Revelation* are a pair of manuscripts written by English nuns in France between 1600 and 1650: one in Norfolk English, the other in an East Midlands dialect (London, BL Sloane 2499 and Paris, Bibliothèque Nationale fonds anglais 41).[1]

These versions give us a bare outline of Julian's biography as a visionary, but tell us little of what her life was like. We know from a will that she was an anchoress at the church of St Julian's, Norwich, by 1393, and from *The Book of Margery Kempe* that she was still an anchoress in 1413, when Kempe visited her: it seems she had a reputation as a spiritual guide.[2] But because we do not know her original name, nobody has found out where she came from or how she came to write what she did. Ignorance on these matters holds back our efforts to understand what is at stake in her book.

One way of dealing with all we do not know about *A Revelation* would be to decide it does not matter, since it parallels the level of generality on which Julian thinks. She instructs readers to 'leve the beholdyng' of her own life to contemplate God, and hears an inner voice advising her to take her vision 'generally [. . .]. For it is more worshype to God to beholde hym in alle than in any specyalle thyng' (*fos. 18r, 62*). Lack of information makes it easy to obey these injunctions. Medieval and modern fantasies about anchoresses as 'dead to the world', living lives of isolated silence, also encourage us to hear the 'I' that speaks in *A Revelation* as a voice without a context: the voice of a solitary woman genius writing mainly for herself.

In practice, the difficulty of Julian's thinking demands that most of this essay spell out her ideas, without much regard for their contemporary context. Yet the book was not written in a vacuum, but composed in one of the busiest cities of medieval England, as part of a nation-wide explosion of vernacular theology, in which opposing views about what is true, what it is to be good, how society should be run, and what ordinary people should be taught were in pitched battle with one another.[3] Julian wrote during the time that the first English Bible was produced, and that the radical group known by its opponents as Lollards was declared heretical by the institutional Church. Despite its use of the visionary 'I', her book is equally an expression of a group, making its voice heard in the debates of the day. Felicity Riddy has shown how the layout of *A Revelation* suggests the presence of an editorial team, and argued that the progressive 'textualization' of Julian's visionary experience is itself a sign of the sustenance her project drew from an authorizing community.[4] Apart from the Lollards, there were other associations of like-minded religious people in late medieval England, from the guilds who formed around a saint's cult, to the network of 'Goddys serwantys' who looked after Kempe as she journeyed around England: 'ankrys and reclusys' (including Julian) 'and many other of owyr Lordys loverys, wyth many worthy clerkys'.[5] The last section of the essay thus moves away from describing Julian's theology, to reflect briefly on what her book tells us about the community in which it was written, as this community sought to publicize its message about the nature of divine love, and about the authority of the visionary medium in which the message was cast.

'By bodily sight and by ghostly sight'

A Vision is the earlier of the versions of Julian's book but is already a polished, gripping, scene-by-scene narrative of an experience it depicts as a dialogic, obscure, but in theory lucid communication between God and his people, with Julian herself acting as representative and a medium. The setting is her death-bed, where she lies, surrounded by friends, forgetting that long before she had asked God to make her undergo, while still alive, the pains of dying and a 'bodylye syght' of Christ's passion: to travel back in time to the pivotal moment in Christian history and forwards to the pivotal moment in her own (fo. 97). As she gazes at a crucifix, held by her priest to protect her from demons waiting to seize her soul, her dying eyes animate the blood painted on Christ's crown of thorns, which begins to 'trekylle [trickle] downe fro undyr the garlande alle hate [hot] – freschlye, plentefully, and lyvelye – ryght as methought that it was in that tyme that the garlonde of thornys was thyrstede [thrust] on his blessede heede' (fo. 98v). Other medieval women, attuned to visualization by the exercise of Passion meditation, saw Christ's death in coherent detail, and at first it seems as if this vision, too, is going to follow this narrative path. But what happens is more unexpected: a string of *allusions* to the passion and what it means about the nature of God, the creation, humankind, and sin: an event richly suggestive, perceived in distinct modes ('be [by] bodylye syght, and be worde formede in myne undyrstandynge, and be gastelye [spiritual] syght', fo. 101r), and full of radical possibilities. These last are made more difficult to interpret by the mix of intimacy and absence – Christ's 'hamly [familiar] lovynge' and moments seen 'hevelye and derkelye' (fos. 99r, 101v) – that characterizes the thirty hours of Julian's spiritual ordeal. *A Vision* goes on to depict Julian's first response to this episode as disbelief, and to suggest lines of interpretation, always generalizing out from 'bodylye syght' to 'gastelye', from the primal scene of the Passion to the order of being as a whole. (This process is figured early in the text by her sight of the 'lytille thynge the qwantyte of a haselle nutte', which represents 'alle that ys made', and a parallel sight, not of creation, but of 'God in a poynte [. . .] by whilke [which] syght I sawe that he es in alle thynge' (fos. 99r, 101v)). But the text never admits the most exciting implication of its fusion of the singular and the cosmic: that sin is a good, and that God's love will save all humankind – that 'synne is behovelye [necessary] [. . .] Botte alle schalle be wele, and alle maner of thynge schalle be wele' (fos. 106r–v). Held back by its commitment to orthodoxy, *A Vision* indeed ends in frustration, implying that it has been thwarted by 'doutefulle drede' [doubting fear] from lucidity: 'I am sekyr [sure] that alle doutefulle dredes God hates' (fo. 114v).

Although often thought of as a mere draft of *A Revelation*, *A Vision* seems at first to have been meant to stand on its own. If it presents God's self-revelation in episodic form, avoiding conclusions even when pointing lessons, this is of a piece with its presentation of Julian's role as visionary, 'styrre[d]' by 'charyte' towards 'evyncrystene' [fellow Christians] to share what she has learned from the 'soverayne techare', not an authority in her own right: 'God forbede that ye schulde saye or take it so that I am a techere. [. . .] For I am a woman, le[w]ed, febille, and freylle' (fo. 101r). In *A Vision*, Julian's reticence in interpreting what she sees is a guarantee that what she says she has from God. Only in its final pages are there signs of the dissatisfaction that underlay her decision to start again.

'Hold thee therein'

A Revelation is a full-scale reworking of *A Vision* and more than four times its length, part expansion, part commentary, part theological *summa*; it must have taken years to finish, and involved research as well as thought and discussion. With its subdivision of Julian's experience into 'sixteen shewynges' (*fo. 1r*) and eighty-six chapters, the text is the result of a systematizing of *A Vision* that derives from two episodes dated to 1388 and 1393. In these, she receives hermeneutic instructions (whether from God or within herself is unclear) as to how her experience can be fearlessly written down, despite the fact that she remains 'a symple creature unlettyrde, leving in deadly [mortal] flesh' (*fo. 3r*).

The first of these instructions, which Julian delays describing until the end of *A Revelation* but which underpins the whole book, explains that God's 'menyng' in the revelation is summed up in the word 'love': 'Who shewyth it the? Love. [What shewyth he the? Love.] Wherfore shewyth he it the? For love.' (*fo. 173v*). This 'gostly understondyng' can be read as a retraction of a passage that may at one point have been intended to become the peroration of *A Vision*, but which Julian eventually left out of *A Revelation*, which suggests that God's meaning has to do not with love but with sin: 'A, wriched synne! Whate ert thou? Thowe er nought! [. . .] And alle tha that [those who] luffez the and lykes the and folowes the and wilfully endes in the, I am sekyr [sure] thay schalle be brought to nought with the, and endleslye confownded' (*fo. 114r*). In an effort to push away the 'doutefulle drede' caused by this emphasis on sin, *A Revelation* begins with an echo of its ending, opening, not with *A Vision*'s cautious 'Here es a vision' (fo. 97r), but with the explosive 'This is a revelacion of love' (*fo. 1r*). In this staking of a claim which must wait eighty-six chapters to be fully justified, Julian also announces that the book is written by one who means to shape what she says: an *auctor*, not the mere *compilator* she is in *A Vision*.

When her account of the revelation begins, she broadens the scope of this hermeneutic of love still further. Medieval theology distinguished between the divine and human natures of Christ, and took the difference between aspects of the Trinity (might, wisdom, and love) very seriously. In doing so, it sustained a view of God as manifesting himself differently at different moments. Julian goes out of her way to elide these distinctions by stating that she means to apply all the revelation shows about the incarnate Jesus' love for humankind not only to the divine person of Christ but to the entire Godhead: 'For the Trinitie is God, God is the Trinitie [. . .] For wher Jhesu appireth, the blessed Trinitie is understand, as to my sight' (*fos. 1r, 7v*). This is a crucial assertion, again based on the visionary episode of 1388, with its tripartite declaration of the 'who', 'what', and 'wherefore' of God's love. For if love is the full meaning of the revelation, and if the revelation is a full manifestation of the nature of Jesus, and if Jesus is a full manifestation of the Trinity, the word 'love' says everything that need be said about God himself.

Medieval accounts of Judgment Day present it as a time of justice, when God's anger against sin is manifest. Middle English bestsellers, like the magnificent *Prick of Conscience*, set out to frighten readers into virtue by evoking the event in all its terror, while English sermons of Julian's time are full of warnings about God's impatience with his corrupted creation.[6] Emboldened by her discovery that Jesus is God's full declaration of who he is, Julian writes passionately against this pessimistic understanding of history, extending Christ's promise that 'alle shalle be wele' (*fo. 50r*) into the trinitarian assertion that 'Oure lorde was nevyr wroth, nor nevyr shall [. . .] it is agaynst the propyrte [inconsistent with the nature] of hys myght to be wroth, and agaynst the properte of hys wysdom, and agaynst the propyrte of hys goodnes' (*fo. 84v*). *A Vision* is already filled with trinitarian cadences; *A Revelation* is suffused with them, as it insists that God is not now one thing, now another – now loving to the saved, now angry at the damned – but always the same, always love.

'Properties and conditions'

The hermeneutic instruction of 1388 empowers Julian to assign her revelation a unitary meaning. The instruction of 1393 shows her in more detail how to do this and cements her role as an *auctor* who can shape what she writes without relinquishing the claim made in *A Vision* that all she says comes from God. This instruction is described in a central chapter of *A Revelation*, as part of its analysis of an obscure visionary 'example' about a Lord and a Servant. In the example – which it is at once clear has to do with God and Adam, but which also proves to be about God and Christ, and about the soul's journey to God – a Lord, sitting on the ground, his Servant standing beside him, 'sendyth hym into a certeyne place to do his wyll' (*fo. 93v*). The Servant, eager to obey, trips, falls to the ground, and is unable to rise. Yet far from being angry at the Servant's failure, the Lord promises to reward him. It seems that, in the very act of falling, the Servant has carried out the task he was set.

The instruction itself consists only of the words: '"It longyth to the to take hede to alle the propertes [modes of understanding] and the condescions [details] that were shewed in the example, though the thyngke that it be mysty and indefferent [cloudy and undifferentiated] to thy syght"' (*fo. 96v*).

Yet from the phrase 'propertes and [. . .] condescions', Julian extrapolates the idea that she can derive information about God's meaning from three sources: not only 'the begynnyng of techyng that I understode therin in the same tyme' (her memory of her original experience), but also 'the inwarde lernyng that I have understonde therein sythen', and 'the hole revelation fro the begynnyng to the ende' (fo. 96r). This trinitarian hermeneutic frees her to find cross-references between moments in the revelation, assured as she now is that its meaning is so integrated that any insight in it can be used to interpret any other. Remarkably, it also encourages her to treat all that she has thought about the revelation since it happened as part of God's message to the world. A Revelation is thus full of passages that begin 'Thus saw I and felt in the same tyme', 'Owre lorde wylle that we have tru understondyng', or 'God shewed in all the revelations', as Julian unpeels layers of interpretation she admits she 'can nott nor may deperte' [distinguish] – since, like the Trinity, these modes of understanding are 'thre as one' (fos. 86r, 76r, 80v, 96r). These add greatly to the length of A Revelation. Despite their claim to be the product of divine revelation, the passages also position Julian in just the role of teacher she disowns in A Vision, as the language of visionary receptivity ('I saw, I understood') is adapted to suit the needs of intricate theological argumentation.

A subtler effect of this instruction and the understanding of the example it enables is that A Revelation becomes preoccupied with self-knowledge, as much as revelation, as a way of knowing God. In taking heed of the example's 'propertes and [. . .] condescions', Julian uses all her faculties: memory, reason, and will. Having done so, she realizes how the 'mysty' quality of the example (its fusion of Adam and Christ, fall and redemption) is a result of mysterious interconnections between the human and the divine. After all, the soul is created in the image of God, who 'made mannes soule to be his owne cytte and his dwellyng place', when the Servant's work is done (fo. 98v). 'For God is endlesse sovereyne truth, endelesse sovereyne wysdom, endelesse sovereyne love unmade' (father, son, and holy ghost), 'and [mans] soule [. . .] hath the same propertes made' (memory, reason, and will), 'and evyrmore it doyth that it was made for: it seeth God, and it beholdyth God, and it lovyth God' (fo. 81r). Seeing, beholding, and loving God, using a trinity of faculties that mirror the divine Trinity, Julian reads God by reading herself – and humanity as a whole. In a remarkable opening out of her experience to include readers, as they develop their own reflections, revelation and meditation become the same. Despite the fact that the soul is a created entity, God uncreated, 'I sawe no dyfference betwen God and oure substance, but as it were all God' (fo. 114r).

'Impossible to thee'

The hermeneutic instructions of 1388 and 1393 thus allow Julian to turn *A Vision* into something new: no longer a thoughtful narrative by 'a woman, le[w]ed, febille, and freylle', but an exposition of a complex theological theory, written by an author who makes no allusion to her gender but presents herself as visionary medium, representative soul, and teacher. In the wake of this complex reconfiguration of a visionary text, personal details tend to fade; details about the vision (its vivid evocations of Christ's blood) are foregrounded; theological problems elided in *A Vision* are faced, even emphasized; and the impossibility of resolving these problems in the present life is theorized.

Above all, *A Revelation* uses the hermeneutic instructions around which it is built to make audacious use of two kinds of *gaps*, filling both brimful of meaning: gaps in the completeness of the visionary experience, the places where Julian cannot see what she wants to see or grasp what she sees; and gaps between her experience and Christian orthodoxy, 'the feyth that holy chyrch techyth me to believe' (*fo. 60r*). In *A Vision*, these gaps threaten the coherence of the project. Here, they are thematized, allowing Julian to understand the human experience of disunity which they figure as part of the process towards unity in which humankind and God are mutually enmeshed.

The first gap opens into an understanding of the distance between God and humankind which is a consequence of creation itself. This gap is given formal expression in the thirteenth revelation's announcement that God's plan to make all things well belongs to his 'pryvy connceyles [secret plans]', into which it is not proper to enquire: 'It longyth to the ryalle [royal] lord-schyppe of God to have hys pryvy connceyles in pees, and it longyth to his sarvanntes for obedyence and reverence nott wylle to [wytte] hys connceyles' (*fo. 54r*). (The passage builds on *A Vision* (fo. 107r) and uses one of Julian's persistent metaphors: God as absolutist monarch.) Such humble acceptance of ignorance, however, is only partial. For as Julian pushes her way closer to the no-go area of these 'prevytes' – as she now understands her revelation, even ignorance is latent with theological truth – this gap reshapes itself as a speculation about a 'deed the whych the [blyssfull] Trynyte shalle do in the last day', in which God will consummate the promises he here makes. In this sequence, Julian's very anxiety to know that God will truly make all things well is enough to generate an optimistic prophecy about the Day of Judgment: sheer human need forces wide open the hope of universal salvation that has haunted her project from the start.[7]

The second gap, between the revelation and 'holy chyrch', defender of all it is necessary to believe, still creates tension in *A Revelation*, but now in a carefully staged way. Responding to her intuition of the deed that God will do to make all well, Julian reconsiders 'oure feyth' and feels it to be 'unpossible that alle maner of thyng shuld be wele'. As often in *A Revelation*, God's response is a variation on Julian's puzzled thought: '"That that is unpossible to the is nott unpossible to me; I shalle save my worde in alle thyng, and I shalle make althyng wele"' (*fos. 58v–59r*). The fascinating possibility of God doing the impossible – preserving the truth of his promise to condemn the wicked, but not in the end condemning anyone – then generates more specific theorizings in the fourteenth revelation, about the kinds of truth and the double nature of human perceptions of God and the self, as Julian works towards her reading of the Lord and the Servant. Building on the separation in *A Vision* of the human will into 'a goodely wille that never assentyd to synne' and 'a bestely [carnal] wille [. . .] that may wille na [no] goode' (fo. 108v), *A Revelation* posits that the soul is divided hierarchically into a 'kyndely [created] substance, whych is evyr kepte one in hym, hole and safe without ende', and a 'channgeable sensualyte, whych semyth now oone and now another', until it is fully united with the substance after death (*fo. 81v*). (The soul is thus created in the image not only of God but of the incarnate Christ.) In souls that are to be saved, sin affects only the sensuality, and can be understood as a process of testing, in which the soul is made fit to be the dwelling-place of God (as the Servant is made fit to honour his Lord). Yet the 'hygher dome' [more absolute mode of understanding] the revelation offers to its readers is not always available to sinning souls, who consider themselves 'wurthy blame and wrath', and need to see themselves that way in order to bring the sensuality back into the 'ryghtfulhede' that is God. (Even so, the fallen Servant's inability to see his Lord is what causes him the suffering that God rewards.) Holy church's teaching about divine anger belongs to the 'lower dome [more provisional mode of understanding]', and is true in the sense of being both necessary and 'groundyd in Goddes worde' (*fo. 58v*), but is transcended by Julian's revelation of love.

Remarkably, *A Revelation* thus deals with the gap between its own and Church teaching on divine anger by subordinating Church teaching to its own absolute vision of divine reality. As the body of Christ on earth, the Church is united with God – 'he it is, holy chyrch: he is the grounde, he is the substannce, he is the techyng, he is the techer' (*fo. 61v*) – and acts with Christ, in his capacity as humanity's mother, to nurture the soul's sensuality: 'For in oure moder Cryst we profyt and encrese, and in mercy he reformyth us and restoryth' (*fo. 125r*). But in Julian's analysis, the Church teaches what people need to hear, not what is finally true, while *A Revelation* offers a necessary supplement to Church teaching: a declaration of the 'prevytes whych he wylle make open and knowyn to us', which is partly provisional but still authoritative. *A Revelation* at once proclaims what is true and shows readers how God wants them to understand 'the prechyng and techyng of holy chyrch' (*fo. 61r–v*).

'His faithfull lovers'

What, then, does *A Revelation* tell us about the role of visionary women in late medieval English religious culture? Clearly, the book's survival in several manuscripts, and the care with which *A Vision* was revised into *A Revelation*, suggests that there was a group who believed Julian's experience meant what she thought it meant. But can we say more? Her life as a parish anchoress and lack of interest in religious institutions suggests that this group was self-selected, like the one that sustained Margery Kempe. But for this very reason, we may never find out much about its members. We do not even know if Julian was in Norwich before the 1390s.

Fortunately, however, the group has left us one revealing passage of writing other than *A Revelation* itself: a set of reading instructions at the end of the Sloane text of the work, perhaps by the cleric who wrote the chapter headings found in this manuscript. This passage seeks to restrict readers of *A Revelation* to Christ's 'faithfull lovers', who 'submitt them to the feith of holy church' and the teaching of 'men that be of vertuous life, sadde age, and profound lerning'. It also warns against selective reading, such as heretics perform; notes that 'hey divinitye and hey wisdam' cannot be grasped by 'him that is thrall to synne'; and claims that Jesus will show any pure soul how 'all is according to Holy Scripture'.[8] In other words, the passage posits that *A Revelation* speaks the truth to those who are in right relation to four different sites of authority: the institutional Church, people of spiritual wisdom, the Bible, and divine illumination. In thus making room for visionary experience, while steering readers between the Scylla of Lollard biblicism on the one hand and the Charybdis of extreme ecclesiasticism on the other, the passage links Julian's supporters to a wider fourteenth-century movement of visionary religiosity. It also holds out the hope that *A Revelation* may give us information about this movement that we cannot get elsewhere.

The role of visions became a matter of import for many English women and men from the 1370s on, as the disrupted state of the Church across Europe (a result of the schism of 1378) and England (a result of the Lollard movement) gave increased anxiety, and proposals for reform grew thick on the ground.[9] English spirituality had traditionally been suspicious of visionary experience. But now certain texts, often associated with the canonization of the prophet Bridget of Sweden (d. 1373), began to be more positive, arguing that 'many men and wymmen have hadde, and have, revelacions and visions, and sum han a spirite of profecie' – as an important late fourteenth-century treatise, *The Chastising of God's Children*, puts it – and suggesting cautious criteria for authenticating these experiences and their recipients. These criteria closely match the qualities the Sloane passage advocates for a true reading of *A Revelation*: the visionary must be a 'goostli lyver', not a 'worldli' one, who submits herself to 'hooli chirche' and 'sum elder, discreet, vertuous, hooli and expert and proved man'; the vision itself must 'accorden with hooli scripture', 'vertuous lyvenge', and 'the feith'.[10] For the most part, such descriptions of how to discern a true vision were theoretical. England never had a visionary of the public stature of Bridget, and efforts to promote visions as a force of renewal remained tentative. Kempe's abandonment of her career as a travelling teacher after her arrests on suspicion of Lollardy is symptomatic of the difficulties advocates of visionary religiosity had in maintaining their delicate position of critical orthodoxy, in a climate of thought dichotomized between a state-promoted mainstream religiosity and everything else. Indeed, were it not for Kempe and Julian, we might be justified in seeing the English visionary movement as conservative, easily co-opted into fifteenth-century orthodoxy, and finding its ultimate expression in Syon Abbey, the sumptuous convent of Bridgettine nuns founded by Henry V in expiation of his father's sins.[11]

A Revelation of Love (like the life and writings of Kempe) gives the lie to this picture, by showing both that formulations of visionary orthodoxy in texts like *The Chastising* were in fact used by Christ's self-styled 'faithfull lovers' and how inventively they were adapted in the process. In its own terms, *A Revelation* accepts the criteria for orthodoxy *The Chastising* or the Sloane passage outline. Its exposition shuttles between the faith, the scriptures and the revelation, as Julian affirms the relevance not only of what she saw in the vision but of what she understood in the years devoted to 'inwarde lernyng', in consultation with holy and learned clerics. (These are figured in the book: partly by juxtaposition of moments of revelation with formal expositions of orthodox teaching, as when a passage critical of prayers to the saints is counterpointed with one about the 'faire and many' ways God desires to be sought; partly by its account of how a cleric is the first to believe the revelation, before Julian herself (chapters 5, 66).) But where *The Chastising* tactfully imagines visions as giving mere confirmation to a singular truth already known from other sources of authority, we have seen how adeptly Julian uses the tension between these sources to make new meanings. It can be taken as read that the supple reinvention in *A Revelation* of what it is to 'submitt [. . .] to the feith of holy church' could not have gained official approval, and that efforts to circulate the book as widely as its appeal to all Christians asks to be circulated would have led to accusations that here was a vision 'enclyned to [. . .] error of hooli chirche', as *The Chastising* puts it: a 'wondir or newe thing', not a true expression of God's purposes. *A Revelation of Love* is not a political work in the same way Lollard writing is political (or as Bridget's revelations are political); it seeks to alter the perceptions of individuals and their relation to Church doctrine, not to intervene directly in how things are run. Yet in its elevation of a woman's experience of God and radical speculations about this experience's meaning to the status of ultimate arbiter of truth, the book does do something extraordinarily daring, reminding us in so doing of the restlessness, indeed the recklessness, of the vernacular religious culture that gave it birth.

NOTES

1. For the manuscripts, see *A Book of Showings to the Anchoress Julian of Norwich*, ed. Edmund Colledge and James Walsh, 2 vols. (Toronto: Pontifical Institute of Mediaeval Studies, 1978). Quotations from Julian are from the Additional and Paris manuscripts respectively; references are to folios of these manuscripts, and are in regular typeface for *A Vision*, italics for *A Revelation*; any emendation to the manuscripts, other than small modifications of spelling, is quoted in square brackets. See the edition in progress by Nicholas Watson and Jacqueline Jenkins, *The Writings of Julian of Norwich: A Vision Showed to a Devout Woman and A Revelation of Love* (Pennsylvania State University Press, forthcoming 2004).

2. *The Book of Margery Kempe*, ed. Sanford Brown Meech and Hope Emily Allen, EETS os 212 (Oxford: Clarendon Press, 1944), chapter 18.

3. Anne Hudson, *The Premature Reformation: Wycliffite Texts and Lollard History* (Oxford: Clarendon Press, 1988); Nicholas Watson, 'Censorship and Cultural Change in Late Medieval England: Vernacular Theology, the Oxford Translation Debate, and Arundel's Constitutions of 1409', *Speculum* 70 (1995): 822–65.

4. Felicity Riddy, 'Julian of Norwich and Self-Textualization', in *Editing Women*, ed. Ann M. Hutchison (University of Toronto Press, 1998), pp. 101–24.

5. *Book of Margery Kempe*, chapter 11.

6. In passus v of *Piers Plowman*, Langland has Reason preach such a sermon; see William Langland, *The Vision of Piers Plowman*, ed. A. V. C. Schmidt, 2nd edn (London: Longman 1995).

7. Nicholas Watson, 'Visions of Inclusion: Universal Salvation and Vernacular Theology in Pre-Reformation England', *Journal of Medieval and Early Modern Studies* 27 (1997): 145–88.

8. This passage is excerpt 3.4 of Jocelyn Wogan-Browne, Nicholas Watson, Andrew Taylor, Ruth Evans, *The Idea of the Vernacular: An Anthology of Middle English Literary Theory, 1280–1520* (University Park: Pennsylvania State University Press, 1999).

9. See Rosalynn Voaden, *God's Words, Women's Voices: The Discernment of Spirits in the Writings of Late-Medieval Woman Visionaries* (Cambridge: D. S. Brewer, 1999).

10. *The Chastising of God's Children*, ed. Eric Colledge and Joyce Bazire (Oxford: Blackwell, 1957), chapter 19, from which all subsequent quotations are also taken.

11. Jeremy Catto, 'Religious Changes under Henry V', *Henry the Fifth: The Practice of Kingship* (Oxford: Clarendon, 1985), pp. 97–116.

15

CAROLYN DINSHAW

Margery Kempe

One of the many ironies surrounding *The Book of Margery Kempe* is its
now canonical status in English literary history. Identified in the modern era
only in 1934, it remained an eccentricity, and a relatively obscure one, until
about twenty years ago. Not that it was entirely neglected: J. P. Morgan is
reported to have read it on his deathbed.[1] But now it is a staple of American
undergraduate English literature education, included in the major anthologies of English literature and routinely taught in introductory classes.
Sparkling new editions for the classroom recently have been produced, not
to mention a website and postmodern gay novelistic adaptation.[2]

But if her *Book* has achieved a place in the literary canon, Margery Kempe
herself has not been taken entirely seriously as a visionary, let alone a can-
didate for canonization by the Church. Being proved divinely inspired was
never far from her mind: she paid a visit to Julian of Norwich, her contemporary, precisely to be reassured as to her contact with the divine. And
canonization was perhaps not absent from the minds of the men who wrote
down her book as she dictated it, shaping her reminiscences to fit into a long
line of holy women. But Margery's mystical and prophetic experiences have
not been subjected to much serious consideration; the inevitable comparison
with Julian of Norwich's austere and theologically ambitious *Revelation* has
heretofore worked to the disadvantage of the rambling *Book of Margery
Kempe*.

What, then, has made it so popular now? What are its claims to modern
secular canonicity? It is the earliest extant autobiographical work in English.
That alone stakes its claim to importance. It is full of the minutiae of everyday
life in late medieval England, and in particular the life and self-fashioning
of a woman – increasingly popular arenas of inquiry after twentieth-century
feminism's impact on the curriculum. Moreover, even as it is comprised of
elements that are entirely of their time, the *Book* is unique, revealing a woman
both deeply situated *in* and profoundly *out* of her time. We demand both such

elements in a canonical literary work, asking that it tell us something specific as well as something general. *The Book of Margery Kempe* not only depicts in brilliant detail the historical moment of a bold late medieval woman, but also tells us about the status of history itself and, further, about our place in it. If Margery is not considered a potential saint, her *Book* nonetheless 'illuminat[es] a life possibility for the present',[3] and its visionary nature is crucial to its new place in the twenty-first-century literary canon.

It was crucial to its sixteenth-century reputation as well. The *Book* as we have it exists in a unique manuscript that is a copy of the mid-fifteenth-century original. (Compare the over forty extant manuscripts of *Incendium amoris* [The Fire of Love], the phenomenally popular devotional work by Richard Rolle that Margery herself mentions.) This copy was owned in the late fifteenth century by the Carthusian abbey of Mount Grace in Yorkshire, the same abbey with which the famous mystic Richard Methley was associated. A brief extract of mystical passages was printed around 1501 by Wynkyn de Worde and reprinted by Henry Pepwell twenty years later; Pepwell identifies Margery as an anchoress.

But Margery was not in fact an anchoress, and *The Book of Margery Kempe* is an immense, sprawling chronicle consisting of stubbornly earthbound as well as visionary materials: eighty-nine chapters in Book 1 (written between 1436 and 1438) plus an additional ten chapters in Book 2 (written starting in 1438) describe her life from early adulthood into old age. Margery was born in East Anglia around 1373, if we can trust internal clues to dating, and died sometime after 1438. Her father was a notable figure in Bishop's Lynn (now known as King's Lynn), having been five times mayor of the town and then alderman of the Trinity Guild. Married at about the age of twenty to a man of lesser social status – Margery indignantly reminds him of her family's importance when he tries to correct her – and with child shortly thereafter, she had a difficult pregnancy and labour, and feared for her life. Chapter 1 tells us the details, and the *Book* unfolds from there: she called for her confessor, because she had something on her conscience – an unconfessed sin. Before she had said what she meant regarding that sin, though, her confessor rebuked her sharply, and she said no more; she therefore feared she would not be saved. She went crazy for over eight months, threatening to hurt herself violently until a vision of Christ restored her to her mind and community. Though she was stirred by this grace to be God's servant, it took more to turn Margery towards a devout life: chapter 2 tells us she continues in her proud and covetous ways, dressing ostentatiously and taking up business as a brewer and then miller. Failing spectacularly in these endeavours, she feels chastised by God, and is eventually converted to a passionately devout life. She thereupon spends her years travelling, witnessing, ministering to people, and furthering her spirituality. Margery is a controversial figure, loud, demonstrative, and disruptive in her devotion, suspected of heresy by some but supported by others, dismissive of secular authority and quick to chide the most powerful churchmen for their spiritual laxness. Her *Book* records meetings and run-ins with just about everyone who was anyone in fifteenth-century ecclesiastical England, among them Thomas Arundel, Archbishop of Canterbury; Philip Repingdon, Bishop of Lincoln; Henry Bowet, Archbishop of York; and the learned Carmelite doctor of divinity Alan of Lynn.

The *Book* is above all a spiritual autobiography: Margery's awakening into the devout life, the content of her devotion, and her struggles to follow Christ's dictates form the matter of the book. 'Þis lytyl tretys [treatise] schal tretyn [treat] sumdeel in parcel [in part] of hys wonderful werkys', says the Proem, 'how mercyfully, how benyngly, & how charytefully he meued & stered [moved and stirred] a synful caytyf [wretch] vn-to hys love'.[4] In this way it does not closely resemble what we call autobiography today. Margery specifically mentions but one of her fourteen children and tells little, for example, about the quotidian ardours of her considerable, long-range travels (pilgrimages to the Holy Land, Rome, Santiago de Compostela, and sites in Germany). As Sarah Salih remarks, 'Margery and her amanuenses assume that she is of interest only insofar as she is not a housewife.'[5] Furthermore, the principle of narrative ordering is obscure: a chronology can be derived from the text, and at least one medieval reader, commenting in ink in the manuscript margins, cared about an orderly temporal arrangement of events. But ordinary chronology, this date following that date and that one, is not the principle here. The *Book* is composed of remembered events; the movement of Margery's mind provides the narrative motion. Thus, even as its primary concerns are devotional, the book is filled with incidental everyday detail that now supplies much of its richness and fascination: what the weather was like on the day she discusses a vow of chastity – really, argues about sex – with her husband, for example; what they were carrying, what they would eat.

Very frequently, individual anecdotes – such as the argument about sex, in chapter 11 – vividly condense Margery's larger concerns in her *Book*. Given the loose overall structure it is not a violation of narrative integrity to single out one chapter and see what its preoccupations are; in fact, such looseness encourages us to do just this. In this essay, then, I shall use chapter 60 as a jumping-off point, to see what it tells us about Margery's *Book* and her world. Finally I shall turn to explicitly methodological questions of how to place this book – and ourselves – in history.

Chapter 60: a visit, with weeping and roaring, to Norwich

Chapter 60 begins with a mention of the 'good preste' who was her 'lystere' –
the good priest who read aloud to Margery. He had fallen sick and people
despaired of his life. Margery is stirred in her soul to take care of him;
as she prays for him, while hearing Mass one day, the Lord tells her that
he will indeed recover and thrive. In an action that points to the complex
temporalities of her life, Margery thereupon decides to visit the grave of a
good vicar, recently deceased, to thank him for the (future) recovery of the
priest. This vicar was Richard Caister of St Stephen's, Norwich, Margery's
frequent confessor and supporter. Taking leave of her confessor at Bishop's
Lynn, she proceeds to Norwich, a town 40 miles (64 km) to the southeast.

When Margery arrives in the churchyard of St Stephen's, she begins the
unsettling vocal and bodily devotion that has become her trademark. Her
performance continues as she enters the church and approaches the high
altar: she is overwhelmed by the spiritual comfort of the Lord, who worked
such great grace for his servant, the vicar. But the violence of her weeping
and wailing, beyond her own ability to contain, irks the people around her,
suspecting her of inappropriate attachment and a prideful sense of her own
singularity:

> Whan sche cam in þe chirch-ȝerd [churchyard] of Seynt Stefyn, sche cryed,
> sche roryd, sche wept, sche fel down to þe grownd, so feruently þe fyer of lofe
> brent in hir hert. Sithyn [Afterwards] sche ros vp a-ȝen [again] & went forth
> wepyng in-to þe chirche to þe hy awter, & þer sche fel down with boistows
> [boisterous] sobbyngys, wepyngys, & lowde cryes be-syden þe grave of þe good
> Vicary . . . And þerfor þe pepil had gret merueyl [marvel] of hir, supposyng þat
> sche had wept for sum fleschly er erdly [fleshly or earthly] affeccyon, & seyd
> vn-to hir, 'What eylith [ails] þe woman? Why faryst þus with þi-self? We knew
> hym as wel as þu.'

But several priests are already acquainted with her extreme devotional style
and are respectful and hospitable to her, as is a lady from the area. Margery
proceeds with this woman to the latter's church, where she sees an image of
the blessed Virgin Mary holding the dead Christ – a pietà. As she is by other
visual experiences of the holy, Margery is overcome by this sight, which
puts her in mind of Christ's Passion and Mary's compassion.[6] The woman's
priest, however, holds a more distanced perspective:

> And thorw þe beholdyng of þat pete [pietà] hir mende was al holy ocupyed in
> þe Passyon of owr Lord Ihesu Crist & in þe compassyon of owr Lady, Seynt
> Mary, be whech sche was compellyd to cryyn ful lowde & wepyn ful sor, as
> þei [as though] sche xulde a [should have] deyd. Þan cam to hir þe ladys preste
> seyyng, 'Damsel, Ihesu is ded long sithyn [ago].'

Margery is provoked by this dismissal, rebuking him for his detachment.

> 'Sir, hys deth is as fresch to me as he had deyd þis same day, & so me thynkyth it awt [ought] to be to ʒow & to alle Cristen pepil. We awt euyr [ever] to han mende of hys kendnes [kindness] & euyr thynkyn of þe dolful deth þat he deyd for vs.'

The woman agrees, finding in Margery an 'exampyl' of God's grace – whether she means that Margery's behaviour conforms to her expectations, or that it is a spectacular exception is not clear – and becoming Margery's 'auoket' (advocate). When Margery returns home to Lynn, her good priest has indeed recovered, as God had told her he would.

This well-structured episode, ordered around her prophetic foresight and its fulfilment, cues us to major preoccupations of *The Book of Margery Kempe* and gives a good indication of her controversial manner of living.[7] First, the chapter tells us about Margery's relationship to reading and the written word. The ailing priest had been her reader for about seven years. It seems that Margery herself could neither read nor write; *The Book of Margery Kempe* was dictated by Margery and written down by three different men. But if Margery was illiterate in our modern terms, she was nonetheless deeply engaged with the written word – even, perhaps, fashioning her life as a text. Second, as we see Margery bustling about to care for her reader, shuttling to and from Norwich, and hear her sharp retort to the priest, the event provides a vivid picture of Margery's mobility, reputation, and interactions with others, and details her aggravating form of devotion. And finally, it suggests that she exists in some sense out of her world's time, in a spiritual time frame (the everlasting *now* of the divine) that is radically separate from the secular chronology governing others around her.

Reading with Margery: books and the *Book*

Margery shows herself deeply committed to this unnamed and ailing priest/reader. Theirs was an important spiritual bond. We get a hint of the intensity of their reading sessions in chapter 58: at their first meeting, the priest invited Margery to his chamber (where he lived with his mother), and read to her about Christ. When Margery heard that Christ wept, she wept too, and loudly. Neither the surprised priest nor his mother knew why, and they marvelled at all the tears and cries. But they were convinced that she was a good woman, and the priest thereafter read to her the scriptures and glosses upon them, in addition to works of devotion in English and in Latin.

Litteratus by the late Middle Ages meant having at least a minimal competence in Latin. Like other lay women, Margery was generally excluded from

Latin 'written culture of commerce and public transactions', as Karma Lochrie has observed, though lay women were increasingly able to read vernacular texts.[8] There are pervasive indications throughout the *Book* that Margery could neither read nor write in either Latin or the vernacular. When she is imprisoned in Leicester under suspicion of sexual misconduct, heresy, and deception, for example, she states that she does not understand when the Steward of Leicester speaks to her in Latin (pp. 112–13). He may be merely trying to intimidate her, of course, since the text mentions that there were many people around waiting to hear how she would respond; and she may be cannily trying to call his bluff. Nonetheless, she still may not know Latin. And in a touching vision narrated late in Book 1 that suggests she cannot read in the vernacular, Margery is granted sight of an angel looking like a child clothed in white, 'beryng an howge boke be-forn hym [bearing a huge book before him]'. It is the Book of Life, she is told. She recognizes the Trinity, all rendered in gold. 'Þan seyd sche to þe childe, "Wher is my name?" Þe childe answeryd & seyd, "Her is þi name at þe Trinyte foot wretyn [written]" (pp. 206–7). This vision neatly expresses Margery's spiritual gifts and her earthly limitations: she is vouchsafed a vision, and moreover is placed in the heavenly scheme of things at the very foot of the Trinity; yet she needs help finding her own name. Perhaps she just hadn't located it yet; she certainly does recognize the power of writing, as Julia Boffey notes.[9] But it may be that she cannot read her own name.

Margery's struggles to get her *Book* written down likewise demonstrate her spiritual gifts and her material constraints. The Proem provides a detailed account of first one, then a second, then a third amanuensis. She initially shared her secrets – her revelations, 'hyr meuynggys & hyr steringgys [her movings and her stirrings]' (p. 3) – with clerks and anchorites, trying to discern their origins and fearing they might be sent by spiritual enemies. These authorities confirmed divine inspiration and urged Margery to have them written down. Some even offered to write them down themselves, but Margery felt commanded in her soul not to write so soon. Indeed, as Alexandra Barratt has demonstrated, such writing would have been virtually unexampled in England at this time.[10] It would be twenty years and more from her first revelations before the Lord commanded her to make her visions and devotion known to all the world through writing.

And then arose the problem of finding a writer who would give credence to her experiences. After her first scribe (perhaps her son) died, a beloved priest promised to rewrite the book, but problems intervened: he could not read it, finding the language and the letters indecipherable (the first scribe lived in German-speaking lands). Moreover, the priest capitulated to the evil talk swirling about Margery, refusing to imperil himself by association with her. Finally, after yet another scribe had tried his hand at the task, the priest agreed to take another look, newly willing to risk his reputation. So at last *The Book of Margery Kempe* could be recopied, and in fact ten new chapters produced. The resultant *Book* contains not only Margery's narrative but the imbedded story of the priest's convictions about her as well.

Producing the *Book* was thus a long and arduous process, political as well as spiritual. Margery seems not merely dependent upon but really at the mercy of others – particularly men – to authorize her and produce her book. Margery's controversial status exacerbated the difficulties. But her need for a scribe, and her aural contact with texts, were not unusual; reading in a manuscript culture was very often an oral (and aural) experience. Even solitary reading was conducted aloud, while reading (hearing) spiritual treatises during meals was common. Margery claims that she has learned scripture through sermons and discussions with clerks (p. 29). Furthermore, composition was often performed orally as well, by dictation; the particular skill of writing down letters and words was more separate from the concept of authorship in Margery's day than in our own. So to say that Margery could neither read nor write does not indicate that she had no access to textual culture. And as Boffey points out, no one seemed to expect that Margery herself would learn to read or write, though these were the obvious solutions to her problems of 'defawte of redyng [inability to read]' (p. 143) and lack of a willing and able scribe to record her experiences for posterity.[11]

Reading and writing were in fact highly fraught activities in Margery's England. The hereticated Lollard sect, opposing clerical privilege in all its forms, advocated direct communication between all Christians and God. One means of such communication was the Bible translated into the vernacular and thus available beyond the clergy. The association of scriptural translations in the vernacular with heresy became so strong that in 1409 it was declared heretical not just to make, but even to own, without diocesan permission, a single biblical verse translated into English. By the late 1430s, as Lynn Staley points out, it was 'dangerous to produce vernacular devotional prose'.[12] Margery, though doctrinally orthodox, was associated with Lollardy because of her direct communication with the divine, her circumventing and correcting clerical authorities, her speaking in public (Lollards considered all Christians to be themselves priests, so that everyone – even women – should be able to preach; Margery was often perceived to be preaching as she travelled around England bearing witness to her Lord), and her generally unofficial and disruptive devotional style. Any priest who undertook to support her, not to mention write down her *Book*, was taking a considerable risk: the reluctance of the second scribe to write down Margery's tale stems not only from his inability to read the manuscript but also his fears – the text calls it cowardice – in the face of what people were saying against her. And since the *Book*, as Kathleen Ashley has shown, was produced outside clerical sanction and through divine grace, it became a 'prototype of the kinds of writing that would eventually undermine clerical textual authority' – thus its relation to Lollardy while being explicitly *not* a Lollard text.[13]

Written texts, Latin and English, are in fact crucial in Margery's *Book*. They not only teach Margery, but they also provide occasions for Margery to exert influence, even perhaps to teach, in turn. In the case of her reader, the priest who became ill in chapter 60, the *Book* stresses not only that Margery's hunger for the word was sated when he read to her, but also that the priest's own knowledge and merit increased. 'Aftyrwardys he wex benefysyd & had gret cur of sowle [was beneficed and had a large cure of souls], & þan lykyd [it pleased] hym ful wel þat he had redde so meche [much] be-forn' (p. 144). Books authorize Margery in her own eyes and in the eyes of others. In one early passage, Margery visits Richard Caister: though he doubts that any woman can occupy the space of an hour in talking about God, she tells him at length how the Godhead dallies with her, instructing her to love, worship, and revere him, 'so excellently þat sche herd neuyr boke, neyþyr Hyltons boke, ne [B]ridis boke, ne Stimulus Amoris, ne Incendium Amoris, ne non oþer þat euyr sche herd redyn þat spak so hyly of lofe of God' (p. 39). In a later passage, her priest/amanuensis had begun to believe slanderous talk about Margery's hypocrisy after a friar preaches against her and many people turn away from her. But this priest/scribe regains his belief in her after he reads of the tears and cries of other holy people, including Mary of Oignies, Richard Rolle, the author of 'Þe Prikke of Lofe,' and Elizabeth of Hungary (pp. 153–4).

At least two of these latter accounts are ones the unnamed priest read to Margery, and we see that they also feature among the works Margery uses to authorize her revelations when she speaks to Caister. As Margery learns of the high contemplation and devotion of these holy men and women through reading, she compares herself to them and understands herself in relation to them; she may live her life as versions of them. Her priest/amanuensis may well use them not only to justify Margery's own experiences in his mind but also actually to fashion her written story on the model of these visionaries.

Margery's resemblance to Saints Mary of Oignies and Bridget of Sweden is particularly compelling: though both were of higher class status than Margery, they were married and persuaded their husbands to live in chastity.[14] Marie, the late twelfth- or early thirteenth-century beguine from Liège, was given to unrestrainable tears, devotion to the Passion, bodily mortification, and miraculous visions. St Bridget, who died around the time of Margery's birth and was canonized in Margery's lifetime, emerges in the *Book* as the most explicit saintly model for Margery. She was a married mystic who lived chastely with her husband for two years, then bore him eight children. When he died on a pilgrimage to Santiago with her, Bridget took up the devout life full-time. She experienced visions, which she dictated, like Margery, to a cleric; she made pilgrimages to the Holy Land and to Rome, where she lived the last two decades of her life. It is in Rome, on her own pilgrimage, that Margery later encounters traces of Bridget, meeting her maidservant and others who knew her and visiting the chamber where she died.

Margery was particularly devoted to Bridget, whose inspiration was doubted by the powerful and authoritative Jean Gerson, Chancellor of the University of Paris, and whose canonization was confirmed in Rome when Margery was there. Typically, though, Margery's devotion to the saint is somewhat self-serving. One day Margery sees the Sacrament shaking and flickering like a dove; she is astonished by this miracle and wants to see more. Christ then says to her, 'My dowtyr, Bryde, say me neuyr in þis wyse [My daughter, Bridget, never saw me like this].' When he goes on to confirm that this is a token of an earthquake (Bridget was renowned for her prophecies), he adds: 'For I telle þe forsoþe rygth as I spak to Seynt Bryde ryte so I speke to þe, dowtyr, & I telle þe trewly it is trewe euery word þat is wretyn in Brides boke' – and here comes the Margery touch: '& be þe it xal be knowyn [by you it shall be known] for very trewth' (p. 47). Through Margery, 'Brides boke' will be proven.

The interplay of written texts and lived lives here is profound. It renders impossible attempts by scholars to separate out the 'learned' elements of the *Book* from the experiential and the everyday. And it forces us to rethink the relationship between text and life. As Mary Carruthers points out, 'A modern woman would be very uncomfortable to think that she was facing the world with a "self" constructed out of bits and pieces of great authors of the past, yet I think in large part that is exactly what a medieval self or "character" was.'[15]

Margery clearly understands some Latin words and phrases, and it may be that she knows how to read Latin after all: Lochrie, tracing the Latinity of the *Book*, suggests that we entertain the possibility.[16] Julian of Norwich's statement about her own unlearned status has not stopped scholars from attributing Latinity to her. But even if this suggestion seems too much for Margery, the point is clear: learning is not just the property of Margery's literate scribes, and the very concepts of literacy and text need to be extended. There is a fascinating blend of voices – written and spoken – in the *Book*. Margery is referred to throughout the text in the third person singular; she is 'þis creature'; but the text includes at least two remarks in the first person, as well as the possessive adjective 'owyr' throughout, and at times it is impossible to untangle the referent. Is it the scribe giving his own brief point of view, or rehearsing Margery's account of someone else's words, or recording Margery's own self-reference? What difference might there be, finally?

'Hir maner of werkyng'

Complicated as the voice of the *Book* is, the persona of Margery Kempe nonetheless emerges powerfully. It comes through loud and clear in chapter 60, with its picture of a parish community that bickers and takes sides, a community whose members have long histories with one another. Margery is indeed a polarizing figure.

The immoderate nature of Margery's devotional display at the vicar's grave causes irritated onlookers to demand, 'What eylith þe woman? Why faryst þus with þi-self? We knew hym as wel as þu' (p. 147). The text explains that her tears respond to divine grace worked in the vicar's life; in fact Margery is 'rauyschyd wyth gostly [spiritual] comfort in þe goodnes of owr Lord', the word 'ravished' suggesting her transportation into a spiritual dimension (as was St Paul in 2 Corinthians). But her neighbours are mired in the flesh, and they accuse her of exaggerating her devotion to the holy man. In the narrative, designed very much from Margery's point of view, their words are snide backbiting, and Margery does not deign to reply; indeed, her spiritual stock rises because of it. As Julian of Norwich told her, 'þe mor despyte, schame, & repref [reproof] þat ȝe haue in þe world þe mor is ȝowr meryte' (p. 43). When people call her a hypocrite for wearing white (the colour of a virgin), though she has borne children, for example; or when there are rumours about her chastity even after she and her husband have taken a vow, her spiritual worth is all the higher: 'þe bettyr xal [shall] I lofe þe,' says Christ (p. 48).

Margery's paroxysm at the sight of the pietà occasions another dismissive remark, this time by the friendly lady's priest. In Margery's memorial rendition here, the cleric comes off as indifferent to the reality of Christ, and Margery is set up for a scorching reproof of him and a ringing declaration of the faith. But viewed from a larger perspective, their interchange may in fact play out theological issues associated with Lollardy and orthodoxy – or even, from a longer historical view, emergent evangelical Protestantism and Catholicism. The priest's words are not necessarily secular when he claims, 'Lady, Jesus died a long time ago.' His liturgical office is oriented around that death,[17] and indeed only the Church has been able to conserve access to that body over the centuries. For Margery, however, as for evangelical Protestants, the point is immediate access to Christ *now*. The conflict here may have theological roots or implications, but for Margery the moment tests her whole reason for living – and she wins. She not only picks up an advocate – someone who speaks for her – but her prophecy proves soon afterwards to be true.

The essence of Margery's piety, in fact, is her living in the presence of the divine. In her first vision – the one that dramatically brings her back to her senses and restores her to community after she has gone out of her mind – Christ appears to her 'in lyknesse of a man, most semly [handsome], most bewtyuows [beautiful], & most amyable þat euyr mygth be seen with mannys eye, clad in a mantyl of purpyl sylke' and says, 'Dowtyr, why hast þow forsakyn me, and I forsoke neuyr þe?' (p. 8). Such an experience (so intimately tied to her own story, yet repeated from Nicholas Love's translation of the *Meditations on the Life of Christ*) focuses on Christ's humanity and is characteristic of her many 'dalliances' with the divine. On a daily basis she has conversations that are deep, familiar, and spiritual. Margery experiences other divine manifestations – she performs miracles, for example (ch. 67) – but according to late medieval devotional traditions, her visions mark her as saintly, and dalliances (with the Lord, Christ, the whole Godhead, our Lady, Saints Peter, Paul, Katherine, and other saints in heaven) are often part of them.[18] Her predictions (as when she foresees in chapter 60 that her ailing reader will recover) channel what God has revealed to her. Such dalliances kindle in her breast the fire of love, a phrase we see in chapter 60.

This direct experience of the divine brings with it tears – of contrition, devotion, and compassion, as Julian of Norwich categorizes them. These dalliances were so sweet, holy, and devout that Margery 'myt not oftyn-tymes beryn it but fel down & wrestyd [wrestled] wyth hir body & mad wondyrful cher & contenawns [wondrous faces and countenance] wyth boystows sobbyngys & gret plente of terys' (p. 40). Later, on her pilgrimage to Jerusalem, she experiences an even more intense form of tears that was to last for years (this is what we see in the church in Norwich in chapter 60): on Mount Calvary she fell down, wrestling with her body, '& cryed wyth a lowde voys as þow hir hert xulde a brostyn a-sundyr [as though her heart should have broken to pieces]' (p. 68). Since she already lives in the presence of Christ, experiencing him in daily conversation, she is overwhelmed when the pilgrimage brings her to the very place where he suffered his agonies: she sees 'veryly & freschly how owyr Lord was crucifyed'. She cannot keep herself from 'krying & roryng þow sche xuld a be ded [even though she should have died] þerfor.' Efforts to hold it in only turn her 'blo as any leed [blue as lead]' (p. 69; also p. 140). A test imposed by uncertain priests proves that these cryings are not done for the sake of publicity (p. 200).

In its emphasis on Margery's emotional experience of the divine, the *Book* finds its place in the tradition of late medieval affective devotion, deeply felt forms of piety focused on the humanity of Christ and often practised by women. Her contemplative experiences contrast with the more austere form of contemplation associated with *The Cloud of Unknowing*. In contrast to what has been called 'negative' mysticism – the work of unknowing that puts a 'cloud of forgetting between you and all the creatures that have ever been made' and that suspects emotionalism and rejects extreme or unnatural uses of the body[19] – 'affirmative' mysticism uses the pictorial imagination in contemplation, focuses the affects on the divine, and experiences other sensory phenomena like sweetness, heat in the breast, and melody. The *Incendium amoris* by Richard Rolle, hermit of Hampole, espoused these affective forms of devotion, and its influence on both Margery and her scribe is pervasive: the work itself is mentioned three times, the phrase 'the fire (or ardour) of love' – popular with mystics – appears throughout the *Book*, and Margery experiences olfactory, auditory, and tactile phenomena such as Rolle describes.

Margery's intricate Passion visions owe much to the tradition of *Meditations on the Life of Christ*, the enormously popular devotional work that directs the worshipper to envision in her soul the Incarnation and life of Christ. Nicholas Love's translation, authorized by no less than Arundel himself as a way of officially controlling such emotional and personal devotional practices (these meditational exercises were originally addressed to a woman, a Franciscan nun), was available in Margery's day. The *Meditations* develops a style of spiritual exercise that contemplates actions in the Lord's life 'as they occurred or as they might have occurred according to the devout belief of the imagination and the varying interpretation of the mind', a contemplative latitude that resonates with Margery's self-authorizing style.[20] Though this emphasis on the visual and affective throughout Margery's book goes much against the negative grain of the contemplative practice of Walter Hilton in his *Scale of Perfection*, Margery mentions 'Hyltons boke' as among those books of high contemplation read to her. (Hilton translated *The Prike of Love*, also mentioned by Margery.) Indeed, *The Book of Margery Kempe* is not without its own negative side, doubt about her corporeal expression of spiritual inspiration being suggested at the very end of Book 1 (p. 220); thus the polarizations around Margery are embedded in the work itself.

'A sort of infection of sensualised mysticism'

Often linked philosophically with Hilton, the author of the *Cloud of Unknowing* feared that 'a sort of infection of sensualised mysticism was creeping over English devotion', as Hope Emily Allen put it.[21] The term 'sensualised' is carefully chosen here, the word applying not only to the senses but to sexual passion as well. For one of the foci of Margery's struggle for spirituality is chaste relations with her husband, while her relation with Christ is expressed in amorous terms: 'dalliance' in Middle English denotes not only spiritual conversation but also sexual union. In this focus Margery is not unique – female mysticism in this period, particularly on the continent, expressed itself often in terms of ecstatic union with the humanity of Christ, perhaps because of the ages-old association of femininity with carnality – but she puts her characteristic spin on it.

Early in the *Book* sex with her husband John has become odious to her. Margery wishes to be chaste, and even before her husband finally agrees to chastity she wears a hair shirt under her garments. Physical relations with John are not so intimate that he even notices. But Margery is increasingly oppressed by her sexual and childbearing duties: 'Lord', she declares, 'I am not worthy to heryn þe spekyn [hear you speak] & þus to comown [have sex] with myn husbond' (p. 48). She grieves that the devout life of dallying with Christ belongs to holy virgins, and that is not she. Contrary to theological tradition, Christ reassures her that he loves wives as well as virgins. Margery at last manages to strike a deal with her husband: if she pays his debts and eats at his table, he will live chastely with her. A measure of their previous physical pleasures is given late in the *Book* when John falls ill in old age and Margery, no longer living with him any more, takes care of him, her penance (she says) after taking venial pleasure in his body earlier.

But if there is no longer human wedded sex, sex, variously understood, is still very much in Margery's life. In an early period of temptation, she yields to a man's demand for sex, only to have him humiliatingly rescind it. Margery constantly fears rape – justifiably – in her travels in England and abroad. But if earthly arrangements are unsatisfying or threatening, in Christ she has found an ideal intimate: she is married mystically to the Godhead (p. 86), but it is the Manhood, Christ himself, who invites Margery into bed with him, reasoning that it is only right that a husband be 'homly' with his wife (p. 90). Margery, he declares, will be the perfect intimate, in turn, 'a very dowtyr to me & a modyr also, a syster, a wyfe, and a spowse' (p. 31). Margery's spiritual life redeems an unsatisfying earthly life, even as the 'gostly [spiritual] labowr' of her body in the throes of writhing, tears, and sobs redeems her multiparous body by re-enacting childbirth on the spiritual level. Margery is so rapt by the manhood of Christ that she weeps and roars if she sees a boy child when she is in Rome, 'as þei [as though] sche had seyn Crist in hys childhode' (p. 86). Screaming on the streets of Rome and causing people to wonder at her, she looks eagerly at handsome men, lest she see him who was both god and man. Indeed, '[t]he threshold between Margery's physical and her spiritual lives is thin', as Ashley puts it, porous or even nonexistent in these instances.[22]

Even the Lord's punitive withdrawal from her is experienced in sexual terms. When Margery (in chapter 59) is deprived of holy thoughts and dalliance for twelve days of vexation, her torment takes a particularly sexual form: among foul thoughts of lechery and prostitution, she thinks various men of religion come before her and bare their genitals. The devil urges her to choose whom she will have first, for she will be common to them all. These horrible sights are delectable to her against her will.

When Margery is deprived of the spiritual element of her devotion, vicious carnality is all that remains. But she has another sort of revelation here as well: she sees through clerical authority as masculine domination, and her vision thus comments on the many ways she *as a woman* is subject to clerical men – from the sharp rebuke of her confessor in chapter 1 at a moment of uniquely female danger (childbirth), to the need for her confessor's permission to travel, to the condescension of Richard Caister. Yet finally it is crucial to the sex/gender dynamics of the *Book* – and a rebuke to simplistic readings of her as a protofeminist – that Margery experiences this clerical demystification as a *horror*.

Margery then and now

The union Margery experiences with Christ, expecting to see him on the streets of Rome, returns us to the priest's comment in chapter 60: to the freshly bereaved Margery he remarks dryly that Jesus died a long time ago. While calendrical time governs the lives of those around her, Margery dwells – at least some of her days – in another time frame altogether, the time of the mystic who inhabits the spirit and participates in the life everlasting of Christ. Aron Gurevich has remarked that all medievals in fact felt themselves 'on two temporal planes at once'.[23] Thus, as do her contemporaries, Margery participates in pilgrimages, retracing the steps of Christ and his family and disciples in the Holy Land, and in Easter pageants, bringing biblical time into the present. Gurevich analyses several different and sometimes contradictory kinds of time perception operating at once in the Middle Ages: agrarian, genealogical, cyclical, biblical, historical. And Ruth Evans in this volume has analysed the weird cultural logic of virginity, its temporality disrupting historical chronology, before and after.[24] But Margery repeatedly experiences herself as set apart from her peers, as she does in chapter 60, joined with the holy but differentiated from her earthly companions. She is an anachronism even in her own (temporally heterogeneous) time.

This condition poses questions for the historian who seeks to place Margery in time. Whose time? The time of the historian, who, while understanding the heterogeneity of medieval chronologies, would nonetheless fit her into a rational historical narrative? Or the time of the mystic, in her everlasting now? I have already suggested that Margery's encounter with the priest adumbrates a historical struggle between Protestantism and Catholicism. Moreover, we could interpret her early failure at business in terms of a lack of adequate life models among bourgeois women. Margery's life, from this point of view, would be seen in terms of the emergence of women's secular models of living. Or we could place Margery in a tradition of English women authors, extending the line already established from Aphra Behn to Jane Austen to Virginia Woolf. In these latter examples we would enlarge the narrative of history to include previously ignored social formations of gender and sexuality. Margery would thus be understood to signify another era, another place, another society, another system of beliefs, and the task of the historian would be to include previously marginalized stories like hers. Such an enlarged history (which includes these 'minority' histories of sex and gender) works in the service of social justice and democracy.

But can we interpret Margery by engaging her own concept of time? I am drawing here on historian Dipesh Chakrabarty's distinction between 'good histories' and what he calls 'subaltern pasts'. Good historical narratives, he writes – those intended to foster democracy and social justice by their inclusiveness – cannot depart from basic disciplinary assumptions and protocols, including the necessity that there be a rational point of view from which the history is told, and that the historian be the subject of inquiry and the archive the object.[25] Good history, even good minority history, cannot be written from inside Margery's own beliefs, that is, from inside the belief that Christ is present physically in the here and now, that humans can touch the divine, that the Godhead motivates all events, public and private. Good history cannot take the supernatural as a cause.

But what if, in addition to fitting Margery into a history inclusive of gender and sexuality, we also asked, following Chakrabarty: 'Is [her] way of being a possibility for our own lives and for what we define as our present? Does [Margery] help us to understand a principle by which we also live in certain instances?'[26] Robert Glück, in his 1994 novel *Margery Kempe*, clearly believes that she does, and thus that her *Book* illuminates a 'subaltern past'. His novel takes seriously her claim to have been invited to sleep with Christ:

it is written from within her belief that she makes daily sensory contact with Christ. Glück adapts her story of passionate love of Christ to his story of a devastating love affair with a handsome boyfriend. What kind of understanding subtends this novel, which mixes fact and fiction? Not rational historical knowledge: it insists on the presence of the divine in the everyday; it believes that a human can touch the divine. Margery becomes 'Bob''s contemporary. To quote Chakrabarty, substituting our medieval English woman for his Indian peasant:

> To stay with the heterogeneity of the moment when the historian meets with [the medieval woman] is, then, to stay with the difference between these two gestures. One is that of historicizing [Margery] in the interest of a history of social justice and democracy; and the other, that of refusing to historicize and of seeing [Margery] as a figure illuminating a life possibility for the present. Taken together, the two gestures put us in touch with the plural ways of being that make up our own present.[27]

'[W]hy bother to remember a past that cannot be made into a present?' Kierkegaard's question about biblical interpretation might as well be Margery's. She lives in a multitemporal, heterogeneous *now*. It might also be *ours*, as we read *The Book of Margery Kempe* and both see her place in a history of medieval women's lives and also experience her contemporaneity with us, understanding her to offer a life possibility for the present. This experience of contemporaneity, Chakrabarty argues, in fact makes historicism possible: if we did not already in some sense connect with her, we could not understand her.[28]

The Book of Margery Kempe allows us to see that modern historical consciousness is but a 'limited good'.[29] In another context its first editor wrote, 'I seem to have always a craving to touch the great human mystery of Time.'[30] In joining the literary canon, the *Book* highlights precisely how a canonical work – if not Saint Margery herself – exists both in and out of time.

NOTES

1. New York *Herald-Tribune*, 13 March 1943, pp. 1, 13; the incident is noted in John C. Hirsh, *Hope Emily Allen: Medieval Scholarship and Feminism* (Norman, OK: Pilgrim Books, 1988), p. 133.
2. Mapping Margery Kempe
   <http://sterling.holycross.edu/departments/visarts/projects/kempe/index.html>;
   Robert Glück, *Margery Kempe* (New York: Serpent's Tail, 1994).
3. Dipesh Chakrabarty, 'Minority Histories, Subaltern Pasts', *Provincializing Europe: Postcolonial Thought and Historical Difference* (Princeton University Press, 2000), pp. 97–113, at 108.

4. *The Book of Margery Kempe*, ed. Sanford Brown Meech and Hope Emily Allen, EETS os 212 (Oxford: Oxford University Press, 1940), p. 1. All subsequent quotations will be indicated in parentheses in the text. All translations into Modern English are mine.

5. See Sarah Salih, 'At Home; Out of the House', ch. 8 in this volume, p. 124.

6. On Margery's relationship to the visual, see David Wallace, 'Mystics and Followers in Siena and East Anglia: a Study in Taxonomy, Class, and Cultural Mediation', in *The Medieval Mystical Tradition in England*, ed. Marion Glasscoe (Cambridge: D. S. Brewer, 1984), pp. 169–91.

7. See Diane Watt, *Secretaries of God: Women Prophets in Late Medieval and Early Modern England* (Cambridge: D. S. Brewer, 1997), p. 28, on the *Book of Margery Kempe*'s self-fulfilling narrative ordering of such episodes.

8. Karma Lochrie, *Margery Kempe and Translations of the Flesh* (Philadelphia: University of Pennsylvania Press, 1991), pp. 97–134, esp. 103.

9. Julia Boffey, 'Women Authors and Women's Literacy in Fourteenth- and Fifteenth-Century England', in *Women and Literature in Britain, 1150–1500*, ed. Carol M. Meale (Cambridge University Press, 1993), pp. 159–82, at 164.

10. Alexandra Barratt, 'Continental Women Mystics and English Readers', in this volume, pp. 240–1.

11. Boffey, 'Women Authors', pp. 163–4.

12. See the *Constitutions* of Thomas Arundel, excerpted in *The Book of Margery Kempe*, trans. and ed. Lynn Staley, Norton Critical Edition (New York: W. W. Norton, 2001), pp. 187–96, and Staley's introduction, p. xi.

13. Kathleen Ashley, 'Historicizing Margery: *The Book of Margery Kempe* as Social Text', *Journal of Medieval and Early Modern Studies* 28 (1998): 377.

14. For fuller discussion of these figures, see Barratt, 'Continental Women Mystics and English Readers'.

15. Mary Carruthers, *The Book of Memory: A Study of Memory in Medieval Culture* (Cambridge University Press, 1990), p. 180. Quoted by Felicity Riddy, '"Women Talking about the Things of God": a Late Medieval Sub-culture', in *Women and Literature*, ed. Meale, pp. 104–27, at 125 n. 72.

16. Lochrie, *Margery Kempe*, pp. 114–27.

17. Thanks to Robert Edwards for this point.

18. Ashley, 'Historicizing Margery', p. 378.

19. See Preface, Introduction and chapter 5, *The Cloud of Unknowing*, ed. James Walsh (New York: Paulist Press, 1981). The quotation is from p. 128.

20. *Meditations on the Life of Christ*, ed. Isa Ragusa and Rosalie B. Green (Princeton University Press, 1961), p. 5.

21. Allen in a letter to E. I. Watkin, excerpted in *Hope Emily Allen*, p. 158.

22. Ashley, 'Historicizing Margery', p. 379.

23. A. J. Gurevich, 'What is Time?' in *Categories of Medieval Culture*, trans. G. L. Campbell (London: Routledge and Kegan Paul, 1985), pp. 93–151, at 139.

24. Ruth Evans, 'Virginities', in this volume, pp. 27–8.

25. Chakrabarty, 'Minority Histories', pp. 98, 108.

26. Ibid., p. 108.

27. Ibid.

28. Chakrabarty quotes Wilhelm von Humboldt in his 1821 address 'On the Task of the Historian': 'Where two beings are separated by a total gap, no bridge

of understanding extends from one to the other; in order to understand one another, they must have in another sense, already understood each other' ('Minority Histories', p. 109).

29. Ibid., p. 112.

30. Hope Emily Allen, 'Relics', in John C. Hirsh, 'Past and Present in Hope Emily Allen's Essay "Relics"', *Syracuse University Library Associates Courier* 24 (1989): 49–61, at 54.

16

ALEXANDRA BARRATT

Continental women mystics and English readers

In 1406 Sir Henry (later Lord) Fitzhugh, trusted servant of King Henry IV, visited Vadstena, the Bridgettine monastery for men and women in Sweden. Vadstena was the mother-house of the Order of the Most Holy Saviour and had been founded by the controversial continental mystic St Bridget of Sweden, who had died in 1373 and had been canonized in 1391. Fitzhugh was so impressed by what he saw that he gave one of his manors near Cambridge as the future site for an English Bridgettine foundation. It was not until 1415 that Henry V, son of Henry IV, laid the foundation-stone of Syon Abbey at Twickenham in Middlesex and Fitzhugh's dream became a reality. But Fitzhugh's generous gesture is an indication of the degree of pious and aristocratic interest in the Swedish visionary and prophet in early fifteenth-century England.

Margery of Lynn; Julian of Norwich

Two years earlier, in 1413, Margery Kempe of Lynn in East Anglia had been granted an interview by Philip Repingdon, Bishop of Lincoln. His visitor intrigued him; he listened sympathetically to her account of her spiritual experiences and then made an unusual suggestion:

> sche schewyd hym hyr meditacyons and hy [high] contemplacyons and other secret thyngys bothe of qwyk [living] and ded as Owyr Lord schewyd [revealed] to hire sowle. He was rygth glad to heryn hem [them] . . . cownselyng [advising] hire sadly [seriously] that hire felyngys [thoughts] schuld be wretyn [written (down)] . . .[1]

To Margery the idea that she should have her spiritual experiences set down in writing had the shock of the new, and she refused, saying that this was not God's will. But to Repingdon Margery must have seemed a fascinating home-grown variety of a species with which he, as a late medieval Latinate and cosmopolitan cleric, would have been familiar: the European woman mystic.

At the time Repingdon made his unsettling suggestion, there were no indigenous, vernacular texts by women mystics in circulation in England. Indeed, it has been convincingly argued that English religious women were actively discouraged from pursuing this type of spirituality, let alone recording the results in writing. The fifteenth-century *Book for a Simple and Devout Woman* cautions against cultivating visions and other paranormal religious experiences, for these open the door to vanity and pride:

> My dere suster, my consaile is þat þu fiȝte aȝeyn [fight against] vayneglorie [vanity], for þerof þu art moste fondud [tempted]. Dremes and siȝtes [visions] þat þu seest in þi slepe, ȝeue to hem no feiþe [credence]. Lyft þyn herte holiche from hem and haue hem alle suspecte, ne tel no worde bi [about] hem to non to wite what þey wolde mene. Soþfaste siȝte [true vision] is, and of parfite mede [(deserving) perfect reward], knowynge of þyself, þorw þe whiche quykneþ [comes to life] knowyng of God and vnyte wiþ hym.[2]

The pursuit of self-knowledge is preferable, and the clerical author urges his charge, rather than trying to scale the dangerous heights of contemplation, to stick to the ascetic, purgative way:

> Of penaunce and of hardschip [austerity] siker buþ [sure are] þe weyes [ways], and of contemplacion vnstabele [uncertain] and somdel to drede [somewhat to be feared]. So perlus hit is on hyȝ [high] to clymbe, and siker wei [sure way] to God hit is þat mon holde hym lowe [one should consider oneself as humble]. Aungeles office [function] hit is heuenliche þyngus [things] to knowe and to wite [know] þe pryuytes [secrets] þat mow not be departed [shared]. Hit is inow [enough] to mon to se his owne lodliche [ugly] synnes.[3]

But such advice was not universally followed. Forty years before Margery's visit, in May 1373, a young woman on the point of death had experienced sixteen visions of the crucified Christ. At the time she was 'thirty and one half years old', and was later to become an anchoress in Repingdon's own diocese, attached to a church just a short walk from his cathedral. Not long after her miraculous recovery, Julian of Norwich described her experiences in the Short Version of *A Revelation of Love*. But there is no evidence that her text, so intensively studied today, circulated widely, if at all, in the Middle Ages. It survives in just one fifteenth-century manuscript, which belonged to a Carthusian monastery, BL MS Additional 37790 (the Amherst Manuscript). Fifteen or twenty years later Julian recast this as the Long

Version, the earliest surviving complete manuscripts of which are as late as the seventeenth century.

Julian is frequently mentioned in Norwich wills: people left her money, but there is not a single piece of evidence that they knew of her writings or her revelations. Margery Kempe consulted her because she enjoyed a reputation as a spiritual adviser: 'the ankres was expert in swech thyngys and good cownsel cowd yevyn' (*BMK*, pp. 42/7–43/20). But in the detailed, and very convincing, account that she gives of their conversations, neither woman refers to Julian's visions, though the irrepressible Margery cannot resist mentioning her own 'many wondirful reuelacyons' (*BMK*, p. 42/14).

Nonetheless, in continental Europe there was a long tradition (or rather several traditions) of women visionaries, quantitatively far more important than the native English strain. Repingdon must have been familiar with some of them, at least, as their texts circulated in both Latin and vernacular versions. They were read and owned by devout lay men and women of the aristocracy, the gentry, and the urban middle class, as well as by monks, nuns, and other religious, as we shall see.

Hildegard of Bingen

The great twelfth-century Benedictine saint and abbess, Hildegard of Bingen (1098–1179), visionary, poet, musician, scientific and medical writer, wrote prolifically if eccentrically in Latin. But she was known in medieval England in her less familiar role as an apocalyptic prophetess (hence her epithet 'the Sibyl of the Rhine'), rather than as a mystic. Possibly Repingdon saw Margery Kempe as a potential 'Sibyl of the Ouse': as a former supporter of the theologian and heretic John Wyclif (though under pressure he had recanted those radical views and had gone on to become a bishop) he would certainly have known of Hildegard and her writings. For she had, particularly in her 'Cologne letter' of c. 1162, apparently prophesied the demands that Wyclif was to make in the late fourteenth century for the disendowment of the Church (that is, that it should be deprived of its extensive lands and temporal possessions). Some of Hildegard's writings were also seen as predicting the rise of the mendicants (principally the Franciscan and the Dominican orders) who owned no property, either individually or collectively, and lived (at least in theory) by begging. Those who disapproved of the new movement were happy to appropriate – even on occasion to forge – her writings.

Consequently, Hildegard probably enjoyed greater fame among the learned than she would have commanded simply as a woman visionary. According to their library catalogue, the brothers of the Bridgettine abbey of Syon had once owned (but had lost) a copy of a prophecy about the mendicants. They still possessed at the time of the dissolution of the monasteries a book containing her *Scivias*, while the Benedictine abbeys of Battle and Glastonbury both owned copies of her complete prophecies. But none of Hildegard's writings were translated into English in the Middle Ages, although in the sixteenth century her Latin texts were printed. So in spite of the renown she has won in the last twenty or thirty years, Julian of Norwich and Margery Kempe very likely knew nothing about her.

Whom else might Repingdon have known? Elizabeth of Schönau (1126–64) was, like Hildegard, a Benedictine nun and abbess. She experienced visions and other supernatural manifestations but did not write them down herself. Egbert, her brother, however, composed a life of his sister which recorded her revelations. A mid-thirteenth-century catalogue of the books belonging to the Benedictine Glastonbury Abbey lists a copy, while the late fourteenth-century catalogue of Dover Priory (also a Benedictine house) lists her vision concerning the Assumption of the Blessed Virgin Mary. But, as with Hildegard, though there is some evidence that her Latin life circulated in England, it was never translated into Middle English.

Beguines

Lives of women visionaries could be important conduits of influence. In the late twelfth and early thirteenth centuries the area around Liège in the north of France and what is now Belgium produced a remarkable flowering of 'holy women'. Many were beguines, that is, women leading a religious life in self-supporting and self-governing communities or sometimes in their own homes, rather than enclosed as contemplative nuns in convents. They were mainly illiterate in Latin, and sometimes even in their vernaculars (principally French and Flemish), but we know of their experiences from their Latin lives or *vitae*, written by their male confessors or disciples. The Dominican friar, Thomas of Cantimpré, and the cardinal/bishop, Jacques de Vitry, wrote a number of these. De Vitry in particular was a prominent apologist for beguine life and for their spirituality, which foregrounded visionary experiences combined with paranormal phenomena and ferocious asceticism.

There is no evidence that the beguine saints were known in England until the end of the Middle Ages. In the fifteenth century the Augustinian canons of Thurgarton in Yorkshire (where Walter Hilton, the fourteenth-century mystic and author of *The Scale of Perfection*, retired) owned a life 'of the three virgins Elizabeth, Christina and Marie'. This could well be identical with Oxford Bodley MS Douce 114, a manuscript connected with the Carthusian order, that contains the only surviving copy of the lives of the beguines

Elisabeth of Spalbek, Christina the Marvellous (she certainly lived up to her name), and Mary of Oignies, all translated from the Latin into Middle English.[4] Around the same time, Margery Kempe's confessor was reading Jacques de Vitry's life of Mary of Oignies (either in Latin or English), and it profoundly altered his negative attitude towards Margery's weeping.

Further evidence of beguine influence (apart from that of the treatise by Marguerite Porete, who will be discussed below) occurs right at the end of our period. Marie of Oisterwijk, a Flemish beguine who died as late as 1547, lived as a recluse under the protection of the Cologne Charterhouse. (Carthusian monks, both on the continent and in England, played a vital role in encouraging women visionaries and in preserving and circulating their writings.) British Library MS Harley 494 contains an English translation of a devotional exercise addressed to the Five Wounds of Jesus, introduced as 'certain prayers showed unto a devout person called Mary Ostrewyk'. Significantly, perhaps, it is found immediately after an extract from another continental mystical text, Mechthild of Helfta's revelations.

This is a rare example of beguine infiltration into England (where, surprisingly, the movement never took root) but it is not unique. In 1533, only months before the execution of the Benedictine nun Elizabeth Barton, the Holy Maid of Kent, *The Mirror or Glass of Christ's Passion*, by the Bridgettine monk John Fewterer, was printed. This vast and scholarly book is largely concerned with identification with Christ through meditation on his Passion, his sufferings on the cross. The author chooses to present Mary of Oignies, whose life he knew through the *Speculum Historiale* of the thirteenth-century Dominican friar Vincent of Beauvais, as a model of the benefits such meditation can provide.

Women of Helfta

In the second half of the thirteenth century a group of women mystics had emerged at the Benedictine monastery of Helfta in Saxony, then under the leadership of its abbess Gertrud of Hackeborn. Her younger sister Mechthild (c. 1240–98), novice mistress and chantress at Helfta, was a visionary but did not herself write down her experiences. This was done in Latin sometime after 1290 by Gertrud of Helfta (1256–1301), a younger contemporary to whom she had acted as novice mistress, and by another (anonymous) nun. Mechthild's collected visions constituted the *Liber spiritualis* (sometimes *specialis*) *gratiae* [Book of Spiritual (or Special) Grace]. Gertrud too was an influential visionary and her experiences are recorded in Latin in the *Legatus divinae pietatis* [The Herald of God's Loving-Kindness]. She wrote Book 2 herself, while others compiled the biography that makes up

Book 1 and the collection of visions in Books 3, 4, and 5. This work was not translated into English in the Middle Ages and was probably not known in England in Latin either.

In contrast, the *Liber spiritualis gratiae* was well known in England and, although Mechthild is not widely read today, her visions had an extensive and understandable appeal. They are vividly visual, very beautiful, and not obviously unorthodox or alarmingly innovative in their theology. Like those of Gertrud, they particularly encourage devotion to the Heart of Jesus as the quintessence of his human nature, within the context of the sacrament of the Mass and the liturgical year. The *Liber* was translated into Middle English, although in an abbreviated form. Two manuscripts of this translation, *The Book of Ghostly Grace*, survive: British Library MS Egerton 2006, which once belonged to Richard III and his wife, Anne of Warwick; and Oxford MS Bodley 220, written by a certain John Wells, who may have been a Carthusian monk.[5] Both belong to the fifteenth century.

Possibly a Carthusian monk translated Mechthild's *Liber* for the Bridgettine nuns of Syon. As we have already mentioned, the Carthusians rather specialized in collecting, studying, and copying the writings of orthodox women mystics. The important Charterhouse (Carthusian monastery) of Sheen was directly opposite Syon on the other side of the River Thames, and relations between the two religious houses were close (though too close for comfort on occasions). Surprisingly, it was the Carthusians, rather than the Bridgettine monks, who seem to have taken the initiative in the spiritual direction of the nuns. Bridgettine nuns, who were highly regarded in fifteenth-century England, took their vocation and the development of their spiritual lives extremely seriously and they needed suitable reading matter in English.

References to Mechthild, known as 'Matilda' or 'Maud' to English readers, and extracts both in English and Latin from her revelations have been identified in a total of nine medieval devotional works and spiritual compilations. These include two in the Bridgettine *Myroure of Oure Ladye* (see further below); another in the *Speculum devotorum*, compiled for a nun by a Carthusian; and extracts and passages attributed to Mechthild in several other manuscripts. Many of these have Bridgettine or Carthusian connections and contain texts by other women visionaries popular at Syon, notably Bridget of Sweden and Catherine of Siena.

Copies of both the Latin original and the Middle English translation of Mechthild seem to have been surprisingly common. In the late fourteenth or early fifteenth century, the local vicar donated a collection of books to Swine Priory in Yorkshire, a house of Cistercian nuns. It included a copy of the *Liber*, probably of the Latin text, even though the gift was made to a house of religious women, who normally could not read Latin. A late fifteenth-century book-list shows that the Augustinian canons of Thurgarton owned a copy of Mechthild's revelations, while Syon Abbey owned four complete copies, one in English, and a text printed in 1513. A manuscript now in Durham University Library (MS Cosin v.iii.16), which belonged to Syon Abbey, contains Latin extracts from the *Liber* together with a letter in English to the sisters, urging them to read the accompanying texts. And as late as the Elizabethan age, Robert Barker, vicar of Driffield, who died in 1581, owned a *Liber S. Matildis*, which had probably come from Byland Abbey in Yorkshire.

Devout lay people also owned Mechthild's revelations. Cicely, Duchess of York, mother of Richard III, who was noted for her piety, is said to have had the book read aloud to her during mealtimes; she bequeathed her copy to her granddaughter Brigitte, a Dominican nun. Alienora (or Eleanor) Roos of York, who died in 1438, owned a text described as 'maulde buke', probably a Middle English version of Mechthild who as we have mentioned was known as Maud in English. This she bequeathed in her will to Dame Joan Courtenay, who was probably a nun.

Marguerite Porete

Marguerite Porete was a contemporary of Gertrud of Helfta. A beguine from Hainault in Flanders, in 1310 she was burned at the stake in Paris for heresy. The treatise that caused her undoing, *Le Mirrouer des simples ames* [The Mirror of Simple Souls], was originally written in French. The Inquisition condemned it as heretical on a number of grounds, notably that Marguerite taught that certain favoured souls no longer needed the Church and its sacraments, nor were they obliged to observe the rules of Christian morality. As part of their investigations, the Inquisition had her book translated into Latin, the better to scrutinize and condemn it. Ironically, four of these Latin manuscripts survive while only one, late and corrupt, copy of the French original has come down to us. Marguerite's book was also translated into Italian and into English.[6]

Like Hildegard, Marguerite fascinates modern readers but was little known in England in the Middle Ages. In contrast to the work of many other continental women visionaries, there is no evidence that her text circulated among women readers, possibly because people quickly forgot that a woman had written it. Indeed, *The Mirror* clearly had a very restricted circulation in England: no wills, catalogues, inventories, or library lists have so far come to light that make any mention of her text. It is true that three manuscripts of the Middle English translation survive, a creditable total for a medieval text. But all three belonged to individual Carthusian monks or to

Carthusian monasteries, a rarefied and exclusive spiritual milieu. (One copy is found in the same manuscript, BL Add. 37790, that contains the only copy of the Short Text of Julian's *A Revelation of Love*.)

Further evidence of Carthusian interest, even sponsorship, of *The Mirror* is the translation into Latin made by Richard Methley who was a monk at Mount Grace Charterhouse in Yorkshire (the house where the only copy of *The Book of Margery Kempe* was held). Presumably he knew nothing of the earlier Latin translation made by the Inquisition. Perhaps he made his own translation so that the text, which he must have admired and valued, could be examined with greater theological subtlety. It would also reach a wider clerical audience throughout Europe, as Latin was the international language of the Church.

The three Middle English copies are remarkably similar, even to the extent of conscientiously transmitting obvious gibberish, for the translation is extremely literal. This suggests that the copies must have been produced under tight editorial control, with strict instructions to the scribes to change nothing. The translator, probably a Carthusian, clearly had no idea that the text was heretical, let alone that a woman had written it. But he did betray some unease with the content and from time to time adds defensive explanatory notes marked with his initials, 'M.N.'

Elizabeth of Hungary

'Elizabeth of Hungary' is a familiar name and a popular saint. She was born in 1207, the daughter of the Hungarian king, and was briefly but happily married to the Count of Thuringia, to whom she bore several children before he departed and died on Crusade. She then became a model of Franciscan piety and poverty, dying exhausted by her austerities before she was twenty-four in 1231. But it is arguable that the Elizabeth of Hungary whose 'treatise' Margery Kempe cites as providing a precedent for her own weeping (*BMK*, p. 154/13–14) was a different person altogether. This other Elizabeth, born nearly a hundred years later in 1294, daughter of another king of Hungary, was a Dominican nun in the Swiss convent of Töss who died in 1336. Margery (or her confessor) probably had in mind, and was familiar with, the so-called *Revelations of St Elizabeth*, of which two Middle English versions survive.[7] This is a brief Latin text that largely consists of highly imaginative dialogues between Elizabeth and the Virgin Mary, and later Christ himself. It seems to have appealed to the medieval mind, for it was translated into numerous European languages.

The first Middle English translation survives in a single early fifteenth-century manuscript, Cambridge University Library MS Hh.1.11. This probably belonged to a community of East Anglian nuns, possibly to the Franciscans of Bruisyard, Suffolk. The other version does not survive in manuscript at all but was printed by Wynkyn de Worde, in or around 1492, and then reprinted c. 1500. It follows a translation of the much longer *Life* of St Catherine of Siena by her confessor Raymund of Capua. Catherine and her writings, as we shall see, were promoted in England by the Bridgettines of Syon Abbey, who may also have suggested the Elizabeth text to de Worde. It is perhaps significant that the brothers of Syon at one time owned a copy of the revelations in English, which was lost or removed. Perhaps they had lent it to de Worde: early printers often destroyed their copy-text after it had been typeset.

Bridget of Sweden

All the visionaries mentioned so far have occupied, as it were, niche positions. By far the best known of the continental women mystics, the only one who was in any way a household name and whose followers could count on widespread brand-recognition, was Bridget of Sweden (1302 or 1303–73).[8] Bridget (or Birgit, or Birgitta) was a very modern saint. Aristocratic; married; a mother (of eight, no less); critic and adviser of popes and kings; foundress of a revolutionary religious order for men and women but never a nun herself; visionary and mystic: she exemplified the 'mixed life' that combined the pursuit of contemplation with active virtue and political involvement, even though the nuns of her own religious order were strictly enclosed. In particular she insistently lobbied for the return of the papacy from Avignon to Rome.

Bridget's writings became increasingly widely read during the fifteenth century, by both lay and religious. The Spanish bishop, Alphonse de Pecha, had definitively fixed the vast Latin text of her revelations, consisting of eight books, some time before 1377. A distinctive and identifiable textual tradition of the Latin prevailed in England, reflected by the two, independent, Middle English translations of the whole text.[9] There were also separate selections of compilations in Latin, and at least seven survive in Middle English. These tended to draw on those revelations with elements of prophecy, or details about the lives of Christ and the Virgin, or instructions about the spiritual life. In addition, short passages from Bridget's revelations were often copied, and recopied, to fill the odd page or half-page in individual manuscripts.

Many of the prophetic revelations criticized the clergy, and are analogous to the Hildegard material that circulated in England. But Bridget's emphasis on the validity of the priestly office, however immoral the individual priest, could also be used against the Wyclifites. Moreover, the Swedish saint had conveniently supported the English claim to the French throne that under-laid the Hundred Years' War: not surprisingly, the relevant revelations were harnessed to the nationalist cause.

Bridgettine material was also absorbed into original works of spiritual in-struction. The anonymous but immensely popular *Contemplations of the Dread and Love of God*[10] contains a great deal of material lifted from the revelations and was in its turn mined by the much-copied *Pore Caitiff* and by a version of the *De remediis contra temptaciones* [Remedies against Temptations] by William Flete, spiritual adviser to Catherine of Siena. Sim-ilarly, a sermon on the Assumption of the Virgin in Cambridge University Library MS Hh. 1.11 (which, as we have seen, also contains the only Middle English manuscript version of Elizabeth of Hungary's revelations) draws on several Bridgettine texts. Bridget's vivid though somewhat old-fashioned vi-sions of Christ's Passion frequently appear in compilations and were recycled in other works such as the Carthusian *Speculum devotorum* and *The Fruyte of Redempcyon*, printed by Wynkyn de Worde in 1514. Other extracts were arranged to constitute the Virgin Mary's autobiography as told to Bridget, found in Oxford Bodley MS Rawlinson C 41.[11]

There is considerable evidence that Bridget's writings were widespread in later medieval England. The donation to the Cistercian nuns at Swine included a Latin text of Bridget's revelations; Durham University MS Cosin V.iii.16, already mentioned as containing Mechthild texts, contains Latin extracts; the Augustinian canons at Thurgarton owned a copy of the Latin revelations; the catalogue of the last prior of Monk Bretton, a Cluniac priory, listed a copy. Cambridge University Library MS ii.6.40, which belonged to Johanna Mouresleygh (fl. 1441, 1460), a Benedictine nun at Shaftesbury, contains a Bridget extract, in English.

Bridget texts are also mentioned in wills far more often than those of any other woman visionary. In 1415 Henry le Scrope, lord of Masham, bequeathed a copy to his brother Stephen, Archdeacon of Richmond. Around 1420 John Dygon, recluse of Sheen, and Johanna, recluse of St Botulph's, London, gave a copy of the revelations to Magdalen College, Oxford. (It is still there, as Oxford, Magdalen MS 77.) In 1432 Robert Semer bequeathed a 'Bridget book' to William Bramley; in 1468 Elizabeth Sewerby and in 1481 Margaret Purdaunce of Norwich left copies in their wills. In 1495 Cicely, Duchess of York, left her copy to her granddaughter Anne de la Pole, while Agnes Vavasour, a Cistercian nun at Swine, was bequeathed books by Bridget, perhaps by her aunt.

Other evidence of Bridget's popularity in England is a verse life, *Salutacio Sancte Birgitte*, written by the poet John Audelay around 1426,[12] in which he praises Syon Abbey, the only English house of the Order of the Most Holy Saviour. There can be no doubt that the presence from 1415 onwards of an extremely pious, wealthy, and well-connected Bridgettine house near London was the primary factor in the circulation of Bridgettine texts and the growth of devotion to the saint. Syon was a focus for pilgrimage, where the famous 'Pardon', or indulgence, could be bought – Margery Kempe herself visited Syon, probably in 1433 (*BMK* p. 245/31–3) – and, given its strong links with Europe, a centre for the dissemination of devotion to St Bridget in particular and up-to-the minute continental cults in general.

Numerous manuscripts of Bridget's revelations and other associated texts directly connected with Syon Abbey are still extant today. Unfortunately, there is no surviving catalogue of the nuns' library (unlike that of the brethren) but much can be reconstructed.[13] For instance, British Library MS Arundel 146 must have belonged to Syon as it contains the Additions to the Bridgettine rule.[14] Cambridge University Library MS Ff.6.33 contains extracts from the revelations and may have belonged to the Syon sisters. Syon owned British Library MS Harley 612, an important Latin manuscript that contains a corpus of Bridgettine writings, including the *Defensorium Sanctae Birgittae* by the Benedictine Adam Easton (d. 1397).

The many early sixteenth-century printed editions of the revelations were aimed at a reading public interested in vernacular devotional literature, in the continental mystics, and in the religious life. This interest extended to the highest in the land: in 1491, Lady Margaret Beaufort, mother of Henry VII, together with his wife, Queen Elizabeth, commissioned William Caxton to print an edition of a spurious but extremely popular text attributed to St Bridget, the *Fifteen Oes* (*STC* 20195). Renowned for her piety and learning as well as for her single-minded dedication to the political interests of her son, Lady Margaret had close contacts with Syon. She herself translated two contemporary European devotional works familiar to the Bridgettines: part of Thomas à Kempis's *Imitation of Christ*, and a penitential text by a Flemish Carthusian monk, *The Mirror of Gold to the Sinful Soul*.[15] These were not however written by women, and are devotional rather than mystical.

Among their many idiosyncrasies, the Bridgettine nuns had a distinctive Latin liturgy that Christ himself had dictated to their foundress.[16] This was translated into English some time after 1435 and was presumably used by the nuns in multiple manuscript copies. In 1530 it was printed as *The Myrroure of Oure Ladye*, perhaps with the aim of allowing every Syon nun to have her own copy – in blissful ignorance that only nine years later they would be turned out of their monastery by Henry VIII and would go into exile in Flanders.

Catherine of Siena

Bridget may have been the best known of the continental women visionaries, but the closest in time to Margery Kempe and Bishop Repingdon was the Italian Catherine of Siena (canonized in 1461). In fact, her dates (1347–80) make her a near contemporary of Julian of Norwich. Although of humbler, bourgeois origins – her father was a wool-dyer – Catherine showed a number of similarities to Bridget. (Significantly, visual representations of the two saints in English early printed books are virtually indistinguishable.) She was an ascetic and visionary, but not an enclosed nun. Rather, she continued to live at home, vowed to virginity as Dominican tertiary (tertiaries were in many ways like beguines) in the midst of her extensive family. She had many followers, both men and women, some of whom acted as her secretaries; she was active in politics, both in urban affairs and in international ecclesiastical diplomacy, demanding (like St Bridget a generation earlier) the return of the papacy to Rome.

Catherine even had a tenuous connection with England, for an English Augustinian friar, William Flete, was her spiritual adviser from 1362 to 1374. (He was succeeded by the better-known Raymund of Capua, a Dominican friar, who wrote the earliest biography of the saint.) This constitutes the only known personal link between the fourteenth-century English and Italian mystics, though there is in fact no evidence that William Flete maintained his links with England or helped circulate Catherine's writings there. But there is evidence for her cult in Britain in the late Middle Ages, including a convent of the Second Order of Dominican nuns, founded in Edinburgh in 1517, and dedicated to her. An early sixteenth-century copy of their constitutions and of the gospels to be read at Mass throughout the liturgical year survives as Edinburgh University Library MS 150.[17]

Catherine's principal mystical work, dictated in Italian in 1378, was known as the *Dialogo*. As the title suggests, it consists of a series of dialogues, between the soul of the mystic and God the Father. Raymund of Capua translated it into Latin and there is extant an English (or Scottish) manuscript of this version, now Edinburgh University Library MS 87, which was perhaps connected with the Edinburgh Dominican convent. In the early fifteenth century the Latin version was translated into Middle English for the benefit of the Syon nuns, as *The Orcherd of Syon*:[18] three manuscripts survive. Wynkyn de Worde eventually printed it for a wider audience in 1519.[19] Syon's spiritual style was very different from the Italian saint's: notably, it lacked the dimension of social activism that made Catherine of Siena a role-model for the nineteenth-century English reformer Josephine Butler. Nonetheless the Bridgettine monastery was closely involved in the dissemination of devotion to Catherine, and of knowledge of her life and writings, and the Bridgettine brothers for their part owned a copy of Catherine's *vita* and two of the *Dialogo*.

Lives of Catherine, such as that owned by the Syon brethren, were also widely disseminated, and because they were relatively accessible may have been more influential than her somewhat demanding visionary writings. The Cistercian nunnery at Swine in Yorkshire owned at one time what is now British Library MS Harley 2409: this includes a life of Catherine and also one of William Flete's texts. The Prioress of Swine, Matilda Wade (fl. 1482), gave this book to a nun at Nuneaton, a house of the order of Fontevrault, another double order of monks and nuns, founded in the twelfth century by Robert of Arbrissel. In 1485–6 another nun at Swine was bequeathed an English life of the saint by her aunt. And the late fifteenth-century book-list of the Augustinian Thurgarton Priory includes Latin texts of the *Dialogo* and of the saint's life.

English women and continental Europe

Such, then, are the women mystics and visionaries of whom Bishop Repingdon might have known. Some at least became known to Margery Kempe herself in due course. This was inevitable: Margery came from Lynn on the Norfolk coast, which in the Middle Ages was an important port with close ties to the Baltic, Scandinavia, and Flanders. She herself travelled extensively in Europe, on pilgrimages to the Holy Land via Rome and to Santiago da Compostela in Galicia, Spain; she also went to northern Germany, possibly via Sweden. She quite blatantly adopted Bridget of Sweden as a role-model – and occasional rival: once when Margery witnessed at Mass the consecrated host flickering in the priest's hands, Our Lord assured her, 'My dowtyr, Bryde, say [saw] me neuyr in þis wyse' (*BMK*, p. 47/26–7). Hope Emily Allen, who rediscovered the unique manuscript of *The Book of Margery Kempe* in the 1930s, was the first to suspect that the continental women visionaries exercised a strong influence on Margery's spirituality. The detailed work of more recent scholars has amply vindicated her hunch. Margery mentions Bridget's revelations ('Bride's book') in the same breath as Walter Hilton's writings, as the *Stimulus amoris* of James of Milan, and as Richard Rolle's *Incendium amoris* (*BMK*, p. 39/23–5): these were all texts read her by her confessor (*BMK*, p. 143/27). Indeed on one occasion God himself vouched for their authenticity – 'it is trewe euery word þat is wretyn in Brides boke' (*BMK*, p. 47/33–4). As a pilgrim in Rome, Margery visited places that Bridget had visited (*BMK*, p. 95/25–9) and interviewed people who had known her (*BMK*, p. 95/10–22). Margery and her confessor also knew the revelations of

St Elizabeth of Hungary (*BMK*, p. 153/13–14), and the latter, at least, had read Jacques de Vitry's life of the Flemish beguine Mary of Oignies, as we have already seen.

More problematic, and perhaps more interesting, is whether Julian of Norwich knew anything of these continental women mystics. Julian was clearly trained, in the English tradition, to eschew visionary experience. She explains that, although her desire for 'mende of [Christ's] Passion' led her to request 'a bodily sight [vision] wherein I might have more knowledge of the bodily peynes [physical sufferings] of our saviour' (that is, perhaps, the kind of detailed vision of the Crucifixion experienced by Bridget), this was the extent of her mystical ambitions: 'Other sight ner sheweing [revelation] of God desired I never none till the soule was departid [separated] fro the body.'[20] Later, when apparently dying, she remembers this desire and again stresses, 'But in this I desired never bodily sight nor sheweing of God.'[21] She never refers to any visionaries by name but the desire she mentions in the course of her revelations for 'ful syte [comprehensive vision] of helle and purgatory' is intriguing. Many such revelations were granted to Bridget of Sweden, though it must be added that accounts of such Otherworld visions and voyages are common in the Middle Ages, such as the fifteenth-century revelation of Purgatory 'showed to a holy woman',[22] (not to mention Dante's *Divine Comedy*). Julian is careful, however, to protest that she did not want any special insight – 'But it was not my mening to maken prive [be confidentially informed] of anything that longyth [appertains] to the feith'[23] – nor was she prompted by lack of faith. When she goes further and wants information about the destiny of a particular person – whether 'a certeyn creature that I lovid' would persevere in virtuous living – she is refused an answer.[24] This kind of curiosity about the fate of individual souls (Julian calls it 'syngular [specific] desire') is characteristic of Bridget and Mechthild, both of whom often sought, and were granted, such privileged information.[25] Julian, in contrast, learns that 'it is mor worship [honour] to God to knowen al things in general than to lyken in onythyng in special'.

Julian, of course, is writing relatively early, in the last quarter of the fourteenth century. Clearly it was from the first quarter of the fifteenth century, particularly after the establishment of Syon Abbey, that continental women visionaries achieved such prominence as they would ever enjoy in England. It is equally clear that without the promotional activities of the Carthusians, as well as of the Bridgettine brethren, they would have made little if any impact on those people, whether lay men and women or female religious, who did not read Latin. As it is, their influence on the latter years of the Middle Ages in England must have been considerable if occasionally deplorable, as in the sad case of Elizabeth Barton, the Holy Maid of Kent.

It is perhaps a measure of Britain's post-medieval insularity (encapsulated in the notorious but possibly apocryphal newspaper headline 'Fog in Channel – Continent Isolated') that we should find it slightly surprising, or intriguing, that writings of continental women mystics circulated in England. In the medieval mind England was, literally, marginalized. The thirteenth-century Mappa Mundi preserved at Hereford Cathedral graphically represents the British Isles as two islands squeezed uncomfortably into the outer circumference of the known world. England was culturally subservient to France, from which it drew its dominant literary and artistic models, and spiritually dependent on Rome. Its rulers harboured extensive political and military ambitions towards France while they cultivated dynastic ties with ruling families all over Europe; its merchant classes were heavily reliant on trade with the greater European market.

But the trade in mystical texts was not all one-way. The Bridgettine mother-house at Vadstena owned a manuscript containing two Latin texts by the mid-fourteenth-century Yorkshire mystic Richard Rolle (now Uppsala MS University C. 1), while the Charterhouse at Enghien in Flanders also owned two Rolle manuscripts, now Brussels, Bibliothèque Royale MSS 1485 and 2103. The existence of Latin translations of the Middle English *Mirror of Simple Souls*, as of *The Cloud of Unknowing*, *The Scale of Perfection*, and the early thirteenth-century guide for anchoresses *Ancrene Wisse*, suggests that some clerics saw great possibilities for English mystical writings, if only they could be disentangled from the obscure and barbarous language in which they usually circulated!

But in the final analysis the continental women visionaries not only offered spiritual guidance: their very existence surely nourished extraordinary and, until then, unthinkable ambitions in their readers. One is tempted to say that these women must have been revelations in their own right. The very existence of the works of continental women visionaries in English translation must have served as a constant reminder that such women, who were not only mystics but also writers, did indeed exist – an existence otherwise only too easily forgotten.

NOTES

1. *The Book of Margery Kempe*, ed. Sanford Brown Meech and Hope Emily Allen, EETS OS 212 (London: Oxford University Press, 1940), pp. 42/7–43/20. All subsequent references by page and line number are to this edition, cited as *BMK*.
2. *Book for a Simple and Devout Woman*, ed. F. N. M. Diekstra (Groningen: Egbert Forsten, 1998), lines 7620–5.
3. Ibid., lines 7633–8.

4. Edited by C. Horstmann, 'Prosalegenden: Die Legenden des Ms. Douce 114', *Anglia* 8 (1885): 134–84.

5. *The Book of Ghostly Grace*, ed. Teresa Halligan (Toronto: Pontifical Institute for Mediaeval Studies, 1979). See also *Women's Writing in Middle English*, ed. Alexandra Barratt, Longman Annotated Texts (London: Longman, 1992), pp. 49–60.

6. M. Doiron, '*The mirrour of simple souls*: A Middle English translation', *Archivio Italiano per la Storia della Pietà* 5 (1968), 247–355. See also *Women's Writing in Middle English*, ed. Barratt, pp. 61–70.

7. Both versions have now been edited by Sarah McNamer, *The Two Middle English Translations of the Revelations of St Elizabeth of Hungary*, Middle English Texts 28 (Heidelberg: C. Winter, 1996).

8. For a brief introduction and for edited extracts from some of the Middle English versions, see *Women's Writing in Middle English*, ed. Barratt, pp. 84–94.

9. One (that found in BL MS Claudius B I) has been edited: see *The Liber Coelestis of St Bridget of Sweden*, vol. 1: text, ed. by Roger Ellis, EETS OS 291 (Oxford University Press, 1987).

10. *Contemplations of the Dread and Love of God*, ed. Margaret Connolly, EETS OS 303 (Oxford University Press, 1993).

11. See *Women's Writing in Middle English*, ed. Barratt, p. 85.

12. See *The Revelations of Saint Birgitta*, ed. W. P. Cumming, EETS OS 178 (Oxford University Press, 1929), pp. xxxi–xxxvii.

13. See Christopher de Hamel, *Syon Abbey: The Library of the Bridgettine Nuns and their Peregrinations after the Reformation* (London: Roxburghe Club, 1991), for a magisterial account of the surviving information.

14. '*The Rewyll of Seynt Sauioure' and Other Middle English Brigittine Legislative Texts*, Vol. 2, ed. James Hogg, Salzburger Studien zür Anglistik und Amerikanistik 6 (Salzburg: Institut für Anglistik und Amerikanistik, 1978).

15. See *Women's Writing in Middle English*, ed. Barratt, pp. 301–10.

16. See *The Bridgettine Breviary of Syon Abbey*, ed. A. J. Collins, Henry Bradshaw Society 96 (Worcester: Stanbrook Abbey Press, 1969).

17. Published as *Liber Conventus S. Katherine Senensis prope Edinburgum*, ed. J. Maidment (Edinburgh: Abbotsford Club, 1841).

18. *The Orcherd of Syon*, ed. Phyllis Hodgson and Gabriel M. Liegey, EETS OS 258 (Oxford University Press, 1966).

19. See *Women's Writing in Middle English*, ed. Barratt, pp. 95–107, for a brief note on Catherine and some extracts from the Middle English translation.

20. *Julian of Norwich: A Revelation of Love*, ed. Marion Glasscoe (Exeter University Press, 1986, repr. 1989), p. 2. Cf. *Julian of Norwich's Revelations of Divine Love: The Shorter Version*, ed. Frances Beer, Middle English Texts 8 (Heidelberg: C. Winter, 1978), p. 39/7, 21–3 and pp. 39/26–40/1.

21. Ibid., p. 4. Cf. *Julian of Norwich's Revelations*, ed. Beer, p. 43/1–2.

22. In *Women's Writing in Middle English*, ed. Barratt, pp. 163–76.

23. Ibid., p. 34. There is no parallel in the Shorter Version.

24. Ibid., p. 36. Cf. *Julian of Norwich's Revelations*, p. 64/16–17.

25. See, for instance, the extract from Mechthild in *Women's Writing in Middle English*, ed. Barratt, pp. 58–60.

17

NADIA MARGOLIS

Joan of Arc

Joan of Arc, or Joan the Maid (Jeanne la Pucelle), as she called herself, exemplifies three powerful female types for the Middle Ages – prophet, virgin martyr, and androgyne – all culminating in one persona, as expressed in her writings: her letters and trial testimony. Given the form and context of her writings, her 'readers' almost inevitably began as her doubters, and often adversaries, in some way. A cult figure even during her brief lifetime, she understood early on, with uncanny insight for a minimally educated person, the essential reciprocity between myth and truth while formulating her mission. For each and every extraordinary attribute she claimed to possess, she could provide some kind of authentication. Such was the recurrent cycle of dialogue between past and present, prophecy and proof, governing her career as controversial saviour of France.

Whether one perceives her as cipher or seer, Joan's entire life (1412–31) was shaped by the Hundred Years' War between France and England, begun in 1337 and eventually ending, partly thanks to her achievements, in 1453. By Joan's time, and despite such hopeful interludes as the reign of Charles V (1368–80), this inter-dynastic struggle between violently self-determining national identities had resulted in two crushing English military victories over the French: Crécy in 1346 and Agincourt in 1415. Strife from within, among the French noble families, also weakened the kingdom, the gravest being the assassination of Louis, Duke of Orleans, by men of John the Fearless, Duke of Burgundy, in 1407. Suffering repeated bouts of insanity, Charles VI could do little to avenge his brother's murder and maintain unity within his kingdom. France was now divided between Armagnacs and Burgundians. The Armagnacs, controlled by Charles's son, the Dauphin (crown prince), took it upon themselves finally to avenge Orleans's murder by killing Burgundy (1419), and thus reinforcing the alliance between the new Duke of Burgundy, Philip the Good, and Henry V of England. The Dauphin's revenge also backfired by casting doubt upon his legitimacy, since, in avenging Orleans's death so recklessly, he behaved more as the son of Orleans – rumoured lover of his mother, Queen Isabel – than as the son of his legal father, Charles VI, thus jeopardizing his claim to the throne.

However, it was Agincourt in 1415 that resounded as the single greatest demoralizer of the French (Armagnac) cause. This 'miracle of St Crispin's Day' (25 October) for the English, led by Henry V, saw a vastly larger French army demolished by nature's seeming complicity with Henry's bowmen. Together with France's internal woes, this defeat underscored the English claim as God's chosen heirs to William the Conqueror's legacy. Thus, with the approval of the aging, mad Charles VI in 1420, the Treaty of Troyes disinherited the Dauphin and named Henry V, hero of Agincourt, the rightful king of France and England. Henry further guaranteed this inheritance by marrying the Dauphin's sister, Catherine of Valois. Himself dispossessed, the Dauphin fled southward, out of Anglo-Burgundian-controlled Paris, to the town of Bourges, to be sardonically named 'King of Bourges', and later to Chinon. Nor was there a chance for the would-be Charles VII when Henry V and Charles VI died in 1422. The Duke of Bedford, chief power behind the English throne, ensured that his nephew, Henry's infant son, inherited both French and English crowns as Henry VI. Bedford and the new king's other uncle, Gloucester, with the Earls of Salisbury and Warwick, continued to conquer more of France with their Burgundian allies. Taking their cue from French monarchic theory, Bedford's propagandists took pains to show the Lancasters too were descended from St Louis, and thus under the fleurs-de-lis – the white lilies associated with Christ and bestowed by King Clovis (c. 496) as a symbol of France's dynastic purity. Such cultivation of ancient symbolism reinforced England's ideal of kingship as one based not only on military might and political strategy but also on divine benefaction. Conversely, France needed, to preserve her sovereignty – that is, all that made her an independent kingdom under God – a military miracle to redress the ravages of Agincourt. Such was the 'grant pitié [great pity]' of the French kingdom, to cite Joan's own words.

Less overtly felt among the masses, but arguably affecting Joan's standing with the Church, the Great Schism of the Church (1378–1417) spawned two (or even three) popes: mainly one in Avignon, in southern France, an 'antipope' to the one in Rome. When the Council of Constance (1415–18) finally ended the Schism by naming Martin V in Rome the sole legitimate pope, the French lost *their* pope. French theologians, largely affiliated with the Sorbonne, or University of Paris, thus relinquished much prestige and influence in Church affairs, which sorely disgruntled them. The pro-Armagnac among them, including some of France's finest intellectuals, were massacred by the opposing faction in 1418. This left the pro-Anglo-Burgundian, reactionary and corrupt 'Sorbonnards' to serve as Joan's judges at the Rouen trial thirteen years later.

Set against this complex political turmoil of which she and her people understood little, even the most banal and basic facts of Joan's life would acquire new meaning during her trial testimony, at which she became her own first biographer. The fourth child of Jacques d'Arc and Isabelle Romée, Joan was born c. 1412, probably on or around 6 January, the feast of the Epiphany, and was baptized in the church at Domrémy, a village in the province of Lorraine, near the German border. Because of their Armagnac loyalty, Domrémy and neighbouring towns suffered raids by Burgundian soldiers. Jacques d'Arc, a native of Champagne, was a peasant farmer, neither poor nor wealthy, and influential in local affairs. Her highly devout mother also provided her only schooling, as was usual for women of Joan's class. Isabelle taught her the basic prayers and such womanly arts as sewing and spinning, at which Joan excelled, but scarcely any reading and writing.

The persistent, affectionate image of Joan the gentle shepherdess – and Shakespeare's negative account of her being sired by a shepherd out of wedlock (*1 Henry VI*, v.4.37–8) – surprisingly enough, is disputed by her in the trial records. Scholars have offered various explanations ranging from Joan's class consciousness to trial-record tinkering by notaries. It nonetheless seems likely, given the prevailing *pâturage* system (shared pastures with communal tending by village children) that she did tend cattle and sheep, though spending more time on domestic duties. Another legendary quality, Joan's extreme piety, would be more pointedly distorted during the trial as evidence of her heresy. In reality, while respecting orthodox Catholicism, she also participated in the mixed Christian/folkloric rituals involving lords and peasants around certain local fountains and trees in celebration of springtime and the autumn harvest, merged with saints' feast days.

At the age of twelve or thirteen, Joan tells us, in her father's garden that summer at noon after having fasted the day before, she heard her voices for the first time, accompanied by a light. Her first vision was of St Michael, who heralded later visions of Saints Margaret and Katherine. All were extremely popular saints for Joan's patriotic, devout milieu; she need not have read such learned hagiographical sources as the *Legenda aurea* [The Golden Legend] to learn of them. These visions initially advised her simply to be a good girl, then gradually revealed that she was the chosen defender of France, despite her youth, humble origins, and gender. The three saints, each in separate fashion, also served as models for Joan's sense of self and future mission. Michael the archangel, slayer of satanic dragons, had become the official protective saint of France.

The legends of her two female saints offer insight into the difficult question of Joan's alleged cross-dressing, a major accusation at her trial, and also her rhetorical prowess. St Margaret of Antioch, a beautiful girl of noble family, so prized her virginity that she eluded marriage by disguising herself as a monk and fleeing home to spend the rest of her life running a monastery in this same disguise. By other accounts she debated with her suitor, then suffered imprisonment and even beheading by him. Like Margaret, Joan too would secretly flee her parents' house at Domrémy to avoid marriage, and don male attire to fulfil her destiny as a virgin, though as an overt sign of divine designation and obedience to her saints rather than a merely protective, practical disguise. Nor did wearing men's clothes respond to an inner desire for masculinity or to be a man.[1] Therefore, recent scholarly opinions to the contrary, Joan did not cross-dress in the sense most often understood now. St Katherine of Alexandria would herald Joan's courageous eloquence at her trials. Katherine's transvestism consisted in dialectical expertise, rather than in an actual change of clothing, to equal and surpass men. She defended her village by successfully debating with the pagan emperor's fifty most eminent philosophers and converting them to Christianity, though she eventually met with a martyr's death, a virgin to the end.

After Joan's eloquence finally won over the originally dismissive Captain Baudricourt, at nearby Vaucouleurs (February 1429), by correctly predicting the outcome of the Battle of Rouvroy well before any messenger could have conveyed the news, Joan obtained the necessary aid and equipment for her journey across France to interview the Dauphin at Chinon, where more tests awaited her. She identified Charles despite his attempts to hide in the crowd at court, then, in private conversation, managed to win his confidence via the famous, oft-disputed 'secret' – either by revealing a sign signifying shared royal parentage; or by a special prayer or prophecy – confirming his legitimacy as King Charles VII.

The gift of prophecy particularly characterized female mystics, whether Christian or pagan. Joan's uniqueness lay in the fact that she could not only prophesy but was herself prophesied, as her self-fashioning merged with such famous pre-existing pronouncements as one of the so-called Merlin prophecies, recounted c. 1135 in Geoffrey of Monmouth's *Historia regum Britanniae* (*History of the Kings of Britain*): *Ex nemore canuto puella eliminabitur ut medelae curam adhibeat* ('A maiden will come out from the oak forest to give care to healing'), and others from mixed Christian/Pagan, historical/mythological traditions. Joan capitalized on the fact that she, a maiden, had often played in Domrémy's Bois chenu ('Oak Forest'), to validate herself through this. Another wave of prophecy declared that France would be lost by a woman and saved by a warrior maiden. To Joan's public, the woman who lost France was Isabel of Bavaria, Queen of France, unfaithful wife of Charles VI, who therefore imperilled their son's succession. Joan's virginity would also link her to another prophecy invoking the Virgin Mary, saviour of the human race by herself and through Jesus. Joan would likewise restore the Dauphin's claim to the throne, as she states in her testimony and letters. In this same vein she would head her letters and adorn her banners with the inscription, 'Jhesu Maria' ('Jesus Mary').

Charles, ever cautious and calculating, nonetheless ordered her prophetic claims questioned and verified by his leading theologians, notably Jean Gerson, at Poitiers, in March 1429. This examination tested for visionary falsehood on two levels: the reality of their outcome and, especially if correct, their source, given the deceptive nature of Satan. It was thus not enough for Joan to be able to predict events and her role in them; her 'enthusiasm' must come from God and not the Devil. Once they determined her to be an instrument of God, then all aberrations – especially her male clothing – were deemed justifiable accoutrements. Gerson's involvement was crucial to furthering Joan's mission because he was the leading authority on *discretio spirituum*, the art of discerning false prophecies. He had also presided over St Bridget of Sweden's canonization deliberations. Since he wrote the most positive opinion on Joan, citing biblical heroines as precedents, the other examiners concurred, though cautiously. Gerson's support, in light of his prestige, facilitated the favourable judgment despite the absence of the validating miracle normally required of visionaries. On the secular, folkloric side, popular acceptance of Joan may owe something to other female mythical figures like Mélusine, recently appropriated as guardian of Poitiers against the English by Charles VI's powerful uncle, the Duke of Berry.[2]

Having won the approval of the Poitiers examiners, Joan was then allowed to ride with the French army. Delivering Orleans from the lengthy English siege (8 May 1429) provided the missing miracle from Poitiers while redressing the loss at Agincourt. Her writing would play a major part in this, now that the Poitiers verdict permitted, indeed privileged, her to write officially as what she claimed to be: the virgin defender of France sent by God against the English. This image would attract further affirmation among a great variety of contemporary authors, most notably Christine de Pizan, who saw in Joan the fulfilment of her feminist, patriotic dreams, as celebrated in her polemical poem, the *Ditié de Jehanne d'Arc* [Tale of Joan of Arc] of 31 July 1429. Joan's Anglo-Burgundian detractors, like the Bourgeois de Paris, Monstrelet's chronicles, and the Duke of Bedford's letters, would brand her a false saint defending a false king, a harlot, yet mannish, and a bloodthirsty witch. Thus was launched an anti-Joan tradition extending through Caxton, Fabyan, Hall, and Holinshed – the latter two major sources for Shakespeare's *Henry VI* – which still persists among some English historians.[3]

Her earliest letters, of which we have only fragments and allusions, are addressed to family and potential allies: (1) to her parents (late February 1429) asking forgiveness for her abrupt departure; (2) to the Dauphin announcing her imminent arrival to aid him (early March 1429); and (3) to the monks at Sainte-Catherine de Fierbois (sent from Chinon, 6 March 1429), requesting them to find and send her the old sword she knew to be hidden in their church. This last represents one of her more mysteriously clairvoyant moments, since she had reportedly never been to Sainte-Catherine. The archives of the town of Compiègne contain references to other lost letters; Joan probably dictated about seventeen in all. Wary of interception by unwanted eyes, Joan devised a code for her captains and royal notaries: an encircled 'X' at the end of a message meant that the order was not to be followed.

In all six of her surviving intact letters, Joan's words speak as loudly as the actions that buttressed them. She usually begins by speaking in the third person singular, then shifts into the first person singular, or official 'we', towards the end.

First and most important among these, the famous *Lettre aux Anglais* [Letter to the English], introduced her, 'La Pucelle' (The Maid), to the English as a real person and not mere rumour. She emphasizes her virginity both as part of her saviour persona and also to dispel straightaway any suspicion of her being a soldiers' harlot or 'camp follower'. Likewise, her imperious tone purports to reflect the infallible will of God and not herself, a humble messenger – an effective ploy. Dictated in March 1429 from Poitiers and later sent from Blois, this letter, addressed to the king of England and 'you, Duke of Bedford' – the real power – contains both a summons, or declaration of war, and a peace proposal, the latter contingent on English withdrawal. In denying the English right to the French throne accorded by the Treaty of Troyes, she also faces head-on the quandary of one Christian nation fighting the other, hoping for victory as God's will. The English had tried to resolve this by simply conquering; Joan, in this letter, appeals to the English as fellow Christians and co-crusaders for the Church against the Infidel, to perform 'the most beautiful deed ever done for Christianity'. Whether the English followed this or not (they understandably accepted neither this arguably specious invitation nor her lopsided terms of peace), Charles VII was the legitimate king of France by divine right, and she hoped that Bedford would see reason to avert God's wrath: 'The Maid begs and beseeches you not to cause yourself to be destroyed.'[4] Like her grasp of politics and military strategy, her keen command of current prophecy, especially for an adolescent only semi-literate at best, impresses us here, since she seems conversant with, while refuting, the main points of the fourteenth-century St Bridget of Sweden's *Revelations* in favour of the English.[5] Joan's first letter disconcerts all who see it by its fiercely confident language, including Bedford, despite his mockery of her as 'that abandoned woman'. By the tone and substantive detail of his reply,[6] he obviously suspects Joan to be no ordinary religious zealot.

The extant letters coming after the *Lettre aux Anglais* equal it in forcefulness but are far narrower in scope and intent. Most of these sought not only safe passage but also supplies for her troops on the way to the Reims coronation (17 July 1429) and for her later campaigns. Her missive to the 'Loyal Frenchmen of Tournai', in what is now Belgium, dated 25 June, was copied thirty-six times for distribution throughout the thirty-six wards of the city. She appeals to their loyalty to the Dauphin while attempting to intimidate pro-English citizens by reporting the deaths or imprisonment of many eminent English knights like Suffolk, Talbot, Fastolf, and Glasdale – and then requests the Tournai citizens' presence at the Dauphin's forthcoming coronation at Reims, along with their welcoming support for her troops when they pass through, 'to keep up the good fight [bonne querelle] for the French kingdom'. Her letter to the burghers of Troyes (4 July 1429) demands the same submission to the Dauphin as king of France by God's command. Though not as bloodthirsty as in letters to other cities on the coronation route to Reims, Joan's language is nonetheless firm: their refusal to obey could cost them their lives.

Her second letter to Philip the Good, Duke of Burgundy, unlike the first, unanswered by him, exists intact. Dated 17 July 1429, it seeks to make peace between Duke Philip and the Dauphin Charles in rather uncompromising fashion. Omitting any conciliatory mention of Charles's role in Philip's father's murder ten years earlier, the chief source of their rift, she instead justifies their proposed truce entirely as God's will, like Charles's right to the throne. While portraying herself on the one hand as supplicant, pleading with Philip to make peace, on the other she threatens bloodshed and misery if he refuses to accede.

In her letter to the people of Reims (5 August 1429), Joan reprises the 'good fight' theme, linking it to her defence of the sanctity of the blood royal, that is, Charles VII, not Henry VI – necessary despite Charles's recent coronation there. She also alludes to the new truce between Charles and Philip of Burgundy, and announces her passage through the town on the way to Paris to safeguard the king. Because she senses this to be an uneasy peace, she requests the Reims citizens' vigilance in case of any traitors, whom she vows to eradicate. Later letters to this city (16 and 28 March 1430), both bearing her actual signature, repeat these themes to reassure the people that she will repay their loyalty by her protection. Letters to the cities of Clermont (7 November 1429) and more threateningly, Riom (9 November), ask specifically for munitions (gunpowder) in preparation for the attack on La Charité, which would fail for lack of reinforcements from Charles.

Her letter of 22 August 1429 to the Count of Armagnac stands alone as the only extant letter by her dealing with religious matters, here the Great Schism. Jean d'Armagnac has asked her, so exceptional in God's grace, for counsel on which of the (now three) popes (Martin V in Rome, Benedict XIV in Avignon, and Clement VIII in Peñiscola) he should revere. Joan replies that she is too pressed at the moment with waging war to answer, and advises him to contact her later, in Paris, whereupon she will consult with God and give him the right answer.[7] Another letter (20 November 1429), now lost, relates to Charles VII her meetings with the mystic Catherine de la Rochelle, whom Joan deems a fraud. A third letter on religious matters, the so-called *Letter to the Hussites* ('Sent from Sully to the heretics of Bohemia'), is no longer thought to be hers, despite its heading, but rather by her confessor at Orleans, Jean Pasquerel, who signed it. This spurious letter affords intriguing evidence of how Church officials tried to exploit Joan's quasi-divine aura to combat heresy.

Once she was captured, however, by the Duke of Luxembourg's men at Compiègne (23 May 1430), this aura would work against her. Luxembourg sold her to Burgundy. After an arduous prison itinerary (fourteen prisons, like Christ's fourteen Stations of the Cross), she was turned over to the Sorbonne inquisitors and brought to trial at Rouen in January 1431. Jealous of her popularity, convinced by scheming courtiers that she had outgrown her usefulness to him, Charles neither offered ransom nor sent a rescue party for her, claiming himself too destitute.

Her trial (9 January to 29 May 1431) was an outwardly proper trial, yet conducted by the chief magistrate, pro-English Bishop of Rouen, Pierre Cauchon, in bad faith, as we might expect from Bedford and Warwick, its true promoters. Outdoing St Katherine, Joan faced 164 ecclesiastical judges and advisers, and yet without a single advocate of her own. Consequently Joan fuelled the case against her with every utterance – whether written or oral. Even earlier positive testimony, like the Poitiers record and the treatise by Gerson (now dead), was transformed into manuals for her condemnation at Rouen. Her truculent refusal to answer certain questions pertaining to her voices did not help either. Repetition, recurrent cycles of questioning, hammering on the same points (her voices and visions; God's favouring the French over the English; her clothing) dominated those months of interrogation, with seventy articles read to her, then compressed into twelve.

In gentler moments like the 'Charitable exhortation' (18 April), the judges feigned concern for her soul, in the manner of priestly confessors, to deceive her into renouncing her voices or admitting her heresy; but more often they snidely insinuated or bullied, with threats of torture, to achieve the same ends. Joan's most dangerous aspect was her refusal to submit to them, the Church Militant (Church on Earth), by claiming to speak directly to the Church Triumphant (Church in Heaven) as represented by her saintly voices and visions. Convicting her as a witch would also help the English cause by nullifying the divine favour confirmed by Orleans and other French victories. Though successful at parrying their attempts to entrap her into admitting witchcraft, Joan was convicted of heresy and blasphemy, plus related charges. At one point, the interrogators almost broke her, in a phase known as the Abjuration (24 May), during which the exhausted heroine signed a paper recanting belief in her voices and promised to wear a dress, to avoid burning. But she quickly renounced this recantation (28 May), so that she who had 'lapsed' in the eyes of her judges had now relapsed by reversing her abjuration of her voices. She was then surrendered to the secular authorities and publicly burned at Rouen on 30 May 1431.

But there, even more than for other martyrs, Joan's story only begins, despite the best efforts of Cauchon and his colleagues. Having conveniently lost the full Poitiers record from 1429, they also destroyed the original French transcript of the Rouen trial, after translating it into official Latin. All that remains of the authentic French testimony is the so-called d'Urfé fragment, containing the minutes of the trial. By circulating only the official Latin version, Cauchon's clever notarial 'translators' again weighted the trial against Joan and the Armagnacs. Nevertheless, once Burgundy rejoined Charles and the English had been essentially expelled from France (per Joan's prophecy) in 1450, Charles initiated the so-called Rehabilitation trial. After five years of royal and papal inquests, the Nullification of Condemnation proceedings took place, rediscovered the d'Urfé fragment and similar documents, re-interviewed witnesses, noted all the procedural errors in Cauchon's trial and overturned the verdict on 7 July 1456. Though purporting to restore Joan's good name, the Rehabilitation more immediately fulfilled its real intention to improve Charles's image, as he went on to rule as Charles the Victorious.

The Church was slower to recover from its malaise in the affair. It took patriotic visionary historians like Michelet and Quicherat in the early nineteenth century – motivated by a culture war with German scholars inspired by Schiller's 1802 play, *Die Jungfrau von Orleans* – to unearth Joan's trial records and other documents from various archives and properly edit them in printed form as part of France's cultural patrimony. Quicherat's epic 1849 edition and translation of all known documents on Joan unveiled the hero-ine's story for all to see. So captivating was this medieval courtroom drama combined with a martyr's passion that readers ranging from Mark Twain to Vita Sackville-West devoured the five erudite volumes to create their own por-traits of her. Joan became an international cultural hero representing a mul-titude of causes, from suffragettes to female gymnasts. In France, Catholic leaders took notice, merging with rightist politicians to promote her can-onization beginning in the 1850s. Many French republican (anti-Church, centrist) nationalists and socialists also favoured Joan, minus her appropria-tion by the right-wing Catholics. Alarmed at her veneration (1896), then be-atification (1909), certain modern sceptics in the tradition begun by Voltaire in the eighteenth century, like Anatole France and, later, George Bernard Shaw, tried to debunk her myth while becoming intrigued with her. After World War I, when French soldiers reported having visions of Joan in the trenches, the Church finally canonized her in 1920. Immune to the Church's hold in France, and other reactionary regimes like Japan, for whom Joan represented ideal female subservience, pioneering English and American fem-inists embraced her as a symbol.

Quicherat's work would be gradually updated and supplemented through-out the twentieth century by Champion, Doncoeur, Scott, Tisset and Lanhers, and, finally, Duparc, furnishing more raw material for some fifty films and thousands of poems, plays, essays, and novels, in addition to an equal pro-fusion of scholarly works on Joan, both favourable and unfavourable, with no end in sight.[8] Doubters still persist, the most recent being Caratini. How-ever, regardless of their opinions after reading her, few readers of Joan have emerged untransformed in some way.

NOTES

1. For opposing views of female transvestism in general, see Judith Halberstam, *Female Masculinity* (Durham, NC: Duke University Press, 1998); for Joan's trans-vestism in particular, see Susan Crane, 'Joan of Arc and Women's Cross-Dress', *The Performance of Self: Ritual, Clothing, and Identity During the Hundred Years War* (Philadelphia: University of Pennsylvania Press, 2002), pp. 73–106.
2. An early snake-goddess figure of multinational origins, Mélusine was transformed into *Mélusine*, a 1393 chronicle romance by Jean d'Arras, at the behest of the Duke of Berry to disconcert English invaders in Poitou. See Jean d'Arras, *Mélusine*, ed. Louis Stouff (Dijon: Bernigaud & Privat, 1932; repr. Geneva: Slatkine, 1974).
3. For summaries and bibliography of English authors on Joan, not all of whom were hostile, see Nadia Margolis, *Joan of Arc in History, Literature and Film: A Select, Annotated Bibliography* (New York: Garland, 1990), pp. 64–77, 154–6.
4. All quotations from Joan's letters are from the texts and notes in Régine Pernoud and Marie-Véronique Clin, *Jeanne d'Arc* (Paris: Fayard, 1986), pp. 377–90, which

also provides a concordance to earlier editions. For English translations, see Pernoud and Clin, *Joan of Arc: Her Story*, rev. and trans. Jeremy DuQ. Adams (New York: St Martin's Griffin, 1998), pp. 247–64.

5. Demonstrated in Deborah Fraioli, *Joan of Arc: The Early Debate* (Woodbridge: Boydell Press, 2000), pp. 69–86, citing from *Sancta Birgitta revelaciones, Lib. IV*, ed. Hans Aili, Samlingar utgivna av Svenska Fornskriftällskapet, 2nd ser., Latinska Skrifter, vol. 7 (Stockholm: Almquist and Wiksell, 1992), bk 4, chs. 104–5.

6. For the text of Bedford's reply, see Monstrelet, *The Chronicles of Enguerrand de Monstrelet*, ed. and trans. Thomas Johnes (London: 1840; repr. 1849), 1: 558.

7. For an analysis and translations of Armagnac's and Joan's letters, see Charles T. Wood, *Joan of Arc and Richard III: Sex, Saints and Government in the Middle Ages* (New York: Oxford University Press, 1988), pp. 126–8.

8. Full references for all authors and scholars mentioned here but not cited in Further Reading, p. 281, may be found in appropriately labelled sections of Margolis, *Joan of Arc in History, Literature and Film.*

FURTHER READING

Placing women in medieval history and historiography

Allen, Prudence. *The Concept of Woman: The Aristotelian Revolution, 750 BC–AD 1250.* Montreal: Eden Press, 1885; rpt Grand Rapids: W. B. Eerdmans, 1997.

The Concept of Woman: The Early Humanist Reformation, 1250–1500. Grand Rapids: W. B. Eerdmans, 2002.

Bennett, Judith. 'Confronting Continuity.' *Journal of Women's History* 9 (1997): 73–94.

'Feminism and History.' *Gender and History* 1 (1988): 251–72.

Blanton-Whetsell, Virginia and Charlene Miller Avrich. *Medieval Women in Film: An Annotated Handlist and Reference Guide, with Essays on Teaching The Sorceress.* Medieval Feminist Newsletter Subsidia series, 1. Eugene: Center for the Study of Women in Society, University of Oregon, 2000.

El-cheikh, Nadia M. 'Describing the Other to Get at the Self: Byzantine Women in Arabic Sources (8th–11th centuries).' *Journal of the Economic and Social History of the Orient* 40 (1997): 239–50.

Gregg, Joan Young. *Devils, Women, and Jews: Reflections of the Other in Medieval Sermon Stories.* Albany: State University of New York Press, 1997.

Harty, Kevin J. *The Reel Middle Ages: American, Western and Eastern European, Middle Eastern, and Asian Films about Medieval Europe.* Jefferson, NC: McFarland, 1999.

Rosenthal, Joel T., ed. *Medieval Women and the Sources of Medieval History.* Athens: University of Georgia Press, 1990.

Schaus, Margaret and Susan Mosher Stuard. 'Citizens of No Mean City: Medieval Women's History.' *Journal of Women's History* 6 (1994): 170–98.

Stuard, Susan Mosher, ed. *Women in Medieval History and Historiography.* Philadelphia: University of Pennsylvania Press, 1987.

Women in the medieval world

Bitel, Lisa. *Women in Early Medieval Europe, 400–1100.* Cambridge Medieval Textbooks. Cambridge University Press, 2002.

Ennen, Edith. *The Medieval Woman.* Trans. Edmund Jephcott. Oxford: Basil Blackwell, 1989.

Fell, Christine E., Cecily Clark, and Elizabeth Williams. *Women in Anglo-Saxon England and the Impact of 1066*. London: British Museum Publications, 1984.

Hambly, Gavin R. G., ed. *Women in the Medieval Islamic World: Power, Patronage, and Piety*. The New Middle Ages series. New York: St Martin's Press, 1998.

Jesch, Judith. *Women in the Viking Age*. Rochester, NY: Boydell Press, 1991.

Jochens, Jenny. *Women in Old Norse Society*. Ithaca: Cornell University Press, 1995.

Klapisch-Zuber, Christiane, ed. *A History of Women in the West*. Vol. 2: *Silences of the Middle Ages*. Cambridge, MA: Belknap Press of Harvard University Press, 1992–4.

LaBarge, Margaret Wade. *Women in Medieval Life: A Small Sound of the Trumpet*. London: Hamish Hamilton, 1986.

Leyser, Henrietta. *Medieval Women: A Social History of Women in England, 450–1500*. New York: St Martin's Press, 1995.

Mitchell, Linda E., ed. *Women in Medieval Western European Culture*. New York: Garland, 1999.

Pernoud, Régine. *Women in the Days of the Cathedrals*. Trans. and adapted by Anne Côté-Harriss. San Francisco: Ignatius Press, 1998.

Shahar, Shulamith. *The Fourth Estate: A History of Women in the Middle Ages*. London: Methuen, 1983.

Skinner, Patricia. *Women in Medieval Italian Society 500–1200*. Harlow: Pearson Education, 2001.

Wemple, Suzanne Fonay. *Women in Frankish Society: Marriage and the Cloister, 500 to 900*. Philadelphia: University of Pennsylvania Press, 1981.

Female childhoods

Barron, Caroline M. 'The Education and Training of Girls in Fifteenth-Century London.' In Diana E. S. Dunn, ed., *Courts, Counties, and the Capital in the Later Middle Ages*. New York: St Martin's Press, 1996. Pp. 139–53

Blumenfeld-Kosinski, Renate. *Not of Woman Born: Representations of Caesarian Birth in Medieval and Renaissance Culture*. Ithaca: Cornell University Press, 1990.

Finucane, Ronald C. *The Rescue of the Innocents: Endangered Children in Medieval Miracles*. New York: St Martin's Press, 1997.

Goldberg, P. J. P. 'Girls Growing Up in Later Medieval England.' *History Today* 45 (1995): 25–32.

Hanawalt, Barbara. 'The Composite Biography as a Methodological Tool for the Study of Childhood in History.' *Marriage and Family Review* 24 (1996): 323–49.

Growing Up in Medieval London: The Experience of Childhood in History. New York: Oxford University Press, 1993.

Orme, Nicholas. *Medieval Children*. New Haven: Yale University Press, 2001.

Shahar, Shulamith. *Childhood in the Middle Ages*. London: Routledge, 1990.

Taglia, K. A. 'The Cultural Construction of Childhood: Baptism, Communion, and Confirmation.' In C. M. Rousseau and J. T. Rosenthal, eds., *Women, Marriage, and Family in Medieval Christendom*. Studies in Medieval Culture series,

37. Kalamazoo: Western Michigan University, Medieval Institute Publications, 1998. Pp. 255–87.

Wasyliw, Patricia Healy. 'The Pious Infant: Developments in Popular Piety during the High Middle Ages.' In Ann W. Astell, ed., *Lay Sanctity, Medieval and Modern*. South Bend: University of Notre Dame Press, 2000. Pp. 105–15.

Virginities

Carlson, Cindy L. and Angela Jane Weisl, eds. *Constructions of Widowhood and Virginity in the Middle Ages*. The New Middle Ages series. Basingstoke: Macmillan, 1999.

Caviness, Madeline H. 'Patron or Matron? A Capetian Bride and a *Vade Mecum* for Her Marriage Bed.' *Speculum* 68 (1993): 333–62.

Dinshaw, Carolyn. *Getting Medieval: Sexualities and Communities, Pre- and Postmodern*. Durham, NC: Duke University Press, 1999.

Dor, Juliette, Lesley Johnson, and Jocelyn Wogan-Browne, eds. *New Trends in Feminine Spirituality: The Holy Women of Liège and their Impact*. Medieval Women: Texts and Contexts series, 2. Turnhout: Brepols, 1999.

Duffy, Eamon. *The Stripping of the Altars: Traditional Religion in England c.1400–c.1580*. New Haven: Yale University Press, 1992.

Elliott, Dyan. *Fallen Bodies: Pollution, Sexuality, and Demonology in the Middle Ages*. The Middle Ages series. Philadelphia: University of Pennsylvania Press, 1999.

Fradenburg, Louise O. 'Criticism, Anti-semitism and the Prioress's Tale.' *Exemplaria* 1 (1989): 69–115.

Freud, Sigmund. 'The Taboo of Virginity.' In *On Sexuality*. Vol. 7 Pelican Freud Library. Angela Richards, ed. London: Penguin, 1977. Pp. 261–83.

Jansen, Katherine L. 'Mary Magdalen and the Mendicants: the Preaching of Penance in the Late Middle Ages.' *Journal of Medieval History* 21 (1995): 1–25.

Karras, Ruth Mazo. 'The Holy Harlot: Prostitute Saints in Medieval Legend.' *Journal of the History of Sexuality* 1 (1990): 3–32.

Kelly, Kathleen Coyne. *Performing Virginity and Testing Chastity in the Middle Ages*. London: Routledge, 2000.

Lewis, Katherine. J. *The Cult of St Katherine of Alexandria in Late Medieval England*. Woodbridge: Boydell Press, 2000.

'Model Girls? Virgin-Martyrs and the Training of Young Women in Medieval England.' In Katherine J. Lewis, Noel James Menuge, and Kim M. Phillips, eds., *Young Medieval Women*. New York: St Martin's Press, 1999. Pp. 25–46.

Meale, Carol M. '". . . Alle the Bokes That I Haue of Latyn, Englisch, and Frensch": Laywomen and their Books in Late Medieval England.' In Carol M. Meale, ed., *Women and Literature in Britain, 1150–1500*. Cambridge University Press, 1993. Pp. 128–58.

Millett, Bella. '*Ancrene Wisse* and the Book of Hours.' In Denis Renevey and Christiana Whitehead, eds., *Writing Religious Women: Female Spiritual and Textual Practice in Late Medieval England*. Cardiff: University of Wales Press, 2001. Pp. 21–45.

'The Origins of *Ancrene Wisse*: New Answers, New Questions.' *Medium Aevum* 61 (1992): 206–28.

Phillips, Kim M. 'Maidenhood as the Perfect Age of Woman's Life.' In Katherine J. Lewis, Noel James Menuge and Kim M. Phillips, eds., *Young Medieval Women*. New York: St Martin's Press, 1999. Pp. 1–24.

Salih, Sarah. *Versions of Virginity in Late Medieval England*. Woodbridge: Boydell Press, 2001.

Wogan-Browne, Jocelyn. 'Chaste Bodies: Frames and Experiences.' In Sarah Kay and Miri Rubin, eds., *Framing Medieval Bodies*. Manchester University Press, 1994, 24–42.

    Saints' Lives and Women's Literary Culture c. 1150–1300: Virginity and Its Authorizations. Oxford University Press, 2001.

Marriage

Brooke, Christopher. *The Medieval Idea of Marriage*. New York: Oxford University Press, 1989.

Brundage, James. A. *Law, Sex, and Christian Society in Medieval Europe*. University of Chicago Press, 1987.

Dockray, Keith. 'Why Did Fifteenth-Century English Gentry Marry? The Pastons, Plumptons and Stonors Reconsidered.' In M. Jones, ed., *Gentry and Lesser Nobility in Later Medieval Europe*. New York: St Martin's Press, 1986. Pp. 61–80.

Donahue, Charles. 'The Canon Law on the Formation of Marriage and Social Practice in the Later Middle Ages.' *Journal of Family History* 8 (1983): 63–78.

Elliott, Dyan. *Spiritual Marriage: Sexual Abstinence in Medieval Wedlock*. Princeton University Press, 1993.

Hughes, Diane Owen. 'From Brideprice to Dowry in Mediterranean Europe.' *Journal of Family History* 3 (1978): 262–96.

Parsons, John Carmi, ed. *Medieval Queenship*. New York: St Martin's Press, 1993.

Richmond, Colin. 'The Pastons Revisited: Marriage and the Family in Fifteenth-Century England.' *Bulletin of the Institute of Historical Research* 58 (1985): 25–36.

Smith, J. H. M., 'Gender and Ideology in the Early Middle Ages.' In R. N. Swanson, ed., *Gender and Christian Religion: Papers Read at the 1996 Summer Meeting and the 1997 Winter Meeting of the Ecclesiastical History Society*. Woodbridge: Published for the Ecclesiastical History Society by the Boydell Press, 1998. Pp. 51–73.

Ward, Jennifer. C. 'The English Noblewoman and her Family in the Later Middle Ages.' In Christine Meek and Katherine Simms, eds., *'The Fragility of Her Sex'?: Medieval Irishwomen in their European Context*. Dublin: Four Courts Press, 1996. Pp. 119–35.

Widows

Barron, Caroline M. and Anne F. Sutton, eds. *Medieval London Widows, 1300–1500*. London: Hambledon Press, 1994.

Carlson, Cindy L. and Angela Jane Weisl, eds. *Constructions of Widowhood and Virginity in the Middle Ages*. The New Middle Ages series. New York: St Martin's Press, 1999.

Cavallo, Sandra and Lyndan Warner, eds. *Widowhood in Medieval and Early Modern Europe*. Women and Men in History series. Harlow: Longman, 1999.

Franklin, Peter. 'Peasant Widows' "Liberation" and Remarriage Before the Black Death.' *Economic History Review*, second series, 39 (1986): 186–204.

Klapisch-Zuber, Christiane. 'The "Cruel Mother": Maternity, Widowhood, and Dowry in Florence in the Fourteenth and Fifteenth Centuries.' In Lydia Cochrane, trans., *Women, Family, and Ritual in Renaissance Italy*. University of Chicago Press, 1985. Pp. 117–31.

Klein, E. 'The Widow's Portion: Law, Custom, and Marital Property Among Medieval Catalan Jews.' *Viator* 31 (2000): 147–63.

Mirrer, Louise, ed. *Upon My Husband's Death: Widows in the Literature and Histories of Medieval Europe*. Ann Arbor: University of Michigan Press, 1992.

Rosenthal, Joel. 'Fifteenth-Century Widows and Widowhood: Bereavement, Reintegration, and Life Choices.' In Sue Sheridan Walker, ed., *Wife and Widow in Medieval England*. Ann Arbor: University of Michigan Press, 1993. Pp. 33–58.

Swaby, Ffiona. *Medieval Gentlewoman: Life in a Widow's Household in the Later Middle Ages*. Stroud: Sutton, 1999.

Between women

Bennett, Judith M. '"Lesbian-Like" and the Social History of Lesbianisms.' *Journal of the History of Sexuality* 9 (2000): 1–24.

Brooten, Bernadette J. *Love between Women: Early Christian Responses to Female Homoeroticism*. University of Chicago Press, 1996.

Hotchkiss, Valerie R. *Clothes Make the Man: Female Cross Dressing in Medieval Europe*. New Middle Ages series. New York: Garland, 1996.

Lewis, Gertrud Jaron. *By Women, For Women, About Women: The Sister-Books of Fourteenth-Century Germany*. Toronto: Pontifical Institute of Medieval Studies, 1996.

Matter, E. Ann. 'My Sister, My Spouse: Woman-Identified Women in Medieval Christianity.' *Journal of Feminist Studies in Religion* 2 (1986): 88–93.

McNamara, Jo Ann. *Sisters in Arms: Catholic Nuns through Two Millennia*. Cambridge, MA: Harvard University Press, 1996.

Murray, Jacqueline. 'Twice Marginal and Twice Invisible: Lesbians in the Middle Ages.' In Vern Bullough, ed., *Handbook of Medieval Sexuality*. New York: Garland, 1996. Pp. 191–222.

Sautman, Francesca Canadé and Pamela Scheingorn, eds. *Same Sex Love and Desire among Women in the Middle Ages*. The New Middle Ages series. New York: Palgrave, 2001.

Schulenburg, Jane Tibbetts. *Forgetful of Their Sex: Female Sanctity and Society, ca. 500–1100*. University of Chicago Press, 1998.

Traub, Valerie. 'The Rewards of Lesbian History.' *Feminist Studies* 25 (1999): 363–94.

Wiethus, Ulrike. 'In Search of Medieval Women's Friendships: Hildegard of Bingen's Letters to her Female Contemporaries.' In Ulrike Wiethus, ed., *Maps of Flesh and Light: The Religious Experience of Medieval Women Mystics*. Syracuse University Press, 1993. Pp. 93–111.

Women and authorship

Bell, Susan Groag. 'Medieval Women Book Owners: Arbiters of Lay Piety and Ambassadors of Culture.' *Signs* 7 (1982): 742–68. Reprinted in Mary Erler and Maryanne Kowaleski, eds., *Women and Power in the Middle Ages*. Athens: University of Georgia Press, 1988. Pp. 149–87.

Cherewatuk, Karen and Ulrike Wiethaus, eds. *Dear Sister: Medieval Women and the Epistolary Genre*. The Middle Ages series. Philadelphia: University of Pennsylvania Press, 1993.

Churchill, Laurie J., Phyllis R. Brown and Jane E. Jeffrey, eds. *Women Writing Latin from Roman Antiquity to Early Modern Europe*. Vol. 2: *Medieval Women Writing Latin*. New York and London: Routledge, 2002.

Classen, Albrecht. 'Female Explorations of Literacy: Epistolary Challenges to the Literary Canon in the Late Middle Ages.' *Disputatio* 1 (1996): 89–121.

Ferrante, Joan. *To the Glory of Her Sex: Women's Roles in the Composition of Medieval Texts*. Bloomington: Indiana University Press, 1997.

    '*Scribe quae vides et audis*: Hildegard, Her Language and Her Secretaries.' In David Townsend and Andrew Taylor, eds., *The Tongue of the Fathers: Gender and Ideology in Twelfth-Century Latin*. The Middle Ages series. Philadelphia: University of Pennsylvania Press, 1998. Pp. 102–35

Macbain, W. 'Anglo-Norman Women Hagiographers.' In Ian Short, ed., *Anglo-Norman Anniversary Essays*. London: Anglo-Norman Text Society, 1993. Pp. 235–50.

McCash, June Hall, ed., *The Cultural Patronage of Medieval Women*. Athens: University of Georgia Press, 1996.

Meale, Carol M., ed. *Women and Literature in Britain, 1150–1500*. Cambridge University Press, 1993.

Mooney, Catherine M., ed. *Gendered Voices: Medieval Saints and their Interpreters*. The Middle Ages series. Philadelphia: University of Pennsylvania Press, 1999.

Smith, Lesley and Jane H. M. Taylor, eds. *Women, the Book, and the Godly: Selected Proceedings of the St Hilda's Conference, 1993*. Woodbridge: D. S. Brewer, 1995.

    Women and the Book: Assessing the Visual Evidence. London: British Library, 1997.

Stevenson, Barbara and Cynthia Ho, eds. *Crossing the Bridge: Comparative Essays on Medieval European and Heian Japanese Women Writers*. The New Middle Ages series. New York: Palgrave, 2000.

Summit, Jennifer. *Lost Property: The Woman Writer and English Literary History, 1380–1589*. University of Chicago Press, 2000.

Tarvers, Josephine Koster. '"This Ys My Mystrys Boke": English Women as Readers and Writers in Late Medieval England.' In Charlotte Cook Morse, Penelope Reed Doob, and Marjorie Curry Woods, eds., *The Uses of Manuscripts in Literary Studies: Essays in Memory of Judson Boyce Allen*. Studies in Medieval Culture series, 31. Kalamazoo: Western Michigan University, Medieval Institute Publications, 1992. Pp. 305–27.

Enclosure

Chewning, Susannah Mary. 'Mysticism and the Anchoritic Community: 'A Time . . . of Veiled Infinity.' In Diane Watt, ed., *Medieval Women in their Communities*. University of Toronto Press, 1997. Pp. 116–37.

Elkins, Sharon K. *Holy Women of Twelfth-Century England*. Chapel Hill: University of North Carolina Press, 1988.

Gilchrist, Roberta. *Gender and Material Culture: The Archaeology of Religious Women*. New York: Routledge, 1994.

Religious Women in Medieval East Anglia: History and Archaeology. Norwich: University of East Anglia, 1993.

Horner, Shari. 'Spiritual Truth and Sexual Violence: the Old English Juliana, Anglo-Saxon Nuns, and the Discourse of Female Monastic Enclosure.' *Signs* 19 (1994): 658–75.

King, Margaret L. 'Book-Lined Cells: Women and Humanism in the Early Italian Renaissance.' In Patricia H. Labalme, ed., *Beyond Their Sex: Learned Women of the European Past*. New York University Press, 1980. Pp. 66–90.

Millett, Bella. *Ancrene Wisse, the Katherine Group, and the Wooing Group*. Cambridge: D. S. Brewer, 1996.

Warren, Anne K. *Anchorites and their Patrons in Medieval Europe*. Berkeley: University of California Press, 1985.

At home; out of the house

Bennett, Judith M. *Ale, Beer, and Brewsters in England: Women's Work in a Changing World, 1300–1600*. New York: Oxford University Press, 1996.

Women in the Medieval English Countryside: Gender and Household in Brigstock before the Plague. New York: Oxford University Press, 1987.

Bennett, Judith M. and Amy M. Froide, eds. *Singlewomen in the European Past, 1250–1800*. Philadelphia: University of Pennsylvania Press, 1999.

Blamires, Alcuin. *The Case for Women in Medieval Culture*. Oxford: Clarendon Press, 1997.

Dillard, Heath. *Daughters of the Reconquest: Women in Castilian Town Society, 1100–1300*. Cambridge University Press, 1984.

Edgington, Susan B. and Sarah Lambert, eds. *Gendering the Crusades*. New York: Columbia University Press, 2002.

Erler, Mary and Maryanne Kowaleski, eds. *Women and Power in the Middle Ages*. Athens: University of Georgia Press, 1988.

Friedman, Yvonne. 'Women in Captivity and their Ransom during the Crusader Period.' In Michael Goodich, Sophia Menache, and Sylvia Schein, eds., *Cross Cultural Convergences in the Crusader Period*. New York: Lang, 1995. Pp. 75–89.

Green, Monica H. *Women's Healthcare in the Medieval West: Texts and Contexts*. Variorum Collected Studies; CS 680. Aldershot: Ashgate, 2000.

Greilsammer, Myriam. 'The Midwife, the Priest, and the Physician: the Subjugation of Midwives in the Low Countries at the End of the Middle Ages.' *Journal of Medieval and Renaissance Studies* 22 (1991): 285–329.

Hanawalt, Barbara, ed. *Women and Work in Preindustrial Europe*. Bloomington: Indiana University Press, 1986.

Harrison, Dick. *The Age of Abbesses and Queens: Gender and Political Culture in Early Medieval Europe*. Lund: Nordic Academic Press, 1998.

Howell, Martha C. *Women, Production, and Patriarchy in Late Medieval Cities*. University of Chicago Press, 1986.

Karras, Ruth Mazo. *Common Women: Prostitution and Sexuality in Medieval England*. New York: Oxford University Press, 1996.

Nicholson, Helen. 'Women on the Third Crusade.' *Journal of Medieval History* 23 (1997): 335–49.

Otis, Leah Lydia. *Prostitution in Medieval Society: The History of an Urban Institution in Languedoc*. University of Chicago Press, 1985.

Richardson, Malcolm. 'Women, Commerce, and Rhetoric in Medieval England.' In Molly Meijer Wertheimer, ed., *Listening to Their Voices: The Rhetorical Activities of Historical Women*. Columbia: University of South Carolina Press, 1997. Pp. 133–49.

Roberts, M. 'Sickles and Scythes: Women's Work and Men's Work at Harvest Time.' *History Workshop Journal* 7 (1979): 3–28.

Beneath the pulpit

Bynum, Caroline Walker. *Holy Feast and Holy Fast: The Religious Significance of Food to Medieval Women*. Berkeley: University of California Press, 1987.

Dor, Juliette, Lesley Johnson, and Jocelyn Wogan-Browne, eds. *New Trends in Feminine Spirituality: The Holy Women of Liège and their Impact*. Medieval Women: Texts and Contexts series, 2. Turnhout: Brepols, 1999.

French, Katherine. *The People of the Parish: Community Life in a Late Medieval English Diocese*. Philadelphia: University of Pennsylvania Press, 2001.

Galloway, Penelope. '"Discreet and Devout Maidens": Women's Involvement in Beguine Communities in Northern France, 1200–1500.' In Diane Watt, ed., *Medieval Women in their Communities*. University of Toronto Press, 1997. Pp. 92–115.

Gibson, Gail Murray. 'Blessing from Sun and Moon: Churching as Women's Theater.' In Barbara A. Hanwalt and David Wallace, eds., *Bodies and Disciplines: Intersections of Literature and History in Fifteenth-century England*. Medieval Cultures series Minneapolis: University of Minnesota Press, 1996. Pp. 139–54.

Lee, Becky R. 'The Purification of Women after Childbirth: a Window onto Medieval Perceptions of Women.' *Florilegium* 14 (1995–6): 43–55.

Lees, Clare and Gillian R. Overing. *Double Agents: Women and Clerical Culture in Anglo-Saxon England*. Philadelphia: University of Pennsylvania Press, 2001.

McNamara, Jo Ann. 'The Need to Give: Suffering and Female Sanctity in the Middle Ages.' In Renate Blumenfeld-Kosinski and Timea Szell, eds., *Images of Sainthood in Medieval Europe*. Ithaca: Cornell University Press, 1991. Pp. 199–221.

McSheffrey, Shannon. *Gender and Heresy: Women and Men in Lollard Communities, 1420–1530*. Philadelphia: University of Pennsylvania Press, 1995.

Morrison, Susan Signe. *Women Pilgrims in Late Medieval England: Private Piety as Public Performance*. Routledge Research in Medieval Studies series, 3. London: Routledge, 2000.

Renevey, Denis and Christiania Whitehead, eds. *Writing Religious Women: Female Spiritual and Textual Practices in Late Medieval England*. University of Toronto Press, 2000.

Riches, Samantha J. E. and Sarah Salih, eds. *Gender and Holiness: Men, Women and Saints in Late Medieval Europe*. Routledge Studies in Medieval Religion and Culture. London and New York: Routledge, 2002.

Rieder, Paula M. 'The Implications of Exclusion: the Regulation of Churching in Medieval Northern France.' *Essays in Medieval Studies: Proceedings of the Illinois Medieval Studies Association* 15 (1998): 71–80.
http://www.luc.edu/publications/medieval/vol15/rieder.html

Shahar, Shulamith. *Women in a Medieval Heretical Sect: Agnes and Huguette the Waldensians*. Rochester, NY: Boydell Press, 2001.

Smith, Julie Ann. *Ordering Women's Lives: Penitentials and Nunnery Rules in the Early Medieval West*. Aldershot: Ashgate, 2001.

Stafford, Pauline. 'Queens, Nunneries and Reforming Churchmen: Gender, Religious Status and Reform in Tenth- and Eleventh-Century England.' *Past and Present* 163 (1999): 3–36.

Watt, Diane. *Secretaries of God: Women Prophets in Late Medieval and Early Modern England*. Woodbridge: D. S. Brewer, 1997.

Wiethaus, Ulrike. 'Sexuality, Gender, and the Body in Late Medieval Women's Spirituality.' *Journal of Feminist Studies in Religion* 7 (1991): 35–87.

Heloise

Blamires, Alcuin. '*Caput a femina, membra a viris*: Gender Polemic in Abelard's Letter "On the Authority and Dignity of the Nun's Profession"'. In David Townsend and Andrew Taylor, eds., *The Tongue of the Fathers: Gender and Ideology in Twelfth-Century Latin*. The Middle Ages series. Philadelphia: University of Pennsylvania Press, 1998. Pp. 55–79.

Clanchy, M. T. *Abelard: A Medieval Life*. Oxford: Blackwell, 1997.

Desmond, Marilynn. '*Dominus/Ancilla*: Rhetorical Subjectivity and Sexual Violence in the Letters of Heloise.' In David Townsend and Andrew Taylor, eds., *The Tongue of the Fathers: Gender and Ideology in Twelfth-Century Latin*. The Middle Ages series. Philadelphia: University of Pennsylvania Press, 1998. Pp. 35–54.

Dronke, Peter. *Women Writers of the Middle Ages*. Cambridge University Press, 1984.

Freeman, Elizabeth. 'The Public and Private Functions of Heloise's Letters.' *Journal of Medieval History* 23 (1997): 15–28.

Gilson, Etienne. *Heloise and Abelard*. Ann Arbor: University of Michigan Press, 1972.

Jaeger, C. Stephen. *Ennobling Love*. Philadelphia: University of Pennsylvania Press, 1999.

Kamuf, Peggy. *Fictions of Feminine Desire: Disclosures of Heloise*. Lincoln: University of Nebraska Press, 1982.

Mews, Constant J. *The Lost Love Letters of Heloise and Abelard: Perceptions of Dialogue in Twelfth-Century France*. New York: St Martin's Press, 1999.

Nye, Andrea. 'A Woman's Thought or a Man's Discipline? The Letters of Abelard and Heloise.' *Hypatia* 7 (1992): 1–22.

Waithe, Mary Ellen. 'Heloise and Abelard.' In Cecile T. Tougas and Sara Ebenreck, eds., *Presenting Women Philosophers*. Philadelphia: Temple University Press, 2000. Pp. 117–28.

Wheeler, Bonnie, ed. *Listening to Heloise: The Voice of a Twelfth-Century Woman*. The New Middle Ages series. New York: Palgrave, 2000.

Marie de France

Bloch, R. Howard. 'The Medieval Text – "Guigemar" – as a Provocation to the Discipline of Medieval Studies.' *Romanic Review* 79 (1988): 63–73.

Broadhurst, Karen M. 'Henry II of England and Eleanor of Aquitaine: Patrons of Literature in French?' *Viator* 27 (1996): 53–84.

Bruckner, Matilda Tomaryn. 'Textual Identity and the Name of a Collection: Marie de France's Lais.' In her *Shaping Romance: Interpretation, Truth, and Closure in Twelfth-Century French Fictions*. Philadelphia: University of Pennsylvania Press, 1993. Pp. 157–206.

Burgess, Glyn S. *The Lais of Marie de France: Text and Context*. Athens: University of Georgia Press, 1987.

Marie de France: An Analytical Bibliography. London: Grant and Cutler, 1977.

Clifford, Paula M. *Marie de France, Lais*. London: Grant and Cutler, 1982.

Dufournet, Jean, ed. *Amour et merveille: les 'Lais' de Marie de France*. Paris: Champion, 1995.

Finke, Laurie A. and Martin B. Shichtman. 'Magical Mistress Tour: Patronage, Intellectual Property, and the Dissemination of Wealth in the "Lais" of Marie de France.' *Signs* 25 (2000): 479–503.

Freeman, Michelle. 'Marie de France's Poetics of Silence: the Implications for a Feminine *Translatio*.' *PMLA* 99 (1984): 860–83.

Griffin, Miranda. 'Gender and Authority in the Medieval French Lai.' *Forum for Modern Language Studies* 35 (1999): 42–56.

Hoepffner, Ernest. *Les Lais de Marie de France*. Paris: Boivin, 1935.

Kibler, William, ed. *Eleanor of Aquitaine: Patron and Politician*. Austin: University of Texas Press, 1976.

Krueger, Roberta L. 'Transforming Maidens: Singlewomen's Stories in Marie de France's *Lais* and Later French Courtly Narratives.' In Judith M. Bennett and Amy M. Froide, eds., *Singlewomen in the European Past, 1250–1800*. Philadelphia: University of Pennsylvania Press, 1999. Pp. 146–91.

Maréchal, Chantal E., ed. *In Quest of Marie de France, A Twelfth-century Poet*. Lewiston: Edwin Mellen Press, 1992.

Maréchal, Chantal E., 'Marie de France Studies: Past, Present, and Future.' *Envoi: A Review Journal of Medieval Literature* 8 (1999): 105–25.

Ménard, Philippe. *Les Lais de Marie de France*. Paris: Presses universitaires de France, 1979.

Mickel, Emanuel J. *Marie de France*. New York: Twayne, 1974.

Mikhaïlova, Milena. *Le Présent de Marie*. Paris: Diderot, 1996.

Parsons, John C. and Bonnie Wheeler, eds. *Eleanor of Aquitaine*. The New Middle Ages series. New York: Palgrave, 2002.

Pickens, Rupert T. 'Marie de France and the Body Poetic.' In Jane Chance, ed., *Gender and Text in the Later Middle Ages*. Gainesville: University Press of Florida, 1996. Pp. 135–71.

'The Poetics of Androgyny in the *Lais* of Marie de France: *Yonec, Milun*, and the General *Prologue*.' In Donald Maddox and Sara Sturm-Maddox, eds., *Literary Aspects of Courtly Culture: Selected Papers from the Seventh Triennial Congress of the International Courtly Literature Society*. Cambridge: D. S. Brewer, 1994. Pp. 211–19.

Sienart, Edgard. *Les Lais de Marie de France: du conte merveilleux à la nouvelle psychologique*. Paris: Champion, 1984.

The Roman de la Rose, *Christine de Pizan, and the* querelle des femmes

Blamires, Alcuin. *The Case for Women in Medieval Culture*. Oxford University Press, 1997.

Brabant, Margaret, ed. *Politics, Gender, and Genre: The Political Thought of Christine de Pizan*. Boulder: Westview Press, 1992.

Brown-Grant, Rosalind. *Christine de Pizan and the Moral Defence of Women: Reading beyond Gender*. Cambridge University Press, 1999.

Desmond, Marilyn, ed. *Christine de Pizan and the Categories of Difference*. Minneapolis: University of Minnesota Press, 1998.

Fenster, Thelma and Clare A. Lees, eds. *Gender in Debate from the Early Middle Ages to the Renaissance*. New Middle Ages series. New York: Palgrave, 2002.

Forhan, Kate Langdon. *The Political Theory of Christine de Pizan*. Brookfield: Ashgate, 2002.

Huot, Sylvia. *The 'Romance of the Rose' and its Medieval Readers: Interpretation, Reception, Manuscript Transmission*. New York: Cambridge University Press, 1993.

Kennedy, Angus. *Christine de Pizan: A Bibliographical Guide*. London: Grant and Cutler, 1984.

Christine de Pizan: A Bibliographical Guide (Supplement I). London: Grant and Cutler, 1994.

Quilligan, Maureen. *The Allegory of Female Authority: Christine de Pizan's 'Cité des Dames'*. Ithaca: Cornell University Press, 1991.

Richards, Earl Jeffrey, Joan Williamson, Nadia Margolis, and Christine Reno, eds. *Christine de Pizan and Medieval French Lyric*. Gainesville: University Press of Florida, 1998.

Solterer, Helen. 'Fiction versus Defamation: the Quarrel over the "Romance of the Rose".' *Medieval History Journal* 2 (1999): 111–41.

Willard, Charity Cannon. *Christine de Pizan: Her Life and Works*. New York: Persea Books, 1984.

Zimmerman, Margarete and Dina De Rentiis, eds. *The City of Scholars: New Approaches to Christine de Pizan*. New York: De Gruyter, 1994.

Lyrics and romances

Barratt, Alexandra, ed. *Women's Writing in Middle English*. London: Longman, 1992.

Boklund-Lagopoulou, Karin. '*Yate of Heaven*: Conceptions of the Female Body in the Religious Lyrics.' In Denis Renevey and Christina Whitehead, eds., *Writing Religious Women: Female Spiritual and Textual Practices in Late Medieval England*. Cardiff: University of Wales Press, 2000. Pp. 133–54.

Bruckner, Matilda Tomaryn. 'Fictions of the Female Voice: the Woman Troubadours.' *Speculum* 67 (1992): 865–91.

Cheyette, Fredric. 'Women, Poets, and Politics in Occitania.' In Theodore Evergates, ed., *Aristocratic Women in Medieval France*. The Middle Ages series. Philadelphia: University of Pennsylvania Press, 1999. Pp. 138–77.

Doss-Quinby, Eglal, Joan Tasker Grimbert, Wendy Pfeffer, and Elizabeth Aubrey, eds. '*Biaus Douz Amis*': *Songs of the Women Trouvères*. New Haven: Yale University Press, 2001.

Goodman, Jennifer R. '"That Wommen Holde in Ful Greet Reverence": Mothers and Daughters Reading Chivalric Romances.' In Lesley Smith and Jane H. M. Taylor, eds., *Women, the Book and the Worldly*. Cambridge: D. S. Brewer, 1995. Pp. 25–30.

Jewers, Caroline A. 'Loading the Canon: For and Against Feminist Readings of the Trobairitz.' *Romance Quarterly* 41 (1994): 134–48.

Kay, Sarah. *Courtly Contradictions: The Emergence of the Literary Object in the Twelfth Century*. Stanford University Press, 2001.

Krueger, Roberta L., ed. *The Cambridge Companion to Medieval Romance*. Cambridge University Press, 2001.

Meale, Carol M. '". . . Alle the Bokes that I Haue of Latyn, Englisch, and Frensch": Laywomen and their Books in Late Medieval England.' In Carol M. Meale, ed., *Women and Literature in Britain, 1150–1500*. Cambridge University Press, 1993. Pp. 128–58.

Meale, Carol M. ed. *Women and Literature in Britain, 1150–1500*. Cambridge University Press, 1993.

Paden, William D., ed. *The Voice of the Trobairitz: Perspectives on the Women Troubadors*. Philadelphia: University of Pennsylvania Press, 1988.

Shapiro, Marianne. 'The Provençal Trobairitz and the Limits of Courtly Love.' *Signs* 3 (1978): 560–71.

Julian of Norwich

Abbott C., *Julian of Norwich: Autobiography and Theology*, Studies in Medieval Mysticism series, 2. Woodbridge: D. S. Brewer, 1999.

Bauerschmidt, Frederick Christian. *Julian of Norwich and the Mystical Body Politic of Christ*. South Bend: Notre Dame University Press, 1999.

Bradley, Ritamary. 'Julian of Norwich: Everyone's Mystic.' In William F. Pollard and Robert Boenig, eds., *Mysticism and Spirituality in Medieval England*. Woodbridge: D. S. Brewer, 1997. Pp. 139–58.

Cré, Marleen. 'Women in the Charterhouse? Julian of Norwich's *Revelations of Divine Love* and Marguerite Porete's *Mirror of Simple Souls* in BL, MS Additional 37790.' In Denis Renevey and Christina Whitehead, eds., *Writing Religious Women: Female Spiritual and Textual Practices in Late Medieval England*. Cardiff : University of Wales Press, 2000. Pp. 43–62.

Jantzen, Grace M. *Julian of Norwich: Mystic and Theologian*, new edn. New York: Paulist Press, 2000.

Lichtmann, Maria R. '"God Fulfylled My Bodye": Body, Self, and God in Julian of Norwich.' In Jane Chance, ed., *Gender and Text in the Middle Ages*. Gainesville: University of Florida Press, 1996. Pp. 263–78.

McAvoy, Liz Herbert. '"The Moders Service": Motherhood as Matrix in Julian of Norwich.' *Mystics Quarterly* 24 (1998): 181–97.

McEntire, Sandra J., ed. *Julian of Norwich: A Book of Essays*. New York: Garland, 1998.

McInerney, Maud Burnett. '"In the Meydens Womb": Julian of Norwich and the Poetics of Enclosure.' In John Carmi Parsons and Bonnie Wheeler, eds., *Medieval Mothering*. New York: Garland, 1996. Pp. 157–82.

Margery Kempe

Ashley, Kathleen. 'Historicizing Margery: the Book of Margery Kempe as Social Text.' *Journal of Medieval and Early Modern Studies* 28 (1998): 371–88.

Atkinson, Clarissa. *Mystic and Pilgrim: The Book and the World of Margery Kempe*. Ithaca: Cornell University Press, 1983.

Bradford, Clare. 'Mother, Maiden, Child: Gender as Performance in *The Book of Margery Kempe*.' In Frances Devlin-Glass and Lyn McCredden, eds., *Feminist Poetics of the Sacred: Creative Suspicions*. American Academy of Religion Cultural Criticism series. Oxford University Press, 2001. Pp. 165–81.

Chakrabarty, Dipesh. 'Minority Histories, Subaltern Pasts.' In his *Provincializing Europe: Postcolonial Thought and Historical Difference*. Princeton University Press, 2000. Pp. 97–116.

Dickman, Susan. 'Margery Kempe and the Continental Tradition of the Pious Woman.' In Marion Glasscoe, ed., *The Medieval Mystical Tradition in England: Papers Read at Dartington Hall, July 1984*. Cambridge: D. S. Brewer, 1984. Pp. 150–268.

Ellis, Roger. 'Margery Kempe's Scribe and the Miraculous Books.' In H. Phillips, ed., *Langland, the Mystics and the Medieval English Religious Tradition: Essays in Honor of S. S. Hussey*. Rochester, NY: Boydell and Brewer, 1990. Pp. 161–75.

Glück, Robert. *Margery Kempe*. New York: Serpent's Tail, 1994.

Lochrie, Karma. *Margery Kempe and the Translations of the Flesh*. Philadelphia: University of Pennsylvania Press, 1991.

McEntire, Sandra J., ed. *Margery Kempe: A Book of Essays*. New York: Garland, 1992.

Pellegrin, Peter. '"I wold þow wer closyd in a hows of ston": Sexuality and Lay Sanctity in *The Book of Margery Kempe*.' In Ann Astell, ed., *Lay Sanctity, Medieval and Modern*. University of Notre Dame Press, 2000. Pp. 91–104.

Continental women mystics and English readers

Bell, David. *What Nuns Read*. Cistercian Studies series, 158. Kalamazoo: Western Michigan University, Medieval Institute Publications, 1995.

Chance, Jane. 'St Catherine of Siena in Late Medieval Britain: Feminizing Literary Reception through Gender and Class.' *Annali d'Italianistica* 13 (1995): 163–203.

Driver, Martha W. 'Pictures in Print: Late Fifteenth- and Early Sixteenth-Century English Religious Books for Lay Readers.' In Michael G. Sargent, ed., *De Cella in Saeculum*. Cambridge: D. S. Brewer, 1987. Pp. 241–4.

Ellis, Roger. '"Flores ad Fabricandum ... Coronam": an Investigation into the Uses of the Revelations of St Bridget of Sweden in Fifteenth-Century England.' *Medium Aevum* 51 (1982): 163–86.

Finnegan, Mary Jeremy. *The Women of Helfta: Scholars and Mystics*. Athens: University of Georgia Press, 1991.

Gillespie, Vincent. 'Dial M for Mystic: Mystical Texts in the Library of Syon Abbey and the Spirituality of the Syon Brethren.' In Marion Glasscoe, ed., *The Medieval Mystical Tradition: England, Ireland and Wales: Exeter Symposium VI*. Woodbridge: D. S. Brewer, 1999. Pp. 241–68.

Glasscoe, Marion. 'Visions and Revisions: a Further Look at the Manuscripts of Julian of Norwich.' *Studies in Bibliography* 42 (1989): 103–20.

Goldberg, P. J. P. 'Lay Book Ownership in Late Medieval York: the Evidence of Wills.' *The Library* 16 (1993): 181–9.

Grisé, C. Annette. '"In the Blessid Vynejerd of Oure Holy Saueour": Female Religious Readers and Textual Reception in the *Myroure of Oure Ladye* and the *Orchard of Syon*.' In Marion Glasscoe, ed., *The Medieval Mystical Tradition VI*. Cambridge: D. S. Brewer, 1999. Pp. 193–211.

Hutchison, Ann M. 'Devotional Reading in the Monastery and in the Late Medieval Household.' In Michael G. Sargent, ed., *De Cella in Saeculum*. Cambridge: D. S. Brewer, 1987. Pp. 215–27.

John, Helen J., SND. 'Hildegard of Bingen: a New Medieval Philosopher?' In Cecile T. Tougas and Sara Ebenreck, eds., *Presenting Women Philosophers*. Philadelphia: Temple University Press, 2000. Pp. 31–9.

Kurtz, Patricia Deery. 'Marie of Oignies, Christine the Marvelous, and Medieval Heresy.' *Mystics Quarterly* 14 (1988): 186–96.

Sister Mary Denise. 'The Orcherd of Syon: an Introduction.' *Traditio* 14 (1958): 269–93.

Newman, Barbara. ed., *Voice of the Living Light: Hildegard of Bingen and Her World*. Berkeley: University of California Press, 1998.

O'Mara, Veronica. 'An Unknown Middle English Translation of a Bridgettine Work.' *Notes and Queries* 36 (June 1989): 162–4.

Petroff, Elizabeth Avilda. *Body and Soul: Essays on Medieval Women and Mysticism*. New York: Oxford University Press, 1994.

Poor, Sara S. 'Mechthild von Magdeburg, Gender, and the "Unlearned Tongue".' *Journal of Medieval and Early Modern Studies* 31 (2001): 213–50.

Stokes, Charity Scott. 'Margery Kempe: Her Life and the Early History of Her Book.' *Mystics Quarterly* 25 (1999): 60–5.

Voaden, Rosalynn. *God's Words, Women's Voices: The Discernment of Spirits in the Writing of Late Medieval Women Visionaries*. Woodbridge: York Medieval Press, 2000.

Voaden, Rosalynn, ed. *Prophets Abroad: The Reception of Continental Holy Women in Late Medieval England*. Cambridge: D. S. Brewer, 1996.

Wallace, David. 'Mystics and Followers in Siena and East Anglia: a Study in Taxonomy, Class and Cultural Mediation.' In Marion Glasscoe, ed., *The Medieval*

Mystical Tradition in England: Papers Read at Dartington Hall, July 1984. Cambridge: D.S. Brewer, 1984. Pp. 169–91.

Watson, Nicholas. 'The Composition of Julian of Norwich's *Revelation of Love.*' *Speculum* 68 (1993): 637–83.

Joan of Arc

Baker, Denise N., ed. *Inscribing the Hundred Years' War in French and English Cultures.* Albany: State University Press of New York, 2000.

Crane, Susan. 'Clothing and Gender Definition: Joan of Arc.' In Denise N. Baker, ed., *Inscribing the Hundred Years War.* Albany: State University Press of New York, 2000. Pp. 195–219.

De Vries, Kelly. *Joan of Arc: A Military Leader.* Stroud: Sutton, 1999.

Fraioli, Deborah A. *Joan of Arc: The Early Debate.* Woodbridge, Suffolk and Rochester, NY: Boydell Press, 2000.

Gordon, Mary. *Joan of Arc.* Penguin Lives. New York: Lipper Viking, 2000.

Goy-Blanquet, Dominique. 'Shakespeare et Voltaire mettent le feu à l'histoire.' In Dominique Goy-Blanquet, ed., *Jeanne d'Arc en garde à vue.* Brussels: Le Cri, 1999. Pp. 9–53.

Krumeich, Gerd. *Jeanne d'Arc à travers l'histoire.* Trans. Josie Mély et al. [from 1989 orig. German]. Paris: Albin Michel, 1993.

Margolis, Nadia. 'Myths in Progress: a Literary–Typological Comparison of Mélusine and Joan of Arc.' In Donald Maddox and Sara Sturm-Maddox, eds., *Mélusine of Lusignan: Founding Fiction in Late Medieval France.* Athens: University of Georgia Press, 1996. Pp. 249–66.

Pernoud, R. and Marie-Véronique Clin. *Joan of Arc: Her Story.* Trans. and rev. by Jeremy DuQ. Adams. New York: St Martin's Press, 1998.

Sullivan, Karen. *The Interrogation of Joan of Arc.* Medieval Cultures series, 20. Minneapolis: University of Minnesota Press, 1999.

Voaden, Rosalynn. *God's Words, Women's Voices: The Discernment of Spirits in the Writing of Late-Medieval Women Visionaries.* Woodbridge: Boydell Press, 2000.

Wheeler, Bonnie and Charles T. Wood, eds. *Fresh Verdicts on Joan of Arc.* New York: Oxford University Press, 1996.

Wood, Charles T. *Joan of Arc & Richard III: Sex, Saints, and Government in the Middle Ages.* New York: Oxford University Press, 1988.

Medieval women on the Web

These links were operative in December 2002. However, some of the links from these sites to others were not.

Feminae (formerly the Medieval Feminist Index):
http://www.haverford.edu/library/reference/mschaus/mfi/ mfi.html

An index of journal articles, book reviews, and essays in books about women, sexuality, and gender during the Middle Ages. Books written by a single author are not indexed. Time period covered is 450 CE to 1500 CE. Geographic coverage includes Europe, North Africa, and the Middle East. Subject coverage for gender and sexuality means that articles on masculinity and male homosexuality are included. Publications in English, French, German, and Spanish are currently being indexed. Links are being added to journal articles available through the subscriptions services JSTOR and Project Muse.

Medieval Feminist Forum Bibliography:
    http://bailiwick.lib.uiowa.edu/smfs/bibguide. html
    MFF Bibliography is a current awareness list of recently published articles, essays, and monographs on women and gender in the Middle Ages with an emphasis on material that appears outside publications covered by the *International Medieval Bibliography* or *Medieval Feminist Index*.

Medieval Women in The Labyrinth:
    http://www.georgetown.edu/labyrinth/subjects/ women/women.html
    The Labyrinth provides free, organized access to electronic resources in medieval studies through a World-Wide Web server at Georgetown University.

Matrix: Resources for the Study of Women's Religious Communities:
    http://matrix.bc.edu/MatrixWebData/matrix.html
    Matrix is an ongoing collaborative effort by an international group of scholars of medieval history, religion, history of art, archaeology, religion, and other disciplines, as well as librarians and experts in computer technology. 'Our goal is to document the participation of Christian women in the religion and society of medieval Europe. In particular, we aim to collect and make available all existing data about all professional Christian women in Europe between 500 and 1500 CE . . . Our editorial intentions in selecting and presenting material are both scholarly and pedagogical – Matrix is designed for use by scholars, students, and anyone interested in the study of women, medieval Europe, or the history of Christianity'.

ORB: The Online Reference Book for Medieval Studies Women's Studies page:
    http://orb.rhodes.edu/encyclop/culture/Women/femindex.html
    The Online Resource Book for Medieval Studies (ORB) is a co-operative effort on the part of scholars across the internet to establish an online textbook source for medieval studies on the World-Wide Web.

International Alliance for Women in Music – Women's Early Music, Art, Poetry page:
    http://music.acu.edu/www/iawm/pages/index.html
    The IAWM site encompasses women in poetry and art as well as music.

Other Women's Voices: http://www.akron.infi.net/~ddisse/index.html
    The site offers an introduction to over eighty women who wrote a substantial amount before 1600 and whose work (or at least a good part of it) has been translated into modern English. All but three entries are on women who wrote in languages other than English; three are on those who wrote in the English of the 1300s and 1400s. Almost all of the entries are on individuals; a few are on more than one woman.

Women's History on the World Wide Web Virtual Library:
    http://www.iisg.nl/~womhist/vivalink.html

    The main purposes of this virtual library are to list women's history institutions and organizations, locate archival and library collections, and provide links to Internet

resources on women's history. In addition, also included are a list of women's studies journals and a few comprehensive link collections useful as a starting point for
searching the Internet for women's studies in general. This section of the WWW
Virtual Library is maintained by the International Institute of Social History in
Amsterdam, The Netherlands.

International Joan of Arc Society/Société Internationale de l'étude de Jeanne d'Arc:
 http://www.smu.edu/ijas/

 The International Joan of Arc Society/Société Internationale de l'étude de Jeanne
d'Arc is a WWW repository of scholarly and pedagogic information about Joan of
Arc collected by faculty, independent scholars, and students.

 For further Joan of Arc materials, of greatest variety and mixed quality:
http://www.stjoan-center.com

Mapping Margery Kempe:
 http://www.holycross.edu/departments/visarts/projects/ kempe/
Classroom-oriented site dedicated to the late-medieval Englishwoman.

INDEX

CAMBRIDGE COMPANIONS TO LITERATURE

The Cambridge Companion to James Joyce
edited by Derek Attridge

The Cambridge Companion to T. S. Eliot
edited by A. David Moody

The Cambridge Companion to Ezra Pound
edited by Ira B. Nadel

The Cambridge Companion to Beckett
edited by John Pilling

The Cambridge Companion to Harold Pinter
edited by Peter Raby

The Cambridge Companion to Tom Stoppard
edited by Katherine E. Kelly

*The Cambridge Companion to
Herman Melville*
edited by Robert S. Levine

*The Cambridge Companion to
Edith Wharton*
edited by Millicent Bell

The Cambridge Companion to Henry James
edited by Jonathan Freedman

The Cambridge Companion to Walt Whitman
edited by Ezra Greenspan

*The Cambridge Companion to
Henry David Thoreau*
edited by Joel Myerson

The Cambridge Companion to Mark Twain
edited by Forrest G. Robinson

*The Cambridge Companion to
Edgar Allan Poe*
edited by Kevin J. Hayes

*The Cambridge Companion to
Emily Dickinson*
edited by Wendy Martin

*The Cambridge Companion to
William Faulkner*
edited by Philip M. Weinstein

*The Cambridge Companion to
Ernest Hemingway*
edited by Scott Donaldson

*The Cambridge Companion to
F. Scott Fitzgerald*
edited by Ruth Prigozy

The Cambridge Companion to Robert Frost
edited by Robert Faggen

*The Cambridge Companion to
Eugene O'Neill*
edited by Michael Manheim

*The Cambridge Companion to
Tennessee Williams*
edited by Matthew C. Roudané

*The Cambridge Companion to
Arthur Miller*
edited by Christopher Bigsby

*The Cambridge Companion to
Sam Shepard*
edited by Matthew C. Roudané

CAMBRIDGE COMPANIONS TO CULTURE

*The Cambridge Companion to Modern
German Culture*
edited by Eva Kolinsky
and Wilfried van der Will

*The Cambridge Companion to Modern
Russian Culture*
edited by Nicholas Rzhevsky

*The Cambridge Companion to Modern
Spanish Culture*
edited by David T. Gies

*The Cambridge Companion to Modern
Italian Culture*
edited by Zygmunt G. Barański
and Rebecca J. West